YOU PAID *HOW* MUCH FOR THAT?!

YOU PAID *HOW* MUCH FOR THAT?!

How to Win at Money Without Losing at Love

Natalie H. Jenkins
Scott M. Stanley
William C. Bailey
Howard J. Markman

JOSSEY-BASS
A Wiley Company
www.josseybass.com

Published by

JOSSEY-BASS
A Wiley Company
989 Market Street
San Francisco, CA 94103-1741

www.josseybass.com

Jossey-Bass books and products are available through most bookstores. To contact Jossey-Bass directly, call (888) 378-2537, fax to (800) 605-2665, or visit our website at www.josseybass.com.

Substantial discounts on bulk quantities of Jossey-Bass books are available to corporations, professional associations, and other organizations. For details and discount information, contact the special sales department at Jossey-Bass.

We at Jossey-Bass strive to use the most environmentally sensitive paper stocks available to us. Our publications are printed on acid-free recycled stock whenever possible, and our paper always meets or exceeds minimum GPO and EPA requirements.

Library of Congress Cataloging-in-Publication Data

You paid how much for that?!: how to win at money without losing at love / Natalie H. Jenkins .. [et al.].
    p. cm.
    Includes bibliographical references and index.
    ISBN 0–7879–5888–3 (alk. paper)
    1. Married people—Finance, Personal. I. Jenkins, Natalie H., date.
HG179 .Y655 2002
332.024'0655—dc21   2002000661

FIRST EDITION
PB Printing 10 9 8 7 6 5 4 3 2 1

CONTENTS

ACKNOWLEDGMENTS

We would like to acknowledge the work of professionals in the diverse fields of family social science, economics, insurance, finance, and tax, which over decades has built a base of knowledge that allows us to develop a book such as this. Specifically, we would like to thank Karl and Amy Locke, insurance professionals at Locke and Associates; David Cordova, CPA; and Mike Gegen, first vice president at Dain Rauscher, Inc., for sharing their specialized knowledge with us. These professionals graced us with excellent feedback on aspects of Part Three in this book. On their behalf, however, we want you to know that we are responsible for the content of the book, and their willingness to give us advice does not imply their endorsement or verification of specific thoughts contained here. We are very glad to have had their feedback.

Unless otherwise noted, the couples here are fictitious, or disguised, but the situations and issues are very real. The "realness" of these examples comes from our years of experience working with couples in research, workshops, and counseling. All identifying information has been changed. We thank all the couples who in varying ways have shared their stories, which have added to the richness of our understanding of the themes we write about here. We can all learn from each other.

The cartoons presented in the book are the work of our friend and collaborator, Ragnar Storaasli. Ragnar has conducted many research analyses with us in years gone by, and he has a wonderful knack for humorously capturing many of the key issues that affect relationships. We thank him for all his efforts, and we hope you enjoy his work.

We can't thank the staff at PREP, Inc., enough for their ongoing support in the effort to reach couples with evidence-based materials—not to mention their tremendous efforts in "manning the fort," which freed us up to write this book. There have been many on this staff who have helped us over the years, and this time, we'd like to specifically acknowledge the work of Nita Wassenaar, Amber Howell, Sheryl Haddock, Mandy Rutt, and Barb Boonstra. A more talented and kind group you could not find.

There are two friends and colleagues of ours whom we esteem most highly in their passion for helping couples build strong and happy marriages. Bill Coffin has been a tireless visionary in supporting prevention efforts for building strong marriages. He has been an especially potent force in helping bring evidence-based materials to couples throughout the U.S. military services. But mostly he's our friend, and we just plain like him. We also thank Diane Sollee for her Herculean efforts to put marriage education on the map nationally. In her development of the Smart Marriages conference and website (www.SmartMarriages.com), she has provided a place for people from widely divergent backgrounds to join together and share knowledge, expertise, and experiences in the common goal of helping build stronger, happier, and more stable marriages. She is a good friend who shares our passion for prevention. If you want to know what's going on in the field of marriage, ask one of these two people we're fortunate to call friends.

Some of the research that we draw on for our work here has been supported over the years by the University of Denver, the National Institute of Mental Health, and the National Science Foundation. We are grateful for the support from these institutions—support that has enabled us to develop the research basis for many of the relationship-building strategies we suggest in this book. Our current research, testing some of the strategies described in Part Two, is supported in part by a grant from the National Institute of Mental Health, Division of Services and Intervention Research, Adult and Geriatric Treatment and Prevention Branch (Grant 5-RO1-MH35525-12, "The Long-Term Effects of Premarital Intervention," awarded to Howard Markman and Scott Stanley).

Our editor at Jossey-Bass, Alan Rinzler, has been immensely helpful and supportive in our work over the past decade. He has aided us in the development of many books now, books that with his support and input are designed to make a real difference in the lives of the people who read and act on them. We greatly appreciate his enduring guidance and wisdom and thank the staff at Jossey-Bass and Wiley for their support and expertise during the book creation process. We are especially grateful for the excellent work of our copyeditor, Michele Jones.

Michele did far more than help us with grammar—she challenged us and helped us make our writing clearer and stronger (though she does seem to have a "thing" with the word "thing!"). We are also grateful to Lasell Whipple and Amy Scott for their unflagging encouragement in getting to the finish line.

It has been many years since the four of us began talking about the possibility of this book. Bill has spent much of his professional life focusing on family economics; he saw the need for a book that could bridge the gap between materials designed to help couples build great relationships and those designed to help people manage money and wealth well. We are all grateful for his ability to see the need to help couples navigate the churning waters at the confluence of money and marriage. Bill would like to acknowledge the help through the years from his friends and academic associates who have taught him about financial matters, especially Tom Garman, Ray Forgue, Jean Lown, Flora Williams, and all his fellow members of the Association for Financial Counseling and Planning Education for encouraging him to work on this project.

Considering Bill's background in family economics, Natalie's background in business and consumer science, and Scott and Howard's backgrounds in both marital social science and business, we believe we are putting into your hands a book that can work in deep and powerful ways in your life. But we never forget that we stand upon the valuable work, insights, and accumulated wisdom of many who have gone before.

To Shawn, for giving me the courage.
To Jessica and Peter, for giving me the reason.
To Scott and Howie, for giving me the opportunity
to make this dream come true.

—N.J.

To those who are always there for me, Nancy, Kyle, Luke, and my
mother and father; my love to you all, and all thanks for your love.

—S.S.

To Jean, spouse, love of my life, dearest friend, and
academic colleague. Thank you for all your love, support,
and teaching how to be almost human.
To our children, Heather and David, and their spouses, Tim and
Amanda, who have also taught me much about life and love.

—B.B.

I want to thank my loved ones, Janine, Mat, Leah,
for their continuing support and for giving me the
opportunity to invest my love in their lives.

I want to thank my parents, Claire and Arnold, for the
love they give all of us from their rich emotional bank account.

Finally, I want to say to my coauthor, Natalie, "Congratulations,
this is the best book by a new author in the field that I have read!"

—H.M.

YOU PAID *HOW* MUCH FOR THAT?!

INTRODUCTION

What I Did During My Summer Vacation

Natalie H. Jenkins

They say life is the best teacher. I'm not sure if it's the *best*, but it sure did teach me some key lessons last summer. We went on a canoe trip down the Colorado River with some friends (Chuck and Vicky, Chris and Traci, and all our kids). Chuck had made this trip before, and he knew things we didn't. He gave us a training video on how to paddle a canoe. Shawn (my husband) and I didn't watch it. (I mean, how hard can it be to paddle a canoe??) We arrived at the river on a gorgeous July day, loaded up our canoes, and were ready to head out. We noticed that the other couples tied all their gear down to their canoes. We didn't—for one thing, we didn't have any rope, and for another, we didn't think we were going to be attacked by a band of canoe pirates who would steal all our gear anyway.

We headed out. During the morning, life on the water was great. We had a blast playing canoe Frisbee. We'd toss the Frisbee from one canoe to another, miss, try to back up, glide over to the Frisbee, and toss it again. We'd also come equipped with massive super-soaker squirt guns. The battles were fierce, and no one was ever dry for any length of time. These were memory-making times.

When the sun was high, we stopped for lunch. The kids played in the sand. Chuck tried to tell me a thing or two about paddling. He said, "Now Nat, the water is going to get a little rougher this afternoon. Here," he said, as he made paddling motions in the air. "This is how to make a J-stroke." At least, I think that is what he said. I politely pretended to listen, but I was far more interested in getting my fair share of the chocolate brownies before the kids got to them.

So, after lunch, we headed out once more. Chuck was right. The water did get a little more exciting in the afternoon. We didn't need to use our squirt guns to stay wet. The river was quite helpful there. Then we stopped again. Chuck and Vicky hiked ahead to scout out the river. When they came back, they said there was a bit of rough water ahead and told us how to navigate through it. "Cool," I thought.

Chris and Traci went first. I watched them disappear down the river. Chuck and Vicky went next. Then it was our turn. Shawn and I were paddling along, and the water started moving faster. Then all of a sudden, "Oh, my GOSH!!! We are headed straight towards a waterfall!!" I started desperately doing my J-stroke. We were still headed for the waterfall. Then I tried other letters. I don't think there is a K-stroke, but I tried it anyway. I'm pretty sure I tried the entire alphabet, but to no avail. That waterfall was getting closer. Then we saw a huge boulder in the middle of the waterfall. "OK, I am NOT having fun."

Shawn tried to go to the right of the boulder. I tried for the left. (Hint: when you're in the same canoe, it is helpful to try to go the same direction.) We managed to hit the boulder straight on. It spun us around. I prayed, "Oh God, please, oh please, I do not want to go down this thing backwards!!!" You know what? There really is a God who answers prayer. We did not go down that waterfall backwards. We capsized instead.

It was one of those slow-motion deals. Whoa-o-o-o-o-a-a-a-a-a, gl-l-l-u-u-u-g-g-g! Next thing I knew I was underwater, unsure which way was up. Then I was splashing around, desperately trying to find our ten-year-old son, Peter. Yep, our son had been in the canoe with us. I'd been in the front of the canoe, Peter was sitting behind me, and Shawn was in the rear. Fortunately, Peter *had* listened when Chuck told him important things like, "If the boat tips over, jump as far away from the canoe as you can so the canoe won't hit you." He'd jumped out of the way. Because Peter was in front of Shawn, Shawn could see where Peter was. He managed to grab Peter and push him toward me. I caught Peter just as I saw Shawn go under. I screamed, but I could do nothing for my husband. The whitewater had swallowed him whole.

I had hold of Peter, and we were headed down the river together. Peter was one scared little boy. I made a lame attempt to tell him everything would be all right—"It's OK, Peter. We'll be OK"—but he wasn't buying it.

We managed to avoid the other hazards of the river—boulders, fallen tress, our gear. It was kind of depressing to see all our gear floating down the river ahead of us. Yep, there goes our tent. Yep, that's your sleeping bag. Hey, that's my Diet Coke floating away!! I realized why everyone else had tied their gear to their canoes. "Oh, God, if you'll just let us get out of this river, next time we'll bring some rope. Really, I promise."

An incredibly l-o-n-g few minutes later, we kicked our way over to an eddy and dragged our scraped and bruised bodies out of the river. "Where's Daddy?" Peter wanted to know. In my mind I replayed the image of Shawn going under. I didn't know where Daddy was, and part of me was afraid he—no, I wouldn't let myself think that. He would be fine. I heard someone say assuredly, "Daddy's probably upriver getting the canoe." I was surprised. That was me who sounded so calm. I managed to keep myself sort of together until I saw Shawn walking up the bank toward us. I could hardly see his smile through my tears, but I remember it as one of the most wonderful smiles I'd ever seen.

We looked around and discovered that our friends were on the other side of the river. Chuck paddled over to pick us up. He reached us and motioned for us to get in. Peter looked at me and said resolutely, "Um, I don't think so."

To wrap this story up, let me say that, thanks to our wonderful friends, no one drowned, we got most of our gear back, Peter is once again willing to get into a canoe with his mom and dad, and we're making plans to go again next summer. And perhaps most important, I learned a few lessons about life.

Five Lessons for the River of Life

1. Watch the video.
2. Bring rope.
3. Head in the same direction.
4. Never take your partner's smile for granted.
5. Get back in the canoe.

Lesson One: Watch the Video

I didn't think I needed to learn how to paddle a canoe. I figured I could just hop in and do it. I was wrong.

Couples often make the same assumptions about both marriage and money. Think about it. Where did you go to "marriage school"? It sounds silly, doesn't it? Our belief that we know all there is to know about marriage or money is so strong that it seems odd to think there might be more to learn. However, with the divorce rate near 50 percent and with 1.2 million bankruptcies in the last year, clearly we do have more to learn. The fact is that most of us learned neither relationship skills nor financial management skills in a direct manner from qualified sources. Most of us simply picked up bits of information from people who had good intentions but lacked expertise. Worse, some of us got advice that was downright wrong.

No one person on the planet knows *everything*. We are stronger when we learn from each other. In fact, that is part of the reason this book has a team of four authors. Howard and Scott are world-renowned marital researchers. They know their stuff. Bill's an expert in consumer science and personal finance. I have been making my mark with one foot in marital education and one foot in marketing and consumer science for over ten years. Combining our expertise from the various disciplines allows us to present to you a well-rounded and well-reasoned approach to marital and financial success.

This book is a great way to learn the ABC's (or J's) of money and marriage skills whether you're single, engaged, or married. Watch the video—or, in this case, read the book.

Lesson Two: Bring Rope

Maybe you're not too happy with your relationship right now, or you're drowning in debt. In that case, we'd love to help you make things better and then maintain your progress. Or maybe your relationship is everything you want it to be, and you're financially independent. That's great, but you have plenty of river ahead of you, right? Have you done all you need to do to protect what you've worked so darned hard to get? What are you doing—intentionally—to keep your love alive? What is your strategy for providing financially for your family? In this book you'll learn specific skills and techniques for cultivating romance, intimacy, and your long-term commitment to each other. We'll share with you the secrets for protecting your financial assets. We'll not only give you the inside scoop on insurance, wills, and safe investments but also show you how to steer clear of the "buy now, pay later" trap. Things you want to keep need to be tied down in some way. You need some rope.

In life, things tend to go from order to disorder. A car goes from clean to dirty, a new dishwasher that works great becomes an old dishwasher that leaks. Have you ever seen a house that's been neglected for a few years? It's not pretty. It's not that the owners *intentionally* meant to destroy it; it's just that no one intentionally meant to preserve it. That's what we believe happens both to marriages and to money. No one says, "It is our goal in five years to become completely apathetic toward one another, and we want to have at least $50,000 in credit card debt," but it happens to couples all the time. It happens not because couples plan for it to happen but because they fail to be intentional about protecting their love and their material assets.

Besides protecting yourselves from everyday wear and tear, you also need to prepare for life's unexpected challenges. Basically there are only two kinds of canoeists: those who have capsized and those who will. It isn't a matter of *if* you will experience tougher times, it's *when*. You don't want to be bobbing down the rapids one day watching all of what you've built together over the years floating away. When you go through rough water, you could end up getting dumped over and losing everything (that could be life or relationship or possessions), or you could be adequately prepared for those times. We want to help you enjoy the good times—as our family did during the morning—but also be prepared for the afternoon.

Lesson Three: Head in the Same Direction

This point may sound obvious, but sometimes we humans manage to overlook the obvious. If you're in the same canoe, you're going to go wherever your partner goes. A single canoeist can head to the right if that's where he wants to go. But for a duo, if one heads left and the other heads right, you'll end up either going in circles or being smashed on the rocks. Regardless, you will do it together. Heavy debt, bankruptcies, separations, and divorce all demonstrate the reality that spouses are financially linked in life. Let's hope you won't need to experience such dire consequences to learn this reality.

Money is an essential in our society. Basic survival requires that we earn it, save it, and spend it wisely. But decisions as to how much money is enough and how to earn it, save it, and spend it wisely are choices that couples face *together.* One of our key goals in this book is to help you and your partner approach your money as a team.

We've found that most financial advice is geared toward individuals as if the "right thing to do" were a one-size-fits-all kind of deal. It isn't. Financial issues for couples are very different from the financial concerns of a single person. For couples, money isn't simply about dollars and cents. If you scratch the surface of almost any money issue, you'll find relationship issues intensifying if not actually driving the problem. Although it is very important to know how to manage the dollars well (and we will show you how to begin), true financial success for couples depends on the seldom explored "why."

The "why" is the deeper, symbolic meanings we ascribe to money. Money issues tend to be manifestations of personal and relationship needs or desires in life, such as power, security, freedom, acceptance, beauty, and fun. We have come to believe that the "why" is the true driving force of our behavior. Partners are most likely to work together as a team in life and maintain some sense of harmony if they can understand and talk openly about the deeper meaning of money and money decisions. In other words, "money" isn't just about money. If you can master money and all of its nuances as a team, the result will be more than financial success. The result will include a deeper level of intimacy within your marriage. This book is more than a superficial discussion of dollars and cents. We'll take you to a deeper understanding of how you can move forward together.

Lesson Four: Never Take Your Partner's Smile for Granted

Some of us obsess over money. "How much do we have?" "Is it enough?" "How can I get more?" We strive for money as if our lives depended on it. But money doesn't help you fall asleep at night. It doesn't help your mother's test results come back "benign." It doesn't help your partner be kind, generous, and appreciative. It doesn't help you feel loved.

Many of us think in terms of acquiring things—a house, furniture, car, boat, clothes, and other worldly things. There's nothing wrong with material goods; however, you may have noticed that although they often bring momentary pleasure, they do not bring deep and lasting fulfillment. More often than not, our question becomes, "Is this all there is?" Many of us get caught in the trap of trying to fill the heart-shaped void within us with a dollar-shaped token. That'll just give you heartburn.

When I saw Shawn sucked under the water, I'd have given everything I had to save him. Money was totally worthless to me at that moment. Money has its limits, and accepting this fact is the beginning of financial freedom.

At the same time, financial success requires that we acknowledge the power of money. Some of us pretend that money doesn't matter at all. We say, "I don't need money" as we head off for another arduous day at the job we hate because it pays well. Of course money is important. Money is not just the currency of stuff, it is the currency of life. Money determines how life is spent. Money determines whether you live in a cardboard box, an apartment, a house, or a mansion. Money is about the basics of life: food, clothing, shelter, health care. Money, or the absence of it, determines whether one or both of you spend your days working at a job or playing on the golf course, whether you spend your retirement eating cat food or caviar. Having an abundance of money means that you have the power to support AIDS research or to work to end world hunger—to make a difference in the world on a larger scale. If you fail to acknowledge the power of money in our society, you will always be subject to it. In denying money's power, many couples refuse to learn to manage money well and thereby end up having money manage them. They end up living without those resources that could greatly increase their quality of life for years to come.

In this book, we want to help you put money into perspective. You'll gain a healthy respect for what money can do for you and what it can't. Once you understand that money has great value but that lasting love is priceless, you and your partner will be well on your way to a prosperous future.

Lesson Five: Get Back in the Canoe

My son, Peter, didn't want to get back in the canoe. He had trusted us to get him down the river safely, and we'd failed him. Adding my newfound love for dry land to my guilt in failing my son, I wasn't particularly excited about getting back into the canoe either. But I wanted to be a good example for my son, so I repeated the old saying, "When at first you don't succeed, try, try again."

"Mom," he said, "the definition of insanity is to keep doing the same thing and expect different results."

"Who told you that?" I asked.

"You," he replied.

"Well, you don't listen to anything else I say; why'd you listen to that?" Then, in a more serious tone, I explained that he was right. To try the exact same thing again would be really stupid. However, the opposite of success is not failure; it is quitting—and that wasn't an option. I then listed all the ways that things were going to be different this time: Chuck was paddling, the water was calm, and we were only going a short way. I also promised to borrow some rope and learn to paddle before we headed into rough water again.

As Peter stepped into the canoe, he asked, "Mom, are you more *against* quitting or *for* getting some dry clothes and a Diet Coke?" He wanted to know why I wanted to get on down the river. "Never underestimate the lure of a cold Diet Coke, Peter," I said. It doesn't have to be an either-or answer. Although most of us don't like the idea of "being a quitter," sometimes the idea doesn't sound so bad. That's when it's most important to remember the "why." Even if the why is nothing more than getting a Diet Coke, reconnecting with the why can help give us the energy we need to get back in the canoe and paddle—one stroke at a time. That is something successful people have mastered in life. Relationship and financial success requires moving forward whether you are driven by a dogged determination *not* to stop or by a specific goal you want to achieve. Get back in the canoe—for whatever reason.

We, the authors, are realists. We know that sometimes life can really knock us around. We may make a huge financial mistake. We may deeply wound the ones we love, and the thought of picking up and trying again can seem crazy. At times we do need to stop and catch our breath—to evaluate how we can do things differently. However, we want to encourage you not to stop for too long. Learn enough to make your next try a bit different and then go for it. If you're like most of us, you'll likely get dunked a time or two. However, we've found that it's important to reward yourself for your efforts—whether you succeed or not—and keep getting back in the canoe. As long as you keep paddling, you'll always be moving forward.

◆ ◆ ◆

It all comes down to this: there are couples who experience financial success but end up in divorce court, there are couples who experience lasting and fulfilling love but end up in bankruptcy court, and there are couples who don't succeed in either domain. Our goal is to show you how to achieve financial success without sacrificing your relationship and how to achieve marital success while reaching your financial goals.

Here's to the journey.

PART ONE

THE INVISIBLE FORCES

CHAPTER ONE

MARRIAGE, MONEY, AND REAL LIFE

The heart has its reason, which reason knows not of.

BLAISE PASCAL

We've met couples who've had great success with money but lost at love. And we've met couples who've lost lots of money, but their love was stronger than ever. Then there are the couples who have had success with both, or with neither. Have you ever wondered what the difference is between these couples? We have.

We believe we've identified the key difference. It has relatively little to do with luck or intelligence, though it has something to do with the answer to another question: Why do smart people sometimes do dumb things with their money? It seems that nearly every family has some story about a silly purchase they've made. There's the one about Ron, who's retired from a very successful career in sales. Ron and Marie are the best of friends and have been married for forty years. Ron's kids and grandkids have all heard the funny story about when Grandma and Grandpa were newlyweds and Grandpa bought a vacuum cleaner for $249.99 from a door-to-door salesman. That was in 1962, when Ron made only $400 per month. Furthermore, they had hardwood floors and not a single rug in the house. "Grandma was so mad at me she could hardly talk to me for a month!" recalls Ron.

Or take Linda, a very smart and savvy teacher who decided to go ahead and visit her girlfriend in Boston even though she and her husband didn't have the money. During her visit, Linda and her friend went shopping, and Linda decided

Understanding these invisible forces and knowing how to manage them are essential to winning at money without losing at love.

to buy a very expensive stereo system for her husband. They couldn't afford the trip, so why did Linda make things worse by buying a stereo?

Why do couples carefully go through their budget in order to figure out how much house they can buy and then let their real estate agent show them houses $5K to $10K more than they had decided they can afford? Have you seen this? Have you done this? Have you become totally obsessed with the house that "is just perfect" and "feels like *home*," even when you'd already decided it was more money than you felt comfortable spending?

Why do we seem to lose our minds when it comes to certain money decisions? Odds are that if you don't have a story to tell, your partner does. Why do smart people sometimes do un-smart things? It's as though there are some invisible forces at work in our lives. Actually, there are. Understanding these invisible forces and knowing how to manage them are essential to winning at money without losing at love. But you won't find these invisible forces mentioned in traditional models of economics.

A Simple Model of Money Decisions

In a most basic model of economics, money behavior can be thought of in four parts:

1. The first part is the person: *you*. You are an individual who wants to reach some particular goal.
2. The second part is the *decisions* you make. How are you going to handle your money? Mainstream economics tends to assert that we make decisions rationally.
3. The third part in this model is your *money:* whether you have a lot of money or a little, whether your income is consistent or erratic, whether your assets are liquid or not.
4. The last part is your goal.

For example, if your goal were to go to a movie, you would decide which movie you wanted to see, go to the theater, buy your ticket, and watch the movie. If we were to draw this simple model, it might look like Figure 1.

Real Life Is More Complicated

The problem is that real life doesn't always follow a simple model. There is often more going on than what is pictured in the figure. In real life, if you wanted to go see a movie and you asked your partner if he or she would like to go with you,

FIGURE 1. A SIMPLE MODEL OF MONEY DECISIONS.

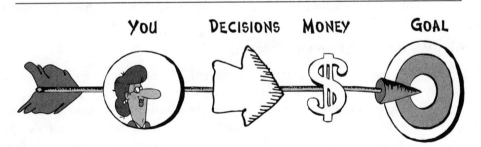

your partner might respond in a way that baffles you. Your partner might say something like, "That won't work because I'm planning to take the kids to the amusement park on Saturday while you are away camping." You might reply, "Um, OK," but you'd be thinking, "Huh?" If you were to ask what one thing had to do with the other, your mate might even criticize you for not planning ahead. Later, when the situation had calmed down, you might find out that your mate was thinking that your plan would require money for the movie, stuff to eat at the movie, and a baby-sitter. Fifty bucks, from top to bottom, and your partner was counting on using that money to take the kids out while you were away on the weekend. In real life, simple things can get complicated pretty quickly.

These baffling interchanges happen all the time to couples, and money tends to have its fingerprints all over them. Money is such an integral part of our lives that it is bound to be mixed up in the interactions between partners. "Want to go to the movies?" "We can't afford it." "The truck needs a new transmission; maybe we should just buy a new one." "Why'd you buy generic ketchup? I like Heinz." "I'd like to cut back to working part-time." "But we'd have to sell the house." "Let's increase our savings for retirement." "But that means we can't afford to go anywhere for vacation." The sheer number of decisions that revolve around money makes it unlikely that two people will always agree about what to do with the stuff.

Why Money Is So Challenging for Couples

Money issues have the potential to ruin or define a marriage like nothing else we know. That's because money is not simply about money. If it were that simple, we could just give you some sound financial advice, and you'd have no trouble following it. Money is complex because money and finance symbolize so much about how we view life, what we think is important, and how we work together—or don't—with loved ones. Let's look for just a moment at that "how we work together—or don't" part.

May We Have the Envelope, Please?

And the winner is . . . money. The topic that is consistently reported to be the number one problem area for couples is not jealousy or sex or chores, it's money. So if you and your partner don't always see eye to eye when it comes to money, you're not alone.

In 1991, Ragnar Storaasli and Howard Markman published a study out of our lab at the University of Denver, which reported how couples rated their top problem areas. In that study, couples were tracked from before they married to long after the wedding bells had rung. People before marriage, people after marriage, people with lots of money, people with little money—all rated their number one area of conflict as money.

In another study from our group, coauthors Scott and Howard devised a nationwide telephone poll that asked people all sorts of questions about their relationships. (You know those guys who call just as you are sitting down to dinner? Yes, that's us!) Among the many questions people answered was this one: "What is the number one thing that you and your partner argue about most?" Figure 2 shows how people responded.

You can see how couples responded, grouped by how long they had been married. The top argument starter for every group, from engaged couples to people married up to twenty-five years, was money. Those who had been married twenty-six years or longer reported that "nothing" started arguments. It's

FIGURE 2. TOP ARGUMENT STARTER BY YEARS MARRIED.

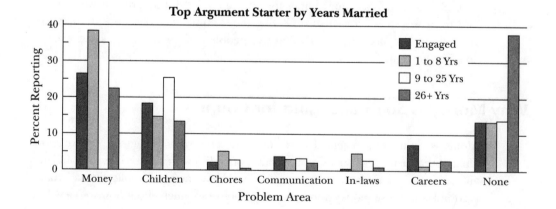

not that they don't argue at all but that on average they argue much less than younger couples. That's understandable, because in studies like this, those who have been married a long time are "survivor" couples who have made it through life's ups and downs that other couples will not make it through. Maybe they were more compatible to begin with, but we think a more likely explanation is that they learned how to work through their differences over the years. That's encouraging news: if other couples have learned to conquer money challenges, then so can you!

Is it fair to conclude that money is the number one cause of divorce? Nope. Surely money and the conflicts surrounding it are the major catalysts behind some divorces. But although this conclusion is often reported, it simply isn't justified. Here's why. Money is the most common conflict area for couples whether they remain happily married or get a divorce. Couples who stay together have money issues. Couples who don't stay together have (and likely continue to have) money issues. The difference between those who stay together and those who don't isn't *whether* they have money issues. The key difference lies in *how* couples manage their money issues. So money per se doesn't cause divorce, but it is the most difficult topic of all for the average couple.

You Are Not an Island

If you don't disagree with me, how will I know I'm right?

ANONYMOUS

Another reason that couples struggle with money is that, compared to singles, couples have additional responsibility and vulnerability when it comes to the financial domain. You get to carry the weight of knowing that your decisions will affect your partner. You also get to know that you're vulnerable to the decisions your partner may make.

Suppose your best friend comes to you and says, "I've decided to quit my job. I don't want to be an advertising executive anymore. I don't want to spend the limited time I have here on earth trying to convince people that they should buy Squirt instead of Mountain Dew. I don't want to be focused on carbonated beverages for the rest of my life. I want to be a teacher. I want to give something to the next generation besides a major sugar high!"

"So what are you going to do?" you ask.

"I'm going to move back home," your friend replies. "I'm going to live with my folks for the next two years while I earn my master's degree in education. They've said they'll let me live there. It won't be easy, but I want to follow my dream."

"Wow!" you say. "Good for you. I'm really proud of you. Not very many people would have the courage to give up such a great-paying job or sacrifice their independence for a bit and live with their folks. Not too many people have the guts to follow their dreams. You're taking responsibility for your future. That's awesome!"

This is all well and good. Good friends are supposed to support you in your life. If they didn't support you in your dreams and aspirations, you'd call them something else. Or you'd stop calling them at all!

Now, suppose that in this case your best friend is also your spouse. This sheds a different light on things, doesn't it? Your spouse comes to you and says, "I've decided to quit my job. I don't want to be an advertising executive anymore. I don't want to spend my few days here on earth trying to convince people that they should buy Squirt instead of Mountain Dew. I don't want to be focused on carbonated beverages for the rest of my life. I want to be a teacher. I want to give something to the next generation besides a major sugar high."

Now, for some reason, you don't feel like being supportive. In fact, you feel panicked. You reply, "WHAT???? ARE YOU CRAZY?!? You can't just quit! You can't just make a decision like this without talking about it with me. We've got a house, with a mortgage, and two kids to support, and car loans, and what are you thinking?? We'll never be able to live on my salary alone."

Your spouse has incredible self-restraint and, instead of getting defensive, says, nicely, "Well, I talked with my folks, and they said we can move in with them for two years while I go back to school. We can sell the house, and the profit we make will cover the cost of my schooling. Look, I know it won't be easy, but I want to follow my dream."

You love your spouse. You want him or her to be able to follow those dreams, but you don't want to lose your house. You don't want to live with your in-laws, and you don't want to have to make the lifestyle changes that you'd have to make if your partner exchanges an advertising exec's salary for a teacher's salary. When a friend makes a financial decision, it is unlikely to greatly affect your life. When your spouse makes a financial decision, you'll live with it for years to come. That's one of the key differences between friendship and marriage.

A spouse is more than a friend and more than a roommate. A spouse is, among other things, a financial partner. Where you go financially, there your part-

A spouse is more than a friend and more than a roommate. A spouse is, among other things, a financial partner.

ner will go, and vice versa. If you've become true teammates, then you are much less likely to feel as vulnerable. If you're true financial partners—real teammates—then you won't feel as burdened in your decisions because you're sharing your lives, and you can relax, knowing that what each of you wants matters to the other. If you don't have teamwork going, then you may have good reason to be fearful of what your partner may do.

Married couples find that they still bear the responsibilities and vulnerabilities of financial partnership even if they try to keep their money separate. When you're married, the IRS doesn't let you say, "Oh, that's my husband's problem" when he didn't pay enough taxes. The IRS seems to think that a married couple is a unit. The landlord or the bank treats married couples as a unit too.

Marriage is a tricky kind of deal. You can't control the decisions your partner makes, but you get to share in the consequences of his or her decisions. You're both vulnerable and responsible at the same time. Your partner can make decisions independently from you, and, for richer or for poorer, you get to share the consequences of your partner's financial behavior. That's partly why marriage can be so difficult for couples who haven't learned to manage money as a team.

Managing money well as a couple is truly a challenge. Money is tough to deal with because it is embedded within so many decisions and because of the additional responsibility and vulnerability associated with those decisions. However, meeting that challenge is not without its rewards. So far in this chapter, it may sound as though you give up more than you get when you choose to commit your life to another. That may be true in some ways when couples don't manage their money well, but for couples who become true financial partners, the benefits are outstanding.

The Good News About Money and Marriage

The security and synergy of a committed financial partnership actually contributes to long-term financial success. Studies show that married people who behave as true financial partners tend to do better financially. Sure, you can find exceptions, but overall, having a strong foundation in commitment increases the likelihood not only that you'll preserve your bond through the ups and downs on life's emotional roller-coaster but also that you'll be financially secure. So although you do take a risk when you tie your financial life to another in marriage, full financial partnership has its benefits.

For example, sociologist Lingxin Hao studied how family structure affects net worth. She compared families raising children, which tend to be mostly young households. (She was careful to make sure she wasn't comparing apples to oranges—for example, young, cohabiting couples to long-term married couples.) Because the families were young, their accumulated wealth was not high. Nevertheless, in Hao's study, married couples with children had accumulated the most money, with a median net worth of almost $26,000. Remarried couples with children were almost as well off ($22,500). The shocker from this study was the median wealth of cohabiting couples with children: just $1,000. Single mothers typically had no financial assets at all.

Young marrieds do better than young singles, whether the singles are living with a partner or not, and as people age, the gap between marrieds and singles becomes a chasm. Economists Joseph Lupton and James P. Smith looked at the net worth of couples on the verge of retirement. The typical married couple had accumulated about $410,000 ($205,000 each), compared to about $167,000 for the never-married and just under $154,000 for the divorced.

By and large, marrieds do better financially than singles. But does that mean that financially successful people get married or that marriage makes people financially successful? Linda Waite and Maggie Gallagher, in their thoughtful book *The Case for Marriage,* argue that people who choose to get married do not display any more financial acumen than those who choose to stay single. In other words, the difference between the two groups isn't just a selection effect; it's a real difference. Marriage itself has the power to alter people's financial destiny.

What Is It About a Healthy Marriage That Promotes Financial Success?

For the purposes of this discussion, we're defining a healthy marriage as one in which both individuals, at the very least, trust the other, are committed to the long-term success of the relationship, and enjoy connection and passion within the relationship. We've found three primary reasons why a healthy marriage contributes to financial success:

1. A healthy marriage provides for healthy checks and balances.
2. A healthy marriage allows for the pooling of resources.
3. A healthy marriage provides security for long-term investment.

Checks and Balances. It can be incredibly frustrating to have someone nagging at you to save more, someone who has the audacity to tell you that you can't spend your money when and how you want to. Yet it isn't without its positive side. In fact, the "constraints" of marriage actually help people stick with what's good for them. Take a look at how single Shelly and married Veronica differ in their handling of similar decisions.

Twenty-seven-year-old Shelly came home from work, dropped her briefcase on the floor, and picked up the mail, mostly a stack of catalogues. She headed to the living room, armed with her cup of Starbucks and her new catalogues. She turned on her stereo, sat down on the sofa, and began to unwind. This was her favorite part of the day. She flipped through the golf catalogue quickly. She wasn't a golfer, but she might want to pick it up someday. She looked through the catalogue of "old-lady clothes," as she called them. "Hey, that's kind of cute. Oh no, did I really find something I liked in there?" she asked herself. She muttered something about soon wearing plaid shorts, black socks, and white orthopedic sneakers, and tossed the catalogue onto the floor.

Shelly picked up another catalogue. This one carried fine china, stoneware, and other kinds of dishes. She wasn't interested in dishes, but as she turned the pages, one pattern seemed to jump out at her. "Ooooh," she exclaimed. "Those are incredibly pretty. I like those. That's what I'm going to spend my bonus on." She picked up the phone and dialed the 800 number. Her dishes would arrive in five to seven business days.

Across town, Veronica, too, was relaxing after work, flipping through a dinnerware catalogue that had come in the mail. Veronica owned a small consulting firm. Her business was both her career and her hobby. She had created a stylish home for her family, but things like dishes hadn't crossed her radar screen since their wedding twenty years ago. She'd never been one to care much about dishes, but when she saw *this* set she was bitten by the I-gotta-have-it bug.

She had her own "mad" money, but she wanted the $300 purchase (for a sixty-piece service for twelve) to come out of the "Household" budget. Ryan and Veronica had an agreement that the Household budget was to be managed on a "consensus" basis, meaning that they both had to agree before that fund was used.

Veronica went downstairs and shoved the catalogue under Ryan's nose. "Pretty dishes, aren't they?" Ryan had never cared one bit about dishes. Not his thing. Certainly not when he was watching basketball and Stanford was three minutes away from making it to the Final Four. As she walked back to the kitchen, Veronica mentioned that she might like to buy the set.

After the announcers had finished ruminating about the game, Veronica grabbed Ryan for a talk. "Hey Ryan, I've been thinking that I'd like to use some Household money to buy some new dishes."

Ryan was watching Veronica "fix dinner." She was microwaving two frozen burritos on paper towels. He was having trouble seeing the need for new dishes. In a good-natured tone, he asked, "Dishes? What do you want dishes for? You don't even cook."

Veronica, tossing a hot burrito from one hand to the other, replied in her sort of serious, sort of joking tone, "Well, when I heat up my Pop-Tarts, I put them on a plate."

Ryan leaned over the counter, kissed Veronica on the forehead, and said, "That you do." He thought buying dishes was a waste of money. However, Ryan was a fair-minded kind of guy. He knew that Veronica could point out his exercise equipment in the bedroom that he used primarily as a clothes rack. "How much would these dishes cost?"

"$300."

Ryan, a bit startled, said, "$300! Holy cow. Do you know how much we'd have if we invested that money instead of spending it?"

Veronica replied, "Yes, I do. (She knew Ryan would ask this question. After all, she'd been married to him for twenty years. So she'd done the math.) We'd have $820 in ten years if we invested the $300 at 10 percent."

"$820!!" Ryan gasped.

"Yes, but these dishes are a particularly good deal. See, I figure that I use a plate, on average, twice a day. So that's two times 365 days times ten years. That is seventy-three hundred uses for only $820. That's only eleven cents per use. You're getting a happy wife for only twenty-two cents per day!! What a deal!"

Ryan smiled. He knew Veronica was a master at rationalizing. (After all, he'd been married to her for twenty years!) He had actually come to find these conversations somewhat entertaining. "So you're saying you'd be happy every day for the next ten years if we get these dishes?"

Grinning, Veronica said, "Well, I'd be happy with the dishes!"

"Since all you want is to have a pretty plate for your Pop Tarts, why don't you just buy one plate? Besides, I thought we were going to remodel the bathroom."

Veronica scowled in mock frustration. "Don't you have another game to watch or something??"

Ryan went back downstairs munching on his burrito, and Veronica put the catalogue in a drawer. She'd decided to think on it a bit more. She knew she could order the dishes if she wanted to. Ryan would be OK with it. And even if he wasn't, she could use her own money, or she might have a serious discussion with Ryan and get him to agree to using the Household money. But somehow her I-gotta-have-it feeling had subsided somewhat during the discussion, and she didn't want to waste the money. She had forgotten for a moment that she and Ryan were trying to save up to redo the bathroom, and really she wanted a new bathroom more than she wanted new dishes.

◆ ◆ ◆

When you're single, you make your financial decisions by yourself, and you affect no one but yourself. You are independent. When you're single, "me" is your entire identity. But all that changes when you commit to someone for the long haul.

Shelly didn't have to discuss her purchasing decision with anyone. That's the positive side of the coin. On the negative side, she didn't have a lifelong partner to listen to her even if she had wanted to talk. Veronica didn't *have* to talk with Ryan either. She didn't need to get permission. Yet she knew that her identity had two facets. She was still fully herself, but she was also part of an "us." Married people face a lifelong challenge: delicately balancing their independence with interdependence. True financial partnership costs a bit of au-

*Married partners
ask a three-part
question: What's
best for me, my
partner, and our
relationship as
a whole?*

tonomy. For married partners, the question is not simply at any given moment "What's best for me?" but a three-part question, day in and day out: "What's best for me, my partner, and our relationship as a whole?"

Asking (and answering) the more complicated three-part question leads to better decisions. Veronica was able to remain connected with her partner and to reconnect with her larger material goal of remodeling the bathroom in the future. Interestingly, it is this very process of interaction, even if heated at times, that often helps marrieds settle for *more*.

What at times may feel to you as though you're being hassled by your partner might actually be part of the key to success in life. This is why most researchers believe that men's health, on average, is so much better in marriage. Their wives get after them about their choices and habits, and literally add years to their lives. The same is true with money. Sometimes, that challenge from your partner about how you are handling money can be the basis of a secure financial future.

Pooling of Resources. True financial partnership requires an interdependent relationship, whereby two independent individuals *choose* to both support and rely on the other. When you combine interdependence with a long-term commitment, then you create an environment that allows for the pooling of resources: money, labor, and time. Pooling, in turn, allows you to lower expenses and raise income, both of which are conducive to financial success. As Waite and Gallagher explain in *The Case for Marriage:*

> Husbands and wives usually need only one set of furniture and appliances, one set of dishes, one lawn mower. They share the heat and light, and each person's use does not diminish the amount available to the other person. Similarly, by pooling their labor, married people lower not only their expenses but also the amount of work that each has to do. Cooking for two is only a bit more time-consuming than cooking for one, for example, and . . . paying the bills for two may take up no more time than paying the bills for one.
>
> This kind of pooling means couples can have the same standard of living for much less money or effort than can an adult living alone. . . . Government poverty guidelines, which are based on actual expenditures of individuals and families, suggest that two people sharing a household, meals, furniture, and a bathroom need only about 30% more income to avoid being poor than one person does.

Theoretically, any two people living together could benefit from pooling. Roommates, for example, do tend to benefit by sharing rent and electricity. The data show a difference, however, between two people who are simply sharing living quarters and those who are committed financial partners. Roommates, for example, don't tend to benefit from pooling in buying groceries, furnishings for the home, insurance, or other such expenses. Sociological data show that roommates and cohabiting couples tend to choose to preserve some degree of financial autonomy but, in so doing, lose out on the economic benefits.

Although married couples are bound by law to be financial partners in many ways, they don't have to live in ways that allow them to benefit from pooling. They can choose to bear all the costs of partnership but enjoy none of the rewards. Many live that very way, and it's not a good path to be on. We believe that the advice in the rest of this book can keep many couples from going that direction. What is the best-case scenario? Two people walking hand in hand through life, with a sense of security in the future of "us," teamwork that permeates all their major decisions, and cooperation in a financial partnership based on respect and knowledge.

Security for Long-Term Investment. Because marriage is a long-term commitment, married couples tend to operate from a long-term perspective. Again, financial partners don't have to benefit in this way, but the opportunity is there. We ran across a study that looked at couples who were happier in marriage compared to those who were not. The less happy couples spent more money on fun stuff like stereos and TVs. Nice things, to be sure. The happier couples spent more money on things like appliances and homes—things you just don't buy with someone you aren't planning to be with into the future. Even the buying behavior of happier couples portrays a fundamental security in the future of the relationship. You're not going to buy a Maytag washing machine with a twenty-five-year guarantee with a partner who doesn't come with even a two-week guarantee.

Because married people plan to live their lives together, they are more likely to plan *for* their lives together. They are more likely to reap the financial benefits that come from making wise decisions, pooling resources, and a long-term perspective toward investment in their future. Smith, the economist we mentioned earlier, found that during a five-year period, couples who stayed married increased their assets by 7 percent per year, whereas the assets of individuals grew by only about 3.5 percent. Those who divorced during that five-year period actually lost assets.

◆ ◆ ◆

Learning to manage money well in marriage is worth the effort because a healthy marriage contributes to financial success. However, it isn't easy. As we said earlier, money is tough for couples to deal with because it is embedded in so many deci-

NOW THIS MODEL ON MY RIGHT MAY BETTER HELP YOU REAFFIRM THE COMMITMENT TO YOUR MARRIAGE.

RAGNAR STORAASLI

sions and because of the additional responsibility and vulnerability associated with those decisions. And as you may have guessed, there are reasons that most couples don't see, reasons that we're calling "invisible forces." These forces are the new element in our model of money and marriage, and handling these invisible forces well is the key to successful money management for couples.

A New Model of Money Decisions

In our model, we still have the same four parts: you, your decisions, your money, and your goal. However, as Figure 3 illustrates, we now reveal the invisible forces.

In Part One of this book, we'll explain these forces—what they *are* and what they *do*.

FIGURE 3. A NEW MODEL OF MONEY DECISIONS.

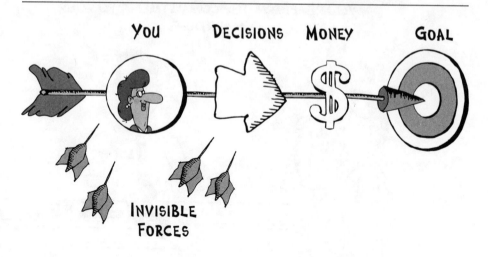

Essentially, as Figure 4 shows, these forces have the potential to push us out of alignment with the direction we want to go in life. When we're off track, we feel that "something is wrong," and we then make decisions that overcompensate for the uneasiness we feel. When we're out of alignment, so are our decisions, and so is the impact on our money, our relationships, and our ability to reach our goals in life. It is the invisible forces that explain why smart people sometimes do un-smart things. It was an invisible force called "the deep desire to protect his wife from severe allergies" that led Grandpa Ron to buy an expensive vacuum cleaner. It was an invisible force called guilt that led Linda to buy a stereo. It is the invisible forces that explain a whole lot about money and marriage.

FIGURE 4. INVISIBLE FORCES CAN PUSH US OFF COURSE.

Now here's where it gets really interesting. What happens when we decide to partner through life with another human being, as in Figure 5? It gets downright complex.

Kind of a dizzying mess, isn't it? We're just getting started! Couples find that their relationship with each other and with money can get confusing at times. Maybe a lot of times. There are a lot of invisible forces at play within a relationship. Oftentimes these invisible forces push couples off course, and they don't even realize what's happening. Take Abby and Ken, for example.

Abby and Ken, as typical newlyweds, were eager to please one another. Abby, seeing how anxious Ken could be about conserving money, went the extra mile to find bargains. Ken applauded her efforts and would say, "I appreciate the way you can pinch a penny until it screams." Abby was delighted.

There were some areas that Abby didn't want to cut out of the budget. If Hallmark had had a poster child, she'd have been it. She loved to browse through all the cards, reading each sentiment and selecting just the right card for the right occasion. Ken, of course, was her favorite beneficiary. After two years of dating and almost nine months of marriage, Ken had quite a collection of cards from Abby. Abby would have purchased small gifts for Ken as well, but she knew money was a big concern, so she'd select a card to say "I love you," and think to herself, "I'm doing so good here, this is only $2.25."

Then came that fateful day. Abby gave Ken a card to celebrate their thousandth-day anniversary. She gave him the card, and he thanked her for it. Then, he added gently, "You know, I'd be just as happy if you told me you love me and saved the

FIGURE 5. INVISIBLE FORCES AT WORK IN MARRIAGE.

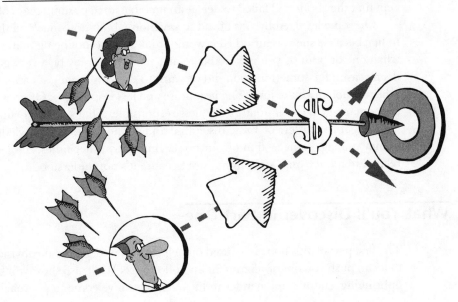

$2.25. Spending $2.25 for a piece of paper that I'll read once seems like a waste." Abby simply said, "OK." But that wasn't what she was feeling. Abby's feelings were hurt. Giving cards was her special way of expressing love for Ken, but his concern for money felt to her like rejection of her love. Furthermore, Abby felt that Ken had chastised her for being wasteful, when she'd been trying to be frugal. Double ouch.

This is a great example of invisible forces beginning to push a couple off course. It doesn't seem like a big deal, does it? But it was. Was Ken was being insensitive or ungrateful? No. Was Abby being overly sensitive? No. The situation was not that simple. For them, just like so many other couples, aspects of money represented many of the deeper themes in life. Where money intersects most deeply with our emotions is a complex and vulnerable place. Money, like nothing else we know of, is the screen on which couples project all their deepest fears, hopes, dreams, and hurts in life. You can learn a lot about your relationship and the deeper longings of each other's hearts if you are able to understand what money symbolizes. We'll go more deeply into that topic in Chapters Three and Four.

Back to Ken and Abby. In this one key story in their lives, Ken was merely being practical, but Abby was operating on a deeper level that Ken completely missed in his analysis of the situation. Sadly, Ken and Abby did not recognize just how significant this particular day was to their future. It was a day like any other, packed full of many small events and interactions. Without sparks or nasty words to demarcate it, this was the day Abby decided, semiconsciously, to withhold from Ken one of her key ways of loving him. Her emotional wound was small, but it would fester. Ken had no idea, and would have no idea for many years, how much he lost in wanting to save $2.25. Neither of them had done anything wrong, except that they both had failed to detect an invisible force pushing them off course.

On some level, Abby was afraid to say more about how much all this meant to her, because she was afraid Ken would think she was not being mature. Often, when one or both of you are unable to articulate what may be a very good, very deep reason for something you did or want to do with money, it can look to the other as though you're just being immature and less responsible. Of course, sometimes many of us *are* immature and less responsible. That's another subject, and we will get to matters of basic discipline and sound financial knowledge in the money management section of our book. But many other times, some behavior related to money only looks immature because it's not understood.

What You'll Discover in Part One

The first part of this book is focused on helping you understand the invisible forces that can push you out of alignment and off course. We'll also show you how your upbringing, culture, and gender influence how you've come to approach money.

This first part is where you may find yourself saying, "Ah ha, now I get it." But you won't find much "what to do about it" kinds of guidance in the first part. That's what the rest of the book is for.

In Part One, we'll delve into several key concepts to help you understand the invisible forces:

- Basic money dynamics in marriage
- The desire for happiness and how that affects you and how you view money
- A model for understanding how events related to money trigger conflicts about issues
- A description of the powerful hidden issues that can either add fuel to the fires of conflict or become a basis of deeper understandings that can forge a stronger connection and partnership in your life together
- A model for how expectations work
- An exploration of where expectations come from, including the influences of culture, family, and gender

As you can see, Part One emphasizes the importance of understanding how meanings and deeper concerns—the invisible forces—affect your relationship. We believe that having a deeper understanding will best prepare you to reach your dreams for your relationship while accomplishing your financial goals.

What You'll Discover in Part Two

Whereas Part One focuses on understanding the invisible forces, Part Two shows you how to tackle these forces. Some of them you'll learn to disable, leaving them virtually harmless. Others really can't be disarmed. We will, however, show you how you can harness their energy and bring them into alignment with the direction the two of you want to go. This will allow you to *use* the invisible forces, to benefit from their energy for your good instead of letting them push you off course. The result would look something like Figure 6.

In Part Two, we will cover strategies for helping you

- Talk without fighting
- Solve problems together in ways that promote teamwork
- Control the issues in your relationship rather than let your issues control you
- Talk through your expectations and plan for how you'll navigate your lives together

Most of us don't usually think of money as a very romantic topic. Yet as you come to understand and harness the energy of the invisible forces, a fascinating

FIGURE 6. INVISIBLE FORCES ALIGNED WITH YOUR GOALS.

thing tends to happen: the process can draw couples closer together. As you dream together of your future, as you look across the expanse of time and see that your partner intends to be there with you, you'll often find the bonds between you becoming stronger. As you plan how you're going to use your money to help each other reach your goals together, you're drawing closer still. We're not suggesting that balancing your checkbook will become a kind of aphrodisiac, but we have found that couples who learn to master money together often find that they gain a deeper level of intimacy as a result. As couples rest in the depths of this intimacy, they create an environment that fosters economic gain. It is a beautiful path to a prosperous future. This is the path that we hope you'll find as you read through the first two parts and move on into Part Three.

What You'll Discover in Part Three

Money is often elusive. It's hard to get your hands on it. It's hard to figure out where it goes and why it doesn't go further than it does. It seems to slip through our fingers easily. Grabbing hold of money can be as challenging as trying to nail Jell-O to a wall. Instead of helping us get where we want to go, money can sometimes be more of an obstacle.

Once you understand and have harnessed the energy of the invisible forces, you are ready for basic money fundamentals; knowledge of these fundamentals enables you to grab hold of it and actually use it to reach your goals. Hence, Part Three covers solid strategies for earning, saving, and spending your money so that you can reach a financially successful future. Because there is so much that could be said on money management, we can't present everything you need to know about handling money wisely, but we do give you a solid foundation and also advice on how to use resources for continued learning.

In Part Three, you'll find specific, usable, and sound financial advice on a wide range of topics, including the following:

- Strategies for getting out of debt
- Advice for creating budgets that work
- Keys to setting financial goals that you can stick with
- Strategies for investing
- Principles for obtaining insurance

What You'll Discover in Part Four

Our new model for money decisions portrayed the goal as the obvious target. Of course, it's often not all that clear what our goals really are, and at times it can be downright vexing to figure out our partner's goals. But simple models are easier to work with than complex ones, and to begin we wanted to focus on the invisible forces. However, by the time you have worked through the first three parts of the book, you will have disarmed or harnessed those invisible forces such that you'll be ready to dream your dreams and define your goals.

In Part Four, we'll attempt to inspire you to move into your future together by presenting keys to building

- Shared relationship goals
- Shared financial goals
- Commitment you can take to the bank

We'll take you through a process to help you define and write out your goals. When you've finished this book, you can know what you want your future to look like and how you and your beloved can get there—together.

◆ ◆ ◆

We started this chapter talking about different kinds of couples. Some succeed with money, others succeed in love, some in neither, and some in both. There are key differences between these couples. Couples who win at money without losing at love tend to be those who don't let the invisible forces push them off course. Both partners value their love and have learned how to nurture and protect it. They tend to understand how to make their money work for them, and they know what they want it to do. Simply put, successful couples do what it takes. We'll teach you what to do.

Questions You Might Have

Before we move on, there are a few questions you might have that we'd like to answer.

Who Is This Book for?

This book is for anyone who wants to better understand relationships, money dynamics, and sound strategies for improving money management. For the most part, we wrote this book with married couples in mind. That's because married couples are most likely to be thinking of their relationship as a long-term union that includes financial partnership and romantic connection. Likewise, this book could be a wonderful tool for engaged couples to use in beginning to plan for their future together—including a solid start on understanding the financial partnership that their marriage will become. Nonengaged dating or cohabiting couples might also find much that is of use here. Even if you have not made a long-term commitment to one person at this time, it's likely that money dynamics have affected relationships that matter to you. And we can guarantee that money dynamics will affect your relationships in the future.

What About Financially Strapped Couples?

We truly believe that many of the ideas presented here can help less well off couples, middle-class couples, and rich couples alike. Every couple has to deal with money, and in every couple, money isn't only about money. Further, every couple can benefit from knowing how to handle conflicts over money more effectively, and every couple, no matter what their financial condition, can benefit by working together in planning for their future.

Having said that, there are ideas here that are less relevant for those of you who might be struggling more with poverty. For example, although we make the point in Chapter Two that having more money does not seem to make most people happier in life, having more money when you are in poverty can make a huge difference. We also realize that some topics in Part Three are not options relevant to all couples at this point in life. For example, you may not be able to afford life insurance when you are having trouble putting food on the table next week. So, if you are in poverty, we hope that at least some of our ideas here will be very helpful for you. We also hope that nothing we say or suggest comes across as being insensitive to your plight. We wish you all the best in life, and hope that your financial situation finds permanent improvement in the years to come.

Should We Read the Chapters in Order?

Although we've organized this book in the order you find it for the reasons we've alluded to in our discussion to this point, you don't have to read it in that order. This is your book, so you should read it in whatever order works for you. For example, if you are reading about hidden issues in Part One and you want some tools right away so that you can discuss them safely, you can skip to Chapter Eight in Part Two. Just be sure to come back and finish Part One, or you'll miss out on some important ideas. Similarly, you may be at a stage in life where one chapter or another does not seem all that relevant. You might sample from those chapters to make sure, but go on to focus your attention on the chapters that match your desires and needs at this point in your lives.

Are All the Stories About the Couples You Describe Real? Really?

We have included many stories of couples in this book. The things the couples say and do in these stories are derived from what couples have told us, what we've seen in our work with couples, themes developed from university research, or situations we've been through in our own lives. Although we've changed details and names so that you could not recognize any couple here as people you know personally, all of the stories are based *in reality.* You may relate to some of the couples more than others, but if you find yourself saying, "Nobody acts like that," think again. People do. People have.

Let's begin.

CHAPTER TWO

THE MASTER KEY

Love is the master key that opens the gates of happiness.

OLIVER WENDELL HOLMES

W hat do you want most in life? Most of us would like the chance to walk through the "gates of happiness"—to live our lives full of joy, fulfillment, purpose, hope, peace, contentment, well-being. As we begin to explore the various invisible forces that push us off our course, we discover that one of the most common forces is our beliefs regarding what we need to become happy. If our beliefs regarding money and happiness are off target, we will certainly have difficulty staying on course, no matter how hard we try or how fast we go. In fact, it does seem that many couples are not merely walking along the path, but sprinting. Perhaps they're sprinting so hard that if they were to come to the gates of happiness, they'd run right past them before they even knew the gates were there.

John and Carol are such a couple. John and Carol were talking to each other on their cell phones one afternoon. They were trying to decide what to do with John's brother, who had lost his job and wanted to live with them for a while. They didn't have time to sit and discuss the situation face-to-face, so they talked while they were both in different cars headed in different directions. John was taking one kid to band practice on his way to work at his second job. Carol was taking the other kid to soccer practice, then going to pick up the dry cleaning, then going to the grocery store, then going home to fix dinner and work on a report that she hadn't finished at work. John came home after midnight just as Carol was finishing up her report. They mumbled "I love you" to each other as they fell into bed. They each hoped to get a bit of sleep before the alarm went off and they got to start all over again.

When Carol woke up, she thought, "What's going on here? That was a *normal* evening. We're so busy trying to make ends meet and keep up with family that we don't know if we're coming or going. Is this all there is? Am I happy living life this way?" The answer welling up within her was a deafening *no*.

Although the day's activities may be different for each couple, it seems that many couples are just racing through life, oftentimes feeling exhausted and rarely stopping to ask if they are truly happy and living life the way they had hoped they might. Are you sprinting through life? What do you really want? Why?

What We Think We Need to Become Happy

Researchers learn about people by measuring either what they think or what they do. When researchers ask Americans what they think about the quality of life, their most frequent responses refer to financial security. In a University of Michigan survey, interviewers asked people what they believed would improve their quality of life. The answer given by the greatest number of people was, "More money." Except for those with the highest incomes, most Americans thought (and still think) that an improved financial situation—for example, having 10 to 20 percent more money–would bring greater happiness in life. In *The Day America Told the Truth: What People Really Believe About Everything That Matters*, surveyors asked, "If you could change one thing about your life, what would it be?" The number one answer was "greater wealth," mentioned by 64 percent.

Those are just two of the surveys that measure what Americans think about how to reach the gates of happiness. Researchers have also looked at what people do. In America, we not only *tell* pollsters that we believe money is the path to happiness but also put our money where our mouths are, so to speak. We live in what may be the most consumer-oriented society in the history of the world. Americans spend three to four times as many hours shopping as their peers in Western European countries. In most countries shopping is a chore. Here it is our national pastime. By the end of 2000, we had developed 5.57 *billion* square feet of land into 45,025 shopping malls. That's around nineteen square feet of store for every American man, woman, and child!

Americans didn't always believe that more money was the way to become happy. But increasingly, we are living out this belief. For example, we didn't always have 45,025 shopping malls. In 1960, there were only 3,000 shopping centers in the United States, and only four square feet of retail space for every American. Here's another example: in just two decades, from 1970 to 1990, the values of students entering college changed dramatically. The American Council on Education conducts surveys on the attitudes and beliefs of college students, including questions about what people hope to gain as a result of their college education. Over this time span, the proportion of students who said they hoped college would help them develop a meaningful philosophy of life dropped from 76 percent to 43 percent. The number who said they hoped college would help them become very well off financially rose from 39 percent to 74 percent. Those numbers reflect a huge shift in values, and what Americans value is increasingly being defined in economic terms.

Americans didn't always believe that more money was the way to become happy. But increasingly, we are living out this belief.

You may be saying, "Oh well, other people may believe that money could bring them greater happiness, but I've always believed that the best things in life are free." OK, you may well be an exception. Yet what do you do when you want to celebrate? Do you go buy a new outfit? A cake? A dinner at an expensive restaurant? What do you do when life doesn't go your way and you need to cheer yourself up? Buy a new electronic gadget? An expensive pen? A quart of Ben & Jerry's? What do you do when you want to impress a new client? Buy him club-level tickets to the Yankees? Pay a golf pro to help you improve your swing? Spend a small fortune on a glossy media kit?

Our point is simple. Most people not only say that more money would make them happier but also live out this belief nearly every day. You could be the exception, but most Americans believe that the way to happiness is to get more money and the things it can buy. Even if that's not true for you, it could well be true for your mate. Whether or not you or you mate currently believe that more money and stuff is the way to happiness (and behave accordingly), there is a bigger question: What exactly *is* the relationship between money and happiness? The answer might surprise you.

Does More Money Mean More Happiness?

Pretend you are walking along a deserted beach and you stumble on an old, tarnished, foreign-looking bottle. It has a cork stuck in the top. You pull the cork off, and suddenly you're engulfed in a cloud of green smoke. When the smoke clears, standing in front of you is a real, live magic genie. He says he can grant you one wish. He's only an apprentice, so he knows how to grant only one particular wish: to double your income. You're not the kind of person who would gripe that you should get any three wishes you choose, so you graciously accept the genie's offer. Poof, you now have twice the income you had before. How much happier will you be?

With twice as much income, would you be twice as happy? Only 50 percent more happy? What about at least 25 percent? We can't say for sure, of course, how much happier you would be, but we can make an educated guess. You see, between 1950 and 2000, Americans' buying power doubled. In 1950, the average family income, adjusted for inflation and expressed in 2001 dollars, was $24,500 ($3,300 in 1950 would be approximately $24,500 in 2001 dollars). By 2000, it was $54,058. Graphically, the growth in average income looks like Figure 7.

Now, if our sense of well-being had increased at the same rate as our adjusted income, then over the same period of time, a graph of our average sense of well-being would look something like Figure 8.

FIGURE 7. AVERAGE INCOME THROUGH THE YEARS.

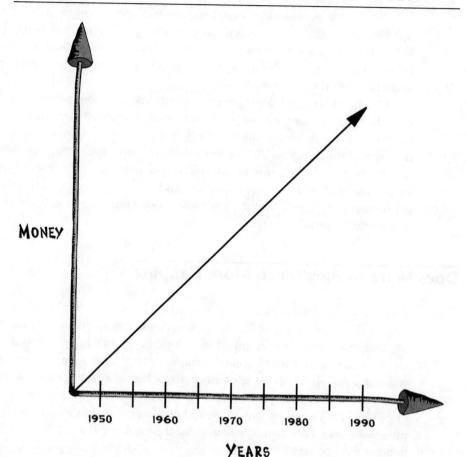

FIGURE 8. EXPECTED HAPPINESS: 100 PERCENT MORE MONEY EQUALS 100 PERCENT MORE HAPPINESS.

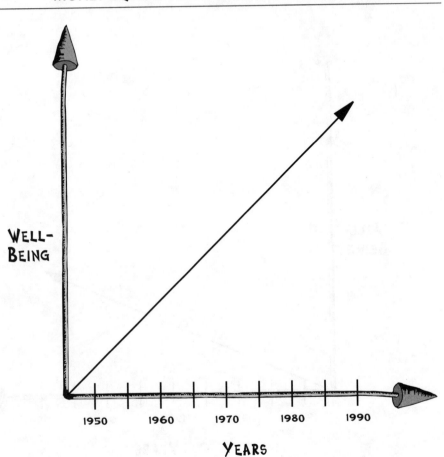

WELL-
BEING

1950   1960   1970   1980   1990

YEARS

But our sense of well-being didn't increase at the same rate as our income. Maybe it increased at half the rate of our income. If that were the case, then over the same period of time, our sense of well-being would look like Figure 9.

But our well-being didn't increase at even half the rate of our adjusted income. The startling fact is that from 1950 to 2000, our reported sense of well-being in the United States looked like Figure 10.

No, your eyes are not playing tricks on you, and, no, we didn't do anything creative with the data. Several different national and international polls have tracked well-being and happiness over different segments of time. Some suggest that happiness peaked near 1957, and others say 1964 and 1974. However, the

FIGURE 9. EXPECTED HAPPINESS IF 100 PERCENT
MORE MONEY EQUALS 50 PERCENT MORE HAPPINESS.

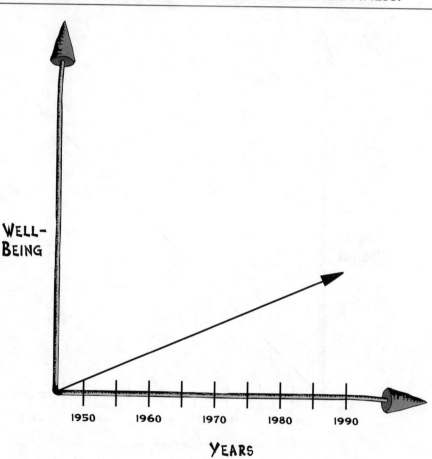

differences are minimal, and all suggest an incredibly flat line. Well-being has, for all practical purposes, not increased at all during these decades. Let that sink in for a moment. Income *doubled,* yet we experienced virtually *no impact* on well-being. Twice the income, and people are, on average, no happier.

So does this mean that money is unimportant or that money doesn't have anything to do with happiness? Nope and nope. Money is extremely important, particularly if you don't have any, which we will get to in a bit. And money does have links to happiness. It's just that the links aren't as simple or direct as many of us Americans apparently believe.

The truth is that researchers are not exactly in agreement about how money and happiness relate to one another. In fact, they spend considerable time dis-

FIGURE 10. ACTUAL REPORTED HAPPINESS.

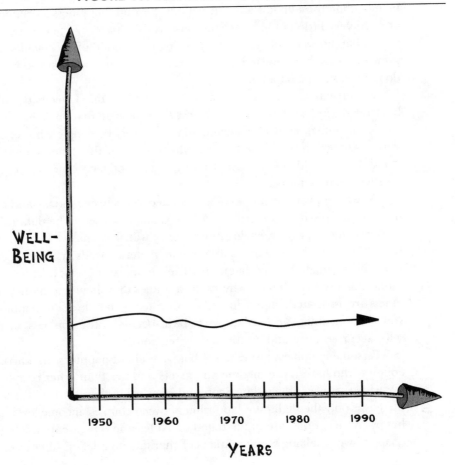

agreeing about what happiness is or about how happiness is different from or the same as well-being, contentment, or satisfaction. Being researchers ourselves, we can admit that we are known for both loving data and loving to argue over the meanings of the data!

If you were to look, you'd find studies that suggest there is little relationship between money and happiness in life. Yet others, including some that have gotten a good deal of attention in recent years, conclude otherwise—that money does buy happiness. Some of the most interesting studies compare nations in terms of well-being and economic status. Ed Diener of the University of Illinois and Eunkook M. Suh of the University of California-Irvine have conducted these kinds of analyses, coming to two important conclusions. First, people in wealthy nations do tend to be happier—or, as researchers put it, to have greater subjective well-being—than those in less affluent nations. Second, happiness so defined has increased very little in the richer nations over the past several decades; in other words, happiness hardly grew at all during that period of spectacular economic growth. So, as these researchers note, as a wealthy nation gets richer, the people do not seem to get happier.

Robert Lane, a professor of political science at Yale University, published a book titled *The Loss of Happiness in Market Democracies*. In that book, he showed how studies document an overall decline in the number of people who regard themselves as happy in the United States, which is one of the richest countries in the world. He concluded that, except for the very poor, larger incomes have almost no effect on happiness.

As we said, various studies of the connection between money and happiness have come up with conflicting results. We make sense of the data this way. If you are living in poverty, having more money will likely make a huge, positive difference in your life. In contrast, if your core material needs in life are met, having more money might be nice, but it's not likely to make you a lot happier. There are diminishing returns. That's why, even in studies that show that money and happiness are associated, money in and of itself tells you little about happiness once you tease out other variables known to be associated with happiness, such as high self-esteem, security, and healthy family relationships.

Personal happiness is one thing, but what about happiness in marriage? Are couples who have more income and assets happier than other couples? A nationwide survey conducted by Scott and Howard in the mid-1990s showed that there was only the slightest relationship between couples' income levels and how happy those couples are in life together. At least in our research, when we say "happy," we're talking about markers of marital and relationship success:

Overall satisfaction

Confidence as a couple in being to handle what the future holds

Dedication to one's partner

Ability to talk as friends

Ability to have fun together

Ability to talk about important concerns without fighting

How often a couple makes love, and how satisfying it is for the partners

When it comes to happiness within marriage, the correlation between income and these relationship dimensions is either not there or so small that it's not worth considering. Again, all bets are off if the couple is struggling with basic financial survival. Couples hovering around the poverty level experience great stress within their relationship as a direct result of the lack of money. More money would help many of these couples cope better with all sorts of other things in life. However, beyond that survival point, your income level will probably have relatively little to do with how happy you are in your marriage.

What Does Lead to Happiness?

So if we can't count on money to make us happy, then what *does* lead to happiness? Through history, poets have known the answer: lasting love with your partner. More recently, researchers have shown that happiness and contentment in life are strongly affected by the quality of our relationships, especially marital and family relationships. For example, we just mentioned the extensive analysis of wealth and well-being conducted by Robert Lane. He concluded that the chief sources of well-being in advanced economies are friendships and family.

The National Opinion Research Center has found that nearly six in ten Americans who rate their marriage as "very happy" also rate life as a whole as "very happy." However, only one in ten who don't rate their marriage as "very happy" rate life as a whole as "very happy."

In *The Case for Marriage,* Linda Waite and Maggie Gallagher demonstrate how people who are married and remain so over time tend to be happier, healthier, and better off financially than others. Obviously, there are many exceptions. Research nearly always speaks to broad averages among groups of people. You could be different. So could your friend across the street. But, on average, people gain tremendous advantages in life by having and investing in a long-term love with their partner.

> *Regardless of how much money people have, people who are in satisfying, secure relationships are also those most likely to be content and happy in life.*

To sum up what we've covered so far, personal happiness is only somewhat affected by having more money but is dramatically affected by relationship success. Regardless of how much money people have, people who are in satisfying, secure relationships are also those most likely to be content and happy in life. Remember our model of money decisions from Chapter One? You can look back at Figure 3.

We show money so prominently because it is one of the two major foci of this book, but we want to be clear. In reality, on the path to happiness, money is just one small component. It is critical that you and your partner put money into perspective. Money is neither unimportant nor all-important. If you were to look at a pie chart of the factors associated with happiness, it might look something like the one in Figure 11.

FIGURE 11. FACTORS ASSOCIATED WITH HAPPINESS.

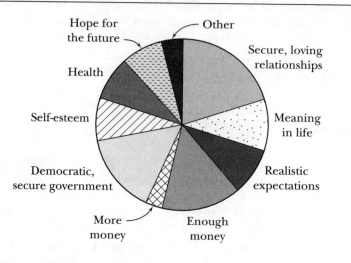

More Money Is a Red Herring

We make a distinction between the pursuit of *enough* money and the pursuit of *more* money and the things it buys, because *more* has turned out to be something of a red herring. If a herring is dragged across a trail that hounds are trying to follow, it throws them off the scent. Couples who thought they were on the path to happiness can find that they're headed down the wrong path. It's very easy to lose the scent by chasing the cents. It's easy to become so busy trying to win at money that you lose at love.

When we invest our energy in obtaining more money and the stuff it buys, the consequences are worse than simply ending up with lots of nice trinkets. The real tragedy is that we too often end up failing to invest our time and energy in ways that could bring real happiness in life.

> *The real tragedy is that we too often end up failing to invest our time and energy in ways that could bring real happiness in life.*

Because for most of us money does not grow on trees, we have to work for it. Many people enjoy their work, and it adds meaning to their lives. Others work solely to get a paycheck. In either case, too many hours at work mean too few hours with your partner. And Americans are working harder than ever. Simply to stay afloat financially, some have to work longer hours. Others are working more in the pursuit of more. In 1977, we spent an average of 47.1 hours per week at work. By 1997 the average number of hours spent at work jumped to 49.9. That may not seem like much, but do the math. One study estimates that the change is equal to one extra month of work a year. That's a month of your life that you could have spent with your spouse or your kids—making a life instead of making a living.

Make no mistake: we, the authors, are not against working hard or earning a living. We ourselves get a big kick out of the work we do—and we enjoy making and spending money like most anybody else. We're not arguing for an austere lifestyle. Wealth is good. Financial security is crucial. We couldn't, in good conscience, write anything like "How to Live Well on Bread and Water." (Pretzels and beer, maybe, but never bread and water!) So you won't find that kind of thing in this book.

No, we're not against work or money. We're simply pointing out that if you believe the myth that money is more important to your overall well-being than your marriage is, you might end up losing your very best chance to walk through the gates of happiness. Love, not money, is the master key that opens the gates of happiness.

The bloodhound that's begun to follow the wrong scent—the red herring—will be on the wrong path. There are two unfortunate consequences to following the wrong path. The first, as we said, is that the wrong path fails to lead the hound where he wants to go (the gates of happiness), so the hound *doesn't* get what he *does* want. The second consequence is that the wrong path leads him to a place he doesn't want to go. The hound *does* get what he *doesn't* want. For example, imagine setting out with your family, intending to enjoy a wonderful picnic by a lake. But you take a wrong turn and end up at a contaminated swamp! You don't get the lake, but you do get the toxic swamp. This is the kind of exchange we see couples making when they believe the myth that more money equals happiness. They not only miss out on joy and well-being, but they also land in places full of stress and less material wealth—the mucky swamp of debt.

Let's look more at what we mean by landing in the swamp. The average household has more than $8,000 on credit cards. More than 1.2 million people went bankrupt in 2000, and it is estimated that by the year 2005, more than 3 million bankruptcies will be filed annually. More than 70 percent of Americans report that they live from paycheck to paycheck. Many indicate that they are constantly worried they will not be able to pay their bills. In fact, many couples are actually living on their credit cards rather than on their current income.

We've not only gotten ourselves into a bind for the present but also mortgaged our future. It was reported in 1998 that for the first time in history, the U.S. saving rate went into the negative. Because families are failing to save for the future, in 1999 the average family reported having less than $10,000 in their retirement account. Many of us are frantically trying to get more, but we're ending up with less. Ironically, instead of bringing people closer to happiness, all the pressure of these pursuits can actually undermine true happiness.

Having It All and Ending Up Losing

How a couple handles—or mishandles—the details of their financial life can ruin a marriage. Let's look at one very common path to unhappiness. In the 1950s, the average American home was a two-bedroom, one-bath, 983-square-foot house. Although the average family size is smaller than it was in the 1950s, by 2000 the average American home had grown to a three-bedroom, 2,265-square-foot house with two-and-a-half baths, a kitchen "nook," a dining room, a study, a "great room," a dramatic "foyer," and a two- if not three-car garage. (By the turn of the millennium, many had to add a fourth garage.) More space is not a bad thing. It's just that the "great room" comes with a great big mortgage. Today's couples carry a financial burden for these homes that is twice if not three times what families carried in the 1950s. In 1950, the average price for a new home was $11,000 ($81,448 in 2000 dollars), compared to $206,400 in 2000.

Jill and David are a typical couple of today. They are a normal, loving couple chasing their dreams in life. Married for three years, they decided it was time to start a family. That meant, first, moving out of their two-bedroom apartment to make room for a growing family. They chose a real estate agent to help them look for the home of their dreams. Their agent referred them to a loan company that specialized in "pre-approvals."

Both Jill and David were working and made pretty good money. He was making $49,000 a year working for a department store chain, and she was making $38,000 working for a company that supplies employee benefits programs to other businesses. The loan officer said that they had great credit. They qualified to borrow up to $235,000 with a monthly payment of $1,800. "Wow," David said to Jill on the way home from the loan company. "I had no idea we'd be able to buy that much house." "Me neither," Jill replied. "That makes me think we could buy a home we'd like to keep for many years to come."

Armed with their pre-approval, Jill and David embarked on several weekends of house hunting with their agent. They tromped through house after house and finally found one that felt like home. The home they sought had a price tag of $243,000, but the owners accepted their offer of $235,000. Although $235,000 seemed like a lot of money, they weren't too anxious. After all, the bank said they could afford that much. They knew they could get the loan. And they did.

Fast-forward two years. Jill and David have just had the first of their family additions—a seven-pound, four-once bundle of baby boy. They named him Jeffrey, and life seemed very good. After taking a couple of months off work to take care of Jeffrey, Jill returned to work. She was fortunate in that her company provided great on-site child care. Even so, Jeffrey didn't adjust all that well. He showed a strong preference for breast-feeding over a bottle, and after a few days, he got his way. Jill would take breaks from work to go feed Jeffrey, and that was really pretty OK. Jeffrey was not the healthiest baby, though, and seemed to easily pick up "bugs" from the other kids at the child-care center. Increasingly, Jill was taking time away from the office to take Jeffrey to the doctor. Yet her workload did not let up one bit, and she was finding herself falling further and further behind.

Jill and David decided that it would be best to look into Jill's dropping to half-time instead of full-time work. They figured this would be for only a few years, and Jill really liked the idea of having more time with Jeffrey while he was so little.

Being flexible, Jill's company went for the plan, and Jill happily began working part-time. Unfortunately, a phrase they had heard before but did not understand came to define their lives: *house rich, cash poor.* They loved their home, but they had maxed out their two-income budget to buy it. Even though David's income had grown to $53,000 over the past couple of years, their health insurance had gone up considerably, wiping out most of the gain. Then there were the costs of child care, diapers, the crib, the car seat, and so forth. When Jill's income dropped to $20,000 after going to half-time, they began to feel the squeeze. There is a big difference between $73,000 and $87,000.

Although both Jill and David were very committed to making sure Jill had more time with Jeffrey, life began to get very painful for both of them. Money became a constant worry. They cut back in all kinds of ways, but still kept falling just a little short. And little-by-little can get to be a lot.

After seven months, they had accumulated $6,300 in credit card debt; before, they had always paid off the balance. If their debt had gotten out of hand quickly, they would have perhaps made what would have felt like a drastic decision to sell their house and buy something more affordable. But, as often happens, their debt had built up gradually, and they believed their situation to be temporary. So they stayed put, and David threw himself into his career with the hopes of a promotion.

Two as Cheaply?

We have all heard the old saw, "Two can live as cheaply as one." Recently, this has led to a series of bumper stickers that say, "Two can live as cheaply as one, for half as long" or "Two can live as cheaply as one, as long as only one eats." Whether or not two can live as cheaply as one, no one disputes that when baby makes three, the costs go way up.

The financial cost of raising children has been calculated by the U.S. Department of Agriculture for at least a couple of decades. It is estimated that the financial cost of raising a child born in 2000 will be about $165,630, or $233,530 when factoring in the cost of inflation. This cost includes all food, shelter, and other necessities until the child is eighteen. This cost does not include a college education, which may cost as much as an additional $150,000 by the time the child enters college in 2017.

David began to volunteer for increasingly high-profile projects in the department. Before, he'd been working about forty-five hours a week; now he was inching toward sixty-seven. He wasn't gone from home all that much more, but even when he was home, he was "gone" a lot. Even though David was home, theoretically available for Jill and Jeffrey, he was distracted, seemingly more focused on his laptop and fax machine. And the bills kept coming.

Stress mounted for Jill and David. Sure, they had their dream home, but their financial situation changed their lives completely. The closeness they had once shared seemed to be gradually slipping away. All the little interchanges that had contributed to their sense of intimacy had virtually ceased, partly because David wasn't around as much and partly because when he was, his attention was spread thin between work, Jeffrey, and Jill.

Things only got worse as David and Jill became more worried about money. This stress showed itself in such ways as David's getting after Jill for how much she spent at the grocery store. "Do we really need to have Jeffrey in that brand of disposables?" "I don't think we can afford to be buying so many convenience food items. Can't you make lasagna from scratch instead of buying it preprepared?" Such comments gave new meaning to the term *food fight*. In reality, their grocery bills were pretty average, and Jill didn't see it as an area where they could make up the shortfall.

Jill and David found ways to make it through these very difficult years, but they didn't come through unscathed. David was rewarded financially for his devotion to his career; however, the distance that grew between him and Jill would be a fact of their marriage for many years to come. Decisions that David had made at work could not be undone. He had created a certain image at work and could not go back to working less without it looking as if he'd become lazy—even if he did outproduce many others in the company. Besides, being successful at work felt good. He'd become the go-to guy, and he felt a lot more appreciated at work than he ever felt at home. Jill increasingly felt that she was raising a family on her own (they had another child, Aubrey, in the mix now). She was mostly right.

There are many pathways to the trap in which Jill and David found themselves. For them, it started simply with a major, mutually agreed-on financial decision: to buy a house at the top end of what the bank told them they could afford. Life does not give you easy ways to undo the effects of decisions that are this big. Jill and David didn't realize at the time that their house purchase was a trade-off. They ended up trading the richness of their relationship for material substance. They have more, but what have they really gained, and what have they really lost?

True Happiness in a Shared Life

If in order to find true happiness you had to choose between investing in your relationship or making more money, you'd be far wiser to put the time and energy into your marriage. Of course, in real life, it's not quite that simple. Couples cannot simply "live on love." You do need to be able to make money, save money, and spend money. The better you are able to do those things together, as a team, the better your future will be. Well-being depends on nurturing your relationship *and* being true financial partners. The two go hand in hand.

Nevertheless, putting money into perspective is crucial. It is not the wealthiest people who are the happiest. It is not the people with the most toys who win. It is the people who have great relationships, and, as we are specifically addressing in this book, people who are mates for life are people who tend to be the happiest in life. Therefore, one of the most important things couples can do to find true happiness in life is to nurture their love. The really good news is that, for most couples, having a strong relationship will most likely to lead to long-term financial security. If couples chase more and more money, they may end up losing their love and never enter the gates of happiness. Yet if they nurture their marriage, they are more likely to find true happiness and to reap financial rewards besides.

You may wake up one morning and ask yourself, "Am I happy with the way I am living my life?" If you've learned that money is valuable but that love is priceless, you're far more likely to be able to answer yes.

CHAPTER THREE

AN INTRODUCTION TO INVISIBLE FORCES

I think a man and a woman should choose each other for life, for the simple reason that a long life with all its accidents is barely enough for a man and a woman to understand each other; and to understand is to love.

WILLIAM BUTLER YEATS

Cathy and Ed managed their money pretty well. They worked hard to make sure they had enough, and in general they agreed on all the necessities. Unlike most couples, Cathy and Ed had a budget. Not only did they keep track of what they spent, but they actually set aside some money every month in an account for special purchases. Their "Special" account was where they kept their money to fund their favorite hobbies. The system usually worked great.

Ed was nuts about classic cars. He and his buddies spent many hours and a great deal of money keeping their cars in tip-top shape. Ed's baby was a cherry-red '57 Chevy. Cathy was content to have Ed play in the garage as long as she could decorate the rest of the house. She liked expensive furniture, rich fabrics, and coordinated colors.

Although their interests were different, they each enjoyed the other's delight in his or her hobby. Cathy enjoyed riding in Ed's cars and attending the special "classics" shows. Ed liked Cathy's panache in decorating the house. If left to his own devices, he'd have spent the money on his cars, but he liked their home. "You make our house grand," he'd tell Cathy, and she would smile from ear to ear.

For many months, Cathy had had her eye on an armoire for their bedroom. It was a beautiful model in rustic oak. She assumed that Ed was fine with purchasing the armoire because she'd talked about it for a long time. But she hadn't talked to him about it recently. Still, they had $1,600 in their Special account, and the armoire was "only" $1,399. In fact, it had come on sale, at long last, and she was ready to pounce.

Meanwhile, Ed was looking forward to replacing all four tires with deluxe, wide-strip whitewalls, straight out of the 1950s. Of course, tires built to look like popular models in the 1950s were a lot more expensive than tires built for newer cars—eight hundred bucks' worth of rolling nostalgia.

There was nothing wrong with either Ed's or Cathy's plans, except that neither had any idea what the other was thinking. The fireworks began for Cathy and Ed one Saturday morning when their desires collided.

Cathy: Guess what? Brandenmoors has that armoire we've been wanting for ages on sale this weekend. Best price I've seen on it yet. Want to come with me to get it?

Ed: Get it? Honey, I don't think we have enough money at the moment.

Cathy: Oh, we do! In fact, we'll still have two hundred bucks left over in our Special account after we buy it.

Ed: Hold on a second. I was counting on using half of the money in that account for some new tires for the Chevy.

Cathy: (with some alarm in her voice) Half of the money in the account? You mean these tires cost eight hundred dollars?

Ed: (sounding defensive and annoyed) I guess.

Cathy: You guess? You've never said anything about getting new tires for the Chevy. We hardly ever drive it anyway. Why does it need new tires?

Ed: Well, it doesn't "need" new tires. But these tires would make it more like the original. I've wanted these for a long time.

Cathy: I'm sure *you'd* like them a lot, but *we* were not planning on buying tires; *we* were planning on buying this armoire, and it's on sale right now.

Ed: (feeling and sounding angry now) That's something *you* want, not something *we* want. And if *you* get what *you* want, *I* don't get what *I* want for a long time.

Cathy: (getting upset and frustrated) I think you're just saying that now because you're angry. You know we've wanted to get this armoire. Or are you saying that you misled me before when we talked about this?

Ed: I haven't misled you. Talking about something you might want in the future is not the same as planning to go out and buy something right now. Now come on, let's try to be adults about this.

Cathy: Adults? (louder) Adults? So throwing a tantrum because you can't wait to buy new tires for your toy car is being an adult???

And off they went. After blowing what could have been a nice weekend, neither could look back and claim to have behaved like mature adults. I (Howard) like to say that we can be young only once, but we can be immature forever! My real point is about the importance of knowing how to play, throughout adulthood. But whereas being playful is a good thing, allowing ourselves to behave like children having tantrums is not. But boy, it sure is easy to do. A happy Saturday morning can suddenly become stressful when a discussion about money transforms into an unpleasant you-versus-me argument. It's almost as if couples find themselves transported into the Twilight Zone.

What in the world happens? Normal people typically do not sit around thinking, "I'm kind of bored. I think I'll start a fight with my partner about money at, say, seven-thirty tonight. Yeah, that'll work." Of course not. Cathy didn't wake up and think, "Hmm, I wonder how I can ruin Ed's Saturday." Like Cathy, most of

WITNESS LILLIAN AND HENRY BATESON, CHARTER MEMBERS IN THE FRATERNITY OF MARITAL BLISS. SHE, A HIGHLY SUCCESSFUL BANK EXECUTIVE, IS ABOUT TO SIT DOWN WITH HENRY, AN UNASSUMING SCHOOL TEACHER, ON AN APPARENTLY QUIET EVENING AFTER AN ORDINARY DAY. THE BATESONS THINK THEY ARE GOING TO TALK ABOUT MONEY, BUT UNSEEN FORCES HAVE OTHER IDEAS, BECAUSE IT ISN'T JUST ABOUT THE MONEY. YOU SEE, LILLIAN AND HENRY ARE ABOUT TO CONFRONT AN ISSUE... ONE THAT LIES IN THE TWLIGHT OF THE **INVISIBLE FORCES ZONE.**

The
INVISIBLE FORCES ZONE

RAGNAR STORAASLI

Many couples have money conflicts, even in loving and usually happy marriages.

us are decent people who enjoy getting along with our mates. Yet many couples have money conflicts like these, even in loving and usually happy marriages. Why? What's going on? If these conflicts become frequent, couples are likely to end up harming their relationship. You can recover from one not-so-nice blowup. Even a few. But month after month after month, the little hurts begin to tear us down, fraying the loving bond that binds a couple together. So it's very important for you to understand why these things happen and to be able to keep them from eroding your love. The first step in preventing these kinds of arguments is to understand what's going on.

Issues and Events

In this chapter, we'll be exploring *issues,* the first of three types of invisible forces we cover in this book. Issues are aptly named invisible, for we tend not to see them. The way we usually feel the pressure of an issue is in the course of an *event.*

An event is an occurrence or incident. Events happen in the flow of time, and they often act as the trigger for an argument. There is no end to possible argument-triggering events when it comes to money. For example:

A check bounces.

The credit card bill arrives and is larger than expected.

It's time for the annual benefits review at work, and you have to decide how much money to have withheld each month for retirement.

One of your parents gets very ill and needs financial help moving into a nursing home.

You have been married for three months when you discover that your mate brought along a few friends with some heavy baggage: Visa, Master Card, and Discover.

An issue is a deeper, ongoing concern. Issues are the enduring themes of conflict in the life of a couple. Common issues for couples include money, sex, communication, child rearing, in-laws, careers, division of responsibilities, and so forth. As you can imagine, there are hundreds of events that could be connected with any of these issues. The possibilities are endless.

For Ed and Cathy, the event on that Saturday morning was the discovery that they both wanted to spend the same money on different things. There would have been no event if, for example, they had had $2,500 in their Special account. The issue of money would not have been triggered at all. They would not have fought at all. In fact, they would likely have been able to enjoy each other's delight in the purchases. Maybe they'd have taken the Chevy out to the furniture store and then to the tire store, and had a great day together. But that was not to be, not on this weekend. The event—each of them having designs on the money in the Special account—triggered a fight about money and about who was going to get what he or she wanted at the expense of the other. The issue was money, and it came to represent a collision of the partners' interests.

Understanding how events can trigger issues helps explain how normal, loving couples manage to find themselves in heated arguments from time to time. As we said, normal, loving couples typically don't *intend* to start arguments. But that doesn't keep us from tripping over events and smacking face-first into issues. Most of the time, things heat up between partners when some event triggers a bigger issue. To use another metaphor, issues are like land mines, and events are the triggers that cause those to explode. Every couple has issues, and every life is full of events. Nearly every couple experiences a ka-boom once in a while, but some couples go KAAA-BOOOOOM! Let's take a look at two more couples and see if you can identify the event and the issue in each case. Here are Jason and Barbara.

Jason: Hi, Hon, how was your day?

Barbara: Oh, pretty lousy, but I stopped off at Foley's to cheer myself up.

Jason: Somehow I don't think that I'm going to be cheered up by this.

Barbara: Now don't start. Foley's had a great SALE!

Jason: Oh, no! The "S" word.

Barbara: *(feeling hurt)* Oh, come on, Jason. I got some stuff for you too.

Jason: *(irritated)* What difference does that make? We don't have money to blow on either of us!!

Barbara: Yeah, right! You just treated yourself to a new super-deluxe Orvis Odyssey 400 fishing rod. The way you fish, a Minnie Mouse pole would have done just fine!

Jason: It wasn't an Orvis . . . I needed that fishing pole . . . a Minnie Mouse pole? What kind of stupid remark was that?

> What we feel, our emotions, need to be taken seriously, even if the content— the words we're saying—don't make much sense or even seem ridiculous.

Jason and Barbara went on to have a rip-roaring argument, but we can stop here. They have already provided us with the opportunity to make several points. First of all, notice how silly this argument seems. To an outsider, many of your arguments might seem pretty silly too. But if you're in the middle of an argument, it usually doesn't *feel* silly, it feels very painful. What we feel, our emotions, need to be taken seriously, even if the content—the words we're saying—don't make much sense or even seem ridiculous. In fact, the silliness of an argument is a clue that there's more going on than what may be obvious—that you're being pushed around by one of those invisible forces.

From Jason's perspective, the event was Barbara's coming home and announcing that she had gone shopping. From his reaction, "Somehow I don't think I am going to be cheered up by this," we can assume that Barbara has gone shopping before, and Jason does not perceive her shopping as a good thing.

From Barbara's perspective, the event was Jason's reacting unenthusiastically to the news that she'd gone shopping. From her statement "Now don't start," we can assume that she's experienced Jason's disapproval of her shopping before, and she doesn't want to experience it again. She's reacting to his reaction—the event for her.

The issue for both Jason and Barbara is money. All the decisions that swirl around spending and saving money form one big issue. Who gets to spend how much and when? When is it OK to break the rules?

Money was the issue for Steve and Macayla too, although the event that triggered their money issue was different. "Rusty had been with me longer than Steve," Macayla explained. "He is the sweetest springer spaniel you've ever seen, and Steve wanted me to have him put down. "I didn't *want* him to be put down," said Steve defensively. "We simply did not have the $1,200 to blow on vet bills."

Three years have passed since the accident, and Rusty has recovered completely, but Steve and Macayla haven't. Rusty, Macayla's then five-year-old "best friend," had run into the street and gotten hit by a car. The damage was extensive, but the vet said Rusty would heal—with expensive surgery. Steve was supportive, until he found out just how expensive it would be. "You have to understand that we didn't have the money. I mean, I'd have sold my truck to keep Rusty alive, but my truck was worth only $500. We did *not* have the money." In the end, Macayla borrowed the money from her parents.

"This was a fundamental disagreement on how you handle things when life gets tough," says Steve. "In the first place, sometimes you have to be willing to do the difficult thing, and in the second, you don't go running back to Mama. There had to be a better way, and we should have found that way together. When I wouldn't give her what she wanted, she went running back to her Mom. That's not how it's supposed to work."

For Macayla and Steve, the event was their dog's needing surgery that would cost more money than they had. As Steve said, he was willing to sell his truck (his most precious material possession) to keep Rusty alive, but it wasn't enough. Steve was willing to go very far in saving their pet, but Macayla was willing to go further—and she was willing to do it without Steve's agreement.

In this book, we focus primarily on money issues and events, but note that there are all kinds of issues that represent all sorts of problem areas. For example, if you have an issue about your in-laws' interfering too much, a phone call with your mother-in-law may be an event that triggers that issue for you. Or suppose the two of you have children, and you tend to disagree about discipline. If your child causes trouble at school during the day, then that may be the event that triggers a big argument over child rearing that night.

Events Happen

You've seen the bumper sticker "Stuff Happens." OK, so maybe you saw a slightly different bumper sticker. But it is true. Events happen as a regular part of life, and there is only so much we can do to prevent them. Cathy and Ed (the armoire/Chevy couple) could have communicated better about their plans before that Saturday. But it just isn't realistic to think that two people are going to be able to tell their partner about every little and big thing they are thinking about, every idea they have, every dream they dream. Sometime, somewhere, one is going to catch the other off guard, and that will be an event.

In the case of Barbara and Jason (the shopping/fishing pole couple), it is possible that Barbara will stop shopping. It is also possible that Jason will learn to jump up and down with glee whenever Barbara goes shopping. But we wouldn't want to bet on either of these possibilities, would you? It is true that people can and do change, and we think that Barbara and Jason could see these events occur less frequently by applying what we teach in this book, but we don't think these events will stop completely. And, even if they did, there would always be other events.

Macayla and Steve's dog ran into the street. No matter how careful we are, some accident is going to happen sometime. The point is this: couples only have so much control over what happens in life. We don't get to choose our circumstances; we only get to choose how we react to those circumstances. It isn't realistic to think, "Well, we will just not experience events." Life doesn't work that way.

> *We don't get to choose our circumstances; we only get to choose how we react to those circumstances.*

Remember the canoe trip I (Natalie) talked about in the Introduction? You don't get to choose when the river is going to take a turn or throw a big boulder in the way. The very first sentence in Scott Peck's best-selling book *The Road Less Traveled* is "Life is difficult." Then he goes on to say, "This is a great truth, one of the greatest truths. It is a great truth because once we truly see this truth, we transcend it. Once we truly know that life is difficult—once we truly understand and accept it—then life is no longer difficult. Because once it is accepted, the fact that life is difficult no longer matters."

You will always face events in your life. We've seen far too many couples either think that there is something wrong with them because there is always something going on, or focus so much on "solving" all these problems that they forget to live. Both of these attitudes rob couples of precious life. There's nothing wrong with you if your life together seems to be just one "thing" after another—that *is* life! Dishwashers break and leak all over the new linoleum. Spouses lose their job. Mothers grow old and need to go to the nursing home.

Part of being financial partners is learning to handle all the events of life together—as a team. At the same time, marriage is not a project; it is a relationship. Couples have told us, "As soon as we get the dishwasher fixed, we'll go spend time together"; "As soon as my partner gets a new job, we'll be able to enjoy a vacation together"; "As soon as we have my mother taken care of, we'll take time for each other." These couples will wake up one day and wonder where their life went. Events will always happen. They aren't always bad either—you might get a bonus check or a tax refund. You might get invited to go on a great vacation with friends. But events will happen. Don't try to stop them, and don't try to handle all of them before you start living.

None of what we've said here means that when events happen, you have to let the issues push you around. We will show you specific ways to handle issues and the other invisible forces in Part Two. (You can skip ahead to Chapter Eight if you're really curious.) Right now we just want you to get a feel for what these forces *do*—how they operate—and to understand that you needn't let them get the better of you. At this point, are you beginning to see how an invisible force such as an issue about money might push a couple off course?

Take Ed and Cathy for example. They were looking forward to a nice Saturday together, but when the event—discovering they had different ideas as to how to spend the money in their Special account—triggered a money issue, they ended up far from enjoying their time together. Have you ever had a similar experience? Can you remember a time when an event triggered a money issue for the two of you, and the issue ended up pushing you off course? If the concept of money issues pushing you around seems a bit fuzzy right now, that's OK. We expect that these ideas will become more clear as we move on. In the next chapter you'll discover the second type of invisible force, which we call *hidden issues*.

Time to Talk

What kind of money events regularly occur in your relationship? We've got an exercise that the two of you can do together that we think you'll find interesting and informative. To get you thinking about how money events trigger issues in your lives, we want you to think about some of the most common events that occur, year in and year out.

Many money- and marriage-related issues tend to become triggered by such events as birthdays, holidays, and vacations. These are times when families are together (providing the opportunity for conflicts), emotions tend to run high (due to unresolved family tensions), expectations are high, and, very often, some money must be spent.

Here's your task. We're going to give you a list of holidays, observations, celebrations, and other important dates. Carve out some time together to talk through the list, using the questions listed here and talking about your perceptions and your sense of history related to the dates.

Holidays and Other Special Days

Valentine's Day

Income tax time (not exactly a holiday, but often an issue-triggering event)

Mother's Day

Father's Day

Christmas or Hanukkah

Your anniversary

Your birthday

Spouse's birthday

Children's birthdays

Other friends' and family members' birthdays and anniversaries

Family vacations

Questions for Discussion

1. What has tended to happen (if anything) on these dates in your relationship? Have you had conflicts? Have things gone smoothly? What events on these days have triggered issues?
2. What are the key issues most often triggered?
3. When you were growing up, were there notable issues and events related to these days in your family?
4. If you have been in a prior serious adult relationship (for example, a marriage or long-term romantic involvement), were there notable issues and events related to these days that might affect you in your relationship at present?

Adjust your list by adding any other special days on which issue-triggering events occur and by subtracting "uneventful" days. Arrange the days chronologically. Once you have your "event calendar" in order, write down what the events were, what issues were triggered, and how you handled the situation. Now take some time to think through how you can work together as a team to handle the events and issues better next year.

You may actually find this discussion kind of fun, especially if you can approach it as two friends, each learning more about the other's views in life. If it seems quite difficult for the two of you—or if you are pretty sure it's not likely to go well—hold off for now until you've read Chapter Eight on making it safer to talk through issues. Practice what we recommend there on easier topics, get comfortable with the model, then return to this exercise and talk it through. You can do it.

CHAPTER FOUR

THE FULL MONTY: EXPOSING HIDDEN ISSUES

Vision is the art of seeing the invisible.

JONATHAN SWIFT

In Chapter Two, you learned how events trigger issues, the first kind of invisible force. You learned that an event is an occurrence or an incident. Events happen in the flow of time, and they often act as the trigger for an issue. Issues are deeper, ongoing concerns; they are the enduring themes for disagreement in the life of a couple. Most of the time, the issues that are triggered by events are very clear, because they are about money-related topics that most of us deal with every day—shopping, paying bills, and so on. Cathy and Ed (whom we met in the preceding chapter) experienced an event when Cathy suggested that they go buy an armoire, which touched off a money issue for them. That one is not hard to figure out. At other times, it's a bit tougher to see what is going on.

Sometimes couples find themselves getting caught up in arguments triggered by events that don't seem to be attached to any particular issue. Or couples don't seem to be getting anywhere when talking about particular problems, as if the relationship were a car stuck on ice, spinning its wheels. These are clues that the second kind of invisible force is at work, what we call *hidden issues.*

When we say these issues are hidden, we mean that they are usually not being talked about openly—but they need to be. Hidden issues reflect the unexpressed needs and feelings that, if not attended to, can cause great damage to your marriage. These are the kind of invisible force that better explains the fury that seemingly innocent events can trigger. As we mentioned earlier, money is a major issue for couples because it, like nothing else we know of, provides the screen on which couples project all their deepest fears, hopes, dreams, and hurts in life.

We see six main types of hidden issues that are often triggered by money- and marriage-related events: *control and power, caring, recognition, commitment, integrity,* and *acceptance.* There are surely others, but these six capture a lot of what goes on as couples struggle with money.

Hidden Issues of Control and Power

We cannot think of any area of life that has more potential than money for triggering hidden issues about control and power. Behind hidden control issues are deeper concerns about status and power. Are your needs and desires regarding money just as important as your partner's, or is there an inequality? Is your input about earning and spending important, or are major decisions made without you? Who's in charge of the money in your household? Do you feel controlled when it comes to money matters? These are common themes for couples and may not be all that hidden, yet they exert a force on you and your partner if the two of you haven't brought them out in the open in a constructive way—if you haven't disarmed them.

Control and power issues are often triggered when various decisions come up—even small ones. A power struggle can result over just about any decision related to money. Lisa and Marvin were newlyweds who had agreed that, unlike most couples, Marvin would be in charge of the grocery shopping. Yet they found themselves constantly arguing over the shopping bill after Marvin came home with the groceries. Instead of saying "Thanks for doing the shopping," Lisa would carefully go over each item and grill Marvin about why he bought such-and-such and why he spent so much money. Marvin felt that he did a great job of shopping within their budget, and after a while he grew angry with Lisa's hawking over him each time he came home from shopping. Without really knowing why, Lisa felt a need to monitor Marvin's shopping decisions, and he fought to maintain control over this household domain.

Some people are motivated to be in control because they're actually hypersensitive about being controlled by others. Usually such a person has experienced a very controlling and powerful authority figure sometime in the past, often a parent, as in the next example.

Harry and Kitty are parents of two daughters ages twenty-one and twenty-three. All his life, Harry has been a control freak. Harry grew up with a controlling father, so Harry assumed that if he were really a man, he should be in control of his family. Daily, Harry let his children know he was the ultimate authority in their family. Kitty, in contrast, is naturally shy and hesitant to say what she really thinks. During the active parenting years, they settled into their respective roles. Harry had the final word. Kitty concentrated on her role as mom and acted as a buffer between Harry and their daughters—especially in the turbulent teenage years.

Harry's big issue was finances, and he controlled the budget. When the kids were still home, this worked well enough. Kitty had a set amount of money each month for food, clothing, and household expenses. She didn't really resent Harry's desire to control everything, but when the last child left for college, she saw no reason to stick to such a rigid budget. Besides, she thought, "the kids have grown up and are on their own; I need to grow up too and make some of my own decisions."

Kitty decided it was time to spruce up their house and one day surprised Harry with a new blue sofa. When Harry came home and saw the sofa, he hit the ceiling. What was wrong with the sofa they had? He hated that shade of blue. And why did she do this without checking with him first? Kitty resented being treated like one of the kids. She had wanted to surprise him. Why didn't he appreciate her thoughtfulness? Why should she have to check out everything with him anyway? The next day, she went out looking for a job. She would earn her own money—then she would decorate the house any way she wanted to! This hidden issue of control had been there for years but didn't really become obvious until Kitty triggered it by buying the blue sofa. Suddenly Kitty realized she was tired of Harry's always having to be in control. It might have been better for Harry and Kitty to decide together on getting the new sofa, but Kitty resented Harry's making all the financial decisions.

In the larger picture, the really big event for Kitty and Harry was the children's leaving for college. David and Claudia Arp, our coauthors on the book *Empty Nesting*, point out that children's leaving home is a major transition point in the lives of couples. Old ways of planning things, deciding things, and doing things may need to change. This transition can feel like a crisis for many couples but can also become a wonderful opportunity to build a stronger, deeper relationship.

For Harry and Kitty, the upheaval led to good changes in the dynamics of their marriage. The couch incident triggered a huge conflict that ultimately led them to counseling and to reevaluating their marriage style and choosing to make some changes. They agreed to start making more decisions together. As Harry began to include Kitty in decision making and financial decisions, Kitty felt less controlled and more loving toward Harry. Originally they had been a living illustration of how power plays in a marriage destroy the potential for love to grow. But when Harry gave up trying to control Kitty, she responded by loving

Every decision you must make together is an opportunity for the hidden issue of control to be triggered.

him more. She felt he must really love her to work on changing such a fundamental part of his personality style.

Every decision you must make together is an opportunity for the hidden issue of control to be triggered. Working together as a team is the best antidote. Hidden issues of control are least likely to damage your relationship when the two of you feel that you are a team and that each partner's needs and desires are attended to in the decisions you make.

Hidden Issues of Caring

The main theme of hidden issues of caring is the extent to which you feel loved and cared for by your partner. Such hidden issues come up when you feel that your important emotional needs aren't being met.

Jill and Nelson repeatedly fought over who should balance the checkbook every month. As you might expect, there was something bigger than the checkbook fueling their arguments. As it turned out, Nelson had always thought of his mother's balancing the family checkbook as one of the ways his mother demonstrated her love and caring for his father. When Jill wouldn't do it for Nelson, he felt she didn't love him. He had a hidden issue of caring.

For her part, Jill was thinking, "Who's he to tell me to balance the checkbook? Where does he get off saying I have to do it?" She resisted doing the task simply because she didn't like being told what to do. She had a hidden issue of power.

For them, exploring their hidden issues and effectively discussing them brought them closer; the checkbook no longer seemed all that important.

Nelson: You know, I never thought much about this before. But when I was growing up, I saw my dad asking my mom to balance the checkbook, and she did. It was one of her ways of showing him that she loved him. I guess I just picked that up. So for me, it really isn't about wanting to control you. I guess I feel loved when you do certain things I ask you to do. So I've put this pressure on you to do it just so I could be sure you love me.

Jill: So you're not trying to boss me around or control me. You just want to feel loved, and having me balance the checkbook feels like me loving you. Is that what you're saying?

Nelson: Exactly, and I'm feeling a bit ridiculous here. I mean, it's not that big of a deal, but it kind of is a big deal to me. And hey, I can see how you'd be feeling controlled without knowing that—I have been putting pressure on you to take care of the checkbook.

> *Jill:* Thanks for telling me this. And I get it. Sometimes little things mean a lot. And you're right. I've really felt you wanted to control me, and that's a real hot button given what I went through before. I do *not* like being told what to do.
>
> *Nelson:* Yeah, I've figured that out! *(smiles)* It really did seem to you that I just wanted to control you, and that's an especially sensitive area for you.
>
> *Jill:* You got it. I want to be your partner, not your servant.
>
> *Nelson:* Oh drag—the only reason I married you was so you'd clean up after me. *(smiling really big)* Just kidding, Honey. Sounds like you want us to be a team.
>
> *Jill:* Ha-ha, you're so funny! Yes, I want us to be a team!

As you can see from the tail end of their conversation, learning to talk about the bigger concerns paved the way for greater connection instead of alienation over who balances the checkbook. Notice that Jill and Nelson haven't really solved the problem as to who is going to balance the checkbook. Maybe they will decide together that Jill wants to take on this task as a way of expressing love to Nelson. Maybe Nelson will decide to take it on, realizing that Jill's *not* doing it doesn't mean she doesn't love him. What's key here is that they have stripped the hidden issue of its power to push them off course and are now free to discuss how to handle the task in whatever way works best for the both of them. Balancing the checkbook is now only about just that—balancing the checkbook. By disarming the hidden issues, balancing the checkbook has lost all its symbolic value and the negative energy it had that was causing so much conflict between them. If these hidden forces were evil little gremlins trying to push Jill and Nelson around, this conversation would have left one of the gremlins down for the count! That's winning!

Hidden Issues of Recognition

Whereas hidden issues of caring involve concerns about being cared for or loved, hidden issues of recognition are more about feeling valued and appreciated by your partner for what you do. Does your partner appreciate your activities and accomplishments? Do you feel that your efforts regarding money in your marriage are ignored?

A common example is that of a couple who has had a pretty traditional division of roles: the man earning the income and the woman taking the major role of day-to-day child care and rearing. For many women, to raise their children and manage the household are their key activities and also their primary sources of recognition.

One such couple is Burt and Chelsea, who have been married for ten years. They have three tow-headed daughters ages two, six, and nine. Burt is a successful computer software salesman, Chelsea a full-time mom. Burt brings home a good income, but Chelsea manages to stretch a dollar farther than anyone we've ever met. They bought a run-down home in a very nice neighborhood, and Chelsea did much of the renovation herself. She bought drywall and windows from the classifieds and saved several thousand dollars. She buys groceries in bulk and pays pennies on the dollar. She keeps the books for the kids' piano teacher in exchange for their lessons. Chelsea takes great pride in the way she contributes to their family's economic well-being. So when she overheard Burt on the phone with the insurance salesman, saying, "No, we don't need life insurance for my wife, just me; I'm the only one who contributes to the finances in this household," Chelsea was crushed.

Likewise, many men tell us they feel that their wives don't place much value on their work to bring home income. One of our colleagues is a best-selling author. One evening when I (Natalie) was having dinner with him, I asked what his wife thought of his book. He said that she hadn't had the chance to read it yet. It had been out for six years and had sold nearly a million copies, but his own wife hadn't bothered to read it. The pain in my friend's expression was palpable. Both men and women need to feel appreciated and can have a hidden issue of recognition.

Unappreciated spouses may try hard for a while to get recognized for what they bring to the family, but will eventually burn out if no appreciation is expressed. How long has it been since you told your partner how much you appreciate the things he or she does? What efforts or contributions does your partner bring to your relationship that you take for granted? Look for ways—now, today—to show more appreciation for those efforts. If it's hard to figure out what your partner feels best about in contributing to your union, ask what he or she is most proud of bringing to your lives. Then go out of your way to consistently show appreciation for those efforts.

Showing real appreciation for your partner's efforts will go a long way toward keeping recognition issues from being triggered in your relationship in the first place. In fact, being proactive is a great way to prevent any of the hidden issues from gaining enough power to push you off your course.

Hidden Issues of Commitment

Commitment themes reflect how confident you are that the two of you are going to be together—no matter what. The key here is the long-term security of the relationship: "Are you going to stay with me?" One couple, Alice and Chuck, were a delight for us to work with. They are a pair of young and vivacious fifty-year-olds. This was the second marriage for both, and each felt lucky to have found the other. Yet, as with most couples, they had to contend with at least one sore spot in their relationship. Alice and Chuck had huge arguments about separate checking accounts. Whenever the bank statement arrived, he would complain bitterly about her having a separate account.

Although the issue was money, the more powerful negative energy in this case came from a hidden issue of commitment. Chuck's ex-wife had a separate account. She decided to leave him after fifteen years of marriage, which was easier for her to do because she'd saved up several thousand dollars in this account. Now, when the statement for Alice's account would arrive, Chuck associated it with thoughts that Alice could be planning to leave him. That was not at all her plan, but because he rarely talked openly about his fear, she wasn't given the opportunity to alleviate his anxiety by affirming her commitment. The monthly event, the arrival of her bank statement, kept fueling their money issue, and they experienced fast-burning conflict around his hidden issue of commitment.

One of the newer trends on the money and relationship scene is that of couples' striking prenuptial (and even postnuptial) agreements. There are advantages and disadvantages to creating such agreements. There are certainly situations in which it seems wise to consider some sort of agreement—for example, when a person is remarrying and wants to protect children from a prior marriage in terms of estates upon the death of the parent or in the event that the couple should divorce. It's this latter prospect that is so painful for many couples to contemplate.

Working through a prenuptial agreement often triggers the hidden issue of commitment. At least in the context of "what-iffing" about divorce, prenuptial agreements require partners, in effect, to plan out the death of their relationship at a time when they are most full of hope for their future together. It's very hard to maintain perspective on commitment when you're talking intensely about the commitment not holding together. It is hard to say, "I will always love you" and "Let's plan for our divorce" at the same time.

One way couples can protect the interests of their children from prior marriages against what the future may hold (for example, the death of a parent) without triggering hidden issues of commitment is to work with an attorney to construct trusts. Creating a trust doesn't require contemplation of the possibility of divorce. We'll talk more about trusts in Chapter Fifteen.

When your commitment to one another is secure, it brings a powerful, peaceful, deep kind of safety to your relationship. This is safety that comes from the lasting promise to be there for one another, to lift one another up in tough times, to cherish each other for a lifetime. Do you worry about your partner's long-term commitment to you and the marriage? Have you talked about this openly, or does this issue find indirect expression in the context of events in your relationship? Do you find yourself acting out a hidden issue of commitment in ways that are counterproductive? Do you let this invisible force push you off course?

Hidden Issues of Integrity

Have you ever noticed how upset you get when your partner questions your intent or motive in a way that implies that your intent isn't really what you say it is? These events can spark great fury. Integrity is triggered as an issue when you think your partner is questioning your motives, values, or standards. Whether this questioning is real or imagined, you feel judged, and this fuels a desire to defend yourself. For Nick and Gladys, arguments about money matters frequently end up with each of them thinking "I know what you *really* mean." Most often, each is sure that what the other meant was negative. Here's a typical example:

Gladys: You forgot to pay for Erica's day camp—it was due yesterday.
  Nick: *(feeling a bit indignant)* You didn't ask me to pay for her day camp, you asked me how much it was. I told you I didn't know.
Gladys: *(really angry at what she sees as his lack of caring about what she needs)* You *did* say you'd put the check in the mail, but you just don't give a hoot about me.
  Nick: *(feeling thoroughly insulted)* I do care, and I resent you telling me I don't.

You can see how their fights are energized by the first kind of invisible force, an issue of money, but the far more powerful forces include the hidden issues of caring and integrity. Her hidden issue of caring is pretty much out in the open here, although the couple is not exactly having a constructive talk about it. Her mind reading triggers a hidden issue of integrity for him.

Keep in mind that Gladys and Nick are not testy people. If you met them, you'd probably like them and find it hard to believe that they could get so nasty with each other. That shows you the power of invisible forces. They can hit us hard, and if you don't know how to handle them (or if you don't choose to handle them well), the scene can get ugly. Don't get us wrong: we're not offering couples excuses for treating each other badly. Nope. You don't get to say, "Oh, it's not my fault I was so nasty—it was an invisible force." No way. It's your job to understand these invisible forces—not so you can excuse bad behavior, not so you can tolerate these painful feelings, not so you can constantly push back, but so you can disarm them. You can convert the negative energy that comes between the two of you into positive connection.

Integrity is about being honest, about character, about being a decent human being. Gladys has impugned Nick's character. She has touched off the hidden issue of integrity by accusing Nick of being a liar. He says he wasn't asked to pay for camp. Gladys says that's a lie. Then she goes further and says that the reason he didn't do what he said he would is because he is uncaring. That's mind reading with a negative interpretation of his motive, and that does not feel good to anyone on the receiving end. The natural reaction of most people when challenged this way is to defend their integrity.

It is always presumptuous to assume that we know what is going on in another person's head or heart. Gladys can't read a person's mind—no one can—yet she states emphatically what Nick cares or does not care about. He feels insulted at her calling him an uncaring, inconsiderate husband who never thinks about her needs. That really offends his sense of himself as a good and loving husband.

It's not wise to argue about what the other really thinks, feels, or intends. Don't tell your partner what's going on inside, unless you are talking about *your* insides. To do otherwise is guaranteed to trigger the issue of integrity. And most anyone will defend his or her integrity when it's questioned.

Some subjects can trigger integrity issues in married couples regardless of whether or not one partner makes negative, mind-reading statements about the other—taxes, for example. We've seen more than a few couples in which the partners differ a lot in how aggressive they are about taking tax deductions. What happens when one partner is pretty sure that their trip to the Bahamas really had very little to do with business and a lot more to do with playing, but the partner knows that his or her mate is deducting it on the tax return—the tax return that the partner has to sign too? You can bet this sort of situation triggers conflicts over integrity.

Here's another example. Luke and Sabrina grew up in very different families, at least from a religious standpoint. Luke's family believed in supporting the church by giving regularly, but the amount of giving was based on what they felt they could afford at the end of the year when they had met their other financial goals already.

Sabrina's family came from a long line of tithers. To many religious people, tithing means giving 10 percent of your income to the religious group *before* taxes. That can be quite a lot of money. And many tithers, such as Sabrina's family, feel that you should give even more, above and beyond the tithe. Do you see some room for conflict here?

Both Sabrina and Luke are honest, hardworking people. Both are religiously observant, too, having come to a place of deep connection in the practicing of their faith together. As a couple, they gave a great deal to their church. Far more than most. Yet they had this ongoing and intense conflict that would surface from time to time about how much to give. Luke was comfortable giving quite a lot, but Sabrina wanted to tithe and then some, and to her, she was failing in following an important religious ideal if they did not do so as a couple. Within herself, she felt that her integrity was at risk by not tithing. Further, at times she'd challenge him to "do the right thing" in ways that, as you can imagine, made him feel that she was challenging his integrity over giving. So here were two moral, observant, dedicated people who, in their monthly financial decisions, could trigger a painful and deeply felt hidden issue of integrity.

For couples, there are better ways and worse ways to handle deep conflict over values. Obviously, the worst thing that can happen between Luke and Sabrina is for Sabrina to express her concern to Luke in a way that implies that he's morally failing by not agreeing with her about tithing. That would very likely push them off course. In contrast, imagine how much better talking about this subject could go if Sabrina were to say something like this: "I have to tell you, I'm still really struggling with this matter about our giving. I know you are a good man, and you are doing the right thing according to your conscience. And I deeply admire these things about you. But I haven't yet found a way to deal with my feelings, month after month, that I'm failing to follow my conscience on this. It's causing me a lot of turmoil, and I haven't seen a way to make it better."

Although a solution might still be hard to find, if Luke can really show her that he hears this concern and that he respects the conflict within her, they will be much better off. They will convert what has been a source of conflict into a source of the deepest kind of intimacy—intimacy founded on the acceptance by one of the vulnerability in the other.

The Bottom Line: Acceptance

We've found that one hidden issue is the driving force behind all the others: the desire for acceptance. Sometimes people feel this more as a fear of rejection, but that is really the other side of the same coin. At the deepest level, people are motivated to find acceptance and to avoid rejection in their relationships, most critically in their relationship with their mate. Every human soul seems to crave acceptance, and in marriage, that would include the need to feel respected and approved of by one's spouse, as well as connected and safe in the other's presence.

This fundamental lack of acceptance or fear of rejection is at the core of most hidden issues. Unfortunately, the fear is real. Marriage involves imperfect people who can deeply hurt one another at times. Given that events and issues around money come up so often, we can say that money is a magnet for our fears of rejection as they come into play in our relationships. Partners may be afraid that if they act in certain ways, they will be rejected. Often people ask for something indirectly because they don't want to risk bringing their desires out into the open and thus becoming more vulnerable. For example, you might say, "Wouldn't you like to

This fundamental lack of acceptance or fear of rejection is at the core of most hidden issues.

buy this special gift for my mother?" rather than "I would like to buy this special gift for my mother."

There are a number of other ways in which people act out their hidden issues around acceptance and rejection. For now, we'll move on to what to do about hidden issues, and we'll revisit the powerful aspects of acceptance in Chapter Eleven, "Accounting for Love."

Recognizing the Signs of Hidden Issues

You can't disarm hidden issues that push the two of you off course unless you can identify them. There are four key ways to tell when there may be hidden issues affecting your relationship: wheel spinning, trivial triggers, avoidance, and scorekeeping.

Wheel Spinning

When an argument about money starts and your first thought is, "Here we go again," you should suspect hidden issues. The two of you never really get anywhere on the problem because you aren't talking about what really matters—the hidden issue. We have all had these arguments in which we have said everything many times before and now feel hopeless as the cycle starts yet again.

Trivial Triggers

When trivial issues are blown up out of all proportion, you should suspect hidden issues. Jill and Nelson's argument over who was going to balance the checkbook is a great example. Deciding on who will balance the checkbook seems like a trivial event, but it triggered horrendous arguments driven by the hidden issues of power and caring.

Avoidance

If one or both of you are avoiding certain topics related to money or levels of intimacy, or if you feel walls going up between you, you should suspect hidden issues. For example, we've talked with many couples in which the partners are from different cultural or socioeconomic backgrounds; these couples often strongly avoid talking about how these differences affect money (and other) issues. We think that this avoidance usually reflects concerns about acceptance—"Will you accept me fully if we really talk about our different backgrounds?" Avoiding such topics not only allows hidden issues to remain hidden but also puts the relationship at greater risk because the partners aren't addressing important differences that can have great impact on marriage.

Other common but sometimes taboo money-related topics in marriage can include what it was like growing up poor (or rich), each partner's feelings about the meaning of money, fears about losing one's job, jealousy about people who make more money, and so on. There are many such sensitive topics that couples avoid dealing with in their relationship, usually out of fear of rejection. What kinds of topics do you avoid talking about? What kinds of hidden issues might be at work?

Scorekeeping

When one or both of you start keeping score—that is, keeping a mental list of all the things your partner does wrong or the times your partner has hurt you or been unfair in how he or she deals with money—you should suspect hidden issues. For example, thinking, "He got to buy a Palm Pilot last month, so I should get to buy a new golf club today," might signal a hidden issue at work. Scorekeeping could mean you are not feeling recognized for what you put into the relationship. It could mean you are feeling controlled and are keeping track of the times your partner has taken advantage of you. Whatever the concern, scorekeeping is a sign that there are important things the two of you are not talking about—just documenting. Scorekeeping reflects that you are working against each other at times, rather than being teammates.

Disarming Hidden Issues

Our goal in this chapter has been to give you a way to explore and understand the second kind of invisible force that can push your relationship off course. You should now have the ability to recognize that when you and your partner find yourselves out of alignment with each other, there are likely issues and hidden issues at work. If you find yourselves arguing about money, you can explore what's happening to see if money is just a smokescreen for a hidden issue. You can prevent lots of damage by learning to handle issues and hidden issues with the time and skill they require.

We are often asked about how to solve hidden issues. Hidden issues aren't solved, per se, but soothed through mutual understanding and respect. These deep feelings are part of who you are and your view of the world, and are the result of your life experiences. They are not things that need to be solved. When you re-

Hidden issues aren't solved, per se, but soothed through mutual understanding and respect.

ally hear each other, situations that have previously been frustrating can turn into opportunities to know one another more deeply.

For all too many couples, the hidden issues never come out. They fester and produce levels of sadness and resentment that eventually destroy the marriage: "We got divorced due to conflicts about money," "We just fought about money all the time," and so on. It just doesn't have to be that way. When you learn to discuss deeper issues openly and with emphasis on validating each other, as you will in Part Two, the negative energy that had been generating the greatest conflicts can be converted into positive energy that actually draws you closer together. That's what we mean when we say that instead of letting these invisible forces push you around, you can harness their power and use it to help the two of you get where you want to go in life. Allow yourself to think back to the times when invisible forces may have pushed you off course. Think about how these concepts may explain some of the disagreements or confusing interchanges that you and your partner may have experienced. Keep these thoughts in the back of your mind as we move on to explore the third kind of invisible force—expectations.

CHAPTER FIVE

GREAT (AND NOT SO GREAT) EXPECTATIONS

Probably the single most important effect of romantic love is that it expands one's universe to include another person.

HENRY GRUNEBAUM

Janice and Rob had been married just a few months. They had had a beautiful wedding and romantic honeymoon, and were just beginning to settle in to their new life together. They were renting a small house and having a delightful time turning their house into a home. One Saturday morning, Rob asked Janice to go get some cinder blocks to make bookshelves for their living room. Janice went to the lumberyard and bought twenty blocks, stopped off at Chevron to fill up the car, and bought herself a super-size drink when she paid for the gas. When she got home, Rob was annoyed. In the first place, Janice hadn't called around to find the best price on the cinder blocks; in the second place, she had bought "expensive" gas; and then, why in the world would she pay so much for a watered-down soda when she could have gotten a whole six-pack for the same price? Janice figured that they were saving over $100 by building the shelves instead of buying them; she had always bought gas from Chevron because her dad had told her that expensive gas was better for the car; and she bought the drink because she was thirsty. "Holy cow!! What's the big deal?"

The "deal" is that hidden issues are born when expectations are not met. Behind *power* issues are expectations about how decisions and control will or will not be shared. Behind *caring* issues are expectations about how one is to be loved. Behind *recognition* issues are expectations about how your partner should respond to who you are and what you do. Behind *commitment* issues are expectations about how long the relationship should continue and, most important, about safety from abandonment. Behind *integrity* issues are expectations about being trusted and respected. And underneath all these expectations are core expectations about being *accepted* by your partner. A hidden issue is pushed to the forefront when an expectation is violated.

What Are Expectations?

To expect is to consider something probable or certain—to assume. Expectations are beliefs about the way things will be or should be—including beliefs about behaviors, roles, decisions, and relationships. You and your partner have specific expectations as to who will go shopping, pay the bills, or balance the checkbook. These are money-related events in your life. Each of you has expectations about common money issues, such as budgeting, savings plans, and retirement plans. You also have expectations for the deeper, often hidden, issues, such as how power will (or won't) be shared around money matters, how caring will be demonstrated through gift giving, or about the ways commitment will be respected or displayed in your dealings with money.

As is true of hidden issues, expectations can cause a lot of damage if you're not aware of them. Unfortunately, often the only time we discover our expectations is when something doesn't work the way we thought it should. Expectations that are not met lead to feelings of disappointment, sadness, frustration, and anger. As our colleague Dan Trathen often says, expectations are like glass walls. You don't tend to notice them until you smack into them. That's often how we discover that the wall is there in the first place. To a large degree, you'll be disappointed or satisfied in life depending on how well what is happening matches what you expected. Therefore, expectations play a crucial role in determining your level of satisfaction in marriage.

Five Key Expectations with Powerful Ties to Money

You have all kinds of expectations. You have expectations about how often you'll spend time with your in-laws, how often you'll make love, how you'll raise your children, where you'll live, and so forth. Those are dealt with in detail in our other books, such as *Fighting for Your Marriage.* Here we want to focus on expectations that are particularly important for "winning at money without losing at love." In that context, there are five major expectations we want to discuss. They are expectations about respect, intimacy, trust, fairness, and autonomy.

Respect

Aretha sang it right. Respect is one of the cornerstones of a great relationship. Without respect, what do you have? For many couples, respect between the partners has very little to do with money. For many others, money themes easily touch expectations about respect.

Let's look at one of the ways that respect and money become linked in expectations. Many men *as well as* women seem to be uncomfortable in marriage when the woman makes more money than the man. While there have been many changes in work patterns, with more women taking on a growing role in family breadwinning, many people have expectations, on some level, for the male to be the primary breadwinner. That may seem silly to you in this day and age, and although it may not matter one bit in your relationship, it's a pretty serious issue in relationships when two people clash in what they expect. What do you really think about this? What do you expect?

With women increasingly likely to have careers right alongside their husbands, the potential for this dynamic to exist is greater than ever. Further, there is some evidence that men are increasingly valuing earning potential when picking a wife. So some men are seeking women who have great income potential, even if they might not be too happy if it's greater than their own.

Nita and Vern fell in love at nearly first sight. They met in college in a class on the analysis of computing systems used in large enterprises. Suffice to say, they were in the right field at the right time if one wants to be both techie and rich. They enjoyed each other, and they enjoyed their work. After college, their careers screamed off into flight; both landed well-paying, exciting jobs with Fortune 500 companies in California.

Nita worked in a fast-moving, lean, and smaller company that was growing fast. Vern worked for an older, more established company that had the slightly more sluggish ways of larger, older businesses. In Vern's company, you got ahead more slowly by advancing in position, authority, pay, and profit sharing. In the company where Nita worked, there were fewer clear lines of authority and a strong sense of a team working together to achieve goals. They also offered stock options, and Nita took all she could.

Although stock options can be risky in some tax situations, the options Nita held and exercised came to have great value. In no time at all, she was bringing in about three times the income Vern could pull down. Furthermore, although Vern was doing fine at his company, he wasn't really advancing the way Nita was. Vern felt that his career was standing still in comparison to hers. He was envious.

Let's be honest. Compared to what many people are dealing with in life, to have a lot of money isn't exactly a huge problem. However, in their case, both Nita and Vern began to feel uncomfortable. Sure, the trips they could take were terrific, and they could drive whatever cars they wanted. Yet deep down, neither felt truly comfortable with the fact that Nita was making so much more money than Vern. On some level, it was turning into a self-esteem problem for Vern. Harder to detect, yet also there, was a growing problem for Nita, who was losing respect for Vern. Daily, she was immersed in a culture that prized drive, energy, creativity, and accomplishment, and she really couldn't see those prized elements in Vern's life. She hated that she felt this way.

When you live in a culture that is so oriented toward money and wealth, your identity and self-worth can be affected by it. Things got even tougher when Nita and Vern started talking about having children. Realistically, they both liked the idea of one parent switching to part-time in order to have more time to attend to the needs of a child. But, on a deeper level, they had both expected that it would be Nita. Now they were faced with the realization that it made less sense for her to cut back than for him to cut back. They'd grown used to spending a good deal of money. They'd have to dramatically alter their lifestyle if she cut back, but wouldn't have to change much at all if he did.

Ultimately, what pulled Nita and Vern through was the ability, after some time, to talk deeply and openly about what each was feeling and thinking. Both were in pain, and both were conscious that Vern has lost some respect in the eyes of both of them—no matter how irrational that seems. Yet respect can be born of many things, including the willingness to look at vulnerabilities openly. What they could not get from their careers they regained through the depth of their relationship.

Intimacy

You might well be thinking, "What's intimacy got to do with money?" Well, it depends on what's intimate to you. It could be that money has nothing to do with intimacy for you—that money can't buy you love. But suppose that the things that bring intimacy to you cost money.

For many people, doing things together is one of the most meaningful ways to build intimacy. If that means taking walks and talking, there's no money needed or involved. Maybe you like to go out to dinner as a great way to be together as friends. Many couples can afford to do that fairly often if it's important to them. Suppose, though, that you had met on a skiing trip and fallen in love, and have been together ever since. What if something that's very exciting and quite expensive is one of the only ways that you really connect?

For couples who fall in love through activities that cost a lot, things can get dicey if they go through times when they have to cut back on spending because of other priorities in life—such as raising children and paying for their clothes, doctors, lessons, and school supplies. Deeper issues, such as your need to know that your partner loves and cares for you, can get triggered if your partner doesn't think you can afford some of the activities that you associate with intimacy. What to him or her might be merely a matter of having realistic priorities might raise deeper, less rational fears in you about your love. An expectation is not met, and it's triggering deep issues.

Maybe you feel closest and most loved by your partner when he or she gets you some expensive gift. Many people grew up in families where love was, in part, expressed by gift giving. This upbringing can set up expectations that can make you feel as though you're not being close if you can't receive or give those kinds of gifts to one another.

Another common scenario occurs when money-related issues cause other changes that have the net effect of reducing intimate connection. For example, people sometimes make financial decisions that directly reduce the amount of time they have to be together. If, for example, you have to work seventy-five hours a week to pay the bills, both you and your mate may resent the lack of time to be together just to talk or play or even make love.

For many couples, money and intimacy are linked symbolically through the ways in which they join or don't join their material possessions and manage their money. For example, some couples see joining their savings and checking accounts as a symbol of their unity. Some ceremoniously open their accounts together after they are married, as part of the ritual of joining their lives. Therefore, for some couples, having separate checking accounts makes them feel as though they aren't a unified team. For other couples, there isn't any symbolic value attached to joint accounts. It is simply a pragmatic matter. For them, separate checking accounts wouldn't feel any different than having separate dressers for their separate wardrobes.

Couples may or may not link prenuptial agreements with intimacy as well. For one couple, creating a prenuptial agreement would symbolize a lack of intimacy or a lack of commitment, and therefore would preempt a happy marriage because at least one partner wanted more on these dimensions. For another couple, signing a prenuptial agreement would be a way of assuring that even when money has been taken out of the equation, the intimacy and desire to be committed for life are still there. How a couple perceives such an agreement will depend on the expectations each partner has for what intimacy will look like in their marriage and on what the symbolism behind the money decisions means.

Trust

For years, Alice drove her husband, Larry, crazy with her constant checking up on their bank accounts, credit card balances, and investments. She would order a credit report almost monthly to make sure Larry hadn't opened up any charge accounts or taken out any loans that she did not know about. She balanced their checkbook every month to make sure that the checks to pay the mortgage had actually been paid.

Alice's behavior both wounded and perplexed Larry. In checking up on all these things, she'd triggered hidden issues of integrity in Larry. Because Alice wasn't a control freak in any other area of their lives together, he didn't think that she had hidden control issues. She was usually fine with his investment ideas and didn't mind when he made the decisions. It was just that she always checked to make sure that he'd done what he said he'd done. She didn't trust him, and that hurt.

When Larry and Alice sat down to talk about their expectations, Larry explained that he had expected to be able to trust Alice and have her trust him. He trusted her, but she didn't trust him. Alice wanted to trust Larry, but a traumatic experience during her childhood made that very difficult for her to do.

Alice's mom had divorced when Alice was five. She married Kevin when Alice was thirteen. Alice's mom had dated Kevin for two years before they got married. She'd wanted to be sure this relationship would last and to be sure that Alice would accept Kevin as a stepfather. Alice had. She'd loved Kevin and was very happy to be the bridesmaid at their wedding.

> *Relationships work best when each partner can trust the other and each partner is worthy of that trust.*

The week after Kevin and her mom returned from their honeymoon, they had gone to the bank and put his name on all her mom's accounts. The next week, Kevin came home with a brand new Cadillac, paid for by money from Alice's mutual fund. Only one week later, Kevin had cleaned out all her mother's accounts and left. Poof. Gone. All gone. All her mom could say was, "Thank God I didn't put the house in his name."

Relationships work best when each partner can trust the other and each partner is worthy of that trust. Sometimes, however, as in Alice's case, a person will have trouble trusting even when her mate is perfectly trustworthy, because of experiences earlier in her life. At other times, one partner has injured the other's ability to trust in financial (or other) matters through some lapse or deception earlier in the relationship.

But I Got a Great Deal on It!

Deception undermines trust. There may be no other area in life where partners are more likely to deceive one another than when it comes to spending money. Many people lie to their partner about some aspect of their finances. About 40 percent of married Americans admitted keeping a secret from their spouses, according to an August 2001 poll published in *Reader's Digest*. The most common secret kept was not about sex or an affair. Of those with a secret, 48 percent said they had not told their spouses about how much some purchase had really cost. Whether or not these types of lies will be problematic for a couple depends on the couple's expectations as to how "big" of a lie they consider acceptable. Trust is a key expectation between most partners.

Do you feel that you have to hide aspects of your spending behavior from your mate? Why? What do you fear would happen if you were perfectly open about how you spent money?

When trust has been damaged, either in the current relationship or sometime in the past, repairing it can be challenging. It can be helpful to keep these three truths in mind:

1. *Trust is a function of trustworthiness.* Trust has the greatest chance to grow when each partner is honest with the other and takes appropriate responsibility for his or her actions.
2. *Trust builds slowly over time.* Trust builds as you gain confidence in your partner's trustworthiness. For example, if a wife has asked her husband to make a specific change, her trust will grow as she sees her husband doing all he can to bring about that change without her prodding and demanding.
3. *Trust is a decision of the will.* Research shows that people vary in their general trust of others. Some find risking trust easier than others, but ultimately trust can be built only by taking the risk. If you need to increase the trust level in your marriage, you have to take a chance—wisely of course, but still a chance.

In Alice and Larry's case, Alice has developed an expectation that she can stay financially safe only through vigilance. But she is allowing fear to damage her marriage. Deciding to trust someone is a real risk. You can't discover whether your partner is trustworthy, and therefore can't really develop trust, unless you are willing to take that risk. Sometimes you will get burned and sometimes you won't. If Alice can't bring herself to trust Larry, the level of intimacy they can achieve will be limited.

Josh and Amanda discovered the very painful truth that when trust is violated, the relationship suffers and, in this case, comes to the point of divorce. Josh was a successful businessman. He and Amanda had been married for thirteen years. They owned a $750,000 home in the mountains. One night, they came home to discover that their beautiful home had caught fire. Though it didn't burn to the ground, nearly everything was lost due to smoke damage or to water damage from the firefighters. When the insurance company came to investigate the damage, Josh discovered that his policy was invalid because he had estimated that the fire hydrant was within a certain distance from the house, which was not the case.

Josh may have been able to fight with the insurance company, but he did not want Amanda to know that he had "failed to protect their home properly." So he did not tell her. Josh simply had the house rebuilt and tried to continue making mortgage payments on the original house while paying for a second home to be rebuilt. Josh wasn't able to keep up the charade, and when Amanda discovered that he had been lying to her, she divorced him.

Many marital experts agree that discovering that one's spouse has lied about finances can be as devastating as an affair. If both partners want to be able to trust each other, then they need to make their relationship a safe place to admit mistakes and faults, and to work together on moving into the future hand in hand.

Fairness

Most people expect fairness in their relationships, especially in marriage. But fairness is in the eye of the beholder. It's a common misconception to equate fairness with *sameness*. They aren't equivalent. People value the same things in different ways. Sometimes *same* is fair, and sometimes it's not.

Trying to be fair can be good for a relationship; however, couples need to hold on to common sense. We know of one couple who went to one of those superstores on a Sunday afternoon. He fell in love with a big-screen TV. She fell in love with a dinette set. He decided he was going to get the TV, so she decided it was only fair that she get the dinette set. The problem was that they couldn't afford either, much less both. So, what's fair? Does it make it fair if one partner gets to overspend in some way because the other partner did?

*It's a common misconception to equate fairness with **sameness**. Sometimes **same** is fair, and sometimes it's not.*

So many money and finance-related issues stem from expectations about fairness. Here are some more examples:

- A husband loses his job and is unable to find another for a long time, putting pressure on the wife to make more money in her work, leading to feelings of failure in him for not contributing the same amount and resentment in her for having to carry the load by herself.
- Although never having agreed to be responsible for recording checks, balancing the checkbook, paying the bills, and the like, one partner always ends up doing these tasks and resents the fact that these things just aren't going to get done unless he or she does them.
- One partner finds it far easier to restrain spending than the other, frequently resisting something special and desired for the good of the budget. But the

other, the one who struggles more with impulse buying, often brings home something like a music CD or electronic device that he or she could not resist. "How's this fair?" the frugal one asks.

- Two people marry who have children from prior marriages. One of the two comes from a family of modest means, the other from a family of wealth. The one will inherit virtually nothing from parents, the other millions. How do they figure out what's fair when it comes to setting up their wills and estates, in determining what will be passed along to whose children?

There are many different ways couples can try to achieve fairness when it comes to pooling (or not pooling) their money. If both partners bring in an income, there are different ideas about what might be most fair. Look at Figure 12, which shows four different ways Sam and Jane could choose to contribute their money to "total savings and expenses." For purposes of illustration, let's say that Sam brings home $2,335 monthly and that Jane brings home about $1,750 monthly. They have kept their monthly expenses and savings to about $3,675. Which option seems most fair to you?

We could give you many other examples, but it's more important that you ask yourselves about expectations that affect your relationship. Before we leave the topic of fairness, we need to warn you about a very destructive tendency that's based in people's expectations for fairness: scorekeeping.

You are scorekeeping when you are keeping close tabs on what you are putting into the relationship compared to what you think your partner is contributing. This can come up around money, chores, expressions of love—just about anything that matters to you. You may ask, "Why not be tuned into what you're getting, and expect to get back what you're putting in?"

Obviously, it's only fair for both partners to pull their weight in a marriage. The problem is that scorekeeping is fundamentally biased in favor of the one keeping score. Of all the positive things you and your partner do for the relationship, you will always see more of what you do and less of what your partner does. You are a continual observer of your behavior, not your partner's. If for no other reason, you'll score many more points on your own scorecard than your partner can possibly score. So even if both of you are doing exactly equal amounts for your relationship, if you're keeping score, you'll look better to you than your partner will, and you'll resent your partner for not doing more.

There are three keys to combating scorekeeping. First, you must be alert to the inherent unfairness of your scorecard. Second, directly counter the bias by looking for specific things your partner does that are good for you. Third, concentrate on what you can do that is good for your relationship, not on what you think your partner *isn't* doing.

FIGURE 12. FINANCIAL POOLING OPTIONS FOR A DUAL-INCOME COUPLE, SAM AND JANE.

	Option 1: The One-Pot Solution	Option 2: Equal Contributions (50–50 split)	Option 3: Contributions based on ratio of contribution to income (Sam 57%, Jane 43%)	Option 4: Contributions with equal spending money
Sam's monthly contribution	$2,335	$1,838	$2,095	$2,130
Jane's monthly contribution	$1,750	$1,750—Jane doesn't have enough	$1,580	$1,545
Spending money	They divide the $410 left, so both have $205 of spending money per month.	Sam has $497 for his own use, though he has to make up the shortfall of $88. Jane has $0 for her own use.	Sam has $240 for his own use. Jane has $170 for her own use.	They both have $205 of spending money per month.

Autonomy

Some of the most basic, core expectations we hold for relationships have to do with the degree of autonomy that is desirable or needed. Here again, money is a key reflector of these powerful underlying themes. Let's look at a couple of significant ways in which expectations about autonomy affect relationships.

In many dual-career couples, one partner will slow her or his career down more than the other during the early years of child rearing—surely not all couples, but many do prefer this if it's possible. In relationships where both partners are highly geared toward autonomy, this career slowdown can be disturbing because expectations for some level of independence are not being met.

When both partners prize autonomy, a change whereby one partner puts her or his career on hold for the benefit of the entire family can lead that partner to feel uncomfortably dependent and the other uncomfortably responsible. Feelings related to autonomy and dependency are often closely tied to other issues we've discussed in this chapter, especially trust and fairness. If you have high confidence in your future together, there will be a greater comfort with the level of interdependence that is part of a marriage over time. If one partner doesn't trust that the relationship will last, it may feel too risky to give up or slow down his or her career. One may be willing to "sacrifice" a career if he or she believes that his or her partner will make another sacrifice later, in all fairness. However, the desire for autonomy may have nothing to do with trust or fairness and may simply have more to do with a person's self-esteem or enjoyment of his or her career. Some couples find themselves in the "You don't trust that I will provide for us" argument when trust isn't the issue at all; the partner simply derives fulfillment from earning an income.

Another area where expectations about autonomy are played out has to do with the ways in which couples handle money. Do you keep separate accounts and divide up responsibility for certain bills, or do you put all you have into one pot? Many couples, especially couples in second or third marriages, prefer to keep their finances separated because doing so allows them a greater sense of autonomy. Many feel they were burned in their prior marriage by allowing their autonomy to slip away. One partner agrees to pay this or that bill, and the other will pay something else: "You do your part and I'll do mine." That works out well for many couples as long as each can fulfill his or her obligations.

There are studies in the field that suggest that couples who do not pool their financial resources are at somewhat greater risk. There are at least two reasons why that could be. One, for some couples, keeping finances separate stems from deeper difficulties in forming an identity as a couple. Two, for others, it stems directly from disagreements over money decisions, and keeping things separate becomes a way to keep the peace. There is no clear agreement, though, on how this all works. Further, research by Kay Pasley at the University of North Carolina at Greensboro, along with Eric Sandras and Mary Ellen Edmondson, suggests that in second marriages, where it's more typical to keep finances separate, whether or not couples pool their finances is not very related to satisfaction in those marriages. The researchers found that couples in second marriages were generally doing just as well whether or not they kept their money separate, pooled, or some combination of the two. There did seem, however, to be a tendency for men in these second marriages to report being happier when the finances were pooled.

What to Do About Expectations

Your expectations about money and marriage can lead either to massive disappointment, even anger, or to deeper connection between the two of you. There are four guidelines for handling expectations well—expectations about money, or anything else for that matter. Couples that do the best in life are usually doing a pretty good job on all four.

1. Be *aware* of what you expect.
2. Be *reasonable* in what you expect.
3. Be *clear* about what you expect.
4. Be *motivated* to meet your partner's expectations, even when you don't share them.

Be Aware of What You Expect

Clifford Sager, a pioneer in this field, noticed how people bring a host of expectations to marriage that are never made clear. In effect, these expectations form a contract for the marriage. The problem is, neither "party" is fully aware of what's in the contract when they get married. Sager went further to suggest that many expectations are virtually unconscious—which means that becoming aware of them is very difficult. We don't mean to say that all expectations are deeply unconscious, but many do become such a part of us that they function automatically. Much of what we do is so automatic, we don't even have to think about it.

Think of the examples we've presented in this chapter. In many cases, such as that of Nita and Vern, people are not even aware of expectations that are having a powerful effect on their happiness. Nita and Vern were able to hang in there and talk it out, reaching a deeper understanding of how each was feeling about her making so much more money than him. Without that awareness, they had very little hope of coping with strong feelings that were beginning to drive a wedge between the two of them.

Be Reasonable in What You Expect

Being aware of expecting something does not make that expectation reasonable. Many expectations that people have about money and marriage just aren't reasonable or realistic. Some unreasonable expectations are very specific. For example, is it reasonable to expect that your partner will never seriously disagree with you about finances? Of course not. Yet you'd be surprised just how many people expect this—or at least act like they do.

Many expectations that people have about money and marriage just aren't reasonable or realistic.

Acting on unreasonable expectations is likely to lead to conflict and hurt. For example, remember Alice, whose great fears and financial insecurities led to a lot of behavior that her husband, Larry, could easily and correctly interpret as a lack of trust. Although it's sad that Alice developed this problem earlier in life, it's not reasonable for her to expect Larry not to be bothered by her hypervigilant, suspicion-driven behavior. Sure, it helps if he can come to understand the origins of her problem. Still, it will be a strain on their relationship if some expectations and behavior do not change.

Many young couples discover that their general lifestyle expectations are unrealistic, and it can be quite depressing when reality sets in. Greta and Luke are one such couple. Greta and Luke both wanted to travel. They wanted to walk the streets of Tokyo, visit the great cathedrals of Europe, and brave the wilds of southern Africa. When they married, they promised each other they would see the world together. Greta was a teacher when they got married. Luke had one more year of college. They went to Australia for their honeymoon. It was an incredible trip, but they'd gone into debt to do it. When they got married, they not only had his-and-her bath towels but also his-and-her school loans and a honeymoon trip on their credit card statement. They reassured themselves that they could easily pay all this off when Luke graduated and got a job.

Luke had expected to command a high salary when he graduated. He was pretty disappointed when he started interviewing and discovered that his business degree didn't open as many doors as he'd thought. Most companies wanted experience too. He finally took a position as an executive trainee with an insurance company. His salary was good, but when he saw what his paycheck looked like after the government bit a chunk out of it and he'd paid for health insurance, he was downright depressed. He and Greta would be lucky to take the bus to the zoo, much less save enough to see Kenya.

Luke and Greta consoled themselves. "We're just starting out. We should expect that it will be rough at first. We can't expect to have all the nice things our parents have taken thirty years to accumulate or to go right away to all the places we want to see. We need to be realistic." So they decided to be patient. They figured it might take as long as two or three years to get their loans paid off, and then they would have more money. Luke would get promotions and raises, and then they'd have more money. They'd get all the basic necessities bought, like furniture, appliances, a good car, some decent career clothes, a better TV set, and then they wouldn't need to spend so much money.

Six months later, Luke finished his trainee program and was assigned to a branch. He got a raise. It was $80 per month after taxes. Luke and Greta were excited. Then they looked through the open enrollment forms for health insurance and discovered that their contribution had gone up $42. Not much, but it took the wind out of their sails. Then, as they were going over their budget, they realized that they had transposed the numbers on one of their student loans. The amount they'd have to pay each month was $242, not $224. That was another $18 per month that they thought they'd have but didn't. They felt pretty deflated as they came to grips with the fact that the raise they'd so looked forward to would amount to only $20 more per month.

A great many couples today often have unrealistic expectations about how easily debt can be paid off, how far their income can go, and how quickly they can accumulate all the possessions their parents took a lifetime to acquire. Unfortunately, because the expectations are so high, both their long-term economic goals and their confidence in their future take a hit.

While acknowledging the very real pain of disappointment, we also want to point out that successful couples do not allow themselves to stay too long in the "poor me" state. This is a good time to follow the old advice and count your blessings. It is hard to stay discouraged when you focus on all that's good. Do you have a strong marriage? Do you have your health? Are you good friends? Visiting a hospital is a good way to put your woes back into perspective. Can you walk? Can you breathe without a ventilator? Can you take a shower without the aid of a nurse? What about friends? Do you have kids? It is important to watch how you let yourself think.

In a study conducted by Jennifer Crocker and Lisa Gallo at State University of New York at Buffalo, subjects who had completed the sentence "I'm glad I'm not a . . ." five times felt happier and more satisfied with their lives. However, those who completed the sentence "I wish I were a . . ." felt worse. Sometimes, counting your blessings is a pretty powerful thing to do.

It's also important to develop a long-term perspective that helps you see that you don't need to solve every financial problem right now. What you really do need is a sense that you can steadily move toward your goals in the years to come. One of the most important ways to feel that you're making progress is to take very careful notice of the ways your life is getting better. Stop and look at the little things. Have you ever tried to take a walk around the block with a toddler? She will stop for five minutes to examine the earthworm that has washed up on the sidewalk. She will touch (and taste if you let her) the blades of grass. She will notice the little droplets of water as they slide down the blade. If you were walking by yourself, likely you'd have missed a whole lot.

Couples need to become childlike in the sense that they need to rediscover the joy of the little things. Have you read a good book? Have you shared joy with a friend? Are you steadily, even if slowly, making progress reducing your overall level of debt? Those are things you can take delight in.

Be Clear About What You Expect

A specific expectation about money and marriage may be perfectly reasonable but never clearly expressed. It's not enough just to be aware of your expectations or to evaluate their reasonableness: you must be able to talk about key expectations together. We all tend to assume that our model of how money and marriage will work is the same as our partner's. Why should we have to tell him or her what we expect? In effect, we assume that our spouse knows what we expect.

This assumption is actually itself a kind of unreasonable expectation. You are assuming that your partner should know what you want, so you don't bother to make it clear enough. For example, how many people make the assumption that their partner should know just what anniversary or birthday gift to get them? We see this over and over again. One or both partners are angry that the other is failing to meet a desire or expectation. But more often than not, they've never expressed their expectation. That's expecting your partner to be good at mind reading.

Some people say to us that if they have to tell their partner what they want, it really doesn't mean much if he (or she, but somehow it's mainly he) gets them what they want. It would mean so much more if he remembered on his own. (Do you hear a hidden issue of caring emerging?) But we say, what could be more loving and caring than for your husband (or wife), when asked to do something that does not come naturally (and not because he doesn't care), to come through and actually do it?

We believe that a great love relationship involves being able to ask for what you want and need and for your partner to make the effort to meet your expectations (as they say in the fairy tales, "Your wish is my command"), but you have to clearly express your wish first!

The Grief of Love

One of the most painful experiences in life is coming to the realization that a very reasonable expectation you hold about money and marriage, one that you've communicated clearly to your mate, is not ever going to come about. For whatever reasons, there will be some things that are reasonable for you to want but that you will not be able to achieve with the partner you chose.

In my book *The Heart of Commitment,* I (Scott) say that we all have a list of things we'd like to have in our relationship. Some items are more important, some less. None of us will get everything we wished for.

When you really want something that is just not going to happen, you can either sulk, get angry, or do what I say every couple needs to do over the long term: grieve the losses that come with commitment. When you commit to one person, you lose the possibilities another person might bring. Simple. At times, painful. Some will experience this sense of loss more and some less, but it would be hard to find someone who was in a long-lasting relationship who did not understand the principle.

People who are maturing in life can acknowledge the pain of what they do not have and grieve about it rather than act out in anger and frustration. Grieving means facing the sense of loss and working to accept it as a part of life and love. The most amazing marriages we've seen are ones in which the partners not only can do this but also have gotten to a point where they can do it together. In other words, they are able to join together in acknowledging things they grieve, and this becomes a way of being more intimate. For example, one partner might say with empathy, "I know this is one of those times when you wish I'd chosen a different career. I know you wanted us to have more money so we could travel and have that large house on the golf course." When you see a couple who can say things like this—and feel closer as a result—you are looking at a deep and tested love.

Be Motivated to Meet Each Other's Expectations

Marital experts have known for years how important it is for couples to understand their expectations. However, the focus has usually been on helping couples understand and *match* their expectations, when that may not be what's most important. Recently, we have learned that it is more important for couples to try to *meet* each other's expectations. Researchers Norm Epstein at the University of Maryland and Don Baucom at the University of North Carolina at Chapel Hill have been studying people's expectations and how they affect relationships over many years. Recently, Norm Epstein told us something very important about what they have found in their work: "Discrepancies between two partners' standards are less problematic than the individuals' being dissatisfied with the ways in which their personal standards are being met within the relationship"—so two people can be different but still work out a mutually acceptable way of meeting their standards.

In other words, it's probably not as crucial for the two of you to hold all the same expectations as it is for each of you to do your best to try to meet the important (and realistic) desires of the other. One of the greatest reasons most relationships go so well early on is that both partners are very motivated to please the other. Both of you try to figure out what the other likes; you try to give to the other in inventive ways. The most powerful element is that you are showing your partner that you are paying attention to what matters to him or her and that you are motivated to try to please. You are sending a clear message: "You are special to me, and I want you to know it." You don't have to let this slip away, and if it has slipped away, you can decide to get it back. You can choose to focus some of your energy on meeting some of the clear and important expectations your partner holds. Try something specific today.

◆ ◆ ◆

Now that you have a grip on what expectations are and how they can be dealt with more effectively, we'll spend the next two chapters exploring in depth where they come from. Again, we're looking at the invisible forces and preparing to bring them into alignment with where you want to go in this life. After that, we'll show you an in-depth exercise designed to help you identify and meet each other's important expectations.

CHAPTER SIX

WHERE EXPECTATIONS COME FROM

Life can only be understood backwards, but it must be lived forwards.

SØREN KIERKEGAARD

Eight-year-old Calvin got out of the shower. His dad noticed that his hair didn't look very clean. In fact, it didn't look very wet. So he asked, "Hey Cal, did you use shampoo to wash your hair?" Calvin, in a surprised tone, asked, "Was I supposed to?" Calvin was escorted back to the shower for a second try.

Learning to use shampoo is just one simple example of the thousands of things you learned as a child that you were "supposed" to do. As children we learn much about how the world is supposed to work. We grow up thinking that life works a certain way, and these beliefs become deeply embedded largely without our questioning whether what we've learned is really the best or only way. We grow up accumulating expectations.

As you learned in Chapter Five, our expectations operate in the present. However, they are based in the past. If you want to understand your attitudes toward money, and those of your spouse, you need to look at the influences that shaped who you have become. Everything you've seen, heard, touched, tasted, or smelled has been stored away in the filing cabinet you call your brain. The mind is a pattern-recording and pattern-repeating contraption. We record what we perceive to be the way the world works or the way it is. Then we translate this information into a "this is the way the world should work" expectation.

Contrary to what economists may like to think, we do not rationally evaluate each economic alternative in order to achieve "maximum utility." Rather, our decisions are driven by what we learned as children: what we were told by our parents; our values, attitudes, and cultural beliefs; even our idiosyncratic preferences—what we find beautiful or pleasing. We believe couples can benefit from thinking about the past so that they can understand and take responsibility for the present.

In this chapter, we will discuss two primary influences on our expectations in general and about money in particular: our previous relationships and our culture. Gender differences also have a profound effect on our expectations regarding money, and we will devote the entire next chapter to them. Now let's delve into how previous relationships and our culture have helped shape who you are today.

Family of Origin

The relationships that have likely had the most influence on who you are and what expectations you hold about *yourself* are those within your family of origin. For some people, family means their mother, father, and siblings above all else. For others, it would include not only those immediate family members but also grandparents, aunts, uncles, and so on. Some had parents who divorced, and they were raised not only by their parents but also by stepparents and stepsiblings. So when we say "family" in this chapter, we simply mean the group of people who were around you most as you were growing up.

Security and Insecurity

Deeper expectations are learned early in life, many having a long-lasting impact on relationships and money. One of the most basic needs we all have is to know that we matter and have worth. From the moment you were born, those who took care of you began immediately to answer your unasked questions: Am I loved? Am I valuable? Will my needs be met? When you cried, if your parent picked you up quickly, and tenderly offered you warmth or a dry diaper or a breast, you learned that you had some impact on your environment and that your needs would be met. If, however, you were met by an irritated or impatient caregiver, you might have absorbed deep within you the nonverbal communication of this irritation or anger. We record not only these messages from those around us but also our own emotional responses of misgiving, anxiety, and insecurity, and then others' responses to our responses. These emotional responses seep into our psyche and are indelibly recorded there.

Thus our basic expectations about such things as self-worth and trust are laid down early in life. Further, our entire childhood is made up of event after event by which we are taught either that what we want is important or that it doesn't matter much to others.

Here are a few more such "lessons." Did you learn . . .

That you were worth paying attention to—or not?

That you were fun to be around—or not?

That you were understood—or not?

That you could count on your parent or parents for safety and security—or not?

That you were able to make things happen when you wanted to—or not?

That you had to perform to be accepted—or not? What kinds of behaviors were most likely to get you the affirmation of others?

That what you did in life was likely to succeed—or not?

We're sure you could add important themes to this list. Stop a moment to think about how these questions were answered for you. Now ask yourself if you see a link between these "messages" and how you approach money. What you want, what you expect, and what you do with money can be affected by such deeper themes. What patterns of belief and expectations did your family imprint on your mind over the years? The linkages between these underlying themes and your adult money behavior can be straightforward or very complex. Here's an "in-between" example.

Mario and Zelda were married a long time, doing well in life, but one little irritant kept cropping up over and over again. Every week for twenty-seven years, Mario would sit down with Zelda to show her a thorough report of where they stood in terms of bank account balances and investments. For reasons that escaped him, Mario often left these little meetings feeling a bit deflated. This was not a big deal, and so much else went right for them in life that he could easily shake off his feelings. Yet it was a weekly event.

In a moment of stunning clarity, Mario left one of these meetings and asked himself, Why am I not happy? We're doing so well. He realized that he wanted Zelda to say something like, "Wow, that's great! You've done so well with our investments." Instead she would usually ask a question or two about specifics, and they would move on with their day.

One day, feeling a bit bolder than usual, he asked Zelda why she didn't react the way he hoped for. Her answer was simply that she had always interpreted these little meetings as just an example of his doing a good job sharing where they stood with their finances. Indeed, she appreciated this a great deal, knowing in talking to friends how many other people's spouses kept things hidden or were simply not conscientious in how they handled money.

Mario expressed to her his awareness that, in part, he had really been looking for her to affirm how well he was managing finances on their behalf. In fact, as the week had gone on since his realization, he'd figured out pretty clearly where it all came from. His parents were the silent type. They were very positive and loving, but not very expressive. There was one major exception. They seemed to be very responsive to evidence of his successes on paper. Report cards and savings account statements (his family heavily promoted saving) were routinely met with expressions of pride and affirmation by his parents. Mario, reflecting on this, felt that he'd nailed down his understanding of what had been a perplexing reaction for years. This pattern was so ingrained in his family that it never occurred to him that Zelda would not understand what he expected when he showed her, on paper, how he was doing.

She heard it, heard it well, and acted on this immediately, including thanking him for sharing something so personal and emotional. The next week, he brought the statements to her for her to look at, just as he'd done for twenty-seven years. But this time, she knew what he hoped for, and it was easy to provide it. "Honey, this is fabulous. I can't believe how well you've done by choosing those mutual funds. It's really wonderful." He beamed from ear to ear. Both knew very well that they were attempting a change in pattern, and he loved her all the more because she was being responsive to what he had said he needed. Walking away afterwards, he winked at her, and she winked back, saying as he left the room, "You da man, Mario!"

Note how Mario and Zelda turned something that was mildly frustrating into something that became a routine but very positive part of each week. Think how differently this might have come out had Zelda said something like this: "That's so childish. I feel like you need my approval for every little thing." In Chapter Eleven, we will discuss how important it is to try to convey love and acceptance to your partner in the ways that have the biggest positive impact on him or her. If you don't expect that you should have to do this, we'd like to suggest that you consider the possibility that that is an unrealistic expectation.

Can You Cut It?

Many children grow up in families that teach them that they are deficient or inadequate in some way, even when they behave well or are high achievers. Most people, as adults, will try to compensate for such feelings of inadequacy, often with strategies that bear directly on money or the value of things. Unfortunately, many of the paths toward acceptance that people choose are actually negative: such strategies both drive others away and lead to poor financial decisions.

Bragging. Bragging is an attempt to gain love based on the belief that "if I am good enough, then I will be loved." So the braggart tries to demonstrate that he

Most people, as adults, will try to compensate for feelings of inadequacy, often with strategies that bear directly on money or the value of things.

or she is "good enough" in order to receive love. People use money to "brag" in many ways. Some will talk about how much money they make or how much money they spend. For some, buying expensive clothes, cars, or homes is a way of saying, "I am good enough." (For others, of course, buying expensive clothes, cars, or homes has nothing to do with a sense of insecurity and more to do with a straightforward enjoyment of nice things.) If as a child you were unsure of your parents' love, you may find yourself buying a new car whenever your best friend does, just to make sure everyone knows you're just a successful as your friend is.

Success and Generosity

In a study at Arizona State University, Robert Cialdini and Kenneth Richardson asked students to take a "creativity test." However, the researchers weren't really trying to discover how creative the subjects were. Rather, they wanted to see if the subjects would react differently when given positive or negative feedback.

So the researchers told some subjects that they had done very well on the test and others that they had done poorly, and then asked the subjects to describe the students at a rival school. How generous or critical would the students be in their descriptions? Those who were told they had done well were much more positive in their descriptions of the rival school. Those who were told that they'd done poorly maligned the rival school. They were not charitable in their descriptions. Studies like this show in very simple terms that how critical or charitable we are toward others can be influenced by our perceptions of our own success in life. When we don't feel successful, we're less likely to be kind in how we think about or describe others.

Excuses, Excuses. People without a sense of personal worth can be overly sensitive to any "evidence" suggesting that what they fear is true—that they are indeed losers. Thus, to cope, these individuals must never admit any kind of failure, cannot admit mistakes, cannot lose an argument—for to admit a fault would be to admit failure as a human being. So they rationalize or hide little details, and sometimes big ones. Such a strategy might sound like this: "Well, it wasn't my fault we didn't make the budget this month, because the washing machine went out and we had to buy a new one. Besides, you played golf twice this month." Or, when having failed to record a large check that causes other checks to bounce, such a person might say, "You should have realized I had to pay that bill and kept that in mind before writing those other checks."

In other words, it's your fault, never mine. Do you see yourself in such examples? Perhaps you see your partner. We're more concerned about whether or not you see yourself, because if you do, you can try to change the behavior. If you are particularly bold about it, you can even ask your spouse to tell you when it seems as though you are making excuses rather than just being matter-of-fact about what happened, even if you fear rejection in the truth. Real humility is rarely met with rejection.

Real humility is rarely met with rejection.

Perfectionism. There are two sides to this strategy. One is to avoid the pain of rejection. If you are perfect, then you won't be criticized. The other is to gain recognition. Those who excel (perfectly) are recognized and affirmed. This is the person who has to balance the checkbook to the penny. Every bill must be paid a minimum of seven days early, and every bill is neatly filed, alphabetically and by date. There's nothing wrong with being neat and organized, but the problem usually comes in when a "perfect" partner marries an imperfect partner and criticizes him or her for not doing things "right."

When feelings of perfectionism are strong enough, the behavior can become compulsive. We've seen relationships in which one partner was absolutely tyrannized by the other's need to account for every penny. For some people, what the money was spent on is not what is so threatening. What they can't handle is that a penny or two may have gone unaccounted for or uncontrolled. As you can imagine, such dynamics can have a powerful negative impact on the level of connection between partners in life. In such cases, hidden issues are easily hooked by all kinds of money events.

Another difficulty for the partner who strives for perfection is spending. Life can be very expensive if you always have to have the "best" of the new gadgets, cars, furniture, clothes, and so on. Perhaps a combination of perfectionism and bragging results in your needing both the nicest, newest SUV that money can buy and needing all your friends and family to see it, ride in it, and go ooh and ah. If that's you, you're going to feel unhappy if your best friend seems hardly to care about your new vehicle. Or worse, he or she might care, but feels envious and so has some internal need of his or her own to diminish what's important to you.

Belittling Oneself. One way to keep others from criticizing you is to get there first. Sometimes this results in others' coming to your rescue: "Oh, no, you couldn't have known that that credit card charges 22 percent interest. They hide all that detail." Sometimes, being self-critical simply keeps others' expectations low so you won't have to suffer loss of respect when you don't meet higher expectations.

The problem with setting lower standards for yourself is that you're likely to meet them. Although there are some people who actually perform better in life when they keep their expectations low—because it keeps them less anxious about performing—other people will simply tend to match their behavior to their own low expectations. This person says, "Oh, I'm just not very good with money. Never have been and never will be." So he or she doesn't try, doesn't learn, and doesn't achieve. The sad thing is that there are very good strategies for financial achievement that the average person *can* use. But you can't succeed if you won't try, and you may not try if you never push yourself to learn. What's worse, extreme self-deprecation can make it hard for your partner to admire you, diminishing your attractiveness over time.

Belittling the Other. A person who feels insecure in himself or herself can easily mask this by taking it out on others—belittling others instead of the self. It doesn't feel so bad to be a loser if others are too. In terms of money, a critical partner may disapprove of the other's spending too much or too little, of the other's not doing enough research before making an investment or not acting quickly enough. Sometimes the criticalness takes the form of outright anger and put-downs. "How could you be so stupid! Don't you know that car dealers charge double or more for simple repairs?" We've seen plenty of couples in which one partner openly disrespects the other's attempts to bring in income because he or she has doubts about his or her own abilities. Such patterns are very destructive to a couple. Instead of going through life as a teammate with his or her partner, an insecure partner not only lets life get him or her down but also tries to take the partner down as well. This need to keep the partner down can be fed by envy, wherein the insecure partner is very threatened by any success of the other. (Many times, patterns of anger have little to do with such deeper themes of insecurity. Some people just get on edge easier, and money problems can cause most people to become anxious. Of course, expressing that anxiety as anger rather than as vulnerability and fear only drives a wedge between partners over time.)

Complete Compliance. An overly compliant person is so desperate to be liked that he or she may rarely assert his or her own needs or wants. Yet—and this is important to realize—this person will still experience disappointment from unmet expectations. Overly compliant people often agree with others in order to be liked and to avoid criticism. It may sound great to be married to a compliant partner, but even agreeableness has its limits. For one thing, an overly compliant partner doesn't contribute to the checks and balances found in healthy relationships. As we said in Chapter One, those checks and balances are a powerful way in which couples are more likely to do well in life when it comes to finances. Further, it can become burdensome to have to make all the financial decisions because the partner abdicates his or her responsibility to contribute.

Money-Specific Expectations

In addition to what your parents taught you about yourself, they also taught you how to think about money. Expectations were transmitted both directly, through what your parents (or stepparents) said, and indirectly, through your observation of what they did. They may have encouraged you to save for a rainy day by taking part of your money and placing it directly into a piggy bank. They influenced your early expenditures by saying yes to this and no to that. Your parents may have directly told you that you must share your money with others through placing "your" money in the offering plate as it passed.

Through indirect learning, you likely came to understand abundance and scarcity. You learned confidence or fear in managing money. You learned whether or not your family was comfortable with money, whether there was usually enough, whether your family tended to see itself as rich or poor. Feeling "rich," "comfortable," or "poor" is a reflection of both the real numbers as well as the expectations you learned as a child. We know couples who make hundreds of thousands of dollars but are still anxious about having enough, and who talk constantly about how they can get more.

Pessimism Versus Optimism

The different messages that our parents give us, and the profound impact they can have, is the major theme of the best-selling book *Rich Dad, Poor Dad*, by Robert T. Kiyosaki. Here are some of the differences in how these two types of parents see the world—and convey this view to their children:

Poor Dad	**Rich Dad**
I can't afford it.	How can I afford it?
Study hard so you can find a good company to work for.	Study hard so you can find a good company to buy.
I'm not rich because I have you kids.	I must become rich because I have you kids.

Rich dad sees life in terms of what's possible—with hard work and effort. Rich dad is not held back by expectations and beliefs that it's useless to try. Rich dad does not make excuses for failing to set goals that stretch him and his family in life. What about you? What messages did you learn from your parents? What messages will your children learn from you?

If you observed your parents avoiding all manner of conflict about money, you may have developed the expectation that couples should seek peace at any price. When you face disagreement and conflict, it may seem to you as though the world is going to end. Or you could learn from such parents that you need to fight for everything, defending each desire, no matter how large or small, when working on agreements with your mate.

If you observed your parents spending freely, you may have come to expect that you and your spouse would do the same, even if you don't have nearly as much money as your parents have or had. If your parents fought fiercely every month when the bills came due, you may have some expectation in the back of your mind that constant fighting is the norm, and you gear up your emotions for a series of events that your partner may not expect or react to in nearly the same way.

One major area of expectations lies in money management. Here are just a few of the areas about which we all have expectations:

Who balances the checkbook, if anyone?

Which accounts are joint, and which are separate?

Who pays the bills, or who pays which bills?

How much is OK to spend on entertainment?

How much do we save, and where?

Who gets the last say if you disagree about a large, important purchase?

How often do we go over the details of our finances? Once a week? Once a month? Yearly? Only on our fiftieth, sixtieth, and seventieth birthdays?

How much is too much before we need to agree on spending money?

The list goes on and on. You formed some expectations about many of these kinds of decisions or situations from your family growing up as well as from key relationships prior to being with your partner. Even these seemingly small expectations can trigger hidden issues and all of those bigger dynamics over time.

Diane and Nolan weren't together a year when they decided to marry. A year later, they were having regular conflicts about money that were threatening their relationship. Growing up, Nolan learned to expect that partners tell each other about almost any purchase over five bucks. In contrast, Diane's family had more money and was a good deal more casual in how they handled it. For her part, she didn't think that she'd need to bother telling Nolan about a purchase if it were under $100. So it was not infrequent that he'd notice something like new shoes or a purse or an accessory for her computer, and feel that she'd broken the rules. To her, of course, there was no such rule, and the only thing that bothered her in the whole matter was that he got annoyed. In her words, "He was going bal-listic over stuff that just didn't matter."

For Nolan, this all triggered hidden issues of caring. He not only saw his way as "just the way it's supposed to be" but also interpreted her behavior as mean-ing that she was less responsible and, worse, unconcerned about his sensibilities. Diane felt increasingly controlled and began to interpret almost all of Nolan's be-havior of this sort as a power trip. The actual basis for this clash was pretty harm-less and didn't really mean all that much. But, as you have learned, these clashes in expectations can grow to take on a life of their own.

Prior Romantic Relationships and Marriages

In addition to learning expectations from your family, you have probably also de-veloped some expectations about money and marriage from all key relationships you've had, including dating relationships, business relationships, and, especially, a prior marriage if you've been divorced or widowed. You have expectations about how much to spend on a date, how much to spend on birthday presents, how to communicate about money problems, whose job is more important, whether or not to combine your income, who should make the first move to make up after a fight about money, and so on.

Many expectations are about such minor things that it's hard to imagine they could become so important, but as you may well know, they can be very impor-tant. It all depends on what meanings and issues are attached to the expectations. For example, newly married Emily told us that her first husband had drilled it into her that he didn't want her spending more than they had budgeted for weekly food shopping, even if there were great sales going on (no stocking up on OJ or spaghetti sauce). She thought, "OK, no big deal." Now, with her second husband, Warren, she was finding quite the opposite. He liked her to buy sale items and buy in bulk, and he'd actually get upset with her if she didn't. Emily was working hard to unlearn the expectation she'd finally learned so well; however, she had gotten into the habit of buying in small quantities and was struggling to change. Warren interpreted Emily's hesitancy to spend money on sale items as a sign that she didn't care about what was important to him. Her devotion challenged, she'd get angry at him. This just confirmed what he was already starting to believe: "I knew she didn't care."

In the case of blended families, the difficult expectations can extend to many more areas. It's very easy to trip over differences in expectations about money when it comes to each other's kids. How much were you used to spending on birth-day presents? Do the two of you clash about that? How about allowance? Do you have the same expectations about when you won't let your children spend some of their money, even if they have it and want to spend it? Does your philosophy lean more toward having kids learn by verbal teaching, or do you think they should learn by personal experience, no matter how painful? How strongly do you feel about that?

Cultural Influences

Just as we have a family background, we all have a cultural background, or even a multicultural background. Many of our expectations about how to handle money are affected by the culture in which we were raised. Almost all of us tend to assume that our upbringing—both our family and our culture—is the basis for how things should be; we fail to appreciate how different things can be someplace else. And if your mate came from someplace else, you have some differences in worldview to factor in if you want to better understand how money works in your relationship—or to understand anything else in your relationship, for that matter. Considering that people are more inclined than ever before to live away from where they grew up, the odds of marrying someone from someplace else have increased dramatically. That means more work to handle issues and events carefully.

As is true of any other culture, we in the United States believe things that are not viewed in the same way in other countries and cultures. For example, when researchers polled citizens all over the world, they found that 68 percent of Americans agreed that both husband and wife should contribute to the household income. However, 98 percent of the Portuguese, 96 percent of the Chinese, 84.5 percent of the Spanish, 45.5 percent of the Japanese, and only 30 percent of the citizens of the Netherlands agreed with the statement.

When asked whether they agreed with the statement, "A working mother can have just as secure a relationship with her preschool child as a nonworking mother," 72.5 percent of Americans, 94 percent of the Finnish, 82.5 percent of the Danish, 73.5 percent of the Swedes, 43 percent of the South Koreans, and 41 percent of the West Germans agreed. These statements express very basic beliefs about money and family that have huge implications for how any one couple might live their lives. Clashes in such basic expectations can cause real fireworks in a marriage.

Industrialization

American culture used to be much different. In the early 1800s, the United States was an agrarian society; social mobility was discouraged, tradition was prized, status was inherited to some degree, and many obligations were communal. In many ways, things moved slowly. People were deeply embedded in their families and communities. By the 1850s, the Industrial Revolution was starting to take hold in the Western world. With it came a new set of cultural expectations—a strong culture shift. The new worldview encouraged economic achievement, individualism and innovation, and increasingly flexible social norms. The top priorities became economic accumulation (for individuals) and economic growth (for societies). Obligations to community and extended family were de-emphasized, social mobility encouraged. Perhaps for the first time in history, people had the opportunity to improve their social status instead of being confined by class membership.

These changes greatly affected people's expectations about marriage and family. Whereas a husband and wife used to be much more likely to be embedded in a family network, marriages increasingly began to be seen as independent entities. Further, the emphasis on capitalism and consumerism placed increased attention on the needs of the individual above all else. People have brought this mind-set into marriages and families in ways that at times have not been altogether good for them. In fact, as historian Barbara Dafoe Whitehead asserts in her book *The Divorce Culture,* prosperity and a focus on self have shredded the traditional meaning of commitment in marriage.

We're not antiprosperity, and neither is Dr. Whitehead. Yet if you absorb the expectation from our culture that you should, above all else, be made happy by your mate—as if your mate were a product to be evaluated and returned if found to be unsatisfying—you will have great difficulty finding lasting, deeper happiness in life. You will most likely lose at love and money if your focus is only on obtaining the most for yourself in either. In the best of all worlds, a couple develops and nurtures a strong sense of couple identity, and from that, the partners support one another in reaching for all the best in life.

Ancestry Groups

Our society comprises many different subcultures, one type of which is the ancestry group. Our ancestry group can influence our expectations. In *The Millionaire Next Door,* Thomas Stanley and William Danko explain that there are certain similarities among people who are rich (beside the fact that they have a lot of money!). One of the interesting similarities is that certain ancestry groups have higher percentages of millionaires than others. The Russian, Scottish, and Hungarian ancestry groups rank first, second, and third, respectively, in percentage of millionaire households. Why? According to Stanley and Danko, the Russian Americans and the Hungarian Americans are far more inclined toward running their own businesses. In general, most American millionaires are manager-owners of businesses.

These authors go on to say that the longer the ancestry group has been in America, the less likely it is that it will produce a relatively high number of millionaires, because they begin to absorb more of American culture, which tends to discourage entrepreneurship and accumulating wealth and to encourage spending.

Different ancestry groups promote different attitudes and behaviors regarding money. Some of these attitudes and behaviors are more conducive to accumulating wealth than others. The following list, adapted from *The Millionaire Next Door*, shows in order of rank (based on the percentage of the ancestry group that is in millionaire households) how the top ten ancestry groups of American millionaires compare.

1. Russian
2. Scottish
3. Hungarian
4. English
5. Dutch
6. French
7. Irish
8. Italian
9. German
10. Native American

As you can well imagine, wealth among cultural groups will be greatly affected not only by traditions but also by opportunity. For example, many African Americans started their life on the North American continent without opportunity or advantages of any sort. Similarly, Native Americans in North America had much taken from them, with few opportunities being supplied to them in return. A strong history of oppression can lead to deeply embedded expectations that it's not worth trying to start a business or reach for more opportunities. Further, even if the opportunities are in no way limited, a given cultural group may simply value material wealth less than another group.

The Generation Gap

Each individual will be most influenced by the prevailing expectations of his or her culture during the teenage to early adult years. So the era in which you grew up will influence your expectations a great deal. *Cohorts* are defined as groups of people who share a common experience by virtue of having grown up in the same time period and similar environment. In 2001, we had cohorts known as Depression Babies, the Silent Generation, the Swing Generation, the Greatest Generation, Baby Boomers, Generation Jones, Baby Busters, Echo Boomers, Generation X, Generation Y, and Millennials.

Each cohort has its own set of values, attitudes, and opinions about the role of money and its use. There are two factors that seem to have the greatest impact on the development of our expectations. The first is the state of the national economy during our adolescence and young adulthood. For example, was the economy expanding, with plentiful jobs, or was there a recession, with layoffs the norm? If the economy was strong when you were a teen, you may be more likely to expect to be able to find work when you need it. You may have a lot of confidence, justifiable or not, that "things will work out." In contrast, someone who grew up when jobs were scarce and money hard to come by might have expectations that include greater pessimism.

One of the greatest events ever to strongly affect a cohort in the United States was the Great Depression of the 1930s. It seems that very few people could go through such tough times without having been affected. Many in this cohort have been particularly cautious and industrious with their financial resources. This group knew how easy it was to see whole fortunes slip away, and by and large they learned to hang on tight. It's probably no accident that this group became such a driving force in the growth of the U.S. economy in the 1950s and 1960s.

The second factor is the rate and types of technological changes that are going on in the marketplace and in financial institutions. For example, the baby boom generation has gone from using cash to credit cards to debit cards to the Internet and online banking services. The number and kinds of changes that you've experienced will influence what kinds of changes you expect to see in the future. If you grew up when change came slowly, your expectations will be violated when changes come rapidly. You might prefer that "things just stay the same," or you might enjoy "all these new and exciting things going on."

Each generation develops it's own expectations as to how money is to be saved or spent. How has that affected you?

How Culture Transmits Its Expectations

There are many ways in which a culture imparts its expectations to individuals. Our culture expects its citizens to learn to read and write, and children attend school to accomplish that goal. Unfortunately, not much about good financial management is taught in schools. The primary way that our culture transmits its expectations about money are through marketing and entertainment channels.

Marketing

Suppose you could travel in a time machine back to New York City in the late 1800s. If you bought a newspaper, what kind of advertisements would you find? Let's say it's the Christmas season. Think about how thick the Christmas paper is now with all the ads. What did the ads look like then? You'd have a hard time finding any. The one or two ads you might be able to scrounge up would be targeted at adults, and they would be for small items, such as a packet of pins or a pouch of pipe tobacco.

OK, get back in your time machine, hop to 1900, and look in a newspaper. Now you will see a good number of holiday ads targeted not only at adults but also at kids, and the gifts that are advertised are becoming more extravagant. There are ads for dolls and trains for children, as well as jewelry for women and waist-coats for men.

Travel once more to 1919 and take a peek at the *New York Times*. You'll find that the newspaper contains quite a bit more advertising than it did twenty years earlier, and the ads are becoming more sophisticated in the messages they convey. They no longer simply demonstrate their wares, but have started speaking to your hidden issues—they speak on an emotional level. For example, an ad on December 15, 1919, says, "Don't give your family and friends frivolous gifts that are sure to disappoint, buy them worthy gifts that will *let them know how much you care*" (emphasis added).

Marketers go to school to learn about the physiological, psychological, socio-cultural, and personality characteristics of their potential customers, all for one purpose: to sell. One of the most powerful strategies that marketers use is one of the most subtle. They woo us; they speak to the deepest cravings of the human heart.

> Marketers don't sell cosmetics, they sell beauty.
>
> Marketers don't sell beer, they sell gusto.
>
> Marketers don't sell insurance, they sell security.
>
> Marketers don't sell a house, they sell a happy home.
>
> Marketers don't sell cars, they sell status, style, performance, and power.
>
> Marketers don't sell a frozen dinner, they sell a happy family having quality time.

Marketers aren't bad people. People who market products are, for the most part, normal people like all the rest of us. It's not their fault that they know us better than we know ourselves. And it's not their fault that we *want* to believe their promises. We want to buy beauty. We want to buy gusto, security, a happy home, power, and quality time. We know it's nonsensical, yet we buy in the hopes that our inner lives will be fuller.

This is how the messages of marketing in our culture can cause significant problems in relationships. Although we want people to aim high in life so that they can reach their dreams together, we also realize that many expectations become so high that no person or couple will reasonably achieve them, and disappointment will result. Take health and beauty. It's terrific to work to stay healthy and in good shape. There is no doubt that your partner will find you more attractive if you give some attention to your health and appearance. In our culture, it's not reasonable to expect your partner not to care at all about how you look. So health is good. But what if your expectations are so high that they're off the charts? You might be susceptible not only to being disappointed with your partner but also to buying the newest gadget advertised on television that promises to make it easy for you to get and stay in great shape. Many of these expensive devices work less well than good, old-fashioned, get-off-your-behind exercise.

Because most of us live in a culture saturated with messages about what we should desire or deserve, it becomes all the more important to be able to talk openly with our partners about what we truly, deeply need or desire. Only with the anchor of such information can you more easily resist the siren song of marketing that suggests you must have things you neither need nor can afford without damaging your relationship as well as your financial status. This is why understanding and talking about your hidden issues and expectations are so important. You increase your potential for intimacy, and you and your partner are better able to meet each other's inner needs. With your inner needs met, you are less susceptible to the temptation to spend money in the vain hope of meeting those inner needs. As you spend less money on things that don't help you get what you want, you end up with more money to spend on the material goods that money *can* buy.

> *With your inner needs met, you are less susceptible to the temptation to spend money in the vain hope of meeting those inner needs.*

Entertainment

Not all the media we take in are directly marketing something. Yet much of it can create expectations for things we want to have in our lives. The movie *French Kiss* with Kevin Kline and Meg Ryan is an example of how very subtle but still powerful money messages can be portrayed in the movies. Meg Ryan plays Kate, a woman who is terrified of flying in an airplane. In the first scene, Kate is in an airplane, ready for takeoff and crying, "We're going down, we're going down, we're going down." The camera shows Kate gripping the arm of her seat, her hands shaking with terror. An astute observer will notice that Kate's engagement ring has a diamond the size of a period. It is one very small diamond.

Kate is dumped by her fiancé and later bumps into him and his new amour. Again, the camera zeros in on a tiny detail. Only this time, the detail isn't so tiny. The new woman has a diamond on her finger the size of a marble. Little details such as this help make this movie delightful, but they also convey a subtle message about money and love. Perhaps if the wandering fiancé had *really* loved Kate, he would have bought her a larger diamond? When he found his *true* love, nothing was too good for her: he bought her the biggest rock he could find. What do you think the message might be?

In research, you know you've influenced something if you see a change in behavior. There is no doubt among marketers that adult buying behavior is influenced by the movies. In the James Bond movie *Goldeneye,* Bond drove a BMW Z3 roadster that was later offered by Neiman Marcus in their Christmas catalogue. They sold their allotment of one hundred of these very expensive little cars by phone in less than two-and-a-half hours. The whole marketing approach left BMW's competitors shaken and stirred. The auto manufacturers fought over what type of car Bond would drive in the next adventure.

Movies and television can even influence what kind of dog Americans favor. When Disney's remake of *101 Dalmatians* was released in 1996, the breed experienced a surge in popularity. The hit TV sitcom *Frasier* costars Eddie, a Jack Russell terrier. Dr. Nicholas Dodman, a leading animal behaviorist at the Tufts University School of Veterinary Medicine, suggests that the show's success may account for the 21 percent hike in registrations for the breed in 2000.

Our key point here is that the messages we take in really do work on us. Maybe not all of them, maybe not even most, but they do work, and they can change what we want, what we think we need, and what we think should be happening in our relationships. For those businesspeople with the resources to learn, there is plenty of marketing research that tells them what works well on us and what does not. Many messages we absorb in the media are not selling anything at all, but they are nevertheless conveying key cultural expectations about the way relationships should be.

What expectations would you absorb about money and marriage, for example, if you watched thousands of hours of TV in the United States? Shows like *Father Knows Best, The Honeymooners, The Price Is Right, The Brady Bunch, The Cosby Show, Roseanne, Home Improvement, Dharma & Greg, Mad About You, Who Wants to Be a Millionaire?, The Sopranos, Sex and the City,* and any number of others all send very powerful messages about the role of money matters in marriages and hence influence our expectations.

In general, the media in America portray couples as having lots of disposable income and few problems dealing with money. How often do we see a couple struggling over whether or not they can afford new tires for the car right now or have to wait because the washing machine is about to go out? Real life confronts us with trade-offs, trade-offs mean we have to make decisions, and decisions mean opportunities for conflict.

Television has also portrayed social changes over time, from the days when Dad worked outside the home and Mom worked inside the home (and got "pin money" from Dad) to the era of dual-earner couples such as the Cosbys. What shows have influenced you most with regard to relationships? What messages have you noticed, and which have you absorbed? Stop for a few minutes. Make this an exercise with your partner. It can be fascinating to discuss what you each think you've learned—or resisted learning—from the media in America.

Take a moment to list five shows that you have watched in the past two weeks. That could include movies, dramas, sitcoms, soap operas, or news shows. Now take the time to think about one or two messages you received from each that relates to marriage, money, or relationships in general. Talk together about what you came up with. What do you notice? What messages have the most effect on you, for good or bad?

Moving Forward

Both directly and indirectly, you have accumulated experiences from your family, your past relationships, and your culture, and translated them into expectations— expectations that you bring to your marriage. Understanding your expectations and how they were formed is an important component in learning to win at money without losing at love. Understanding and expressing your expectations can bring closeness to your relationship and help you be a more sophisticated consumer.

Several experts in cultural trends suggest that our society may be on the verge of another culture shift, that the emphasis on economic achievement is giving way to an increased emphasis on the quality of life. We may be moving to a time when culture conveys the increased importance of such values as spirituality (despite the wide range of definitions), friendship, and connection with others. We think such shifts would be good for people overall. As we said early in this book, nurturing the friendship between the two of you may be one of the most powerful ways to increase your overall well-being.

Wherever our culture is headed, understanding your expectations allows you to choose your future rather than simply to live on automatic pilot. We hope you create the future you've dreamed of—together.

CHAPTER SEVEN

JUST HOW OPPOSITE IS
THE OPPOSITE SEX?

When women are depressed, they eat or go shopping. Men invade another country. It's a whole different way of thinking.

ELAYNE BOOSLER

When I (Natalie) teach workshops on money and marriage, I usually introduce myself by saying that for more than ten years I've kept one foot in consumer science and one foot in marriage education. But, as often as possible, I keep both feet firmly planted in the malls. I freely admit that I love to shop. I don't go to the mall often. I don't have time to do that. But when I do get to go shopping, I enjoy the heck out of it.

Whether you shop online or at the old-fashioned brick-and-mortar store, whether you clip coupons, buy in bulk, or get it on sale, when all is said and done, somebody's going to take some money out of your bank account and put it in theirs. Shopping is the process through which you give up money and get stuff in return. For years I have tried to explain to my husband why this is a spiritual experience. He doesn't get it.

Over the years, however, we have come to understand each other a bit better. I remember one afternoon when we were supposed to be going to some friends' house for dinner. Shawn was engrossed in a basketball game on TV. It was "the most important game of the season." I could never figure out how the most important game could be on every week, but some things in life may forever remain a mystery. Anyway, I kept nagging Shawn, "Honey, how much longer? We're going to be late." I remember distinctly that he told me, "There's three minutes left in the game."

Silly me. I thought that three minutes meant three minutes. But he meant *basketball minutes*. According to the official spouse-translation dictionary, three basketball minutes can be anywhere from seventeen to thirty-two real-time minutes. Maybe this is what Einstein meant by relativity in time. I'm not sure.

The next day we were at the mall. Shawn had been a good sport, but he was ready to go home. I wanted to hit one more store. As I headed into the store, I told him I'd be "just a couple of minutes." He found a chair among the other good-sport husbands at the mall that day and bummed a sports page off of a guy who was ready to get out on parole—um, I mean, was about to get to go home. A good thirty minutes later, Shawn found me still wandering around the store.

"Nat, I thought you said you'd be just a couple minutes."

"Oh, Honey, didn't I tell you? This is NBA shopping! And we could be headed for double overtime!" *That* was a spiritual moment. He and I truly understood one another!

When I tell this story at my workshops, some women become annoyed with me. We women have been fighting the stereotype of mindless shoppers, and they say that I'm not helping any by presenting myself as one. But I don't see it that way. I'm not afraid to admit it: once in a while I "devolve" into a mindless, stereotypical female shopper. I have told my husband, "Honey, I've had an extremely rough day, and I'm going shopping. It's cheaper than therapy." When I bring home all my purchases, he points out that therapy would have been *much* cheaper. I tell him that he has no idea just how much therapy I really need. Of course, I am more than a mindless shopper. I am also a competent and responsible human being. The fact that I am not perfect does not cancel out my value as a human being, nor does it diminish my expertise in marital and money issues.

I think the best way to fight unfair stereotypes is for both men and women to acknowledge the fragments of truth that allowed the stereotypes to develop in the first place. A little humility never hurt anyone. No one behaves perfectly all the time. If with a healthy sense of humor we acknowledge the areas where we tend to be "flawed," then we can transcend the stereotypes and become flesh-and-blood, multidimensional human beings.

Humor and humility—not denial—are two of the best weapons against stereotypes. Humor has been defined as a gentle way to celebrate our human frailty. I like that. I think laughing at ourselves is a healthy thing. We shouldn't *just* laugh, however. A healthy approach to our human frailty involves something of a paradox: we admit and accept our flaws and, at the same time, work to improve in the areas where we need to improve. Accepting ourselves warts and all doesn't absolve us of our responsibility to continue to grow.

So I laugh at myself as I head to the mall to soothe my frazzled nerves. And I work to find better (less expensive and more healthy) ways to deal with stress. Shawn wants to know when I'll find a better way. "Well, Sweetheart, I keep getting better every day, and I'll finally succeed right after the last 'most important game of the season'!" We all, men and women, have reason to laugh at ourselves and reason to keep growing. You're kinda funny, too, aren't you? In some ways?

Men and Women: The Great Divide?

There are a lot of stereotypes out there. We often hear that men are this way and women are that way, but what's true and what's hype? Is there a great divide between the sexes? What do you think? We've got a quiz for you. True or false?

1. Women shop more than men.
2. Boys get larger allowances than girls.
3. Mothers teach their sons more about money than they teach their daughters.
4. Women save less than men.
5. Women are more willing to stop and ask for directions.
6. Men and women are equally committed to their marriages.
7. Women handle more of the finances than men.
8. Women are less risk tolerant.
9. Men, being more competitive, are more likely than women to have already looked at the correct answers below so that they can get a higher score on this quiz.
10. In dual-earner marriages, men do as much of the housework as women.

Go ahead and write down your answers. We'll wait for you. Before we go through the answers, we want to clarify what researchers mean when they talk about differences between groups. When researchers talk about differences between groups of people, such as men and women or married and single, they are talking averages. They're talking about differences that tend to be true for many people, but there will be a great number of exceptions. Think about all the different kinds of people there are just in America. There's rural versus inner city. There's East Coast versus West Coast versus South versus Midwest. There are doctors and lawyers and teachers and construction workers and salespeople and farmers. There are huge generational differences between the people who grew up in the World War II era and the Baby Boomers and Generation X and Generation Y.

When we talk about averages among diverse groups, such as when we say that one gender tends to do this or think that, you could very easily be the exception. So you should add the words *on average* to just about any sentence in the rest of this chapter. You may or may not behave or think like many people of your gender. There are far more differences between individuals in how they think and act than can be explained just by knowing the sex of the individuals.

Nevertheless, although there are differences *within* each gender, there are real differences *between* the genders as well. You've probably noticed that. Let's go through the true-false quiz briefly. First, the answers. Look back to the questions. In order, the correct answers are true, true, true, true, true, true, it depends, true, did you? and false! Before we go on, note that nearly all these questions deal with expectations that can lead to conflicts if the expectations are not made clear or if there's no agreement about how differences will be handled.

Now let's look more closely at each item from the quiz.

Women Shop More Than Men

Baby boys and baby girls start out with similar instincts. Newborns of both sexes will grip fingers when given the opportunity. When we get older, though, things change. Men grip the remote control, and women grip the charge card. The data we found showed that there's some truth to this. Guys tend to be more enamored with electrical gadgets, and women do shop more often than men.

We're not convinced that women are "born to shop," however. It may be that women tend to shop more than men as a consequence of the role they often play in the family. Although there is an increasing number of men taking more responsibility for the everyday running of families, most of the job still tends to land with women. It is usually the woman who knows that Johnny needs to go buy some green felt and a plastic spoon for the science project tomorrow. It is often the woman who knows that the kids' underwear looks like Swiss cheese and that it's time to head to the store. It's commonly the woman who knows you're out of milk—again—and runs to the store to pick some up, along with two bags of groceries.

We know of one husband who took the credit card bill and highlighted all of his purchases in blue and hers in pink. The bill was seven-eighths pink. He then proceeded to scold her for shopping so much. She needed to be more frugal—like him. But that was unfair: he worked outside the home, she didn't. It was her job to manage the family. She had bought exciting things like pajamas for the kids and oil for the car and charcoal for the grill. She had done the job of shopping. If she had been "at work," he'd have had to make more blue marks on the Visa bill. We think that both men and women can be unfair at times when evaluating the shopping behavior of their partners. Both sexes take turns behaving badly. We think that this guy used up two (maybe three) of his turns in this case! According to one study, 61 percent of the food shopping is done by women and only 11 percent by men (28 percent say "both" do the grocery shopping). If you're going to scold your spouse for shopping, you might want to be ready to start making out your own grocery list!

For many women, shopping is a "job" they would rather not do. In the 1980s, the "shop till you drop" mantra was more prevalent. But experts assert that women's priorities shifted dramatically between the 1980s and the 1990s. Now, if a woman has free time, she is far more likely to want to spend it at home than in a store. The *Women's Market Handbook* states that one in three female consumers would rather do housework than shop, and according to the highly respected 2001 Yankelovich Monitor, 45 percent of women even consider shopping for clothes to be a chore rather than a pleasure.

There are differences in how much men and women spend on different items. We know that women spend three times more than guys on household textiles (yes, that's the guest towels and the dust ruffle). Sixty percent of Starbucks customers are women. But men consistently out-shop women when buying beer, junk food, chips, and other entertainment food—not to mention the big-screen television to go with those items. Only one in four first-time motorcycle buyers is a woman, and only one in five truck buyers is a woman. Women aren't the only ones who get that glazed look in their eyes and start chanting, "I gotta have it. I just gotta, can we please have it, oh can we please?"

Boys Get Larger Allowances Than Girls

This is also true. Many children receive allowances by the age of eight or nine. Research suggests that despite income differences among families, most families give about the same allowance amounts to children of the same age. However, within the same age group, when comparing boys' allowances to those of girls, boys win out.

There are interesting gender differences in how parents approach allowance. Research has found that fathers tend to want to associate the payment and amount of allowance with chores and behavioral performance. The more chores performed and the better the behavior or grades in school, the more likely Dad will shell out the dough. Moms, in contrast, usually want to give the kids money as a sign of affection and to meet their basic wants and needs. Dads want their kids to learn about the relationship between income and work, whereas moms simply want their children to feel loved through access to money.

Mothers Teach Their Sons More About Money

True. I (Bill) conducted a study at the University of Arkansas comparing the financial education mothers provided to their sons with that provided to their daughters. The majority of the mothers in the study were under the age of thirty, and more than 80 percent had college degrees. My colleagues and I asked these

mothers to report when and how much they would tell children about both simple and complex financial issues—for example, at what age they would tell a child about banks or allow a child to open a bank or savings account. The women were given two questionnaires, one for a boy and one for a girl. Sons were most often taught about money concepts earlier, and they were taught more than daughters. Twenty percent of the mothers reported that they would never tell their children what the family income was.

That sons are taught more about money than daughters has some implications for how knowledgeable men and women might be about money when they enter into a relationship. However, studies also show that when provided with the information, women close the gap very quickly.

Women Save Less Than Men

On average, this is true. Studies show that women tend to save less than men and also less as a percentage of what they make. According to the National Center for Women and Retirement Research, women normally save 1.5 percent of their pay versus the 3 percent typical of men. The guys don't have any reason to act smug about this, though. Financial advisers recommend saving 10 to 15 percent of one's income, so neither sex is doing particularly well in this area. How about the two of you?

Women Are More Willing to Stop and Ask for Directions

You've probably heard the joke, "Why is it a good thing there are female astronauts?" "So someone will ask for directions if the crew gets lost in space." Ha-ha, sort of funny. But is it true? Are women more willing to ask for directions than men? In certain situations, yes. Particularly when it comes to finances.

In one study, men and women were given a list of investments and asked if they would invest in each of the items. The researchers pulled a fast one, however. They included on the list some bogus items—investments that don't exist. Men marked that they were willing to invest in the bogus investments far more often than women. Women were willing to say, "I don't know what this is. What is it?"

In 1999, the American Savings Education Council cosponsored a study with Employee Benefits Research Institute and Mathew Greenwald & Associates. They discovered that working-age women are more likely than their male counterparts (62 percent versus 49 percent) to hire a professional planner. When it comes to asking for help with finances, women are more willing to ask for directions.

When it comes to shopping, females again are more willing to ask for help. Retail anthropologists (those are the people who spy on shoppers to learn about shopping behavior) have actually timed shoppers to see how much time they spend

LET ME GET THIS STRAIGHT, JACK, YOU WENT OUT AND SPENT ALL OUR GROCERY MONEY ON SOME "MAGIC BEANS"?

BUT JEAN, THE GUY SAID THESE BEANS HAVE REAL GROWTH POTENTIAL!

JACK AND JEAN TALK

in a store. They report that men nearly always move faster through the stores than women do. Women walk at a relaxed pace, interact with the sales staff, and ask questions. Guys don't. They look around quickly, and if they don't find the section they're looking for, they leave the store without asking for help.

This doesn't mean, however, that men don't want information; it simply means they are less likely to *ask* for it. Studies show that men will walk right up to displays and signs, and read intently. They will stand in front of an instructional video. They will take brochures and study them. Men are just as willing to become informed consumers as women are; it's just that their method of obtaining that information is different.

Men and Women Are Equally Committed to Their Marriages

Over the years, there have been a number of studies that have looked at the subject of commitment. One of the most important kinds of commitment is what we call dedication. In two large studies, we have found almost no differences between the dedication levels of husbands and wives.

Women Handle More of the Finances Than Men

It depends on how you define "handle the finances." A study by Prudential Securities found that men still do most of the investing for families. Only 15 percent of married women describe themselves as the main decision maker regarding investments. However, 78 percent said they share the decision-making responsibility. Among married men, about one-third say they are the main decision maker, and two-thirds say they share the responsibility.

Women Are Less Risk Tolerant

When it comes to finances, virtually all studies demonstrate that women are more conservative in investing than men. Men are more likely to be more active and assertive investors. They are willing to take bigger risks, and more often. Women are closing the gap, however.

A report from Prudential Securities in March 1999 described how things are changing in this area of risk tolerance. In 1995, 45 percent of women considered investing risky; by 1995, that number had dropped to 25 percent. In 1995, 72 percent of women said they were open to considering new investment opportunities and strategies. Yet by 1998, the percentage of women open to considering new opportunities had grown to 80 percent. In 1995, 41 percent of women said they often put off making financial decisions for fear of making a mistake. In 1998, that number had dropped to 32 percent. Another study found that the gap still exists between men and women in their comfort level with financial risk: 11 percent of men are willing to take substantial financial risks, whereas only 5 percent of women are willing to do so.

Men Are More Competitive About Things Than Women

Did you look ahead at the answers? There really does seem to be a difference between men and women when it comes to some types of competition (and we're only joking, not seriously implying that men cheat more than women on quizzes). Surely there are many women who love to compete and win, but men more often seem to be the ones who are driven toward the kind of success that comes from competing and winning.

As Carol Gilligan notes in her book *In a Different Voice,* when women are in conflict with others, they are more likely than men to put the goal of preserving relationships ahead of winning. Such matters are complex and vary greatly from relationship to relationship. When it comes to financial matters, men tend to be more aggressive investors; however, as women gain knowledge and experience, they tend to become more aggressive. When it comes to being competitive in the workplace, men are still viewed as more aggressive, although women seem to be changing that perception as well.

Increasingly, we have seen partners competing with one another—for example, competing over whose job is more important or who should sacrifice more so that the other can get ahead in his or her career. Such competition is usually not a good sign, as it leads to scorekeeping and resentment between two people who should be working from the perspective of being a team in life.

In Dual-Earner Marriages, Men Do as Much Housework as Women

Nope. It sounds like a nice idea, but it just isn't so. Even though more women than ever before work outside the home, they have generally not been able to reduce a lot of the traditional workload at home. In a study published in 2001, Stevens, Kige, and Riley from Utah State University found that women spend an average of 15 hours a week in household labor, compared to 6.8 hours for men.

Do men do less housework simply because they are lazy or because they feel that they are entitled to have their wives clean up after them? We don't think so. Although married men generally do less housework than their wives, it's not as if they suddenly changed when they got married. For the most part, they were not into housework when they were single, either. Single men also report spending less than women do on cleaning supplies. Are you shocked? Nah. Compulsively clean men must surely exist, but generally, housecleaning is not as high a priority for most men as it is for women. Figure 13 shows how much, on average, single men and single women spend annually on cleaning supplies.

FIGURE 13. AVERAGE SPENDING BY SINGLES ON CLEANING SUPPLIES.

	Single Men	Single Women
Housekeeping supplies	$151	$258
Laundry and cleaning supplies	40	56
Other household products	66	105

We can conclude that on average, women spend more time and money on household chores than men do, whether they are married or not. Clearly, there is real potential for conflict here when the man and woman get married. He's upset with her for spending so much more money than he ever did, and she's upset with him because he's not doing more housework.

American women expect to find in their husbands a perfection that English women only hope to find in their butlers.

W. SOMERSET MAUGHAM

For many couples, housework is an area where differing expectations and poor problem solving collide to create a lot of heat. We also would do well to keep in mind that there are many, many tasks to do in keeping a home running smoothly. Sometimes we can focus on "housework" and forget that our partner contributes by going to the bank or mowing the lawn or changing the oil in the car. Couples can negotiate for better equality with the chores. The division of labor need not follow traditional gender lines. But it is also wise to keep our expectations realistic. The same Utah State University study found that the discrepancy between the amount of housework each partner does was not nearly as important as the couple's satisfaction with how the tasks were divided up. In other words, given our responsibilities in life, it's more important for a couple to be comfortable with how they divvy up the chores than for the work to be neatly divided right down the middle.

The Spice and Sparks of Love

So there you have it. There are some ways in which men and women are indeed different. These differences, we think, are the spice of life. It would be terribly boring if we were all exactly the same. As you contribute your different insights, hopes, understanding, and knowledge to your financial and intimate partnership, you create a much stronger future. We think your differences are to be celebrated and enjoyed.

However, we need to be honest here. Although it's true that we should celebrate our differences, sometimes our differences cause sparks—and not the happy kind. It's pretty amazing how we can love someone so deeply and be mad as heck at them at the same time, but we manage to pull it off. The differences between men and women—or, more to the point, the differences between the two of you— allow both to bring something unique to the relationship, but they also can make the blending of two lives into one something of a challenge. Now more than ever before, there is much to be negotiated as two different people try to forge one path in life together.

The Dance

There's one more stereotype that we want to discuss in some detail. It's this: when conflicts arise, men are more likely than women to shut down or pull away. As you know from what we've said earlier—and very likely from what you have experienced—money is an area of life that is rife with conflict for couples, or at least the potential for it. The pattern we'd like to discuss now is not unique to money conflicts, but because money conflicts are common for couples, these dynamics of one pursuing and one pulling away are going to be common as well. So let's look deeper into those dynamics and what extra features money issues bring to the dance.

Her Concerns, His Concerns

Women often voice concerns about withdrawn, avoidant husbands who will not open up and talk. When that happens, women feel shut out and get pretty unhappy. This is the most common complaint we hear from women who come in for marital counseling. In our experience, women value and seek communication about how the relationship is going more than men do.

In contrast, men frequently complain that their wives get upset too much of the time, griping about this or that and picking fights. Dare we use the "N word"? (Hint: rhymes with "bag.") Usually men feel hassled and want peace—at any price. Often that price is way too steep for women. We hear men saying, in one way or another, that they want some way to stop having fights with their wives. It seems very important to them to have harmony and calm in their marriage.

Who's Raising the Issues?

Although many researchers have done an admirable job of bringing more light to this whole topic of how issues get pursued and dealt with, two whose work stands out are Andrew Christensen of the University of California-Los Angeles and Christopher Heavey of the University of Nevada-Las Vegas. In addition to doing excellent research on the topic of acceptance in marriage, they've conducted a long-term study of what happens between two partners when one pursues and one withdraws. They call this the *demand-withdraw pattern*.

One of the fundamental points that Christensen and Heavey make is that this pattern is most often triggered when one partner wants some kind of change or wants to discuss some issue that she or he feels the couple needs to talk about. Whether it is the female or the male who desires the discussion, males are more

Women raise issues more often than men, in part because women tend to feel more responsible for how relationships are going.

likely than females to withdraw when things get heated up. Christensen and Heavey have found that this pattern of male withdrawal is strongest when the woman is the one asking the man for changes. Further, there is a lot of reason to believe that women raise issues more often than men, in part because women tend to feel more responsible for how relationships are going and therefore feel that it's their job to bring "things" up. Things like issues. Like problems. Like conflicts. And lots of things about money.

Mel and Sandy had been married ten years when we saw them. Mel was a restaurant manager, and Sandy was a schoolteacher who was taking a few years off to be at home with their children while they were young. Money was tight, as it is for many couples. Mel worked long hours to make ends meet. Sandy was torn between her desire to be home with the kids and her longing to be teaching again and bringing in some income. Sandy badly wanted to talk with Mel about her conflicted feelings, but he never seemed interested in hearing what was on her mind about this. Sandy's frustration grew daily. She felt that he was avoiding talking with her about anything more important than the weather. The following conversation was typical, taking place one Saturday morning while the kids were outside playing.

Sandy: *(sitting down by Mel and looking at him)* I sure wish I could relax about money. When I see you worrying so much, it's just . . . I wonder if I'm doing the right thing, you know, being here at home.

  Mel: *(not looking up from the paper)* It'll all work out.

Sandy *(thinking, He doesn't want to hear it. I wish he'd put that stupid paper down.)* I don't know. Am I really doing the right thing, taking time off from teaching? I think about it every day. Some days, I . . . you know, I'm not sure.

  Mel: *(tensing while thinking, We always end up fighting when we talk about money. Why is she bringing this up again now? I thought we'd settled this.)* I really think you are doing the right thing. It's just harder to make the budget work, but we'll get back on track. I don't think we need to hash it out again.

Sandy: *(thinking, Why can't he relax and open up more? I want to talk and know that he's listening.)* I can tell that you really don't want to talk about it. It bugs me that you can't talk with me about this. You always either change the subject or get real quiet.

  Mel: *(He takes a deep breath and lets out a loud sigh. He wants to say something to stop the escalation, but no good idea comes to mind. He says nothing. He feels tense.)*

Sandy: *(feeling very frustrated, with anger growing)* That's exactly what I mean. You just close me out, again and again, and I'm tired of it!

  Mel: *(thinking, I knew it. We always fight when we talk about money.)* Why do you do this? I'm just sitting here relaxing. It's the only time I have all day to sit still, and you pick a fight. I hate this! *(He throws the paper down, gets up, and walks into the living room.)*

To be blunt, she wants him to open up, and he wants her to shut up. At face value, it sounds like they have very different goals for their relationship, but it's not that simple. She's looking for a way to connect, to be intimate with Mel, and he cuts her off because he thinks a fight is coming.

Is Withdrawal About Comfort with Intimacy?

Are men afraid of, or uninterested in, intimacy? Is that why they are more prone to withdrawal? We don't think so. Yet that is the most common interpretation of the difference between men and women in marriage. We think that both men and women want intimacy but that they tend to define it differently. There is little doubt that men and women naturally seek out different kinds of intimacy, but that is not the same as saying that men are not as interested in it. You can pursue this topic more deeply in your relationship when you get to Chapter Eleven, on the ways you can express and receive love together.

Both men and women want intimacy, but they tend to define it differently.

We believe that withdrawers are not avoiding intimacy; they are avoiding conflict. Men simply don't seem to handle conflict in marriage as well as most women. This difficulty can show up in different ways, including problems with anger management or this tendency to clam up and close down. This is not to say that this kind of pursuing and withdrawing dance has more lasting negative effects on men. Quite the contrary. Janice Kiecolt-Glaser of the Ohio State University College of Medicine has been studying the physical reactions people have to conflict in marriage. She has found that poorly handled marital conflict has negative effects on the functioning of the cardiovascular, endocrine, and immune systems. Further, she finds that whereas men tend to show more negative effects when it comes to general life stress, women tend to be more negatively affected, physiologically, by marital conflict.

It is sad but true: men and women who are doing this dance really want similar changes to make their relationship better. For example, in counseling, when we ask couples to list their goals for therapy, people who put "to talk more" as their first goal often have "to fight less" as another major goal, and vice versa. We want to help the two of you do both. This goal underlies much of the advice we have for you in Part Two of this book.

The Damage Being Done

Although the pursuit-withdrawal dynamic is not motivated by an avoidance of intimacy, it can nevertheless have serious consequences for intimacy, because when men go into conflict avoidance mode, their choices concerning intimacy become more limited. If an argument seems at all likely, the effort to prevent (or avoid) the fight too often diverts energy away from connecting. Feeling comfortable talking as friends is a feeling that can rapidly evaporate if a withdrawer thinks storm clouds are beginning to appear on the horizon. This in part explains why pursuers so often feel as though withdrawers are avoiding intimacy. But if someone were watching the couple's interaction carefully, the observer would see that the withdrawal usually kicks in only when the nature of the talking starts to shift.

Think more about Mel and Sandy. His withdrawal is very frustrating to her. She wants to talk about the fact that their decision that she should stay home with their young children for a few years was increasing the level of stress on both of them. Mel wasn't pulling back from talking because he did not want to change, nor did his withdrawal have anything to do with power, though at times withdrawal can be rooted in the power dynamics of a relationship. His withdrawal was driven by his discomfort in having these kinds of talks with Sandy. Over their years together, he'd come to believe that talking about issues like this usually led to fights between them, and he did not want to fight with Sandy. He loves her.

There is irony here, and we think it is a common one. She wants to express her concern about him and feels that he won't let her do that. He wants to avoid a fight with her at all costs, and yet his pulling back guarantees the fight. So, as with most couples, when one withdraws, the other tends to up the ante and push harder. This can be motivated by frustration that nothing is going to get resolved. On a deeper level, it can be motivated by panic—panic that the partner is detaching from the relationship.

Mel and Sandy are finding pursuit and withdrawal a painful dance.

Imagine how much more destructive the situation can become if each partner starts thinking the worst of the other. A pursuer can think her mate's withdrawal means "he doesn't love and care for me." That's terribly serious, if true. A withdrawer can think the pursuer likes to stir up conflict—to control him or nag him. These kinds of interpretations are devastating, and they are usually off base. Once you start making negative interpretations like these, it's very hard to get your relationship back on track. You can do it, but you have to work at it—by looking hard for evidence that is contrary to the unfair view of the other. Push yourself to think the best, not the worst.

Rates of Male Versus Female Withdrawal: A National View

In conjunction with a project of our friend and colleague Gary Smalley, we (Scott and Howard) conducted a nationwide random phone survey in 1995 of people who were married (most of the sample), engaged, or cohabiting. One of the questions we asked was this: "Who tends to withdraw more when there is an argument?" Surprisingly, the answers of both men and women were virtually identical as to who was most likely to pull away.

42 percent said the male.

26 percent said the female.

17 percent said both.

15 percent said neither.

For many couples, who withdraws mostly depends on what the topic is. Regardless, we think the advice we have to offer will apply to any couple who finds one partner or the other withdrawing about some issue.

> *There was no area where the couples in which one or both withdrew were doing as well as the couples in which neither withdrew.*

We did something very simple with these data. We compared the people who said "neither" with those who said either the male or the female tended to withdraw. We compared them on overall happiness, sense of friendship, commitment, sensual satisfaction, fun, and their reports of the danger signs (which we discuss in Chapter Eight). In each and every way, those who said that neither tended to withdraw were doing better than those who said either might withdraw. There was no area where the couples in which one or both withdrew were doing as well as the couples in which neither withdrew.

Withdrawal is both common *and* a bad sign for your relationship. There are many experts around who suggest that men are just this way and women are just that way, and that the key is just to accept these differences. Acceptance is great—usually. However, when experts suggest that there is something OK about men's (or women's) tendency to withdraw, the message goes too far in light of what's best for the two of you.

Spenders and Savers

Pursuit-withdrawal dynamics have special implications when it comes to how spenders and savers get along. Savers are often pursuing spenders about how they spend money, and especially about how much they spend. Spenders often pursue savers for permission or approval for purchases that they want to make.

The pursuit-withdrawal dance is very frustrating and painful for a couple to engage in.

The Bottom Line

In our book *Fighting* for *Your Marriage,* we (Scott and Howard) and coauthor Susan Blumberg sum up what we believe with regard to the pursuit-withdrawal dance:

- The person more likely to withdraw in any talk is the one who feels more anxious about the topic or tone of the talk.
- The person who withdraws is very likely the one who feels less confident that something good for the couple is about to happen.
- Our avoidance and withdrawal in relationships is often similar to our behavior in other areas of life: most of us pull away from things that we're not sure we can handle well.
- In most marriages, pulling back has far more to do with conflict than with a lack of commitment or caring.
- Partners have to work together to stop this dance.

The bottom line? If you are both committed to staying close, being friends, and being a team in dealing with life, you have to be able to talk safely about the issues that come up and that are more difficult to talk about. We'll show you how you can do just that in Chapter Eight.

GOING DEEP

What Lies Beneath?

Here at the end of the first part of this book, we want to help and encourage you to explore the deeper themes in your relationship as they relate to the topics of the preceding chapters. To get the most out of what is presented here, you should plan some time to think, write down your thoughts, and talk through what you come up with, together. There are three major exercises here: Examining Expectations, Exploring Hidden Issues, and Your Money-Relationship Style. We do not assume that each one will be equally valuable for every couple. You might look all three over and make a decision as to which seem most useful to you. If you are up for it, go for all three.

Examining Expectations

This exercise is one we have recommended to couples in many of our works over many years. Here, however, the focus is on the specific themes of this book: meaning in life, money, and what money means to the two of you and the future of your relationship. The examination of expectations will focus on expectations as they relate to your family background, culture, and gender.

As you work through each of the specific expectations we ask about here, spend some time carefully thinking things through. As you do, write your thoughts down so you can share them with your partner after your own reflection on the questions. Each point is meant to stimulate your *own* thinking. You won't get much out of this exercise unless you are able and willing to really put some time into it.

The goal is to consider your expectations for how you want the relationship to be or how you think it should be, not how it is and not how you guess it will be. Write down what you expect, whether or not you think the expectation is realistic. The expectation matters, and it will affect your relationship regardless of whether or not it's realistic. Consider each question in light of what you expect and want for the future. It's essential that you write down what you really think, not what sounds like the "correct" or least embarrassing answer.

For each aspect of money and meaning in life listed here, consider these questions: What do you want regarding this subject? Or how do you think things should be?

1. *Happiness in life.* Even the U.S. Constitution speaks to the importance of people's right to life, liberty, and the pursuit of happiness. Surely the framers of that document were not speaking of some frivolous focus on happiness in the absence of responsibility. But what do those words say to you? Whether you are American or of some other nationality, you have some concept of what happiness in life means to you.

- What does bring or would bring you the greatest happiness and contentment in life?
- What did your family upbringing teach you about happiness? How it is obtained? What makes one really happy in life? What would make you happy in life?
- What does your culture teach about happiness in life? Give thought to your religious background and beliefs, the entertainment media's messages, and other aspects of the culture in which you live.

2. *Wealth and financial status.* How important to you is gaining or having financial wealth? Do you want to be rich? Do you want to be comfortable (we can't imagine anyone saying they'd not, but think about it anyway)? What would be a comfortable financial position for you at this point in life? How about ten and twenty and thirty years from now? What does financial security mean to you?

- What did your family upbringing teach you about financial position and wealth? What would financial security look like to you? Is it possible?
- What does your culture teach about financial position and wealth? What does your culture teach you about financial security? Is it possible? Does that security come about through your efforts or from the government, or is it simply not seen as possible or desirable?

- What do you think about money and wealth? What is important to you in terms of financial position in life? What are your goals?

3. *The meaning of life.* What does life mean? What is most important in life? What values are most enduring?

- What did your family teach you about the meaning of life?
- What does your culture teach you about the meaning of life? Which influences affect you?
- What do you believe? Why? How do your most basic beliefs affect how you live your life?

4. *Children.* Do you have them? Do you want to have children? How important is raising children to you, in the grand scheme of life? What is more important to you, how your children turn out or how your work, career, or financial status turns out? Many people say that children are very important to them, but they don't live their lives in ways that reflect that sentiment. What do you believe, and how do you live?

- What did your family teach you about children and what they need in life?
- What does your culture teach you about children?
- What do you believe about children and child rearing? How important are these beliefs? How do (or would) your beliefs affect how you manage money in life?

5. *Blended family issues.* Do you have children from a prior relationship? Do you have contact with them? Do you have financial responsibility for them? Where do these children live? Where would you like them to live, and for how much of the time? What do you believe is the way the two of you should share in their parenting or financial support?

6. *Work, careers, and provision of income.* Who will work in the future? Whose career or job is more important? If there are or will be children, will either partner reduce work time out of the home to take care of them?

- What did your family teach you about work and careers? What did you observe in the lives of the adults around you?
- What does your culture teach you about work and career matters? What about the media or other aspects of the culture in which you live?
- What is most important to you regarding your work life?
- Is what you believe or expect in these matters affected by gender issues? Who should do what? Is it comfortable for you or not if the female makes more money than the male? Why?

7. *Team and couple identity.* Do you approach life as a team, with a strong sense of an identity as a couple, or do you view things more from the perspective of the two of you as individuals? What takes priority if there is a conflict: the needs of the individual or the needs of the couple? What does "equality" in your relationship mean to you? How important are these beliefs?

- What did your family teach you about teamwork in marriage? What did you observe in the lives of the adults around you?
- What does your culture teach you about being identified as a team? What about the media or other aspects of the culture in which you live? If you have a strong sense of "us," does that mean you are being codependent?

8. *Power and control.* Who has more power in what kinds of decisions? Is this arrangement in keeping with what you expect? Is it what you prefer? For example, who will control major money decisions: you, your partner, or both of you equally? Does it depend on what type of decision? What happens when you disagree in a key area? Who has the power now, and how do you feel about that?

- What did your family teach you about power and control? What did you observe in the lives of the adults around you?
- What does your culture teach you about power and control? What about the media or other aspects of the culture in which you live?
- Is what you believe or expect in these matters affected by gender issues?

9. *Money tasks.* When it comes to money management, who do you expect will do what? Who pays the bills? Who makes the deposits? Is this arrangement in keeping with what you expect or desire? Who balances the checkbook? (If you are asking "What does that mean?" just move on to the next question!)

- What did your family teach you about who does what? What did you observe in the lives of the adults around you?
- What does your culture teach you about who does what? What about the media or other aspects of the culture in which you live?
- Is what you believe or expect in these matters affected by gender issues? Why? Is that OK with you?

10. *Charity and religious giving.* Even people from similar backgrounds can find that they have very different expectations in this regard. Do you give to a charity or religious group? How much? What guides your decisions? Do you give 10 percent of your gross income to a religious group? Do you give less? Or more?

- What did your family teach you about charity and religious giving? What did you observe?
- What does your culture teach you about how much you give and to what institutions?

11. *Retirement.* What do you want life to be like when you retire? How do you expect your retirement to be? What lifestyle do you expect to have? How much financial security do you hope for, and why? How old or young or young at heart will you be when you retire? Will you ever retire? Do you want to retire? What do you expect it will take to reach your goals for retirement?

12. *Passing it on.* Do you expect to inherit much wealth from anyone now living? What do you expect might happen? How will that affect your life? When you pass on, what do you plan to leave to whom? If you have children from different past relationships, what do you expect will happen when one of you passes on, in terms of how the children are taken care of financially in the future? Do you expect your assets to go to your children or to your partner's or both?

13. *Spending versus saving.* Are you more of a spender or a saver? What do you expect happens in life to spenders as opposed to savers? Do you expect your partner to be like you in this regard? Or at least tolerant of you? What do you expect happens in life to someone who errs too far either way? In your mind, can you err too far in saving?

- What did your family teach you about spending and saving? What did you observe in the lives of the adults around you?
- What does your culture teach you about spending and saving? What about the media or other aspects of the culture in which you live?
- Is what you believe or expect in these matters affected by gender issues? Why? Is that OK with you?

14. *Anything else?* List all the other expectations you can think of that relate to money or meaning in your relationship so that you can share these thoughts with one another. As you did with the other questions, give thought to what you learned from your family or what you've come to expect because of the culture in which you live.

After you and your partner have finished thinking through these questions, plan time to discuss the expectations you have identified. You should probably plan on a number of discussions. Also talk about the degree to which you each feel that the two of you had clearly shared the expectation in the past. For some couples, it may make more sense to talk about these themes after you've read

Chapter Eight on communicating safely and clearly, and after you've had time to practice the Speaker-Listener Technique taught there.

At the end of the book, we'll suggest that you work through identifying specific goals for your future together. That exercise will overlap with various expectations you have in the areas you've been looking at here.

Exploring Hidden Issues

We recommend that you first work through these questions individually, then sit down and talk together about your impressions.

1. Here's a list of the signs that hidden issues may be affecting your relationship. Think through each of these signs. Do you notice that one or more of them come up a lot in your relationship? What do you notice? Are any of these particularly common when the two of you are dealing with money events?

- Wheel spinning
- Trivial triggers
- Avoidance
- Scorekeeping

2. Next we'd like you to consider which hidden issues might operate most often in your relationship. There may be some big issue you'd like to add to our list here. Consider each hidden issue and to what degree it seems to affect your relationship negatively. Also, how hidden are they for you?

Note if there are certain events that have triggered or keep triggering the hidden issues. Make a list in the right-hand column. Think about all manner of issues, but also focus on money in particular.

Hidden Issue	**Common Triggering Events**
Power and control	
Caring	
Recognition	
Commitment	
Integrity	
Acceptance	

3. Plan some time together to talk about your observations and thoughts. For most couples, there are certain hidden issues that repeatedly come up. Identifying these can help you draw together as you each learn to handle those issues with care.

Your Money-Relationship Style

Do you have style? No matter what your friends and family may think, we believe you do have style. We're not talking about how you dress but how the two of you deal with money as a couple. We want you to think about what we call your *money-relationship style*. Over our many years of researching how couples manage their lives, we've observed five key dimensions that determine how a couple's relationship affects their finances and how finances affect their relationship. As you will see, these dimensions run through the topics and examples of this entire book. Here are the five dimensions:

1. Teamwork level
2. Blending level
3. Agreement level
4. Conflict level
5. Structure level

Each dimension ranges from low to high; the middle zone would represent where the average couple would land. After we describe these dimensions to you in more detail, we'll ask you first to rate where you see your relationship on each and then to rate where you would like it to be on each. As you will see, these dimensions are not completely independent of one another, but they each capture a part of your money-relationship style as a couple.

Teamwork

As you make decisions about finances, do you approach money issues as a team, looking for what is best for you as a couple? Or do you each focus more on what is best for you as an individual? If you tend to buy costly items without talking with your partner—or even thinking all that much about how it might affect him or her—you likely rate lower on the teamwork scale. If you discuss significant purchases with one another and make your decisions based on what you both think best, you likely rate higher on the teamwork scale.

Blending

This one is simple to assess. Do you keep your money and assets separate or together? On the high end of this scale are couples who keep all their finances jointly held and managed; on the low end, each partner's money is kept separate from the other's. You are somewhere in between if you have some financial accounts that are separate as well as some that are together. If you both work at places with retirement accounts, those assets are likely kept separate regardless of the other areas mentioned here, as that's just the way it's done with retirement accounts. So don't give your job-associated retirement assets much consideration as you think about this dimension—unless one or both of you are feeding these individual retirement accounts at the expense of any needed, nonretirement savings in the present. Rather, do you have separate savings accounts and checking accounts? Credit cards with both names on the accounts or some cards with only one name?

Another important way to understand where you are on this dimension is by considering how you pay your bills. Are most of your bills paid with money from both of you, or do you have the bills divided up into who is supposed to pay which, out of his or her own money? We bet you get the idea.

Agreement on Money Issues

Do you have similar philosophies and sensibilities about savings, major purchases, and the use of debt? Or do you have very different ideas about how much to save for retirement and how to go about it, how expensive a house to buy (or whether to rent or buy), when it's time to buy a new car, or how much to spend at this point in life versus how much to save for the future?

Conflict

Do you have conflicts about how you manage money and what you spend money on? How intense are these conflicts? We're not referring to disagreements about how to spend money and what to spend money on, as in the prior dimension. Here we're focusing on fighting and negativity. You can disagree quite a bit on money philosophy, but that doesn't mean you have nasty fights about your differences. If you are able to talk about money and spending decisions calmly and with respect, you are low on this dimension.

Structure

Some couples have their money lives highly ordered, and others struggle to get checks recorded in the register. Do you balance your checkbook, or do you call the bank to find out how much money you have today? Do you save in some sys-

ACCORDING TO THESE MARITAL RESEARCHERS, OUR DIFFERENCES AREN'T AS IMPORTANT AS OUR WAY OF HANDLING THEM.

RAGNAR STORAASLI

tematic way or save here and there when you can (or not at all)? Do you pay all your bills on time? That would be higher structure.

For some of these five dimensions, there is not necessarily a right or wrong place or a better or worse way to be. On others, there is. For example, it's not likely that many couples do better with higher rather than lower levels of conflict about money. On other dimensions, the position on the scale may not be as important as the difference between the two of you. If the two of you feel comfortable with your level of blending, for example, you could be anywhere on the scale. In contrast, if one of you would like to keep money more separate and the other wants it more combined, there will be some tension and perhaps increased conflict for the two of you.

What About Your Style?

We want you to think about where your relationship falls on the five dimensions. Take some time thinking through each, looking back at the descriptions if you like. First, in the book or on separate paper, mark on the scales how you think your relationship actually is right now, not how you might wish it would be. If you and your partner are working through this book together, we suggest you each do this independently on separate pieces of paper. Don't share your answers until you've both made your ratings.

How It Is

Teamwork Level

Low ├──┤ High

Blending Level

Low ├──┤ High

Agreement Level

Low ├──┤ High

Conflict Level

Low ├──┤ High

Structure Level

Low ├──┤ High

Now we'd like you to mark each dimension again, but this time, mark how you wish things would be. If money and all it touches could be handled better in your relationship, where would your marks be? Take some time now to make those ratings.

How You Would Like It to Be—Your Ideal

Teamwork Level

Low ├──┤ High

Blending Level

Low ├──┤ High

Agreement Level

Low ├──┤ High

Conflict Level

Low ├──┤ High

Structure Level

Low ├──┤ High

Unless the two of you are positioned very high on the conflict scale, we'd like you to share your answers with one another. If you do have a very high level of conflict over money, wait to share your answers until after you've worked on Part Two of this book—after we've taught you some ways to talk more openly and safely about these volatile themes. Otherwise, if the two of you think you are up to it right now, go ahead and take some time to talk through the ratings you both made. How are your ratings similar? Where are the differences? How closely do your "ideal" ratings line up?

PART TWO

NOW THAT WE UNDERSTAND, WHAT DO WE DO?

CHAPTER EIGHT

TALKING THINGS OUT

Aren't the only people who really listen to an argument the neighbors?

ANONYMOUS

Now that you understand how the invisible forces—issues, hidden issues, and expectations—can affect your relationship, we're ready to show you how to harness their energy to make sure these forces affect your relationship in a positive way. This is the first of three chapters that give you the highlights of our communication and problem-solving skills for couples. These come right from our decades of research and work with couples, helping partners learn more effective ways to work together as a team. You may be surprised by the simplicity of some of the techniques we present. Don't be fooled. There are certainly more complicated ways of doing things, but, in all the research, we've not found anything more powerful. We're interested in helping you get results, not in impressing you with complicated methodology. In our other books, most notably *Fighting for Your Marriage*, we spend a great deal of time explaining our research and showing evidence of why what we'll say here truly works. Here we'll briefly introduce you to the PREP approach.

PREP, the Prevention and Relationship Enhancement Program, is one of the most extensively researched programs for couples ever developed. For more than two decades, researchers have been studying the key risks couples face as well as the most promising avenues for helping couples lower those risks.

Some of the most important research on the PREP approach has been conducted at the University of Denver. Over the years, our research has been supported by grants from the National Institute of Mental Health, the National

Institute of Health, and the National Science Foundation and has resulted in more than fifty scientific and professional publications. Here we will give you a brief example of findings from these studies and those of colleagues we've been privileged to work with over the years. Those colleagues include such fine researchers as Kurt Hahlweg at the Technische Universität Braunschweig, in Germany; Kim Halford at Griffith University in Queensland, Australia; Don Baucom at the University of North Carolina at Chapel Hill; and a long list of talented colleagues at the University of Denver.

We have seen from a number of long-term studies very solid results for helping happy couples stay that way. Depending on the specific study, we see evidence of couples communicating more effectively, decreasing the use of negative interactions, maintaining higher levels of satisfaction, and having a lower incidence of relationship breakup and divorce. Of the seven most significant studies, five show significant positive results, though not all studies show the whole range of possible positive results. Although PREP has had impressive results, no program or model is ideal for every couple. Years from now, we in the field of marital research will know even more about which couples benefit, and how much, from what strategy. We continue to learn more and refine the PREP program so as to bring couples a state-of-the-art program based on the best information in the field. If you would like to know more about research on PREP, we suggest that you pick up the book *Fighting* for *Your Marriage*. But for now, we're going to jump right in with some of our communication and problem-solving skills for couples.

Feeling Safe to Be Open

When do most couples have the greatest difficulty talking well? When they have a disagreement or a conflict or when they are talking about something very sensitive, such as when they are talking about feelings of loneliness or disappointment. What do these two situations have in common? One or both partners may fear that the conversation will not go well—they fear conflict, frustration, rejection. The antidote to these kinds of fear is safety. What we really mean here is emotional safety.

Every couple needs to have a safe way to talk about everyday disagreements as well as deeper, more sensitive hidden issues or expectations.

Every couple needs to have a safe way to talk about everyday disagreements as well as deeper, more sensitive hidden issues or expectations.

There are things you can do that will make your relationship feel safe, and there are things you can do that will show your partner that it isn't emotionally safe to be around you. We're going to talk first about the things you can do to destroy the sense of emotional safety in your relationship (as in *don't do these!*), and then we'll discuss ways that you can nurture the emotional safety in your relationship.

The Four Danger Signs

The real art of conversation is not only to say the right thing at the right time but also to leave unsaid the wrong thing at the tempting moment.

ANONYMOUS

There are many ways a couple can poison their love, but marital research has led us to believe that the following four behavior patterns are among the most potent. We call them the four danger signs.

The Pursuer-Withdrawer Pattern

The pursuer-withdrawer pattern, which we discussed in Chapter Seven, is so important that we'll review it again here. You will recall that we said this pattern looks something like a dance. When the withdrawer withdraws, the pursuer feels

more anxious, so she pursues harder. When the withdrawer feels her pursuing more aggressively, he pulls away more. In this way, both "dancers" contribute to what research has shown is one of the most destructive patterns couples have for handling—that is, mishandling—conflict and disagreements.

As if this dynamic weren't frustrating enough, we often create in our minds negative reasons for our partner's behavior. Pursuers often interpret their partner's unwillingness to discuss issues as not caring about the relationship. Withdrawers tend to think that their partner wants to discuss issues just because she enjoys fighting.

Many women are withdrawers and many men are pursuers, but on average, it's more common to see women pursuing and men withdrawing from dealing with issues. Nevertheless, the pattern is equally destructive to a relationship regardless of who takes what role. For many couples, who pursues and who withdraws changes depending on who is more concerned about what issues.

Money is a powerful trigger of the pursuit and withdrawal dance because so many money situations have great urgency to them. For example, some checks really do need to be covered right now. Some creditors can threaten pretty immediate consequences. And some decisions about investing for retirement many years from now might have to be made before your tax return is filed on Friday. Because situations involving money often have true urgency, each partner will tend to feel that stress but may react to it differently. One may respond to the stress by withdrawing, the other by pursuing. The urgency can add intensity to the situation, which makes another danger sign likely: escalation.

Escalation

A couple begins to escalate when one partner says something, and the other partner, instead of responding gently, decides to respond negatively. Then each partner takes turns behaving more and more negatively to each other. Instead of listening with the desire to understand, each person continually ups the ante so that conditions get worse and worse. A tit-for-tat effect kicks in, with negative comments spiraling into increasing anger and frustration.

There are two really good ways to fuel escalation (in other words, if you really want to blow out an entire evening, try these):

1. You can insult your partner by calling him or her a name or saying something to put your partner down—for example: "You're lazy!" "You act just like your mother!" "You *never* think about anyone but yourself!"

2. You can try Kitchen Sinking. Instead of sticking to the issue at hand during an argument, drag in complaints about everything but the kitchen sink! For example:

Partner 1: I'm fed up! I'm always having to pick up the house, we never doing anything fun, and our sex life is the pits!!

Partner 2: Well, you're always too tired to go anywhere, and you always dress like
a slob.

Couples who are happy now (and more likely to stay that way) are less prone
to escalation; if they do start to escalate, they are able to stop the negative process
before it erupts into a full-blown, nasty fight.

Invalidation

You invalidate your partner when you say or do things that ignore or put down
your partner's ideas, opinions, or feelings. Invalidation can include anything from
rolling your eyes to sighing to outright personal attacks.

Invalidation can often lead to escalation. Feeling invalidated, each partner
may try harder and harder to get his or her point across. Instead of taking the time
to listen to each other, each partner is focused on proving the "rightness" of his or
her point of view.

Negative Interpretations

A partner is making a negative interpretation when he or she believes that the motives of the other are more negative than is really the case. When partners consistently engage in negative interpretations, they create a very destructive pattern in
their relationship, one that will make any conflict or disagreement harder to deal with.

Margot and David have been married twelve years and are generally happy
with their relationship. Yet their discussions at times have been plagued by a specific negative interpretation. Every December they have had trouble deciding
whether to travel to her parents' home for the holidays. Margot believes that David
dislikes her parents, but he is in fact quite fond of them in his own way. She has
this mistaken belief because of a few incidents early in the marriage that David
has long forgotten. Here's how a typical discussion around their issue of holiday
travel plans goes:

Margot: We should start looking into plane tickets to go visit my parents this holiday season.

David: *(thinking about their budget problem)* I was wondering if we can really afford it
this year.

Margot: *(in anger)* My parents are very important to me, even if you don't like them.
I'm going to go.

David: I would like to go, really I would. I just don't see how we can afford a thousand dollars in plane tickets and pay the bill for Joey's orthodontist, too.

Margot: You can't be honest and admit you just don't want to go, can you? Just
admit it. You don't like my parents.

David: There is nothing to admit. I enjoy visiting your parents. I'm thinking about
money here, not your parents.

Margot: That's a convenient excuse. *(storms out of the room)*

Given that we know David really does like her parents, can you see what a
bind Margot has put David in? David wants to address the holiday plans from the
standpoint of the budget, but Margot's interpretation will overpower their ability
to communicate effectively and will make it hard to come to a decision that will
work for both of them.

No matter what David says or does, Margot will believe that he dislikes her
parents. If he says he wants to go visit her folks, then she'll believe he's only being
nice for her sake. If he says he doesn't want to go, then she takes that as proof that
he doesn't like them.

A strong negative interpretation can be something of an impenetrable fortress.
Only from the inside can these walls be overcome. In this case, David cannot reach
Margot. He cannot prove that he likes Margot's parents. Margot holds the key.
She can push herself to look for evidence that challenges her beliefs, or she can
choose not to. It's up to her. If you've formed a negative interpretation of your
spouse, your spouse can't change it. It's up to you. Scary thought, isn't it?

Furthermore, negative interpretations can lead each partner to feel more justified in behaving badly. When wounded, whether it is a perceived hurt or an actual wound, we tend to justify taking revenge. Although most people don't like
to think of *revenge* in a marital context, it's a perfectly accurate word for what so
commonly happens. Each partner, feeling wounded, feels entitled to hurt back.
Partners can remain in this vicious cycle until they've completely destroyed all the
love and joy they once shared.

In the financial realm, negative interpretations can lead to a kind of self-
justification for spending money on what each wants, because it seems so fair. It's
common for partners to feel justified in spending money recklessly when they think
their spouse has done so. Or, thinking that their partner is trying to control them,
spouses will spend simply to prove their independence. That's a bad path to go down.

◆ ◆ ◆

Withdrawal, escalation, invalidation, and negative interpretations—these are four
key patterns that are almost guaranteed to destroy intimacy in your relationship.
Engaging in these danger signs has been shown, in research all over the world,

to have very negative consequences for couples. To turn this harsh truth around, *not* doing these things is a great way to protect your love.

Adding Structure for Safety

For your relationship to grow as you talk as friends, reveal inner feelings, and handle unavoidable money issues, you need to work together as a team to prevent escalation, invalidation, withdrawal, and negative interpretations from happening. One way to do this is to use agreed-on strategies and techniques to help you in important conversations. We call this adding structure to your discussion. Structure acts like a guardrail along a treacherous highway. If your vehicle is in danger of careening off the road, certain to cause injury and destruction, then the guardrail adds a valuable element of safety.

The Speaker-Listener Technique

We'll warn you right up front. In our research, this technique is the one that couples are most often hesitant to try—we hear words like "hokey" and "artificial." However, when couples try it out and give themselves a chance to get the hang of it, the Speaker-Listener Technique turns out to be the skill that couples say helps them

> **When couples try it out, the Speaker-Listener Technique turns out to be the skill that they say helps them the most.**

the most. Any conversation about money (or any relationship issue) in which you want to enhance clarity and safety can benefit from this technique. We hope you'll give it a try. If you decide it's not for you, so be it. If you have another way of talking about particularly sensitive issues *that works,* then stick with what works. If you do not, here you go. Try it out and then make it yours with practice.

Let's look at the rules (or structure) for this way of talking.

Rules for Both of You

1. *The Speaker has the floor.* Use a real object to designate the floor: the TV remote, a silver dollar, a pen, your checkbook—anything at all. The point is that you have to use some specific object, because if you do not have the floor, you are the Listener. As Speaker and Listener, you follow the rules for each role.

2. *Share the floor.* You share the floor over the course of a conversation. The Speaker is the first one who holds the floor. After the Speaker talks, you switch roles and continue as the floor changes hands. The point is for each of you to have enough time with the floor that you feel able to express what is important to you.

3. *No problem solving.* When using this technique, you are going to focus on having good discussions, not on trying to come to solutions. When you focus on solving a problem, you are far less likely to really hear what each other thinks about that problem, so it is best to save solution seeking for later.

Rules for the Speaker

1. *Speak for yourself. Don't mind-read.* Talk about *your* thoughts, feelings, and concerns, not your perceptions of the Listener's point of view or motives. Try to use "I" statements. "I was upset when you forgot our date" is an example of an "I" statement. ("You didn't care about our date" is not.)

2. *Don't go on and on.* You will have plenty of opportunity to say all you need to say. To help the Listener listen actively, it will be very important to keep what you say in manageable pieces. If you are in the habit of giving monologues, remember that having the floor protects you from interruption. You can afford to pause to be sure your partner understands you.

3. *Stop and let the Listener paraphrase.* After saying a bit, stop and allow the Listener to paraphrase what you just said. If the paraphrase is not quite accurate, you should politely and gently restate what you meant to say in a way that helps your partner understand. This is not a test! You want to make it possible for your partner to understand you as well as he or she can.

Rules for the Listener

1. *Paraphrase what you hear.* You must paraphrase what the Speaker is saying. Briefly repeat back what you heard the Speaker say, using your own words if you like, and make sure you understand what was said. When you take the time to restate what you heard, you show your partner that you are listening. If you truly don't understand some phrase or example, you may ask the Speaker to clarify, but you need to limit yourself to just asking for explanations.

2. *Don't rebut. Focus on the Speaker's message.* While in the Listener role, you may not offer your opinion or thoughts. This is the hardest part of being a good Listener. If you are upset by what your partner says, you need to edit out any response you may want to make, and *pay attention* to what your partner is saying. Wait until you get the floor to make your response.

Frequently Asked Questions

Before showing how the Speaker-Listener Technique works in a conversation, we want to answer two commonly asked questions.

What's a Good Paraphrase? Suppose your spouse says to you, "I am so stressed out by all the gifts we have to buy for our kids and relatives, I can hardly breathe. And today at work I learned we're not getting our regular holiday bonus." Any of the following might be an excellent paraphrase:

> "Sounds like you were feeling a ton of financial stress already, and you had a really tough day on top of it."
>
> "So you are feeling we won't have enough money to buy nice presents this year."
>
> "Bad day, huh?"

Any one of these responses conveys that you have listened and displays what you have understood. A good paraphrase can be short or long, detailed or general. At times, if you are uncertain how to get a paraphrase started, it can help to begin with "What I hear you saying is . . ." Then you fill in what you just heard your partner say. Another way to begin a paraphrase is with the words "Sounds like you think [feel, want] . . ."

Who Decides If the Listener Understands? When using the Speaker-Listener Technique, the Speaker is always the one who determines if the Listener's paraphrase was on target. Only the Speaker knows what the intended message is. If the paraphrase is not quite on target, it is very important that the Speaker gently clarify or restate the point—not respond angrily or critically. Remember that you and your partner may be dealing with expectations that make it difficult to paraphrase accurately. This is your best opportunity to correct any misperceptions or misunderstandings before they interfere with your communication efforts.

When in the Listener role, be sincere in your effort to show you are listening carefully and respectfully. Even when you disagree with the point being made by your partner, your goal is to show respect for—and validation of—his or her perspective. That means waiting your turn and not making faces or looking angry. You can completely disagree with your mate about something and still show respect.

Using the Speaker-Listener Technique

Here is an example of how this technique can change a conversation that is going nowhere into a real opportunity for communication. Brad and Regina are in their mid-thirties, with four kids ages two to ten. For years they have had a problem dealing with financial issues. Brad consistently avoids discussing any problem areas that have to do with money, and if cornered by Regina, he withdraws by pulling into himself. They know they need to communicate more clearly and safely on tough topics, and have agreed that the structure of the Speaker-Listener Technique can help.

In this case, Brad and Regina have been locked in the pursuer-withdrawer cycle about the issue of sending their son Jeremy to a costly private preschool. However, they have been practicing the Speaker-Listener Technique and are ready to try a different way of dealing with the issue. Let's see what happens.

Regina: I'm really getting tired of leaving Jeremy's preschool up in the air. We have got to deal with this, now.

Brad: *(not looking up from the TV)* Oh? I'm not up for this now.

Regina: *(walking over and standing in front of the TV)* Brad, we can't just leave this decision hanging. I'm getting really ticked off about you putting it off.

Brad: *(recognizing this would be a wise time to act constructively and not withdraw)* Time out. I can tell we need to talk, but I have been avoiding it because it seems that talking about anything to do with money just leads to us fighting. I don't want that. Let's try that Speaker-Listener thing we've been practicing.

The conversation proceeds, with Brad picking up the "floor"—in their case, it is a refrigerator magnet they got from one of our workshops, with the Speaker-Listener Techniques rules printed on it.

Brad (Speaker): I've also been pretty concerned about sending Jeremy to the Mountainside preschool. It's just so expensive, and I'm not sure if we can afford it.

Regina (Listener): You have been concerned, too, and you're very concerned about our ability to pay for the tuition.

Brad (Speaker): Yeah, that's it. We're both working as hard as we can, and we still can't get ahead of the game as it is.

Note how Brad acknowledges that Regina's summary is on the mark before moving on to another point.

Regina (Listener): You're worried that we will get further in debt, and we are already concerned about the amount of time we spend away from each other and the kids, right?

Regina is not quite sure she has understood Brad's point, so she makes her paraphrase tentative.

    Brad (Speaker): Well, partly that's it, but also I'm feeling so bad that I'm not doing my job as a man, that I should be earning more so that this wouldn't be an issue for us.

Note how Brad gently clarifies, and as he feels safer and understood he is naturally starting to talk about deeper issues. He's moving forward in the conversation, rather than backward. In general, whenever you as Speaker feel that clarification is needed, use your next statement to restate or expand on what you're trying to get across.

    Regina (Listener): So you are feeling upset about your expectations for yourself.

Regina really wants to jump in as the Speaker and reassure Brad, but she stays in the Listener role; Brad notices and suggests that she take the floor.

    Brad (Speaker): Yes. That's right. Here. Why don't you take the floor; it seems like you want to say something. *(He passes the floor to Regina.)*

    Regina Well, I feel you're the best man I can imagine, in terms of everything.
    (now the Speaker): Actually, I hadn't realized your feelings were this deep about this. I thought when you didn't want to talk, you didn't care about how I felt about Jeremy going to a good preschool.

As the Speaker, now, Regina validates Brad in the comments he has made.

    Brad (Listener): Sounds like you're feeling better about me than I am, and you were afraid my not wanting to deal with it meant I didn't care about you.

    Regina (Speaker): Yes. This really helps a lot to understand you. I can sense how hard this all is for you.

    Brad (Listener): It's making you feel better that we are talking this through.

    Regina (Speaker): Absolutely! I want to hear more about how you are feeling about yourself and also want to let you know that I appreciate how hard you work and what a great husband and father you are. I realize, as I am talking, that I do not tell you this enough.

    Brad (Listener): Wow, that makes me feel good! Oh, back to the structure. So you're saying that you really think I'm doing OK.

Note how Brad initially breaks out of the structure and starts to speak (express his reactions) to the really nice comments his wife has shared about him. This is natural, and even the most practiced couples using the Speaker-Listener Technique do this once in a while. But also note how he quickly gets back into the structure.

Regina (Speaker): Well, not exactly. I feel you are doing more than just OK. I know you could be earning more money if you invested more time in work or if you had taken the promotion you were offered last year. But you've told me that our family is more important to you than being the best lawyer in your firm and having all that money, and I love you all the more for sacrificing success on the job for us!

Note how Regina clarifies her intent and how she directly responds to Brad's concerns.

Brad (Listener): So you understand that I'm making sacrifices for our family, and that means a lot to you, and you love me!

Regina (Speaker): Yes, and I also love your listening to me like this. But I know you have more to say about how you're feeling, and I don't want to hog the floor.

Regina feels good with Brad listening so carefully, and lets him know it.

Brad (Listener): You like how we are talking now and want to know about how I'm feeling. Can I have the floor?

Regina (Speaker): Right. Here, you take the floor again. *(They pass the floor again.)*

Brad (Speaker): You know, we've gotten away from talking about Jeremy's preschool, and I'm starting to feel more like making love than talking about my conflicts about earning money. How about we talk some more tomorrow about how we can afford the best possible preschool for Jeremy and then later on about where we both are in terms balancing earning money, job status, and our family.

As you can tell, they have been practicing quite a bit. They are both doing an excellent job following the rules and showing concern and respect for each other's viewpoints. Couples can have discussions like this on difficult topics, even when they disagree. The key is to show respect for your partner's thoughts, feelings, and opinions. With practice, the process can become far more natural than it will seem at first. Although not all conversations end like Brad and Regina's, using the technique with a genuine desire to connect does tend to help couples connect in very positive ways.

> *Couples can discuss difficult topics, even when they disagree. The key is to show respect for your partner's thoughts, feelings, and opinions.*

Brad and Regina used the technique to their benefit. Note that what initially seemed like a simple conflict and disagreement (about

something very important, though) really had a lot more to it than it looked. It's only because they were talking safely that they got to two critical pieces of information. One, Brad was more deeply affected by all of this because the preschool money issue triggers the deeper issue of how he feels about himself and the degree to which Regina accepts him for who he is. Two, she was starting to make a pretty negative interpretation of why he was avoiding the topic, thinking that maybe he just didn't care about her. The technique helped Brad and Regina detect these invisible forces and harness that energy positively.

Some Helpful Hints

To ease into the use of the technique, you will find it helpful to focus on a non-stressful, nonloaded, totally easy topic. The point of your first practice sessions is to learn to talk in this new way, not to resolve your biggest issues. By talking about the last movie you saw, your dream vacation, ways the two of you might spend $500 over a weekend, or the project you are doing at work, you keep some of the stress out of the conversation until you are more skilled with the process. In the exercise at the end of the chapter, we will take you through a progression of issues, moving at the speed with which you are comfortable as you gain confidence in your skills.

Our research shows that couples benefit from learning to use structure when handling conflicts about money and finances. Agreed-on rules like the Speaker-Listener Technique add some degree of predictability, and that reduces anxiety and avoidance, helping both of you win rather than lose when dealing with conflict. You need to work together to fight negative patterns rather than each other.

For the Skeptical at Heart: Common Questions or Objections

We often hear what we think are really legitimate questions about this technique. Sometimes the questions aren't so legitimate and are coming more from avoidance than from a genuine desire to find a better way to talk about difficult or sensitive things. Here's how we sum up our perspective: every couple needs a way to communicate safely and openly about important thoughts, feelings, and desires, but the situation doesn't always feel safe enough or calm enough to do this well. You don't need to adopt our suggestions, but we know that all couples need some way or ways to have talks that go deeper. This is one of the most powerful ways to get at the invisible forces that can pull the two of you all out of joint.

So if you are wanting to learn how to go deeper in your talks, but still have some questions, read on, then get started trying things out.

It's So Artificial

Probably the number one criticism we hear about this technique is that it's artificial and just not natural. It's not a normal way for people to talk to one another. Very true. Note, however, the assumption that is embedded in this criticism—that how we naturally talk to one another is usually superior to ways we've learned to talk with one another. If you have children, you already know how often you show that you don't really believe this assumption. There are many "natural" ways children communicate with others, ways that you try to help them overcome by teaching them principles and rules for how to treat others.

If you and your partner naturally do those negative behaviors we call danger signs when discussing conflicts and problems, what's so hot about being natural? The danger signs are exceedingly natural for many people. Try being unnatural for a bit. You might really like it. It's kind of like budgeting: it's not a natural act (spending is), but it provides a structure for handling finances and promoting teamwork.

It Goes So Slowly When We Talk like This

Yes, it does. That's a big part of why it works. Stop to think about all the time couples waste fighting over and over again about the same money issues without the partners' really hearing one another. That's very sad and very unproductive. Yes, a talk with this technique is on the slow side, but that may be the fastest you've ever dealt with a difficult topic in your relationship. Sometimes the fastest route is the slow lane.

We Have Trouble Sharing the Floor

So, one or both of you tend to want to hang onto the floor once you have it? We have a simple suggestion to solve this. Add a rule that you will switch the floor after every three or four statements of the Speaker that are paraphrased by the Listener. This assures that each of you will know your turn to talk is coming up soon. You will be a better Listener when you know you are going to have a chance to respond with your point of view soon.

Although it may be frustrating to have to pass the floor when you are in the middle of building a point, rest assured: you will get the floor back quite soon. Too often, people feel they have to get everything in while their partner is finally listening, before the door shuts. If the two of you get in a habit of talking more and doing a good job of it, that sense of urgency will go away. Don't try to get so much through each open door that you make it unpleasant for your partner to keep the door open whenever you are around.

This is really a simple one, though simple is not always easy to do. Share. Take turns. It's not magic; it's being polite. It's about honoring your partner.

I Really Hate Rules

Many people can relate to this one. Some people really dislike structure more than others. Some people feel truly confined when trying to follow these kinds of rules. We value that input. Keep in mind something we cannot stress enough: we do not recommend talking like this when you are just being together as friends and you are not talking about things that are difficult. That would be unnatural and constraining in ways that we don't think would benefit your relationship.

However, suppose one of you really does not like this structural idea for any kind of talk. We have a couple of points in response to your concern. First, the primary message in this chapter is that every couple needs to have a way to talk about the most difficult things. If you have another way, or develop another way, you'll do fine. You can safely ignore our ideas in this chapter and move on to the next— as long as the two of you agree that you have another way to talk safely, and you both agree about what that other way is. If this describes you, we bet you've already figured out some ways to talk without fighting that work well for you.

Second, over the years, we've noted that if one partner is not so wild about trying this and working at it, it's usually the one who is otherwise most comfortable with conflict. That does not necessarily mean the person is handling conflict well; rather, we're talking about the partner who is less negatively affected by the conflict. If that sounds like you, give this a lot of thought. *You* might not feel intimidated by talks about anything. But if one of you benefits a lot from using structure to make talking safe, both of you will gain. Like the rules in most any setting, these rules level the playing field to make it fairer to all in terms of how things will proceed.

What If My Partner Isn't Interested?

We feel strongly that any change in either partner will have a positive effect on the relationship. Your effort to try these skills and bring safety and structure to your communication will be helpful and will perhaps even encourage your partner to participate, as he or she comes to feel validated and accepted by you.

Time to Talk

The Speaker-Listener Technique does not work miracles, but it does work well. If it is going to be useful, you have to practice. As is true when you are learning any new skill, you'll likely be a bit unsure at the start. You need to learn this technique so well *together* that the rules are automatic when you have something really difficult to discuss.

If you were learning to play tennis, you would not try to perfect your backhand at center court in Wimbledon. Instead you would hit backhands against the back wall for hours to get it just right. Trying to learn a new skill in a high-stress situation is not advisable. Here we suggest a good method for learning the Speaker-Listener Technique most effectively.

1. Practice this technique *several* times a week for fifteen minutes or so each time. If you do not set aside the time to practice, you will never find this powerful technique very helpful.

2. For the first week, try the technique with only *nonconflictual* money-related topics. Talk about anything of interest to either of you: the meaning of money to your parents, financial news, how much money sports figures are earning, your dreams for the future if money were no object, concerns you have at work, and so on. Your goal here is not to resolve some problem but to practice new skills. When you practice with these topics, it doesn't matter what topic you choose, only that you try to stick to the technique.

3. After you have had three successful practice sessions about nonconflictual money topics, choose money-related areas of minor conflict to discuss. Sometimes couples are poor at knowing what will and will not trigger a fight. If the situation gets heated on a topic you choose, drop it. It won't go away, but you can deal with it when you have practiced more together.

Practice several discussions in which you both exchange some thoughts and feelings on these issues. Don't try to solve problems, just have good discussions. Your goal is to understand each other's point of view as clearly and completely as possible. Problems are sometimes solved in the process because all that was needed was for each of you to understand where the other was coming from. That's OK, but don't intentionally try for solutions. You'll learn and practice problem solving in another chapter.

4. When you are doing well with smaller issues, move on to tougher and tougher issues. As you do, remember to work at sticking to the rules. They work if you work at it.

5. As you feel more confident, talk about less conflictual but more sensitive issues, such as the psychological meaning of money to you, or the money-related values you want your children to develop.

CHAPTER NINE

REAL SOLUTIONS FOR REAL PROBLEMS

First, have a definite, clear, practical ideal—a goal, an objective. Second, have the necessary means to achieve your ends—wisdom, money, materials, and methods. Third, adjust all your means to that end.

ARISTOTLE

All couples have money problems, and even the happiest couples don't ever solve some of their key money problems. Let's repeat that in case it wasn't clear: some of the happiest couples we've seen still struggle with significant money issues over many years.

This is true of the couples with the most money, couples with the least money, couples who start out poor and end up rich, and couples who start out rich and end up poor! So why do we start this chapter on problem solving by telling you that some of your money problems may never be solved? Simple. We'd like to adjust your expectations to be more in line with reality.

Many partners believe that there is something wrong with their marriage if they have problems with money (or other issues) that are not readily solvable. This belief can be very damaging to a relationship. One of the pathways to unhappiness or divorce lies not so much in having problems with money but in believing that there is something seriously wrong with your relationship because you've not resolved all your financial issues. As we've made clear, most couples struggle with issues about money and finance. For some, this means disagreements over spending or issues about earning potential. For others, money may be a magnet attracting the deeper invisible forces: expectations born in your culture or family of origin, and such hidden issues as those of recognition or acceptance.

In the preceding chapters, we have tried to clear the fog that surrounds many money problems by helping you understand the invisible forces that surround money and by providing a safe way to talk without fighting. Now your money-related issues should be clear for you, and we will provide a simple model for solving some of them.

Hallmarks of Great Problem Solving

There are many things that go into great solutions. Two of the most important are teamwork and patience. When making the bigger decisions in life, couples who make the best solutions, the solutions most likely to last, go slowly but hand in hand.

The Team's the Thing

We consider teamwork to be one of the core themes of this entire book. All kinds of money and other relationship problems are made worse when two partners have lost— or have never learned—the ability to work together as teammates. Allan D. Cordova has conducted research at the University of Denver on teamwork with couples in the transition to parenthood. Whether or not a couple is having a baby, teamwork is crucial. Here's what he told us about his research as well as other studies in this area:

> Research suggests that teamwork—how coordinated, committed, and "in sync" couples feel and act—is a cornerstone of marital adjustment. The stakes of thinking and acting like a team may be the highest under stressful circum- stances, such as when trying to talk about a "hot" topic. But being a "team" may mean different things for husbands and wives. In my work, I've found that couples who score higher on measures of teamwork are couples who also score highly on general marital satisfaction, commitment, confidence in the ability to constructively solve relationship problems, and communication quality. In another teamwork study conducted by R. Carols and Don Baucom, women responded more positively to specific, recent supportive events, whereas men tended to be relatively more affected by more general and historical relationship support. Similarly, in my research, I discovered that both men's and women's marital happiness was related to "feeling" like a team. But for women, and not for men, marital happiness was also related to the frequency of actual team-like behaviors (for example, doing a chore you don't normally do in order to help out your spouse; saying "thank you" to acknowledge your mate's efforts). This may mean the difference between "talking the talk" (saying you feel like a team player) and "walking the walk" (acting like a team player).

Among other things, what all this means for handling money problems is that part of teamwork is following through on things you've agreed to do. It's far less likely that you will follow through if your decisions were not well made in the first place. You have the best chance of working together as a team if you slow down and take the time to understand the roots of your money issues from each of your perspectives.

What's Your Hurry?

Haste makes waste. Just because it's a tired old saying doesn't mean it isn't true. There are two major factors that propel couples to rush to solutions about money problems: time pressure and conflict avoidance.

Time Pressure. We live in a "give-it-to-me-now" world of instant solutions to problems and desires. In fact, we use the saying *time is money* to justify doing things quickly. Although this way of thinking might work fine when it comes to wanting a certain brand of shaving cream or a particular color of draperies at the store, it doesn't work so well for relationships. For resolving the problems most couples struggle with, hasty decisions are often poor decisions. You may have heard the expression "you can pay me now or pay me later" when it comes to car maintenance, and it's all too true when dealing with money problems in relationships.

Conflict Avoidance. Sometimes people rush to solutions because they can't stand to deal with the conflict. Frances and Bjorn have been married twenty-four years, with one child through college and one a senior in high school. Bjorn is an insurance salesman, and Frances works as a nearly full-time volunteer with a local religious charity. They've always had enough money, but things have gotten much tighter with college bills piling up. An issue for Bjorn is Frances's devoting so much time to a job that doesn't pay. The following exchange is typical of their attempts to solve the problem.

Bjorn: *(testy)* I noticed that the Visa bill was over $3,000 again. I just don't know what we are going to do to keep up. It worries me. I'm doing all I can, but . . .

Frances: *(gives no indication that she is paying attention to Bjorn)*

Bjorn: *(frustrated)* Did you hear me?

Frances: Yes. I didn't think we spent that much this time.

Bjorn: How many clothes did Jeanne need, anyway? *(really annoyed now)*

Frances: *(annoyed but calm)* Well, we figured she needed one really nice outfit for applying for jobs. I guess we got more extras than I thought, but it was all things she can really use. It's really important to her to look good at interviews. And you know, the sooner she gets a job, the better off our budget will be.

Bjorn: *(settling down a bit)* I can understand, but this kind of thing adds to my worry. *(long pause)* We aren't saving anything at all for retirement, and we aren't getting any younger. If you had some income coming in for all your work, it would help a lot.

Frances: Why don't we just get rid of that credit card? Then you wouldn't have to worry about it anymore.

Bjorn: We could do that, and also plan to put aside an extra $150 a month in my retirement plan. That would help a lot to get us going in the right direction. What about a part-time job?

Frances: I can think about it. What I'm doing seems a lot more important. For now, let's try to get rid of the credit card and save more. That sounds good. Let's try it out.

Bjorn: OK, let's see what happens.

End of discussion. The one good thing about this discussion is that they had it. However, what are the chances that they came to a satisfactory resolution of their money problem? Two months later, nothing was changed, no more was saved, the credit card was still being used, interest was accruing, and they were no closer to working together on the budget.

This example illustrates what couples do all the time: make a quick agreement so that they can avoid conflict. In addition, the lack of discussion precludes the exploration of the invisible forces that are also at work. Solutions arrived at in this manner rarely last because all the important information is not "on the table." In the case of Bjorn and Frances, they did not really address his central concern about her volunteer job. Furthermore, there are no specifics about how they will implement their agreement.

When you settle prematurely on a solution, you are likely to pay for the lack of planning with more conflict erupting about the issue later on.

Do Men Want to Solve More Than Women?

Countless men have told us that when they perceive their wife's concerns as being unfixable, they feel helpless, which leads them to withdraw. This scenario can come up a lot, too, as in many marriages women are the ones more frequently bringing up the issues that they think need to be dealt with. But that does not mean that their greatest goal is usually solving the problem. When we ask wives what they want, the answer is simple: "I want you to listen to me, not fix things for me." It's not just men who want to fix things; ours is a problem-solving-oriented society, and it rewards people who are good fixers. Both men and woman tend to go for the problem-solving jugular, and feel helpless and hopeless when that doesn't work. It's better to resist this urge and listen as a friend might to what is upsetting your partner. For many problems in life, especially concerns about money that are not readily solvable, just being heard, really heard, can make the "problem" go away. That's why it's so important to start with really hearing one another before even trying to solve a significant problem.

In our seminars, we often shock couples by announcing that our experience indicates that approximately 70 percent of the issues couples face do not need to be solved as much as just aired out. It's hard to appreciate this point unless you have experienced the power of good talk. The truth is that we often want something much more fundamental in our relationships than solutions to problems: we want a friend. Friends make great mates and great teammates. Investing in talking without fighting pays off.

Handling Problems Well

If you have been reading carefully, it will come as no surprise that the approach we take here to solving money and marriage problems is structured. In other words, we recommend a specific set of steps for you to follow together as a team. As we said in Chapter Eight, we think that you're most likely to benefit from added structure when you're dealing with topics that are difficult to handle. We have featured these steps in our various materials based on the PREP approach. Similar models are contained in such works as *We Can Work It Out* (1993), by Notarius and Markman, and *A Couple's Guide to Communication* (1976), by Gottman, Notarius, Gonso, and Markman—from which we have adapted a few ideas.

Although these steps are very straightforward, don't be misled by the simplicity of the approach. You must be willing to work together, be creative and flexible, and be willing to experiment with change. We think of this structure as a scaffold around a building under construction. You need the support to complete the project. Full discussion clarifies the issues, identifies the invisible forces at work, removes conflict, and increases the feeling of teamwork. Solutions to problems flow naturally from working together against the problems rather than working against each other. Here are the steps to handling problems well:

I. Problem Discussion
II. Problem Solution
   A. Agenda setting
   B. Brainstorming
   C. Agreement and compromise
   D. Follow-up

We've learned over the years that some couples really like to follow explicit steps like these—and greatly benefit—and others don't care for quite as much structure when working on problems. We are going to strongly recommend practicing these steps because we believe doing so can fuel a sense of confidence that the two of you can deal with problems in the future. Then, over time, you can decide how and when you want to use the specific guidelines.

As you read what follows, give a lot of thought to the principles reflected in these steps. The themes here are the essence of how people get to great solutions on difficult issues in life.

Problem Discussion

Problem solving is easiest when the two of you have created an atmosphere of mutual respect and acceptance. Therefore, we recommend discussing problems before trying to solve them. In the Problem Discussion step, you are laying the foundation for a solution to come. Whether the problem is large or small, you should not move on to Problem Solution until you both understand, and feel understood by, the other. We recommend you use the Speaker-Listener Technique for this step, though the technique itself is not as critical as having some kind of good discussion before attempting to find solutions to the problem at hand.

> *Problem solving is easiest when the two of you have created an atmosphere of mutual respect and acceptance.*

Problem Solution

We have found that the following steps work very well for couples after the work of Problem Discussion has been done.

Agenda Setting. The first step in the Problem Solution phase is to set the agenda for your work together. The key here is to make it very clear what you are trying to solve at this time. Often your discussion will have taken you through many facets of an issue. Now you need to decide what to focus on. The more specific you are at this step, the better your chances of coming to a workable and satisfying solution.

Many problems in marriage seem insurmountable, but they can be cut down to size if you follow these procedures. Even a great mountain can be leveled in time if you keep chipping away at it.

Let's say you've had a Problem Discussion about money, covering a range of issues, such as credit card problems, checkbooks, budgets, and savings. The problem area of "money" can contain many smaller problem areas to consider. So take a large problem such as this and focus on the more manageable pieces, one at a time. It is also wisest to pick an easier piece of a problem to work on first. You might initially decide who should balance the checkbook each month, then deal with budget plans later.

At times, your Problem Discussion will have focused from start to finish on a specific problem. In this case, you won't have to define the agenda for problem solving. For example, you may be working on the problem of which spouse's family you'll visit for the holidays. There may be no specific smaller piece of such a problem, so you will set the agenda to work on the whole of it.

Brainstorming. Brainstorming is where people get together and throw out any idea they can think of, no matter how silly it seems. As far as we know, the process referred to as brainstorming has been around forever. However, it seems to have been refined and promoted by NASA during the early days of the U.S. space program. NASA needed a way to bring together the many different engineers and scientists when looking for solutions to the varied problems of space travel. Brainstorming worked for NASA, and it came to be frequently used in business settings. We have found that it works very well for couples, too.

There are several rules regarding brainstorming:

- Any idea is OK to suggest.
- Write the ideas down as you generate them together.
- Don't evaluate the ideas during brainstorming, verbally or nonverbally (this includes making faces!).
- Be creative. Suggest whatever comes to mind.
- Have fun with it, if you can. This is a time for a sense of humor; all other feelings should be dealt with in Problem Discussion.

The best thing about this process is that it encourages creativity. If you can edit out your tendency to comment critically on the ideas, you will encourage each other to come up with some great stuff. Wonderful solutions can come from considering the points made during brainstorming. Following the rules here helps you resist the tendency to settle prematurely on a solution that isn't the best you can find. Loosen up and go for it.

Agreement and Compromise. In this step, the goal is to pull from the ideas generated during brainstorming and come up with a specific solution or combination of solutions that you both agree to try. We emphasize the word *agree* because the solution is not likely to help unless you both agree to try it—sincerely. We emphasize *specific* because the more specific you are about the solution, the more likely you will follow through.

Although it is easy to see the value of agreement, some people have trouble with the idea of compromise. From time to time we've even been criticized for using the term. Obviously, compromise implies giving up something you want in order to reach an agreement. To some, compromise sounds more like lose-lose than win-win. But we mean to emphasize compromise in a positive manner. The two of you will see some things differently. You would, at times, make different decisions. However, many times, the best solution will be a compromise in which neither of you gets everything you want.

> *The more specific you are about the solution, the more likely you will follow through.*

Follow-Up. Many couples make agreements to try a particular solution to a problem. It is just as important to follow up to see how the agreement is working out. Following up has two key advantages. First, solutions often need to be tweaked a bit to work in the long term. Second, following up builds in accountability. Often we don't get serious about making changes unless we know there is some point of accountability in the near future.

At times you'll need a lot of follow-up in the Problem Solution phase. Other times it's not really necessary: you reach an agreement, it works out, and nothing more needs to be done.

A Detailed Example: Bjorn and Frances

It did not take Frances and Bjorn very long to realize that their problem solving about the credit card, her volunteer work, and their retirement savings was not working. They decided to try the steps we are suggesting.

First, they set aside the time to work through the steps. A couple may not need a lot of time, depending on the problem, but setting aside time specifically for working toward solutions is very wise. Let's follow them through the steps:

Problem Discussion Using the Speaker-Listener Technique

Frances (Speaker): I can see that we really do have to try something different. We aren't getting anywhere on our retirement savings.

Bjorn (Listener):   You can see we aren't getting anywhere, and you are also concerned.

Frances (Speaker):   *(letting Bjorn know he had accurately heard her)* Yes. We need to come up with some plan for saving more and for doing something about the credit cards.

Bjorn (Listener):   You agree we need to save more, and can see that how we spend on the credit cards may be part of the problem.

Frances (Speaker):   I can also see why you are concerned about my volunteer work, when I could be spending some of that time bringing in some income. But my volunteer work is really important to me. I feel like I'm doing something good in the world.

Bjorn (Listener):   Sounds like you can appreciate my concern, but you also want me to hear that it's really important to you. It adds a lot of meaning to your life. *(Here, he validates her by listening carefully.)*

Frances (Speaker):   Yeah. That's exactly what I am feeling. Here, you take the floor, I want to know what you're thinking. *(She hands Bjorn the floor.)*

Bjorn (Speaker):   I have been anxious about this for a long time. If we don't save more, we aren't going to be able to maintain our lifestyle in retirement. It's not all that far away.

Frances (Listener):   You're really worried, aren't you?

Bjorn (Speaker):   Yes, I am. You know how things were for Mom and Dad. I don't want to end up living in a two-room apartment.

Frances (Listener):   You're worried we could end up living that way, too.

Bjorn (Speaker):   I'd feel a lot better with about three times as much saved.

Frances (Listener):   Too late now. *(She catches herself interjecting her own opinion.)* Oh, I should paraphrase. You wish we were much further along in our savings than we are.

Bjorn (Speaker):   *(This time, he feels he is really getting her attention.)* I sure do. I feel a lot of pressure about it. I really want to work together so we can both be comfortable. *(letting her know he wants to work as a team)*

Frances (Listener):   You want us to work together and reduce the pressure, and plan for our future.

Bjorn (Speaker):   *(suggesting some alternatives)* Yes. We'd need to spend less to save more. We'd need to use the credit cards more wisely. I think it would make the biggest difference if you could bring in some income.

Frances (Listener):   You feel that to save more we'd need to spend less with the credit cards. More important, you think it's pretty important for me to bring in some money.

Bjorn (Speaker):   Yes. I think the income is a bigger problem than the outgo.

Frances (Listener):	Even though we could spend less, you think we may need more income if we want to live at the same level in retirement. Can I have the floor?
Bjorn (Speaker):	Exactly! Here's the floor. *(He passes the floor to Frances.)*
Frances (Speaker):	*(responding to Bjorn's clarification)* Sometimes I think that you think I'm the only one who overspends.
Bjorn (Listener):	You think that I think you're mostly at fault for spending too much. Can I have the floor again? *(Frances returns the floor to Bjorn.)*
Bjorn (Speaker):	Actually, I don't think that, but I can see how I could come across that way. *(validating Frances's experience)* I think I overspend just as much as you do. I just do it in bigger chunks.
Frances (Listener):	Nice to hear that. *(She validates his comment, and is feeling good hearing him taking responsibility.)* You can see that we both spend too much, just differently. You buy a few big things we may not need, and I buy numerous smaller things.
Bjorn (Speaker):	Exactly. We are both to blame, and we can both do better.
Frances (Listener):	We both need to work together. *(Bjorn passes the floor to Frances.)*
Frances (Speaker):	I agree that we need to deal with our retirement savings more radically. My biggest fear is losing the work I love so much. It's been the most meaningful thing I've done since the kids got older.
Bjorn (Listener):	It's hard to imagine not having that. It's so important to you.
Frances (Speaker):	Yes. I can see why more income would make a big difference, but at the same time I would hate to lose what I have. I really like running those programs for the kids—especially when I see one of them open up.
Bjorn (Listener):	You enjoy it, and you are doing something really useful. I can hear how hard it would be for you to give it up.
Frances (Speaker):	Exactly. Maybe there would be some way to deal with this so that I would not lose all of what I am doing, but where I could help us save what we need for retirement at the same time.
Bjorn (Listener):	You are wondering if there could be a solution that would meet your needs and our needs at the same time.
Frances (Speaker):	Yes. I'm willing to think about solutions with you.

They discontinue the Speaker-Listener Technique.

Bjorn:	OK.
Frances:	So, are we both feeling understood enough to move on to Problem Solution?
Bjorn:	I am, how about you?
Frances:	*(She nods her head yes.)*

Here they are agreeing together that they have had a good discussion and are ready to try some problem solving. They are consciously turning this corner together to move into the Problem Solution step.

Problem Solution

Bjorn and Frances now go through the four steps of Problem Solution.

Agenda Setting. Choosing a specific piece of the whole increases the couple's chances of finding a solution that will really work this time.

Frances: We should agree on the agenda. We could talk about how to get more into the retirement accounts, but I think we also need a discussion on the credit cards and how we spend money.

Bjorn: You're right. We are going to need several different stabs at this entire issue. It seems we could break it all down into the need to bring in more and the need to spend less. I don't want to push, but I'd like to focus on the "bring in more" part first.

Frances: I can handle that. Let's problem-solve on that first, then we can talk later this week about the spending side.

Bjorn: So we're going to brainstorm about how to boost the income.

Brainstorming. The key here is to generate ideas freely.

Frances: Let's brainstorm. Why don't you write the ideas down—you have a pen handy.

Bjorn: OK. You could get a part-time job.

Frances: I could ask the board of directors about making some of my work into a paid position. I'm practically a full-time staff member anyway.

Bjorn: We could meet with a financial planner so we could get a better idea of what we really need to bring in. I could also get a second job.

Frances: I could look into part-time jobs that were similar to what I'm already doing, like those programs for kids with only one parent.

Bjorn: You know, Jack and Marla are doing something like that. We could talk to them about it.

Frances: I feel this list is pretty good. Let's talk about what we'll try doing.

Agreement and Compromise. Now they sift through the ideas generated in brainstorming.

Bjorn: I like your idea of talking to the board. What could it hurt?

Frances: I like that too. I also think your idea of seeing a financial planner is good. But I don't think it is realistic for you to work more.

Bjorn: Yeah, I think you're right. What about talking to Marla and Jack about what they're into?

Frances: I'd like to hold off on that. That could lead them to try and get me involved, and I'm not sure I'm interested.

Bjorn: OK. What about exploring if there are any kinds of part-time jobs where you could be doing something that has meaning for you and makes some bucks, too?

Frances: I'd like to think about that. It'd be a good way to go if they don't have room in the budget where I'm volunteering now. I sure wouldn't want to do more than half-time, though. I would hate to give up all of what I'm doing now.

Bjorn: And I wouldn't want you to. If you could make a part-time income, I'll bet we could cut back enough to make it all work.

Frances: So, how about I talk to the board, you ask Frank about that financial planner they use, and I'll also start looking around at what kinds of part-time jobs there might be.

Bjorn: Great. Let's schedule some time next week to talk about how we are doing in moving along for the solution we need.

Frances: Agreed. *(They set a time to meet for follow-up.)*

Follow-Up. At the end of the week, Frances and Bjorn met to discuss what they were finding out and what to do next. To Frances's surprise, the board member she talked with seemed eager to try work out something. In the meantime, she'd gone ahead with looking into various part-time jobs that would meet her needs. Bjorn had scheduled a meeting for them with a financial planner for the following week.

Even though they haven't completely solved each component of their problem at this point, Bjorn and Frances were finally moving forward on an issue that had been a problem between them for a long time.

Later, they went through the steps again and came to a specific agreement about spending less. They decided how much less to spend and agreed to record all the credit card purchases in a checkbook register so that they would know how they were doing compared to their target. In contrast to their problem solving about income, which was a process lasting several weeks, this specific solution on spending was implemented right away without much tweaking required.

When It's Not That Easy

We'd like to tell you that this model always works as well as it did for Frances and Bjorn when it comes to handling money issues, but there are times when it does not. In our experience with couples, there are a few common difficulties that come up when dealing with problems. We have a few suggestions for what to do next.

Cycling Back Through the Steps

If you get bogged down, simply pick up the floor again and resume your discussion.

You can get bogged down and frustrated during any segment of the Problem Solution phase. If you do, you need to cycle back to Problem Discussion. Simply pick up the floor again and resume your discussion. While you're getting used to the process or when you're dealing with more complex and difficult issues, you might cycle through the steps several times.

Halfway Can Get You All the Way

The best solution you can reach may not always be the end solution. At times, you should set the agenda just to agree on the next steps needed to get to the best solution. For example, you might brainstorm about the kind of information you need to make your decision. Which of you can find out what answers, and from whom? Divide and conquer, and move on.

Staying the Course

I (Howard) saw a client recently who had just left a high-paying job to follow his dream to play on the pro golf tour. He was a two-handicap player and everyone told him he had a chance to make it on the tour. He and his wife came in during the time he was making this decision, and we used the basic discussion-solution model to structure how they dealt with this complicated issue that would affect both of them in the short and long run. They used the model well and reached a joint decision after spending one session discussing the issues and another working together as a team to solve it.

They decided that he would give up his job as a vice president at the phone company and invest two years in trying to make the tour. They agreed that they would use money from their savings to give this a go. They also agreed to evaluate how things were going every three months, first by meeting to talk about each of their perspectives (discussion) and then by doing any problem-solving refinements if necessary. After about nine months, the husband called for an individual session, saying his wife supported his coming in alone. He complained about being depressed and anxious, although his new golf career was going as well as could be expected. He said he was often thinking about how he wasn't supporting his family, and he was comparing himself with his former coworkers as well as more successful golfers in terms of financial success. He was feeling like a loser. In the session, we talked about how such comparisons almost always result in feeling bad, as there are always going be to people who are doing better than us on dimensions important to us.

I shared with him that I would sell my soul (check e-Bay) for a chance to play major league baseball. Yet if I were to make it, I'd not be happy to be a player who occasionally came off the bench to pinch hit or run. I'd want to start. But if I were a starter, I'd not be happy with just that for long. I'd want to make the all-star team. Maybe from there, I'd want to be the highest-paid player at my position—not because I'd need the money but because I'd want to be at the top. There's nothing wrong with wanting to be the best at what you do, but sometimes we focus on things that make us miserable. We talked about how he needed to stop doing "comparison shopping" and start using a "thought-stopping" procedure to put brakes on his negative thinking and to think more realistically and positively about his life.

Most important, this couple needed to keep talking, regularly, about how the decision was working out. This is best done at intervals you choose, not randomly. If you do it randomly, you may either skip the follow-up or do it too often, second-guessing the decision too much and not allowing it to have the best chance of playing out. Sometimes you just need to reaffirm the decision and stay the course. This couple had decided, with the wife fully supporting the husband, to go through tight times financially to give this a go. Even though he was having serious doubts about the decision—and feeling somewhat guilty for not bringing in the money he had brought in—their willingness to look openly at the solution and the plan in light of what they'd decided gave her a good opening to reassure him that she remained behind him and the decision. When they look back years from now, they may or may not see their decision as having been wise. But they protected their relationship, regardless, by working on the solution as a team and reaffirming their mutual commitment to see how it played out.

When There Is No Solution

There are some money problems that do not have solutions you'll both be happy about. Suppose you've worked together for some time using the structure we suggest, and no clear solution is emerging out of your work together. You can either

let this lack of a solution damage other aspects of your marriage, or you can plan for how to live with the difference. If you have an area that seems unsolvable, you can set the agenda to protect the rest of the marriage from the fallout from that one problem area. You might state the agenda this way: "How can we protect the rest of our relationship from the problem with _____?" You would be literally "agreeing to disagree" constructively. This kind of solution comes out of both teamwork and acceptance.

◆ ◆ ◆

In this chapter, we have given you a very specific model that will work well to help you preserve and enhance your teamwork in solving the problems that come your way in life. We don't expect most couples to use such a structured approach for minor problems. We do expect that most couples could benefit from this model when dealing with more important matters, especially those that can lead to unproductive conflict.

Exercises for Moving Forward

We've got some work for you to do. If you want to take some giant steps forward in your ability to work on problems as a team, give this exercise a try.

Money and Marriage Problem Area Assessment

The following is a simple measure of common money and marriage problem areas that most couples will face in relationships. This type of measure was originally developed by Knox in 1971, and we have used versions of it for years in our research as a simple but very relevant measure of the problem areas in couples' relationships. This is a new version focused on money, which we developed especially for this book. As we'll explain, filling out these forms will help you practice the problem-solving skills we have presented. Use separate pieces of paper so that you can each fill out your own form independently.

Problem Inventory

Consider the following list of money-related issues that all couples must face. Please rate how much of a problem each area currently is in your relationship by writing in a number from 0 (not at all a problem) to 100 (a severe problem). For example, if the amount of time spent working is somewhat of a problem, you might enter 25 next to "time spent working." If time spent working is not a problem in your relationship, you might enter a 0 next to "time spent working." If time spent working is a severe problem, you might enter 100. If you wish to add other areas not included in our list, please do so. *Be sure to rate all areas.*

_____   Spending habits

_____   Time spent working

_____   Retirement planning

_____   Differences in long-term money goals

_____   Not having or making enough money

_____   Savings issues (not enough, different preferences, too much?)

_____   Money chores (recording checks, balancing checkbooks, paying bills, and so on)

_____   Credit card debt

_____   Tax matters

_____   Housing (rent versus purchase issues, housing payments, and so on)

_____   Fairness of how money responsibilities are divided up

_____   Overall debts

_____   Money and in-law dynamics

Practice Problem Solving

For practicing this model, it is critical that you follow these instructions carefully. When dealing with real problems in your relationship, the chances of conflict are significant, and we want you to practice in a way that enhances your chances of solidifying these skills.

1. Set aside time to practice uninterrupted. Thirty minutes or so should be sufficient to get started with using the sequence on some of the problems you want to solve.

2. Look over your problem inventories together. Construct a list of those areas in which you each rated the problem as being less serious. These are the problem areas we want you to use to practice the model at the start.

3. We recommend that you set aside time to practice the sequence of Problem Discussion and Problem Solution several times a week for a couple of weeks. If you put in this time, you'll gain skill and confidence in handling problem areas together.

4. Keep this chapter open when practicing, and refer back to the specific steps we recommend.

5. As you gain confidence, move from the easier topics to the more difficult.

Remember, you are a team.

CHAPTER TEN

THE GOLDEN GROUND RULES

We have committed the Golden Rule to memory; let us now commit it to life.

EDWIN MARKHAM

W hen the two of you disagree or one of you is unhappy with the other— these are the times when you are most likely to do or say something that will damage your relationship. The choices you make at these moments can make the difference between being happy and connected or distant and angry. Remember: money is embedded in nearly every decision a couple makes, so it is highly unlikely that you will always agree. There are just too many opportunities for differences to surface. Conflicts about money are inevitable; what matters is how the two of you handle those conflicts.

> **Conflicts about money are inevitable; what matters is how the two of you handle those conflicts.**

At this point in the book, you understand how the invisible forces may try to push you off course, and you have some strategies for talking safely so that you can disarm these forces and work toward solving problems as a team. Now we're going to tie these strategies together by sharing with you our six ground rules for building a great relationship and protecting it from the destructive effects of conflict.

We use the term *ground rules* to highlight the importance of having a mutual understanding of, and commitment to, how the two of you will deal with difficult money and marriage matters. For us the term originates with the game of baseball. Every major league baseball park has its own ground rules, agreements that are particular to that park. These rules tell the coaches, players, and umpires whether a ball is considered in or out of play when it hits the top of a particular fence and bounces back onto the field, whether such a hit counts as a home run or a double, and the like. You get the idea. Essentially, these rules are designed to minimize conflicts about what's fair and to allow people instead to focus on enjoying the game.

That's what we want for you. We want the two of you to customize some rules to minimize conflicts that occur in your home park. We want you to be safe at home. Many couples tell us that these ground rules level the playing field in that they are clear and easy to follow; agreeing on them before disagreements come up helps the couples feel safe at home. In addition, these ground rules can protect you from the influences of the invisible forces that can push couples into "foul" territory.

Ground Rule 1

When conflict is escalating, we will call a Time Out and either (a) try it again, using the Speaker-Listener Technique, or (b) agree to talk later at a specified time about the issue, using the Speaker-Listener Technique.

Here is a secret. Happy couples tend to do something well that almost all couples, happy or not, can learn to do better: they have ways to signal each other when they need to take their interaction in a different direction. In other words, they have ways to put the brakes on, and they use those brakes.

Many couples who do poorly over time do not have ways to exit damaging arguments, or the ways in which they try to exit these fights (for example, by withdrawing) cause further conflict. Happier, healthier couples have ways to *cue or signal* each other when it's time to calm it down and rein in the negative feelings and harsh words. The clearer your cue and the firmer your agreement to use it, the better your odds of handling your most difficult marriage and money issues well. The cue that we suggest is Time Out.

Ground Rule 1 can help you counteract the danger signs, especially escalation. It's a way to prevent the two of you from damaging your relationship when you know that's what you're about to do—or may already have started to do. We suggest that you also agree on the specific signal that will mean Time Out for the two of you. It is necessary that both of you know what the other is trying to do when you hear the signal. Even if one of you calls Time Outs more often than the other, you both need to understand the signal as something the two of you are doing together. That's the whole point. Otherwise, it can look like one partner is just avoiding the other, and that will only fuel more escalation and anger.

One couple we worked with used names of food for their conflict management cues. "Hamburger" came to mean Time Out for them. So if they found themselves escalating and getting snippy, one would say, "Hey, let's grab a burger."

Sometimes this would get them not only to cool it but also to start laughing—and many experts do believe humor helps in just about any situation!

Regardless of who gives the signal, each of you must use the cue to take responsibility to calm yourself down. Mutually agreed-on signals are not an excuse to control your partner but a way to mutually take control of your conflict. So it's not OK to drop a nasty word bomb on your partner and then throw out a quick Time Out to stop things right there.

Using Time Outs gives withdrawers confidence that conflict won't get out of hand. Some withdrawers even find they are better able to tolerate conflict, knowing they can stop it at any time. However, Time Outs will not work for pursuers at all if the two of you don't come back to talking about issues that you've temporarily paused. We realize that for many couples, we're addressing this last comment to men. Even though we can joke (and have) that when men call for Time Outs, it's a kind of "men-o-pause," it's no joke at all to a pursuer if a withdrawer never comes back at another time to talk. You have got to make that talk happen, and in general it's probably more important for the one who called a Time Out to be especially diligent about following up.

If you are a pursuer, this part of the ground rule addresses your concern that Time Outs mean withdrawal and avoidance. The two of you do need to discuss important money-related (or other) issues, but in a productive manner. By agreeing to use the Speaker-Listener Technique when you come back to talking about an issue, you are agreeing to deal more effectively with the issue that got out of hand.

When you do decide to talk later, try to set the time right then. Perhaps in an hour or maybe the next day would be a good time to talk. If things were really heated when the Time Out was called, you may find that you can't even talk right then about when you'll come back to the discussion. That's OK. You can set a time after things have calmed down between the two of you.

What If My Partner Does Use Time Out, but Only to Withdraw?

We are often asked this question. We have come to believe that unless you are in a relationship that is physically dangerous, you are likely better off pursuing the issue assertively—yet without hostility. In fact, a couple of studies hint that some marriages do better in the future when women are more negative in the present. This may sound inconsistent with some of the other things we've said, but in one way it makes perfect sense. Many of us in this field believe that such findings suggest it's generally better for women to raise issues, even if it means more conflict in the short run, if *not* doing so means that important issues are going to be ignored. The other critical point here is that the pursuit must really be motivated by wanting to do what's best for the relationship.

It's better to deal with matters head on than not at all.	It is truly important for each of you to raise concerns that you have about your relationship. Yet we hope you are learning (or have already learned) constructive ways to do so. *Constructive* does not mean peace at any price. It's better to deal with matters head on than not at all. If you are prone to withdrawal and are even using

Time Out to avoid issues, fight that tendency within yourself. Don't put your partner in the bind of having to decide whether to pursue you or not. In the long run, that will be far harder on both of you than facing issues as a team in the here and now.

A Look at Time Out Working Well

Here's an example of a couple using this ground rule to save an important evening from potential disaster. Jules and Alexandra had been married for six years, and had no children. They both wanted kids, but Jules wanted to wait until he felt financially secure enough not to have to worry about kid-related expenses, whereas Alexandra felt her biological clock ticking away and was afraid they might have trouble getting pregnant. This had added plenty of strain to their marriage. They had decided to take a weekend trip to the mountains, to get away and spend a relaxing—perhaps romantic—couple of days together. They had both been looking forward to this time together for months. This conversation took place on their first evening, as they got into bed together:

Alexandra: *(feeling romantic and snuggling up to Jules)* It's so nice to get away. No distractions. This feels good.

Jules: *(likewise inclined, and beginning to caress her)* Yeah, we should've done this months ago. Maybe a relaxed setting'll help you get having a child off your mind.

Alexandra: *(suddenly upset)* I wasn't even thinking of our baby issue! Why did you have to bring that up?

Jules: *(anxious and annoyed at himself for spoiling the moment)* I don't know, it's just that you always seem so tense these days and so far away.

Alexandra: *(angry)* You are the one who is distant and selfish and not caring about what I want.

Jules: Hold on. Time Out. I'm sorry I mentioned the child issue. Do you want to talk this through now, or set a time for later?

Alexandra: *(softening)* If we don't talk about it a little bit, I think the rest of the evening will be a drag.

Jules: OK, you have the floor. *(He picks up the remote control on the nightstand and hands it to her.)*

Alexandra (Speaker):	I got all tense when you brought up my feelings about getting pregnant. It's such a difficult topic for me, and I do think about it a lot.
Jules (Listener):	So mentioning that subject raised unpleasant feelings, and more so because you tend to think about it a lot.
Alexandra (Speaker):	Yes. That whole thing has been just awful for us, and I was hoping to get away from it for the weekend.
Jules (Listener):	It's been really hard on you, and you wanted to just forget about it this weekend.
Alexandra (Speaker):	And I wanted us to focus on rediscovering how to be a little bit romantic, like it used to be.
Jules (Listener):	Just you and me making love without a care.
Alexandra (Speaker):	*(feeling really listened to and cared for)* Yes. Your turn. *(She hands Jules the floor.)*
Jules (Speaker):	Boy, do I feel like a jerk. I didn't mean to mess up the moment, though I see how what I said affected you.
Alexandra (Listener):	You feel bad that you said anything. You did not mean to screw things up between us tonight.
Jules (Speaker):	You got it. And I really do want to have a child with you, and hugging you earlier and talking like this now makes me want to even more. Maybe I have been too concerned about money and not enough about your feelings.
Alexandra (Listener):	*(with a smile)* You didn't mean to be a jerk.
Jules (Speaker):	*(chuckling back)* That's kind of blunt, but yeah, that's what I'm saying. I think we should just avoid that whole topic for the weekend.
Alexandra (Listener):	You think we should make talking about having a child and other stuff an off-limits topic this weekend.
Jules:	Yes! *(He hands her the floor.)*
Alexandra (Speaker):	I agree. OK, where were we? *(Tossing the remote on the floor.)*
Jules:	*(big smile)* You were calling me a jerk.
Alexandra:	*(playfully)* Oh yeah. Come over here, jerk.
Jules:	*(moving closer to kiss her)* I'm all yours.

Notice how effectively they used the Time Out to stop what could have turned into an awful fight. Alexandra was too hurt to just shelve the issue. She needed to talk right then, and Jules agreed. Doing so helped them diffuse the tension and come back together, and it saved their special weekend. Talking without fighting also gave Jules the chance to say that he was placing too much emphasis on money and not enough on his family. The Time Out allowed Jules and Alexandra to control how they were going to react to the event of Jules's mentioning the child issue. Time Out gives couples the power to keep events from dragging them into issue discussion at the worst of all times.

Self-Regulation: A Fancy Way of Saying "Staying in Control"

Most of what we've suggested in Part Two so far can be summed up this way: you need to work together to manage negative emotions and disagreements well. How well you can do this depends in large measure on your ability to manage your own emotions when things are going downhill. There are two keys of doing this: watching how you think and knowing what you can do to relax your body.

Watching How You Think. Imagine this. Your partner has just said something that you find incredibly hurtful. Whether or not he or she meant to is one thing. How you choose to think about it is everything. Most of us react more to *our interpretation* of what was said than what our partner actually meant and did say. What we have been calling negative interpretations researchers might call maladaptive attributions. That's a technical way to say that some people tend to make consistent, negative judgments of their partner's motives.

Take Barb and Max. They have not been doing so well lately. Married for seven years, they are fighting so much about money and work and kids that it's hard for them to remember why they fell in love nine years ago. It's Tuesday night, and Barb has just come home from work. Max was there already. Their boys, Georgie and Frankie, had been told by Max that they could play Nintendo until dinnertime. Enter Barb.

Barb: *(not sounding particularly upset yet)* We'd agreed that the boys needed to clean up their rooms to earn their allowance before they could play Nintendo or computer games.

Max: *(remembering that he'd forgotten this, but also feeling pretty tired from work)* Oh yeah. I forgot.

Barb: *(Interpreting his simple tiredness as noninterest and invalidation, she is now feeling insulted.)* I guess you think I'm just trying to teach my kids the value of money for the sake of hearing myself think out loud, eh? *(She is not really looking for a response to this charge, but now that she's made her negative interpretation overt, Max responds with his defense.)*

Max: You are so darned sensitive. I just forgot that we said that this morning. I didn't mean anything by forgetting.

Barb: *(Here they go, moving this event into a full-blown issue.)* You forget a lot, you know. I think that's your way of undermining my authority. *(neatly expressing another negative interpretation)*

Let's give Max and Barb a big benefit of the doubt here. Let's say they are able to put the brakes on this escalation before any more damage is done. Max suggests a Time Out, which sounds very good to Barb. Which set of thoughts gives them the best chance of getting back on track?

Max: "She's always dissing me in front of the boys. She must think I'm an idiot."

Barb: "What a jerk. He must have the most pathetic memory on the planet—or else he does this just to frustrate me. Arrgggghhh!"

Or:

Max: "I bet she's had a pretty tough day. Maybe I can give her some space and then look for a way to tell her I do care about teaching the boys the value of money and of doing their chores, and that I really do agree with her."

Barb: "Maybe that comment about always forgetting things was a little out there. That's not so fair of me. I forget some things, too."

In their book *We Can Work It Out,* Clifford Notarius and Howard Markman labeled the kind of thoughts expressed in the first set "hot thoughts." Want to stay angry? These will do the job. You have little or no chance of handling times of escalation well if you choose to think in these ways. Avoiding these kinds of thoughts is not easy, though: you have to put aside your righteous indignation and have the humility to give the other the benefit of the doubt. Your call. Your choice. Your relationship.

Calming Down That Runaway Train (Your Body). John Gottman and his colleagues have been making the case that part of what is important in handling conflict well is controlling the bodily reactions that come along with it. Once you are upset, it's not just your thoughts you are trying to get a hold of; it's your body, too. Gottman's research team has found, for example, that when couples are upset, if they just read magazines for twenty minutes or so before continuing to talk, the rest of the talk is far more likely to go better. Got *Money* magazine? Got *Sports Illustrated* (not *that* issue, guys!)?

To be prepared for those times in the future when you'll need to calm yourself down, you need to think now about what you can do to help you relax. These may be very different for each of you. Here are some ideas:

- Lying down, eyes closed, thinking "better" thoughts
- Taking a walk

- Reading a novel that already has you hooked
- Playing with the kids
- Cleaning (works for some people)
- Taking a hot shower or bath
- Weight lifting

◆ ◆ ◆

If you are a couple that is particularly prone to volatile escalating arguments about money and other matters, you'll find that you have to be that much more specific with one another about how you take Time Outs and what you will do during them. Remember, it's especially important that you work on calming both your thoughts and your body.

Ground Rule 2

When we are having trouble communicating, we will "engage" the Speaker-Listener Technique.

It's so important for every couple to have at least one good way to talk when it's hardest to do so. With this ground rule, you are agreeing to use more structure when you need it. The earlier example of Jules and Alexandra highlights this point. However, there are many times when you may not need a Time Out but do need to make the transition to a more effective way to talk. Remember, talking without fighting is key.

For example, suppose that you wanted to talk about a problem such as how the two of you are spending money. You know from your history that these talks usually get difficult. You would be wise to follow this ground rule, raising the issue in this way: "Dear, I'm pretty concerned about money right now. Let's sit down and talk using the floor." Such a statement cues your partner that you are raising an important issue and that you want to talk it out carefully. This is the most common use of this ground rule.

There are other situations where things have already escalated and a Time Out might have helped, but you skip right to using the Speaker-Listener Technique. The point of this ground rule is that the two of you are making a decision to handle difficult or sensitive topics more effectively and with increased structure, rather than using old, destructive modes of communication.

Ground Rule 3

We will completely separate Problem *Discussion* from Problem *Solution*.

Too often, couples rush to agree to a solution, and the solution fails. It makes no sense to hurry when doing so only moves you backward. Only after the two of you have had a good discussion and each of you have expressed your concerns and feel understood should you begin discussing solutions. Making the transition between Problem Discussion and Problem Solution might look something like this:

Partner 1: I think we are ready for problem solving, what do you think?
Partner 2: I agree. I'm feeling like we had a good talk and got a lot out on the table. Now working on some solutions would be great.

Discussion and solution are different processes: whenever you start to solve an issue, stop and ask yourself, "Do I really understand my partner's perspective? Do I feel understood?" If either answer is no, you are probably not ready to move to solutions. This ground rule is a simple reminder of the need to talk first, solve second.

Ground Rule 4

We can bring up issues at any time, but the "listener" can say "this is not a good time." If the listener does not want to talk at that time, he or she takes responsibility for setting up a time to talk in the near future.

This ground rule accomplishes one very important purpose: it ensures that you will not have an important or difficult talk about an issue unless you both agree that the time is right. How often do you begin talking about a key issue in your relationship when your partner is just not ready for it? Most couples talk about their most important money and marriage issues at the worst times—dinnertime, bedtime, when you're getting the kids off for school, as soon as you walk in the door after work, on a date, while making love, when one is preoccupied with an important project or task—you get the picture. These are times when your spouse may be a captive audience, but you certainly don't have his or her attention. Because these tend to be stressful times in the routine of life, they are not good times to talk things out.

Most couples talk about their most important money and marriage issues at the worst times.

RAGNAR STORAASLI

This ground rule assumes two things: (1) you each are responsible for knowing when you are capable of discussing something with appropriate attention to what your partner has to say, and (2) you can each respect the other when he or she says, "I can't deal with that right now."

You may ask, "Isn't this just a prescription for avoidance?" That's where the second part of the ground rule comes in. The partner who doesn't want to talk takes responsibility for making the discussion happen in the near future. This is critical. Your partner will have a much easier time putting off the conversation if he or she has confidence that you really will follow through. We recommend that when you use this ground rule, you agree that you will set up a better time within twenty-four to forty-eight hours. This may not always be practical, but it works as a good rule of thumb. Many couples also often agree that some times, like bedtime, are just never a good time to deal with important issues.

Ground Rule 5

We will have weekly "couple meetings."

Most couples do not set aside a regular time for dealing with key issues or problems. The fast-paced lives so many of us lead can make this hard to do, but the advantages of having a weekly meeting time far outweigh any negatives. First, by carving out time for the upkeep of your marriage, you are placing high priority on it in a tangible way. We know you're busy, but if you decide that this is important, you can find the time to make it work.

Second, following this ground rule ensures that even if there is no other good time to deal with issues, you at least have this one regular time. You might be surprised at how much you can get done in thirty minutes or so of concentrated attention on an issue. During this meeting, you can talk about the relationship, talk about specific problems, or make plans about what's coming up.

A third advantage of this ground rule is that having a weekly meeting time takes much of the day-to-day pressure off your relationship. This is especially true if you are snared by the pursuer-withdrawer trap. If something happens that brings up a gripe for you, it's much easier to delay talking about it until another time if you know there will *be* another time.

You may be thinking that a couple meeting is a pretty good idea. If you like it and start doing it, you'll find it tempting to skip the meetings when you are getting along really well. Don't succumb to this urge. Do many of our successful couples actually have meetings? Some do and some don't. Many couples love the idea, have meetings religiously for a while, and then taper off. Things go well for a while due to their increased confidence and skills. Then conflict starts creeping back into the relationship; with luck, the couple realizes that they need the meetings to help contain and control the conflict, and they start them up again. Other couples are really dedicated and maintain meetings on an ongoing basis, but perhaps only a couple of times a month instead of weekly. You can be flexible and customize the ground rule to fit your needs.

Ground Rule 6

We will make time for the great things: fun, friendship, and sensuality. We will agree to protect these times from conflicts and the need to deal with issues concerning money and marriage (as well as other issues).

Just as it's important to have time set aside to deal with issues in your relationship, it's critical that you protect positive times from conflicts over issues. You can't be focusing on issues all the time and have a really great marriage. You need some times when you are together relaxing—having fun, talking as friends, making love, and so forth—when conflict and problems are off-limits. Putting time into nurturing the great things in your marriage will be the best investment you can make for your future. This is such a key point that we'll devote the entire next chapter to investing in your love.

For now, we'll emphasize two points embodied in this ground rule. First, make time for these great things. After all, that's what brought you together in the first place. Second, if you're enjoying special time together, do not bring up issues that you have to work on. And if an issue does come up (that is, if it's triggered by an event), table it until you have your couple meeting to deal with it constructively.

The example we presented earlier in this chapter with Alexandra and Jules makes this point well. They were out to have a relaxing and romantic weekend, and this wasn't the time to focus on one of their key issues. Using Time Out and the Speaker-Listener Technique helped them get refocused on the real reason they had gotten away. It would have been better still if they had agreed to keep such issues off-limits during such positive times in the first place, consciously deciding to protect their relationship.

◆ ◆ ◆

One of the most destructive things that can happen to a marriage is to have the growing sense that you are walking in a minefield. You know the feeling. You begin to wonder where the next explosion will come from, and you don't feel in control of where you're going. You no longer feel free to just "be" with your partner. You don't know when you are about to "step in it," but you know right away when you just did. Your relationship just doesn't have to be this way or ever get this way in the first place. These ground rules will go a long way toward getting you back on safe ground. They work. You can do it.

Time to Talk

Relationships need ground rules to level the playing field and to ensure that both partners are playing by the same rules. Rules are not one-size-fits-all. It's very important that the two of you talk about these rules and customize them in ways that make them best fit your relationship.

Here again are the six ground rules. Talk about each one, what you each think about it, and how you might use the rule in your relationship.

1. When conflict is escalating, we will call a Time Out and either (a) try it again, using the Speaker-Listener Technique, or (b) agree to talk later at a specified time about the issue, using the Speaker-Listener Technique.
2. When we are having trouble communicating, we will "engage" the Speaker-Listener Technique.
3. We will completely separate Problem *Discussion* from Problem *Solution*.
4. We can bring up issues at any time, but the "listener" can say "this is not a good time." If the listener does not want to talk at that time, he or she takes responsibility for setting up a time to talk in the near future. (You need to decide how to define "the near future.")
5. We will have weekly "couple meetings." (Schedule the time now for your weekly couple meeting. There is no time like the present.)
6. We will make time for the great things: fun, friendship, and sensuality. We will agree to protect these times from conflict and the need to deal with issues.

CHAPTER ELEVEN

ACCOUNTING FOR LOVE

If you have built castles in the air, your work need not be lost; that is where they should be. Now put the foundations under them.

HENRY DAVID THOREAU

Remember when the two of you first fell in love? Many couples seem to live in the clouds for a while, each believing that their beloved is perfect and that their love knows no bounds. Of course, even in the beginning, we know that our partner isn't *really* perfect. She can see that he worries a bit too much, and he can see that she doesn't take responsibilities as seriously as she might. But new love tends to see those things as endearing quirks. He thinks, "She's so fun and carefree." She thinks, "He's so dependable and responsible." Some couples experience an almost euphoric state of supreme happiness for a period, each longing to be with the other, each able to think only of their beloved, each completely devoted to ensuring the other's happiness. Other couples seem to keep their "heads" to a greater degree. No matter how your relationship started out, after a time, reality likely set in. By "reality" we don't mean that your love became less valuable, but that your partner's flaws became more real to you. What was once endearing could become downright annoying. This can be a frightening and disappointing time for couples, particularly if they had unrealistic expectations about "living in the clouds" forever.

Although passion can last a lifetime, at some point love will face a "reality check." If you haven't already, you and your partner will each move from seeing each other's flaws vaguely and not caring much to seeing clearly and caring very much. When this shift happens, there are different ways you can handle that stage of your relationship.

Some marital experts suggest that couples need to understand that once the euphoric state is over, it's over. The deep passion—the burning flame—has gone out, so get over it and learn to live without those feelings, or go find a new partner and start all over again. We don't think that's the truth of love at all. We'd agree more with Henry David Thoreau when he said, "If you have built castles in the air, your work need not be lost; that is where they should be. Now put the foundations under them."

We believe that passion and deep love can last for a lifetime. It doesn't always. In fact, it doesn't often. Deep, lasting love is not common, but it is a treasure worth pursuing, protecting, even fighting for. If your love castle seems to be falling to the ground, don't just stand there and watch it collapse. Build a strong foundation underneath it. You could think of learning to recognize events, issues, hidden issues, and expectations as part of building your foundation. The same goes for learning to use the Speaker-Listener Technique, the problem-solving model, and ground rules. Yet there's more. There are two more strategies for keeping your castle from falling to the ground, and we focus on them in this chapter. First, you need to keep your partner's "love account" full. Second, you need to learn to accept your partner fully. Let's look at these two strategies in some detail.

> *Deep, lasting love is not common, but it is a treasure worth pursuing, protecting, even fighting for.*

A Banking Metaphor

Sometimes, when couples are afraid that their love castle is going to fall to the ground, they react by running. If the thing is going to fall, they want to get out from under it so they don't end up smashed by the debris. This kind of thinking makes some sense, except that if you really want to keep your castle in the clouds, then running—emotionally withdrawing or physically leaving—is the worst thing you can do. The best thing you can do is to run toward your castle and do all the things you did to build your castle in the clouds in the first place. Fortify your foundation. Because this is a book about money and marriage, we're going to switch metaphors here and start talking about making wise investments in your relationship. We're going to talk in terms of a banking metaphor.

The idea of an emotional bank account as a key metaphor for understanding marriage has been with us for some time. Clifford Notarius and Howard Markman made excellent use of the idea in their book *We Can Work It Out*. They noted that withdrawals are all the ways we hurt our partners, whether intentionally or through neglect. It's in the nature of intimate relationships that withdrawals will grow over time. The number of events and the depth of issues they can trigger guarantee it. All of these events and issues of life become potential withdrawals from your most important asset: your friendship and bond of love.

It's the nature of accounting, no matter what kind of account: if you take out more than you put in, you end up in debt. In previous chapters, we focused on helping you limit your withdrawals from your emotional bank account. Here our focus is on making deposits.

We want you to be bullish on investing in your relationship. There is no more important kind of investment you can make than those that draw the two of you closer together. We know you can go through bear markets with your love, in which your efforts don't seem to matter, but you need to take the long view, just you would when investing in stocks. You are investing for the long haul, and if you are both genuinely trying to give it your best, you are likely to reap great rewards.

Investing in the Bonds of Love

When someone invests wisely, it's not just a simple matter of making any ole deposit into any ole account. Instead, the deposits are well considered. How much, when, and where are the questions of smart investing. By investing thoughtfully and directly in your marriage, you'll not only find your love becoming stronger but also experience powerful indirect benefits when it comes time to discuss financial issues. The more loved and secure you both feel, the more you'll be able to function as a team in other key aspects of life. You'll be operating from a position of relational wealth.

Elizabeth Barrett Browning penned the famous words, "How do I love thee? Let me count the ways." We want you to think about the ways you show your love to one another. Take a piece of paper and list ten things you have done in the last month to convey love to your spouse.

Was it hard to come up with items for this list? That would be something to think about. What does that mean to you?

Now we'd like you to go back and circle the items for which your primary motivation was to show love. For example, if you listed "I cooked a certain meal for my partner," you should circle that item only if you wouldn't have cooked the same way if you were single. In other words, you did it (or regularly do it) as a specific and thoughtful investment in your love.

Did you list something like "I go to work every day" as something you do to convey your love? This action may well be something that your spouse should greatly appreciate about you in life, but for our purposes here, you have to ask whether your work pattern would be much different if the two of you were not together. We're not suggesting that everything you do needs to be solely for the benefit of your partner. But the point here is to see how much effort you are really investing in showing your spouse love just for the benefit of your spouse. How many of the items on your list were you able to circle?

Now let's reverse Elizabeth Barrett Browning's famous line: How do *you* love *me?* Let me count the ways." List ten things your partner has done in the last month that conveyed love, most powerfully, to you. We're less interested here in things that you appreciate or that you know are good for you and your family. Rather, what really said "I love you!" most clearly?

If you've been struggling a bit as a couple, please don't get hung up right now on how incomplete either of these lists seems to be. Our job is to help you make the lists more effective for you.

Accounting for Love

Although the number of loving things you do for your partner is important, it's not the only factor. In other words, it's not just the number of deposits that determines good investing. It's the different ways you can make those deposits that matter. Here, we're going discuss the major ways that people tend to give and receive love.

In his work *The Five Love Languages,* Gary Chapman focuses on the difficulties that come from differences in how two partners understand the ways to communicate love. We're not using his model, but we were inspired by his core idea: that there are various ways we all prefer to give and receive love and that misunderstandings between partners about their differences in this area can cost them opportunities to fully invest in their relationship—and, in many cases, can cause outright withdrawals. We highly recommend his book for those of you who want to go deeper in understanding how you can best show your love to your unique partner.

In our work, we've come to believe that there are six primary ways individuals complete the statement, "I feel loved when . . .":

1. I feel loved when you do something for me.
2. I feel loved when you touch me.
3. I feel loved when you give something to me.
4. I feel loved when you tell me I'm wonderful.
5. I feel loved when you spend time with me.
6. I feel loved when you talk with me.

Each item on this list is like a love account in which you can make a deposit. For each of the six different love accounts, each person needs some minimum balance in order to feel fully loved. Different accounts are more important than

others to different people. It's likely that the two of you have similarities in pre-
ferred investments, but you may experience some significant differences as well. If
those differences are undetected or are not acted on, you risk losing some of the
capital in your relationship. Let's look in more detail at each of the six accounts.

I Feel Loved When You Do Something for Me

Your partner may be deeply affected when you do something for him or her. That
may be the way of saying "I love you" that pierces to the depths of the soul.

If your partner feels loved when you do something for him or her, think of all
the opportunities you have every day: going to the grocery store, picking up the
dry cleaning, throwing a load of laundry in the wash, getting the leaves out of the
gutter, mowing the grass, cleaning out the hamster cage, washing the chunk of
toothpaste out of the sink, putting a new roll of toilet paper on the holder (the
right way—you don't earn points for putting it on backwards!), putting the toilet
seat down, painting the spare bedroom, putting the milk back in the refrigerator—
the possibilities are almost endless! I (Scott) discovered that cleaning the spider
webs out of our window wells made my wife, Nancy, a very happy woman. You
never know until you really know someone what will trip his or her trigger.

Maybe a great way to keep your love feeling like new is to keep doing the little things for your partner. Or the big things. Think about it. That's what thoughtful investing means.

I Feel Loved When You Touch Me

*It doesn't take much: a shared shower in the morning, a sexy message on his answering
machine at work, a little note in this lunchbox, a long hug before we turn off the lights.
These are the little-things-that-go-a-long-way.*

ELLEN SUE STERN

Little things can go a long way if they are the little things that count most to
your partner. All of us need physical touch—some more, some less, some one way,
some another, but everyone needs physical contact with others. Studies show that
humans fail to thrive without physical touch. Touch can mean a celebratory pat
on the back; a sympathetic caress on the cheek; a playful nibble on the neck; a
long, a reassuring hug; or making love. Some people don't feel loved without an
abundance of touch. With it, they feel secure in the love of their spouse.

When it comes to touching, your most knowledgeable instructor will be your
partner. Be sure to ask and listen to direction from your spouse on what feels good

and what does not. Don't blunder in thinking that what feels good to you will feel good to your partner, and don't expect that what feels good one time will feel good the next. Part of the power of touch to communicate love is your caring enough to learn what is pleasurable and what is not. That means communicating and paying attention to what your partner is telling you.

If sexual intercourse is the primary manner in which your mate experiences love, then taking initiative in sexual involvement might sing out love to him or her. And when you are not making an advance, you can make a consistent effort to give a recognizable "green light" when your partner makes sexual advances. We've learned over the years that when one partner is more sexually motivated than the other, it can be difficult for the highly motivated partner to discern if (or when, where, how often) it's OK to communicate the desire to his or her partner. If you are married to a person who really craves your love in this way, help him or her know when it's OK to pursue you.

Maybe you're thinking, "Wait a minute! Are you saying that I should have sex whenever my partner wants to? Even if I don't feel like it?" Not really, although there are likely many times when love pushes itself to meet the other's needs, even if you're not experiencing the same need at the same moment. Sometimes your partner's account needs some deposits even if yours does not.

When learning to give to your partner sexually, it can help to understand sexual desire. You can think about the desire for sexual intercourse as a combination of a desire for physical release, a psychological desire to "take," and a psychological desire to "give." We believe that nearly everyone will, at times, desire sexual intercourse in which only one or two of these components come into play. For example, at times, one may desire only physical release and to take. One may simply desire to give. Two partners can meet very different desires in the same physical acts.

We believe it is perfectly OK for a mate simply to "want" his or her partner at times, without primarily desiring to give. However, if this is "typical" of one partner, then there will be issues. This love account is one for which consistent taking without giving does not tend to go over very well.

If you are not in the mood, jumping into bed is not your only option. Doing so can leave you feeling used instead of feeling good about giving to your mate. You can give without being taken. For example, as an expression of your love, you can take care of your partner sexually by some other activity designed for your partner's benefit or pleasure, such as a quick shower together or something else that works for the two of you. It's a sign of an open, safe relationship if each of you can tell the other things like this: "You know, I'd really like it if you'd sometimes do A, B, or C just for no reason at all other than that you want to show me how much you love me."

When it comes to lovemaking, many couples can improve their investment strategies by getting some advice from experts—a point not unlike one we'll make when we get to specific financial advice later in this book. You can read books that give you new ideas or watch videos that are designed to teach you more. Go to a large bookstore and browse the relationship, romance, or sexuality section. That in itself might be a lot of fun. Pick out a book or two that appeals to both of you in terms of the tone and content, and make a promise to read it together.

I Feel Loved When You Give Something to Me

Gift giving can be hard work. Some of us don't tell our partners exactly what we want. What kind of gifts do you like? Expensive? Handmade? Store-bought? Something practical or something that's a "luxury"? Do you like tools or clothes or art? Some of us are very hard to please. Some of us just hate to see our partner spend money on us. If one of you is deeply affected by thoughtful gifts, large or small, it will be very important for the two of you to understand this and have some sense of what kinds of giving convey love the most clearly.

If you are one who feels loved when you receive gifts, help your partner learn what kind of gifts you like. We find that, as in so many other areas of relationships, some people expect their partner to read their minds about what pleases them. Further, some add to this mix the belief that if their partner can't figure it out, he or she really doesn't love them. It's hardly fair to ask your partner to pass a test when you haven't helped him or her study for it.

If you are one who really responds to tangible gifts, find ways to help your partner understand what you like best. You could do that by making a list and sharing it. Or you could sit down together and go through a favorite catalogue or two, pointing out the kinds of things you really like. It can help one partner know how he or she might surprise the other if the two of them have already shared some clear ideas. Another way to help your partner understand what kinds of gifts you like is to be extra appreciative of the things you like best.

June and her husband have had quite a time of getting it right. When first married, June didn't know much about tools, and Marv, you guessed it, is Mr. Tool-Man to the max. For Christmas one year, he asked June for a wonder bar. She went to the hardware store and bought him one. He found it in his stocking Christmas morning. In July, he explained to her that he hadn't wanted a crow bar; he wanted a wonder bar. "Oh—sorry, Honey." So, next Christmas, June went back to see her friends at Ace Hardware. She bought Marv a set of wonder bars. He very sweetly thanked her for the six-inch miniature wonder bars and asked if next Christmas she could get the standard size. "Oh, heck." So, next year, June went back to Ace and got him a set of cat's claws, a set of all sizes of wonder bars, some crow bars, and a set of screwdrivers for good measure. (Marv admitted to us that the previous summer he'd bought a wonder bar, but he still hasn't told June. Smart guy!)

Often money becomes a real hang-up when it comes to gift giving. It's very easy for deeper issues to get triggered around gifts. For example, savers, in particular, tend to feel resistance to the idea of spending money as an expression of love. You don't buy stuff for yourself, so why should you buy stuff for your spouse? Recognize that you actually are buying something for yourself when you save, whether it's security or a sense of self-worth. Sure, it's responsible and desirable to save money. But it's also wise to make deposits in this gift account if it means a lot to your partner.

But what if you're just not a gift giver? Maybe you didn't receive many gifts growing up. Maybe you don't have the knack for selecting good gifts. Well, the good news is that you've now discovered something new that you can learn so as to become a better lover. Start giving gifts immediately. It's likely that you're overdrawn in this account.

I Feel Loved When You Tell Me I'm Wonderful

Mark Twain once said, "I can live for two months on a good compliment." If you are Mrs. Twain, all you have to do is compliment your husband six times a year, and you're all set. Everyone else probably has a bit more work to do.

Learning to tell your partner about how special he or she is and how much you appreciate him or her is like almost any other skill we can learn. Some of us are naturally talented, and some of us have to work at it, but all of us can learn to do it well.

You can start by saying things like "You're handsome [beautiful]." Then you can be more specific: "You have incredible eyes." Try to increase your repertoire of adjectives. If you say, "You look nice," your partner may be pleased with the compliment for the first couple of years, but then you might want you to throw in "You look hot!" for a bit of variety.

Try not to get into a rut by always complimenting the same characteristic. Don't just focus on how your partner looks, for example. Tell your partner what it is about who he or she is and what he or she does that you believe is wonderful. You might try saying,

> "I'm glad I met you."
>
> "You're fun to be with."
>
> "I like talking with you; I always feel better after we've talked."
>
> "You're wise."
>
> "I'm glad I married you."
>
> "Thanks for going to work today."
>
> "Thanks for doing the dishes."
>
> "Thanks for being so focused on the kids when I'm out with my friends."

Saying thank you can be very powerful. How long has it been since you thanked your partner in some specific way? One of the most common mistakes we see people make is to cling to the attitude that you should say thanks only for extraordinary behavior. "Why should I thank him for doing what he should do?" We respond to this question with a query of our own: What's *should* got to do with it? There are a lot of people who . . .

Should do their share of the housework, but don't.

Should pay the bills, but don't.

Should put gas in the tank when it's empty, but bring it home with the big E flashing.

Should tell you how much they appreciate you, but don't.

If you married someone who does what he or she should, maybe it's something you *shouldn't* take for granted.

I Feel Loved When You Spend Time with Me

Doing something together can be a way to express your love and friendship. You can cook dinner together, paint the house together, go shopping for a car together—any of these activities might qualify. Watching a television show together may or may not qualify as a deposit for the two of you. You'll have to ask your spouse. For one spouse, doing chores won't count as doing something together. For another, it will. For one spouse, doing something together might mean not having the kids or other friends along. For another, it may feel like time together only if the couple leaves the home.

How Long Has It Been?

In the nationwide random phone survey we conducted with our friend Gary Smalley in 1995, we asked each respondent how long it'd been since they'd gone on a date with their partner. On average, couples were going close to two months without having a date. While this may seem a short time to some of you, we believe it's one sign that most couples are not having enough fun together.

The most intriguing result from that survey was that men reported going out on dates substantially more frequently than women. In some groups, women said it had been twice as long as what the men reported. Why is that? Our best guess is that men and woman have different definitions or standards for what a date is. Use this finding to stimulate some conversation about what a date means to each of you or, more generally, what kinds of time together mean the most to each of you.

You don't both have to enjoy each kind of activity together in the same way or to the same degree. If your partner is a golfer but you're not, go take golfing lessons and then make a date to show off all you've learned. If you're not an opera lover but your partner is crazy about it, surprise your mate with two tickets to *Porgy and Bess.*

I Feel Loved When You Talk with Me

We (Scott and Howard) see couples in counseling in addition to the research we do on marital success and failure. When a couple comes into either of our offices, it's common for the wives to complain about husbands who don't open up and talk—or listen. Women who complain that their spouse does not talk do not mean literally that their husband never says a word. They mean that he seldom takes part in intimate conversation.

There are different kinds of conversations. There's small talk about such topics as the weather. There's pragmatic talk about who's taking which kid to baseball practice. There's planning talk about how you'd like to handle the next vacation. There's teaching talk about how to work the new VCR. There's opinion talk, during which you discover that your partner thinks a landscape painting would look better in the living room than the still life you just bought. These are all different kinds of talking, and they're all fine in their own way. However, if you are married to a partner who feels loved when you talk with him or her, none of these kinds of talk are likely going to cut it. What your spouse is after is intimate talk.

For many of us, to disrobe in front of our partner is a deeply intimate act. We are allowing our partner to gaze upon us. In a similar fashion, to talk and reveal ourselves emotionally is a deep form of intimacy. When two people open their minds and their hearts, each allowing the other to gaze upon him or her, and when each gazes in total acceptance, that is the deepest of all forms of human connection. That is intimacy of the soul.

One obstacle to intimacy is fear. The possibility of rejection is a risk some feel is too high. That is your choice. We think that people vary in risk tolerance emotionally just as they vary in risk tolerance in financial investing. We cannot guarantee that your partner will accept you fully. We can only guarantee that if you do not take the risk, you will not find intimacy.

Often couples ruin their ability to remain close and connected through conversation by failing to talk the way best friends talk. Most couples start with some ability to talk together about all kinds of interesting things, including hopes, hobbies, dreams, fears, and interests. Unfortunately for many couples, these talks that fuel the development of love and commitment are often replaced through the years by talks that focus mostly on problems and issues. Sure, you have to talk about those things or else you are asking for trouble. But do you also make time to just relax and talk as friends?

Asset Allocation

Now we invite you to take stock of your investments in the six love accounts. To help you work through this, we'll borrow a device often used in statistical analyses of money: the pie chart.

Here's the idea. We want each of you to make pie charts and then talk about them. As an example, Figure 14 shows a graph of the six love accounts in the case where a person values each equally.

For nearly all of us, some types of deposits matter far more than others. Figure 15 shows what a graph might look like for a person who is deeply affected by touch and verbal affirmation and less affected by other types of deposits.

Figure 16 shows what a person might draw who is so affected by talking and being heard that anything else is small potatoes in comparison.

Now that you have the idea, take out a piece of paper and make four circles on it. If you are both doing this exercise, please do this first part on your own, before comparing answers. On the piece of paper, divide up each circle to reflect the pieces of the pie for the following four questions. Label your four circles 1 through 4 to keep track of which one is reflecting what question here:

1. Draw the pieces of pie 1 to reflect what kinds of love affect you most.
2. Draw the pieces of pie 2 in a way that reflects how you think your partner loves you. In other words, what does he or she actually do?
3. Now draw the pieces of pie 3 in the way that reflects what you think affects your partner most.
4. Finally, draw the pieces of pie 4 in a way that reflects what you tend to do to show love to your partner.

FIGURE 14. SIX LOVE ACCOUNTS OF EQUAL VALUE.

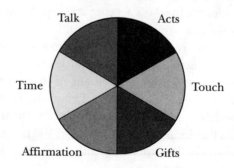

FIGURE 15. HIGH VALUE FOR TOUCH AND VERBAL AFFIRMATION.

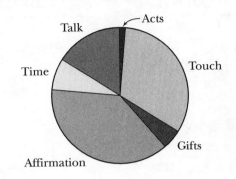

As you have probably realized by now, there are differences in both the *types* of deposits and the *amount* of deposits that matter in your relationship. In other words, within a given pie, the size of the different pieces can vary. And the entire pie can be smaller than you wish it were, even if the pieces were nearly in the right proportions. What we're saying is that the chart in Figure 17 is going to feel very different from the one in Figure 18, even though the proportions are the same.

As you can readily see, this way of thinking can help you understand why, even though you may be doing things specifically to express love to your partner, your partner may still not feel loved. And vice versa. You may not be expressing love in the ways or in the amounts that mean the most to each other. Do you want to live large? Go for the bigger pie.

FIGURE 16. HIGH VALUE FOR TALKING AND BEING HEARD.

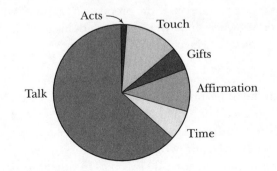

FIGURE 17. LARGER PIE OF LOVE ACCOUNTS.

FIGURE 18. SMALLER PIE OF LOVE ACCOUNTS.

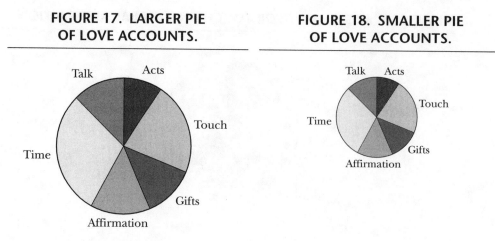

For your partner to feel deeply loved, you need to be making the right kinds of deposits in the right amounts. With your piece of paper and your thoughts that have been building throughout this chapter, we'd like the two of you to plan some time to sit down and compare notes. Carve out some time that will allow some fruitful discussion and exploration of these themes. You'll want to pick some time when you are not otherwise stressed and when each of you can be at your best to really hear what is in the other's mind and heart. Here are some questions that can help you in this discussion:

- How accurate were you in estimating the sizes of the pieces of pie in your partner's picture of what means the most to him or her? And how accurate was your partner in knowing what means the most to you?
- Do the efforts you see yourself making match what your partner has perceived you as trying to do, even if the proportions are not those your partner prefers?
- How do you each think you have been doing as a couple in expressing love in the total picture? Have things been slipping?

Most important, talk through—and take some time doing—the things you each wish the other might do more often that would have the greatest impact on your love accounts. One way to do this is for each of you to consider the two largest sections of the pie you drew to show what expressions of love mean the most to you (pie 1), and write out three very specific things your partner can do that fit in that category. Be specific. In other words, don't just say, "I wish you'd talk with me more." Say something specific enough that you'll both know whether it happened or not—something like, "On Thursday night, instead of watching *Star Trek*, I'd like for us to sit in the living room and talk about our favorite vacations."

If you've done what we suggest here, you now have two key pieces of information that we want you to act on, regularly: the pie chart that best reflects what your partner wants and needs most from you, and six specific ideas from him or her about meeting those desires. Put this information somewhere where the two of you will see it often. Commit to putting serious effort into making these things happen in the coming weeks, and watch what unfolds.

It's the Thought That Counts

Too often we try to make deposits with our partners by focusing only on the accounts that mean the most to us personally. For example, if she needs a deposit in her "talk with me" account, she'll grab her guy for a talk. She'll feel loved, which is great. What's not so great is that she assumes that because she's feeling loved, he must be too. But he's a different human being with different needs, so he may not be feeling loved. He may be desperate for a deposit into the "touch me" account instead.

Let's be honest: most of us are not as thoughtful in our giving of love as we could be. It's just too easy to be lazy and to focus on our favored account, which may not be our partner's most important account. Our hope is that both of you would learn to express love in the ways that mean the most to your partner. But we'd also like for you to be gracious in allowing your partner to express love for you in ways that feel natural to him or her, too. You don't always have to express love in ways that feel most natural to your partner. Nor should you insist on receiving love in only the accounts that matter the most to you. It is also loving to accept your partner's love even when it's not expressed in ways that mean the most to you. If you really think about what the love account exercise can teach you, you'll be better able to recognize when your partner is trying to show love to you, whether it is in a key account or a minor one.

Keeping Accounts Versus Making Deposits

If you've been doing a good job of loving your partner, hooray for you! Just don't let up. But beware of a trap that many of us fall into from time to time: the trap of thinking that you are the one who's making all the deposits and your partner isn't. You can get to feeling like a martyr who's giving and giving without recognition.

It's generally bad for a relationship when one or both partners are closely keeping score as to who is doing what for whom.

Once you are thinking that way—once you are carefully comparing account balances—you're in trouble. As we talked about in an earlier chapter, scorekeeping is fundamentally unfair because you will always be aware of everything you do, so you'll give yourself more points. Because you can't see everything your partner does or thinks, he or she will lose the competition, even if in reality the score is the same. Look hard and thoughtfully at the various ways your partner shows love to you—and don't look only at the accounts that mean the most to you.

If you've lost your way as a couple, the work you did on your pie charts gives you powerful ways to get back on track. Maybe you're saying, "Yeah, but my partner hasn't been doing anything for me, so I shouldn't have to do anything for him [her]." Maybe you're angry or hurting. Feeling unloved can hurt deeply, and you have our sympathy. We, the authors, have all had times when we felt unloved, and we know how hard it is. But if you are struggling with such thoughts, ask yourself: How will thinking "I won't do anything for my partner because he [she] doesn't deserve it" help you? If you *won't* do the things you *can* do, then you are truly stuck. Take the chance to live differently.

You could easily read this book and come up with an excuse as to why nothing here would be helpful to you. But that will mean you've wasted the money you spent on this book, and all you'll get is to continue complaining to your friends, "Poor me. I've tried everything, and my husband [wife] just doesn't care." Instead, if you have the courage to admit that you're human and that you can do better in loving your partner, then you can make a difference. Your partner may or may not respond, but you will feel better knowing that you're behaving in a loving way. You'll be doing your part in keeping your love castle in the sky.

Acceptance and Love

Love is the heart's immortal thirst to be completely known and all forgiven.

HENRY VAN DYKE

The focus of this chapter is on two of the essential components of keeping love and passion alive. The first is keeping your partner's love account full. The second is learning to accept your partner fully. We didn't include acceptance in the love account model because it is more than simply another way to *express* love. Acceptance is actually a part of love itself. One way that you accept your partner, for example, is by respecting that his or her key ways of giving and receiving love may be different from yours. If you are unable to appreciate and accept that difference, you'll miss out on "seeing" some of the loving things he or she does for you. You'll also miss out on acting on the most potent ways you can show your love to your partner.

You express your love to your partner during the new-love phase and during the later stages as well. Acceptance, in contrast, can only come into play once you've hit that "reality check" when you can see your partner's flaws clearly. Love isn't very special if each partner is loving someone who is "perfect." How hard is it to adore something that is wonderful in every way? How hard is it to want to do something for someone who always has your best interests at heart and always

Love doesn't get a chance to use its muscles until you can each truly see the flaws of the other.

thinks of you first? Love doesn't even get a chance to use its muscles, so to speak, until you can each truly see the flaws of the other.

Although it is nice to have a partner who thinks we're perfect, that is nothing compared to the powerful connection that arises from being fully loved and accepted even though the other knows we are not perfect. Acceptance is so potent a force in a relationship that in Chapter Four we said it is the driving force behind all hidden issues. Here we'll show you how it is one of the most potent forces of love. Acceptance is where love gets to develop some muscle. To be fully known and yet loved anyway—that's the strong foundation on which lasting passion can be built. Judith Viorst explains it this way: "Infatuation is when you think that he's as sexy as Robert Redford, as smart as Henry Kissinger, as noble as Ralph Nader, as funny as Woody Allen, and as athletic as Jimmy Connors. Love is when you realize he's as sexy as Woody Allen, as smart as Jimmy Connors, as funny as Ralph Nader, as athletic as Henry Kissinger and nothing like Robert Redford—but you'll take him anyway."

Acceptance Takes Two

To make deposits into your partner's love accounts, you need only one: you. You just do it. Either of you can decide on any given day to express your love without the other's having to do anything but be around for it to happen. In contrast, acceptance requires something of both of you. One of the deepest forms of acceptance requires a special opportunity—usually something that makes your partner vulnerable or that puts his or her idiosyncrasies on display—and you choose to accept instead of reject your partner at this vulnerable moment.

Sadly, many people won't let their partner be vulnerable, whether because they don't want to see weakness in their partner, because hearing their partner be vulnerable raises anxieties in their own minds, or because they just have no idea what to do when their partner's pain or sense of failure is oozing out. This is sad because it means that the couple is missing an opportunity to go deeper in terms of love and intimacy. Let's look at an example of how one couple handled a vulnerable moment.

George and Suzie were typical newlyweds planning their life together. They'd known each other for a couple of years, and both felt that the choice to marry was very right. If you will, they'd done their due diligence. They knew each other well. They knew what their dynamics were like. They knew how to work though complex issues. But they didn't know how to talk about deeper vulnerabilities—at least, they hadn't really tested this out.

The problem was that George had racked up about $23,000 in credit card debt before he met Suzie. He felt awful about it, too. He could not imagine how he'd ever pay those debts down, and the shame of it left him unable to face it within himself, much less able to tell Suzie about it. So he didn't tell her.

This couple's situation may not be a part of your experience, but it's an increasingly common occurrence. Because the average person is waiting till he or she is a bit older to get married—compared to years ago when people married younger—the average person has more time to accumulate debts prior to marriage. Research conducted at the Creighton University Center for Marriage and Family has demonstrated that the discovery of the indebtedness of one's partner has become a common, major problem for couples in the first year of marriage.

Suzie found out about George's debts the hard way, about three months into their marriage. He had to take a business trip and was not able to do what he'd so successfully done up to that point: intercept the mail before she saw it. And in came the statements.

Warts and All

James Cordova is a psychologist who conducts research on intimacy at the University of Illinois at Urbana-Champaign. He's done a lot of thinking about what intimacy is. Although there are many answers, he suggests that the deepest kind of intimacy occurs when one partner shares something he or she feels vulnerable about and the other partner responds in a positive and accepting manner. This kind of warm acceptance can transform a relationship.

When the two of you can talk on this level, you've got something that many people don't. You have the kind of safety that allows you to be fully known by one another. If you cannot now share on this level, don't despair. Many couples cannot. But it's something you can shoot for, something you can learn. We believe that doing so is a great goal for any couple. Using something like our Speaker-Listener Technique might help the two of you get there. However you go about it, if this is a very powerful way one of you would like to receive love from the other, take the risk to share that with your partner. Then, with care and compassion, try making it happen over the next month and see how it goes.

Suzie figured, "We're married now. I'm sure he won't mind if I open any of the bills when they come in." Oops. Suzie was stunned, then crushed, then depressed as she got a clear vision of the level of debt George had developed before they met. She felt betrayed. It's not that George had intentionally wanted to deceive her—though he did intentionally deceive her. Rather, he was simply too embarrassed to tell her what was going on with his financial situation.

Once the facts were in the open, George handled it as well as anyone could. He was not defensive, and he owned up both to the problem and to his having hidden it from Suzie. That's where the surprise set in for him. Suzie was deeply hurt, but she was also greatly accepting once he was fully open and vulnerable. She told him that she was hurt and angry that he'd kept such a secret from her. She didn't mince words. Yet she also told him, "I know you. I know that you are capable of deep caring and wonderful fun. I also know that you are capable of making pretty big mistakes. And I love all of you. You don't love people in pieces." He never felt so accepted, so loved, in all his life.

That experience, though unpleasant for a time, became a key to their abiding love for years to come. In this example, George could not bring himself to be that vulnerable, but circumstances sort of forced it on him. Yet, with the opportunity at hand, Suzie showed George just how completely she loved him by accepting him in this.

In using this example, we're not suggesting that all couples could walk the same path to deeper love that Suzy and George did. For example, suppose that prior to marriage Suzy had specifically asked him, several times, about his debts, and he had lied to her about them. That situation would require them to walk a whole different path—one involving a deep look at forgiveness. Whether or not there has been deceit, a person who hasn't been open with his mate or fiancée about debts needs not only to come to that point and take that risk but also to make sure he is changing the spending behaviors that got him into that much debt in the first place. Acceptance of vulnerability is an extremely powerful part of love, but it's not one to be taken advantage of time and time again. We are encouraging you to accept your *partner*, not to accept consistently inappropriate *behavior*.

Acceptance meets the most fundamental of human needs: to know that you are lovable just as you are.

We're not talking about tolerance, either. We make a distinction between tolerance and acceptance. Tolerance is allowing someone to be themselves without necessarily fully approving. It is merely enduring. Acceptance, in contrast, is much richer. Much deeper. Acceptance is receiving with approval. It is saying, "You are a person of value." Acceptance meets the most fundamental of human needs: to know that you are lovable just as you are—that you, the real you, is enough. Imperfect, yes; inadequate, no.

Suzy and George got through this difficult time in their lives because they learned how to talk, and to talk deeply. George, when his mistake became known, chose to own up to it. He allowed himself to face this vulnerability, and Suzie chose acceptance. They chose to add to the strong foundation that would keep their castle in the clouds.

Moving Forward

We said at the outset of this chapter that passion can last a lifetime. One of the keys to making this happen is to learn to love your partner in ways that mean the most to him or her. With your understanding of the ways of expressing love that mean the most to your partner, think about how you can express your love most effectively. These are likely the kinds of things you did when you first experienced deep intimacy and passion together. If you are doing well, these expressions play a crucial role in keeping your foundation strong. If your foundation has started to crumble, they are ways you can fortify it once again. And always work toward fully accepting your partner—warts and all.

PART THREE

SHOW US THE MONEY

INTRODUCTION TO
MONEY MANAGEMENT

Did you know that it doesn't take a fortune to achieve financial independence? It doesn't take a winning lottery ticket either. Really. There are normal, average couples all over America *deciding* to become financially independent. They are not hoping, wishing, or trying. They are deciding to go for it, and they are doing it.

The Average Family's Guide to Financial Freedom is the financial autobiography of Bill and Mary Toohey. In 1991, they had a combined income of $34,000 and a net worth of around $63,000. They were an average couple in their thirties. They had a daughter in high school, a son with severe disabilities and health problems, and a daughter in elementary school. They had a mortgage, car payments, and college bills to look forward to. By 1999, the couple had paid cash for a new car; covered the costs of many medical expenses and orthodontia; helped their daughter pay for her wedding and get a debt-free college education; extensively remodeled their son's room; and made some expensive home improvements and repairs, including all-new kitchen appliances, a new roof, and new central heating and air conditioning. During that time, Bill's salary never broke through $40,000, and Mary had just topped $20,000. Yet in just eight years, the couple added more than $400,000 to their bottom line. They are just a few years away from achieving financial freedom; according to the Tooheys, "A family has achieved financial freedom when they are able to pay for all of their living expenses, for the rest of their lives, utilizing their assets and 10 to 15 hours of work per week, per spouse, until Social Security, Medicare, and pension eligibility."

The Tooheys did not follow any get-rich-quick scheme. No gimmicks were involved at all. They did it without winning the lottery. They did it without buying the year's number one stock. No fancy investment schemes. Not even a financial planner. They did all this without suffering. The Tooheys are a great example of what teamwork and sound money management can do. They could *not* have done what they did if they had allowed their issues, hidden issues, and expectations to push them off course. They could not have done what they did if they had spent their time and energy fighting about money instead of managing it as a team. It isn't rocket science. The Tooheys did it by knowing what to do, and doing it. You can too.

A Fresh Look at Income and Expenses

Because a picture is often worth a thousand words, let's look at some money graphs to see where we are going in the chapters ahead. Pretend that what we have depicted in Figure 19 is your income and how it will likely go up for some years to come. No matter what your level of income, we've assumed that your income will tend to rise slightly over the years. Your actual line could be less steep or straight up; it may even go down over time. But this is a pretty good way to think about how it plays out for most people.

Figure 20 shows how most couples go through life. As their income rises, their expenses rise, so they never seem to get ahead.

In Figure 20, the expenses are equal to income, which means the couple is at least staying even. Unfortunately, some couples aren't even making more than they spend. For those who are spending more than they have, and getting deeper and deeper into debt, their graph might look something like Figure 21.

FIGURE 19. INCOME OVER TIME.

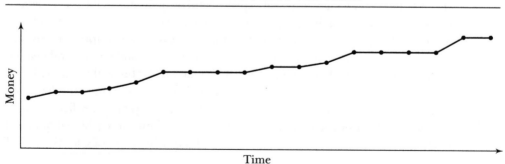

FIGURE 20. INCOME AND EXPENSES OVER TIME.

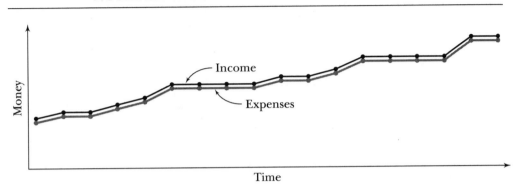

FIGURE 21. EXPENSES SOMETIMES GREATER THAN INCOME.

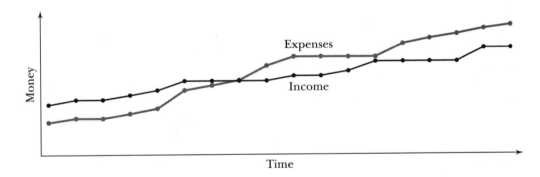

Now we want to make a point about money that we've never seen made in any better way than in the book *Your Money or Your Life,* by Joe Dominguez and Vicki Robin. Look at Figure 22; it shows what happens when you start lowering your expenses.

That space between your income and your expenses represents *your money.* That's the money that you don't hand over to the credit card companies or the car salesman or anybody else. It's *yours.* And that means that you can use that money to invest. Investing means you can own things that grow in value (we hope!) and *pay you.* In Figure 23, we've added a new line for investments.

That new line may or may not be very exciting for you. We'd be surprised if you hadn't heard this before. But have you *seen* it? Have you ever seen what that money can do for you? Do you see that new, third line on the graph in Figure 23? That's the investment income that you get when you invest your money over time.

FIGURE 22. INCOME GREATER THAN EXPENSES.

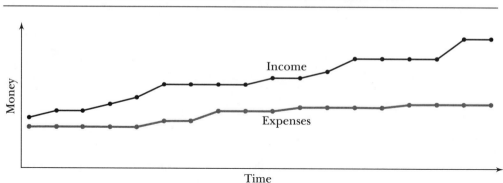

FIGURE 23. BRINGING INVESTMENT INTO THE PICTURE.

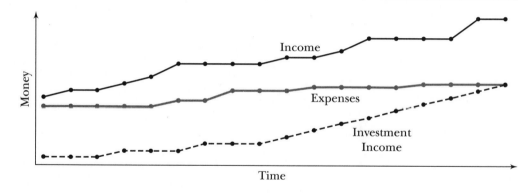

Sometimes it feels as though saving or investing is just throwing money into a black hole, and you'll never see it again. That may be true if you stuff it under your mattress. But if you make sound investments, then you'll start to see your money working for you.

Although it may take quite a while (or it may not), look at what can happen when that investment income line goes even higher. It's going to cross over and above the expenses line, as shown in Figure 24.

Look at Figure 24 for a moment, please. This shows what happens when your investment income becomes greater than your expenses. It's called financial freedom. You have enough income coming in from your investments to cover your expenses, so you're not dependent on your job anymore. You don't have to quit your job, but you *could*. Or you could cut back from how hard you are working to spend

FIGURE 24. FINANCIAL FREEDOM: INVESTMENT INCOME BECOMES GREATER THAN EXPENSES.

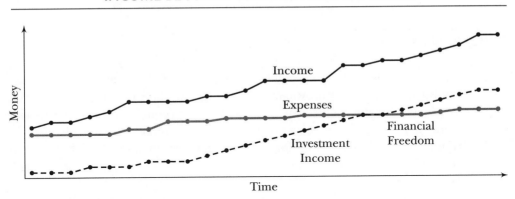

more time enjoying your partner and your children. You decide. You'd have the freedom to do whatever you wanted with your time—you could be a volunteer, you could start a new career, you could spend all day on the golf course or going fishing, or you could continue living just as you are, but you'd know that you didn't *have* to anymore.

That's just what the Tooheys did. They lowered their expenses and increased their investment income. In eight years, on a salary that never topped $60,000, they had reached the point where they could, without lifting a finger again to earn an income, pay for their food, clothing, shelter (house, heat, air conditioning, utilities, phone, house maintenance and repairs, house insurance, property taxes, appliances, household furnishing, cable TV, and Internet access), transportation (car, car insurance, car license, and maintenance), dental care, miscellaneous expenses, and some medical expenses. They were planning on dropping down to working ten to fifteen hours per week in the next couple of years, except that they decided they wanted to buy a house by a lake, so they're going to work a couple years beyond that. That's freedom.

Maybe financial freedom isn't what you're after. Maybe it is. The point is that whatever your financial goals are, you have a real shot at achieving them. What you long to have happen may be more possible than you think, especially if you are great teammates in life. Now that the two of you understand the forces that tend to push couples off their course, and how the two of you can work together to create teamwork within your relationship, you're ready to tackle the fundamentals of money management. The two of you *can* decide what you want, go after it, and get it. We don't mean to imply that all of life falls under your control, like some puppet on your string. Of course there will always be much that is beyond your control, but the combined forces of teamwork and sound financial knowledge are very powerful. The two of you *can* decide what you want, go after it and get it.

Where We're Headed

We're headed wherever you want to go. We're going to help the two of you figure out what it is that you really want, and how to get it. There is a catch, though. (You were expecting this, right?) The catch is that you're going to have to learn about some things that may not be all that exciting to learn about. You might enjoy it. You might not. You're also going to have to do some things that might not qualify as *fun*. They might even be considered *work*. So consider yourselves warned. Success is *not* for wimps.

We're headed into the money management section of this book. We're going to go through all the nitty-gritty of how to get what you want. Then, when you really believe that you *can* do it, we'll help you figure out what it is that you want to go after. Here's what we're going to cover in Chapters Twelve through Eighteen:

> **Success is not for wimps.**

Getting It Together: We'll start by helping you figure out how to organize all your financial documents.

What Do You Have? You'll learn to create a balance sheet and figure out how much money you've got coming in and how much you've got going out.

Smart Borrowing, Dumb Debt: Here we'll talk about the wise use of credit cards and loans.

Insurance: How to Protect What You've Got: We cover the basics of how to protect what you've got.

Taxes: Keeping More of What You Make: We'll talk about how to keep more of what you earn.

A Penny Saved Is . . . Not Much! How to Control Spending: This is where we dare to use the "B word"—budgeting.

Investing: How to Get More: We introduce you to the various ways to make your money work for you.

Are you ready to look at how the two of you can master your money together instead of being controlled by it? Then, as our editor so often says, *onward!*

CHAPTER TWELVE

GETTING IT TOGETHER

The ability to simplify means to eliminate the unnecessary so that the necessary may speak.

HANS HOFMANN

In this chapter, we're going to help you get organized. For some, "Let's get organized" sounds fun. For others, it sounds like as much fun as a root canal. No matter which category you fall into, the two of you need to come up with a system for keeping things organized—at least organized just well enough to get the job done.

Here's some good news for you. Many professionals in the financial industry are similar in their preference for rather compulsive organization. Two of the four authors of this book have these tendencies and are grinning broadly as they acknowledge this strength (weakness?) in themselves. The other two authors are *not* this way—sad for them, we know. Perhaps for the first time in history, a couple of authors of a financial guidance book are going to publicly shout, "WE ARE GREAT FANS OF THE 'DON'T TOUCH MY PILE ON THE FLOOR' SYSTEM, AND IT WORKS QUITE WELL, THANK YOU!" So, to maintain our own integrity, we want to recommend that the two of you choose a system that works for *you*, not insist on one that works for at least some of us.

Your system is working for you if your important financial documents are in a location that is accessible and convenient so that the two of you can use the information on a regular basis, you don't waste a lot of your time trying to find something, and you both like it. If you like your system, you can skip the rest of

"HEY, LOOK, NO BIG DEAL, IF YOU'RE TIRED OF HANDLING THE BUDGET, I COULD TAKE IT OVER AGAIN."

this chapter if you want. Or you can keep reading to see if you can pick up any tips that might make your system even better. If your system isn't working (or if the two of you don't agree), then keep reading.

Quick Quiz: Do You Know Where It's at?

We're not asking that question as a throwback to the 1960s, wanting to know if you are hip or not. We know you are hip and groovy, or you wouldn't be reading this book. But do you know where all your key financial documents "are at," right at this moment? We recommend you each write down your answers to this question about each of the following items, and then compare notes. This may be a good exchange of information for the two of you. So, where do you have the following information?

Bank accounts

Insurance policies

Tax records

Records of house purchase

Listing of major possessions for insurance purposes (in case your home burned or was robbed)

Information on loans, including home, auto, and credit cards

While you're at it, can you name each of the following people, and do you know how to contact him or her?

Insurance agent(s)

Tax professional or accountant

Health insurance adviser

Often, one of the partners knows far more than the other about these basics. This is a good time for the two of you to make sure that both of you have at least a good sense of what's where and who to call if you need help.

Here's some more good news. As we've talked with different couples over the years, we've noticed what seems to be a common misconception about what it takes to manage their finances well. Couples seem to assume that it takes a whole lot of time. It can, but we don't think it should. In fact, let's see if you've learned one of the key points of this book yet. It's a one-question quiz:

1. Once a couple has spent the minimum amount of time needed to manage their finances well, a wise couple will spend an extra fifteen minutes:
   a. Reviewing their bank statement again.
   b. Making love.

If you chose "a," go directly to Chapter One, do not pass Go, and do not collect $200! No, our goal is not to convince you to start spending lots of time on your finances. There's a minimum level of management necessary to financial success; beyond that, your relationship is far more important. Our goal is to help you spend as little time as possible managing your money well so that you can go do other, more fun kinds of things (as in answer b). It's different if you *enjoy* organizing your finances and gaining financial expertise. In that case, you can almost make it a hobby that you enjoy together. You can spend lots of time on it, and it can be fun.

However, if paying bills or researching mutual funds isn't your thing, then you don't have to spend tons of time on it to succeed.

> *There's a minimum level of management necessary to financial success; beyond that, your relationship is far more important.*

In his book *Ordinary People, Extraordinary Wealth*, best-selling author Ric Edelman states, "If my clients are any guide, then time is perhaps the one thing that's not a prerequisite for achieving wealth. Indeed, according to the findings of our research, our clients spend on average 2.4 hours per month on money matters. And that includes the time they devote to paying their bills." It also includes balancing the checkbook, making deposits, and anything else. So let's go over the basics of organizing your financial documents so that you don't spend one more minute of your life managing money than you want to.

Getting It Together

Some financial documents are pretty important to keep. Start by sorting all those documents into different categories. If your partner doesn't want to help, that's OK. You can do this on your own. Put each category into a separate pile, pizza box, file folder, or whatever you fancy. The following categories work pretty well for most couples:

I. Personal Papers
   A. Birth certificates
   B. Marriage license
   C. Medical records
   D. Divorce settlements (if any)
   E. Wills
   F. Power of attorney
II. Insurance Policies
   A. Health
   B. Life
   C. Auto
   D. Homeowners
   E. Disability

   III. Banking
      A. Account statements
      B. Cancelled checks (if you still receive them)
      C. Certificates of deposit (CDs)
   IV. Bills
      A. To be paid
      B. One pile or file for each company you owe
      C. Telephone
      D. Gas and electric
      E. Cable TV
      F. Other
   V. Credit Cards and Other Loans
      A. Terms
      B. Statements
   VI. Income Statements
   VII. Investment Records
      A. IRA account records
      B. Brokerage records
   VII. Major Appliances
      A. Receipts
      B. Warranties
      C. Operating instructions
   VIII. Taxes
      A. Receipts
      B. Returns

What to Keep and What to Toss

Some financial documents you have to keep for a long time. Other papers are just clutter, and you can toss them out. Which is which?

You don't have to keep the bills from your insurance policies, and be certain to toss all your old policies if you have no outstanding claims against them. You don't have to keep bills for your telephone, cable TV, or the like once you know your current statement is correct. You don't need to keep your pay stubs more than a year, because if you ask nicely, your employer can reproduce them.

It might be easiest to keep everything for a year and then once per year toss out what you don't need and put into archives what you do need. Many financial professionals now recommend that you shred any financial papers when you throw them out because of the increasingly rampant crime of identify theft. Shredders are quite inexpensive, and repairing the damage done if someone has stolen your financial identity is anything but.

Bank statements and cancelled checks should be kept for seven years in case the IRS audits you. Brokerage records are very important. Both brokers and the SEC contend that you should keep all statements forever. However, after you have checked them carefully and confirmed that they're accurate, there is little reason to keep them longer than seven years. Records for investments that are taxable are very important. Be certain to keep your trade confirmation slips. When and if you make a trade, you can match the buy and sell records and prepare your taxes knowing that you have documentation for all trades and the material for calculating your capital gains. Your IRA account records are also important, especially those for which you used after-tax dollars for your contributions.

Hold on to all information regarding terms and conditions for your credit card accounts. Essentially, these are loan documents, and you occasionally may need to compare the documents when interest rates go up or down. You don't necessarily have to keep all of the monthly statements, but if you have lost a receipt, these statements are important when you need a proof of purchase. Other loans, such as your mortgage and car loans, can be placed with your credit card material.

Many of us have numerous documents associated with our real estate transactions. For tax purposes, you need to know the original cost basis of your house if you sell it. In addition, you need to keep records of the costs of any major capital improvements or repairs in your home, such as adding a pool, deck, extra room, and so on. In addition, keep all the inspection reports made on your home before you bought it. Occasionally, an inspector might miss something that needs repair, and you may be able to go back to the previous owner for these costs.

According to the IRS and numerous state laws, you are required to keep all tax records for a minimum of three years. Many of us have our income taxes done by professionals, and they give you back all of your W-2 forms, 1099 forms, and other paper along with your 1040 when you file your taxes. For some, keeping the tax material returned by your accountant is sufficient for the IRS.

Where Should We Keep All This Stuff?

You can keep everything in one place, or you can keep the current year's documents in a more convenient place and archive the other papers. That's up to you.

We do suggest you keep your really, really important papers in a small fireproof box or fireproof file cabinet. Your passports, mortgage, wills, trusts, birth certificates, marriage license, and other significant documents should be kept in a safe deposit box at your bank. However, remember that in many states, in the event that one of you die, a jointly held safety deposit box cannot be opened without a court order—unless you have power of attorney for each other.

Natalie's Nightmare

In 1995, Natalie and her family ended the summer with one last camping trip. When they returned and opened the front door, they were greeted with a great big whoosh of water. Their stairway was a giant waterfall. While they were away a water pipe had broken in the upstairs bathroom, and water had been gushing through their entire house for four days. Ceilings had caved in from the weight of the water, crushing the furniture below. The walls had water inside them. Nearly everything they had was destroyed.

Did they have all of their important documents in a safety deposit box? Nope. And reading your insurance policy is darned hard when it's dripping wet. In addition to all the stress and tremendous work in rebuilding their home, they had the hassle of rebuilding all their files of important documents.

Natalie learned the importance of keeping your most valuable documents in a safe place. But what she learned was the *most* valuable might surprise you. It wasn't the birth certificates or the mortgage papers or even the insurance policy. It was their photographs. People who have had their homes destroyed will often tell you it wasn't the financial loss that was so devastating (if they had adequate insurance!) but the emotional loss. There are some things that can't be replaced, and your photos are one of them. If you have irreplaceable items like photos, consider doing something like putting the negatives into a safety deposit box (a fireproof box is unlikely to protect negatives—they'll melt). If you take digital pictures, periodically put them all on something like a CD-ROM and put that in your safety deposit box.

Does Your System Work for You?

Now for the most important part. If you now know where your important financial papers are located, let's see if your system is really working for you. Here are some questions to ask yourselves:

- Are you paying all your bills on time?
- Have you incurred any finance charges on credit cards?
- Have you bounced any checks lately?
- Have you been paying your taxes on time?
- Do you know how much you pay for utilities, groceries, clothes, and other items each month?

- Does it take either of you more than two minutes to find your latest IRA statement?

Time to Talk

If it turns out that your system isn't working for you or you want to make improvements, then you need to grab your partner and talk about what you want to do differently. You can use the problem-solving model from Chapter Nine. Here are some topics to cover:

- Who's in charge of paying the bills? Do you want to keep it that way?
- Do you pay your bills as they come in, or do you save them up and pay them once per month? Does one of you need to call to change the billing dates so that everything comes due at around the same time?
- Is the one balancing the checkbook, savings, and other accounts comfortable with this task? Does the task need to be reassigned?
- Is there a problem with remembering to record ATM withdrawals or checks written? How do you want to solve that problem?
- Who checks the bills for accuracy every month? If there is a discrepancy, who calls the company and gets the bill fixed?
- Who will file all the incoming paperwork each month? By when?
- What is happening to your investments, 401(k) contributions, and IRA accounts?

A Honey-Do List

After you've talked and decided how you want to handle the routine tasks, here are some more action items for the two of you to consider. These tasks will be easier if you have now organized all your information.

- Gather all your insurance policies and make a list of policies, companies, agents, phone numbers, death benefits, cash values, and insurance loans, if any. Copy this list and keep a copy in a few special places.
- Look over your monthly salary and benefit statements and discuss how to coordinate and maximize your benefit plans.
- Look over your current retirement and pension plans. Anything to pursue at this point?
- Reconcile all bank statements, saving accounts, and credit card bills to the present, or decide to start doing this today.
- Cancel all but two or three credit cards. If you each want to use a card separately, that is one way to easily keep track of who is spending what. It is a good

idea to keep an extra card that you never use; as long as there are no fees associated with it, it won't cost you anything if you keep your hands off it. You can use the card in emergencies (a sale on that big-screen TV you want is NOT an emergency!) or take it with you if you travel.

- Set a monthly date to pay all bills, or pay all currently due bills today.
- Computerize your financial information system or plan to do it soon. Software like Quicken or Microsoft Money is very easy to use and can help you a great deal in your goal of being organized.

If you want more information on how to organize, read Julie Morgenstern's *Organizing from the Inside Out: The Foolproof System for Organizing Your Home, Your Office, and Your Life.*

CHAPTER THIRTEEN

WHAT DO YOU HAVE?

They say that money talks. Why is it that all mine ever says is goodbye?

ANONYMOUS

Now that you have a good system for organizing your financial documents and for keeping up with your bills, it's time to get a picture of how well the two of you are currently doing with your money. To succeed in almost anything in life, you need to know where you are, where you're going, and how you're going to get there. Financial success is no different. To succeed financially, you need to start by knowing where you are. That's what we're going to help you discover in this chapter. One way to get a picture of how you're doing is to create a balance sheet.

The Balance Sheet

A balance sheet is a way to list all your *assets,* which are anything you own, and your *liabilities,* which are everything that you owe. The reason for doing a balance sheet is to figure out your *net worth.* Your net worth is the amount that you would have if you sold everything you own and paid off every debt you owe. It's a way to keep track of whether or not you're gaining wealth or not. We've found that most couples rate how well they are doing by how much their income goes up or down. If they are making more this year than they were last year, then they feel they're doing well. You may be surprised to hear that this isn't the way most wealthy people think. Most millionaires rate their success based on how much they *keep,* not on how much came *in.* Interesting to think about, isn't it? If you had more come in this year than last year, but you kept less this year than last, you're not really moving forward, are you? Because you likely want to improve your net worth over time, completing a balance sheet will give you a way to see how far you've come in a year, when you do this process again. Let's look now at an example; Figure 25 shows a balance sheet for the Jones family.

FIGURE 25. BALANCE SHEET FOR THE JONESES.

Assets	1995	2000
Liquid Assets	$ 600	$ 500
Cash	1,200	1,500
Money market accounts	8,000	10,000
Cash value of life insurance	0	0
Fixed Assets		
Certificates of deposit	$8,000	$8,000
Bonds	0	0
Mutual Funds	2,500	20,000
Variable Assets		
Stock	$750	$2,000
Real estate	0	0
Collections of stamps	0	0
Retirement Assets		
Employee retirement plan	$ 0	$ 0
IRAs	5,000	30,000
Roth IRAs	0	0
401(k)s	5,000	30,000
Personal Assets		
House	$150,000	$190,000
Cars	20,000	15,000
Furniture	15,000	17,000
TOTAL ASSETS	$216,050	$324,000
Liabilities		
Home Mortgage	$118,000	$105,600
Car Loans	18,000	6,000
Student Loans	120,000	4,500
Credit Card Balances	6,000	0
Investment for Which We Owe	0	0
Total Liabilities	$262,000	$116,100
NET WORTH (Total Assets less Total Liabilities)	−$45,940	$207,900

You can see that from 1995 to 2000, the Joneses' net worth increased from *negative* $45,950 to *positive* $207,900. The Joneses have done well. This is one instance when keeping up with the Joneses would be a *good* idea.

Assets

To create a balance sheet for your family, you need to determine the value of all of your family's financial assets. There are five types of assets:

1. Liquid assets are those that can (theoretically) be turned directly into cash within a twenty-four-hour period. They include the money you have in the bank, savings accounts, money market accounts, credit unions, and the cash value of your life insurance policies.
2. Fixed assets are those that take a little longer to turn into cash, such as CDs, certain types of bonds, money owed to you by someone, and most types of mutual funds.
3. Variable assets are items whose value changes from day to day and take more than twenty-four hours to turn into cash. Some examples are stock; certain types of real estate; collections of coins, stamps, or other valuables that you hold as investments; business ownerships; and certain types of stock option plans.
4. Retirement assets are the financial resources that you and your spouse plan to use for retirement, such as your employee retirement plan, IRAs, Roth IRAs, and 401(k) holdings. In many cases, when you turn these into cash, they lose cash value because there are penalties associated with their early withdrawal as well as massive tax liabilities associated with them.
5. Personal assets are those items that could be turned into cash if you could find a buyer. These assets include your home, cars, household furnishings, noninvestment collections, recreational vehicles, and most real estate.

Using these five categories as guides, write down and add up the cash value of all of your assets. You have now determined your total assets.

Liabilities

The next step is to write down all of your liabilities. Liabilities are what you owe others for the goods and services you have bought in the past. For many of us, our liabilities are our home mortgage, car loans, student loans, and credit card balances. Some of us will also have liabilities associated with stock purchases or real estate purchased for investment purposes. To determine your total liabilities, you need to add up all the money you owe.

The Average Net Worth of the American Family

In 1999, the Consumer Federation of America (www.consumerfed.org) and the investment firm of Primerica (www.primerca.com), a member of the Citigroup, reported on a study of wealth in America. The study used 1995 data and determined that the typical American household has a net worth of about $35,500. The vast majority of the net worth is due to equity in their homes.

The reason given for the low net worth is that the average household has consumer debt that equals more than half of the gross financial assets. Most of this debt was in the form of credit cards with high interest rates. The families in the lowest 20 percent of net financial assets were households with *median*, not low incomes. Those families with the lowest levels of net financial assets were making about $32,000 a year. Generally, those who made less money had more financial assets.

Determining Your Net Worth

In order to complete your balance sheet, you need to subtract your total liabilities from your total assets. When you have done that, you have not only completed your family's balance sheet but also found your family's net worth.

Many Americans spend most of their lives in a state of negative net worth. Most of us have borrowed money to purchase our homes and cars. Many of us borrowed money to get our education or our children's education. These may all be very good reasons to borrow, yet the average person does not emerge from a state of negative net worth until his or her fifties. It's normal to have a negative net worth until age fifty; however, normal does not mean good. As we have seen, average couples don't *have* to wait until they are fifty to have a positive net worth. Average couples don't have to wait until they are fifty even to reach financial freedom.

We'd guess that you bought this book because you want to succeed financially and enjoy sharing that success with your beloved. As you look at your balance sheet, you may be quite distressed that it doesn't look better than it does. Good. Yes, good. The first step in making your future better is realizing that you're not happy with where you are. Now you can start thinking about reasons why making things better is important to you. Without those reasons, you won't change. Having a basic benchmark like a balance sheet makes it a lot easier to hold yourselves accountable for goals you may set.

We'll talk more in the next chapters about what you can do to get where you want to go, but now you have a tool to help measure your success in the area of money. If you are pleased with what you've accomplished thus far, that's wonderful. You can hold on to your balance sheet and periodically take your financial temperature, to make sure you stay on course.

Tracking Income

Time seems to fly by all too quickly, and if you're living paycheck to paycheck, it's easy to lose track of how much money has really passed through your hands.

Keeping track of how much money comes into your family may be a simple task if you receive one paycheck on the fifth of every month and that's it. However, as time goes on, you will likely increase the number of sources of income. Some couples are paid weekly, or biweekly. Some couples receive sales commissions or bonus money at various times of the year. For some, keeping track of when and how they're getting paid can become complicated.

Different people like to keep track of their income in different ways, depending mostly on how much detail they like. If you want to know how much income you've had coming in, you can pull out your tax returns and see what your adjusted gross income has been, provided, of course, that you were honest and accurate when you filed your taxes!

However, that figure may not include income such as child support or certain parts of your previous year's tax refund, which you'll want to include when it comes time to figure out how much money you have to spend each month. Knowing how much you have coming in on a yearly basis may not be too helpful when you need to figure out how much you can spend on a daily or monthly basis.

It can help to record your income in a chart like the one shown in Figure 26, to get a feel for how much is really coming in, and when. A detailed chart like this can serve two purposes: one is to compare over the years how much more money really is coming in; the other is to compare your income to your expenses.

When designing and using your own chart, you will need to decide if you want to record *net* or *gross* income. Gross income is the total amount you earn before the government takes a big chunk out of it and before any other deductions like health insurance or 401(k) investments are taken out. It doesn't matter how you want to record your income, as long as you are consistent. If you record your gross income in your income chart, then you'll need to include the categories for taxes and other deductions in your expense chart (discussed in the next section). If you include your net income in the income chart, then you don't want to record the deductions in your expense chart, because you've already taken those deductions into account.

FIGURE 26. MONTHLY INCOME CHART.

	Jan.	Feb.	Mar.	Nov.	Dec.	Average	Year Total
Income							
Your salary							
Partner's salary							
Rent income							
Interest income							
Tax refunds							
Capital gains							
Dividends							
Child support							
Other income							
Other income							
Other income							
TOTAL							

How Wealthy Are You?

Another way you can use both your income chart and your balance sheet is to see how well you're doing in accumulating wealth compared to other Americans. In *The Millionaire Next Door*, authors Thomas Stanley and William Danko provide an interesting calculation to see how wealthy you are compared to others in your age group with similar income. In other words, compared to other folks who make about as much as you do, and who've had as long to save as you have, how are you doing?

What the authors did was to divide people into three groups. Those who are in the top 25 percent for wealth accumulation are called Prodigious Accumulators of Wealth (PAWs). Those in the middle 50 percent are Average Accumulators of Wealth (AAWs). Those in the bottom 25 percent are Under Accumulators of Wealth (UAWs).

Here's what you do. Multiply your age by your total annual income before taxes. (That's the total you recorded in your income chart from all sources except inheritance.) Then divide that number by ten. This is what your net worth *should* be.

Compare what your net worth actually is (from your balance sheet) to what it should be. If your net worth is twice what it should be, then you are a PAW. If it is half what it should be, then you are a UAW. How are the two of you doing?

How Much Money Is Going to Pass Through Your Hands?

Figure 27 shows how much money will come into your family over the next several years depending on how much income you make.

Stop to think about how much money you have earned in the last five years. How much closer to getting what you want in life are you now than you were five years ago? How much are you going to earn in the next ten years? Are you going to do something differently so that you're much closer to getting what you want? There will likely be a lot of money going through your hands. Are you going to make it work for you? If you're going to see your money work for you, you're going to have to get a handle on your expenses.

Tracking Expenses

There are many ways to keep track of your expenses. Again, how you track what you spend will depend on how much detail you like. You can keep a notebook with you and write the date on top of each page, then jot down what you spend. You can keep all your receipts in an envelope and transfer the expenses to a chart

FIGURE 27. THE AMOUNT OF MONEY YOU MIGHT EARN IN THE YEARS AHEAD (IN DOLLARS).

Monthly Income	5 Years	10 Years	15 Years	20 Years	25 Years	30 Years
1,000	60,000	120,000	180,000	240,000	300,000	360,000
2,000	120,000	240,000	360,000	480,000	600,000	720,000
3,000	180,000	360,000	540,000	720,000	900,000	1,080,000
4,000	240,000	480,000	720,000	960,000	1,200,000	1,440,000
5,000	300,000	600,000	900,000	1,200,000	1,500,000	1,800,000
6,000	360,000	720,000	1,080,000	1,440,000	1,800,000	2,160,000
7,000	420,000	840,000	1,260,000	1,680,000	2,100,000	2,520,000
8,000	480,000	960,000	1,440,000	1,920,000	2,400,000	2,880,000
9,000	540,000	1,080,000	1,620,000	2,160,000	2,700,000	3,240,000
10,000	600,000	1,200,000	1,800,000	2,400,000	3,000,000	3,600,000

like the one shown in Figure 28 later in this section. The more accurate you are in keeping track of what you spend, the better chance you'll have of finding money to invest when we get to budgeting later.

Many people don't want to keep track of "every little expense" because it seems too inconvenient. Tracking every penny can, indeed, be quite cumbersome. There are several ways around this, however. If you use checks (with carbons) or a credit card for everything you purchase, you'll have a record to help you more easily keep track of spending. You can round to the nearest $1 or $5 or $10 depending on your need for accuracy. Using software programs such as QuickBooks or Quicken can greatly simplify things. Some credit cards and banks can download your statements right into your computer-based bookkeeping system so that with a click, everything you purchased is accounted for by category.

Other individuals are reluctant to track their expenses because they really don't want to know how much they are spending. Somehow having a number in black and white would make them feel frightened or guilty, and they would rather avoid the pain. Although it is normal for humans to want to avoid pain, remember what we said: success is not for wimps! If you want to take charge of your money, then you're going to have to take a look at what you're doing, whether it feels good or not. Even though you might be a bit shocked to discover how much you're spending on certain items, most couples find it comforting to finally feel that they have a grasp of what is going on with their money. There's nothing quite like that feeling of being in control. It is wonderful.

If the two of you have a history of blaming each other for your money woes, then keeping track of your expenses might feel as though you're giving your partner ammunition, and that doesn't sound so good. If your partner thinks you spend too much on recreation, for example, then you may not want to show him or her exactly how much you spend on recreation and thus possibly prove your partner correct. But it would also be nice if you could show that you haven't spent as much as he or she thought. Likely you'll find that each of you has areas where you might want to do better. If you're not ready to share with your partner how you've been spending money, then we suggest that you each complete your own expense chart. You don't have to share the information with your partner until you're ready to do so.

Honesty at Any Price?

In the July 2001 issue of *Good Housekeeping*, there was a humorous article by Joanne Kaufman titled "Lies We Tell Our Husbands." Kaufman asserts, with tongue embedded firmly in cheek, that harmless fibs about money can actually be beneficial to a marriage. She gives the five rules for twisting the truth, the second of which is "It doesn't count if it's cash." She stated that this is the case when it comes to the high cost of "girl maintenance" that is not placed on credit cards. She goes on to say, "My concerns on this issue are twofold. If my husband knew I spent $60 on a haircut, he would be sure to point out that the money could have been more profitably spent on pruning shears. Worse, if he knew what I was really paying, I'm afraid he'd wonder why I don't look a whole lot better."

Although we can laugh about human behavior, there are situations where just because everyone is doing it doesn't mean it's really best for you. Think carefully about lying to your loved one about any issue. Perhaps you can establish a "don't ask, don't tell" policy for certain situations if you don't want to be *completely* honest but don't want to be deceitful either. For example, "We agree not to ask or try to find out how much we spent on each other's birthday present, though it will not exceed _____ (amount)."

We've found that *motivating* couples to keep track of their expenses is really the hard part. It's a lot like getting couples to try the Speaker-Listener Technique. It just doesn't look like something that is worthwhile, but the experience is so powerful that once they give it a serious try, they make some adjustments, adapt it to their own unique situation, and enjoy the great results.

Figure 28 shows a sample expense chart. You may have more categories or fewer, and you are likely to have different categories. You can organize your expenses however you want to. We've listed these alphabetically. Some couples prefer to list their expenses according to whether they are *fixed* expenses, those for which you pay the same amount on a monthly basis, or *variable* expenses, those for which you spend an amount that varies from month to month.

Some couples prefer to group their expenses into *nondiscretionary* and *discretionary* expenses. Nondiscretionary expenses are those expenses for which you are obligated. You owe this money to someone. For example, you signed up for cable, so now you owe the cable company. If you have a mortgage, you have to pay it. Discretionary expenses are those for which you might spend money but have not yet obligated yourself. For example, if you usually spend $100 per month on eating at a restaurant, you would list that under discretionary expenses because you could choose to eat at home that month and spend the money on something else. In reality, all of your expenses are discretionary in the sense that you could choose to sell your house so you wouldn't have a mortgage to pay, or you could cancel cable TV and then wouldn't have to pay that bill. But as long as you are obligated to pay an expense, it should be kept in the nondiscretionary category.

FIGURE 28. MONTHLY EXPENSE CHART.

	Jan.	Feb.	Mar.	Nov.	Dec.	Average	Year Total
Expenses							
Books, CDs, tapes							
Car insurance							
Car maintenance							
Car payment							
Child care							
Christmas							
Clothes							
Credit card interest/fees							
Emergency							
Entertainment							
Gas and electricity							
Gasoline							
Haircuts							
Health club, racquetball							
House							
Housecleaning							
House maintenance and furnishings							
Kids sports, lessons, clubs, books, etc.							
Life and disability insurance							
Mad money							
Medical, dental							
Miscellaneous							
Monthly presents (birthdays, etc.)							
Paper, soap, detergent, toiletries, etc.							
Pets							
Recreation							
Restaurant food							
Telephone							
Tithe							
Tuition							
Vacation							
Water/sewer							
TOTAL							

Who Would Go to Such Trouble?

As you look at Figure 28, you may think, "Oh, good grief. Who would ever keep such detailed records? Life is too short for that!" Here's an answer that may surprise you: 62 percent of millionaires, that's who. Stanley and Danko, whose book *The Millionaire Next Door* we mentioned earlier, are noted for their expertise on the behaviors of people who have successfully accumulated wealth. In their research, they found that 62.4 percent of millionaires answered yes to the question, "Do you know how much your family spends each year for food, clothing, and shelter?" However, only 35 percent of those who earned a high income but had low net worth were able to answer yes to this question. Why on earth would someone with a million or more (most in the study had far more) go to the trouble of keeping track of how much he or she spent for "food consumed at home, food consumed away from home, beverages, birthday and holiday gifts (for each category of recipient), each category of clothing for each household member at each store, baby-sitters, day care fees, line of credit use, charitable contributions, financial advice, club dues, motor vehicles and related expenses, tuition, vacations, heating and lighting, and insurance"? Stanley and Danko are blunt in their assertion: "They became millionaires by budgeting and controlling expenses, and they maintain their affluent status the same way."

Other Reasons for Tracking Your Expenses

The truth is that some couples don't keep track of their expenses the way we're showing you, but some do. Many who are very wealthy do. It's up to you whether you want to see if something like this might work for you. It might not. One of the benefits of keeping careful track is that doing so often eliminates conflict between partners. Yep, it does. Here's why. Naturally we have to spend money on necessities, and then there isn't as much left over for the things we want. We think, "Well, I know I didn't spend money on anything fun, so my partner must be the reason we don't have any money." If one or both of you are thinking this, well, you can see that's not such a happy path to be on. Oftentimes we're just so busy that we forget what we spend money on. We forget that the dog had to get his annual shots ($100—poof, gone), that we had to pay Roto-Rooter to clean out the sewer ($150, bye-bye), that both kids needed new cleats for soccer ($75), that one needed a new uniform ($40), that the nephews had a birthday party ($40), and that you donated $25 to the Police Officer's Charitable Fund, and on and on. Those things add up, and it is reassuring to see that neither you nor your partner let $430 vanish into a black hole.

Keeping track of expenses also lets you see the areas where you don't feel you're getting your money's worth. One couple we know was frustrated because they never seemed to have enough money to eat at nice restaurants. But when they looked at their monthly expense chart and discovered that they were spending $23.50 per week (about $1,100 per year) to have pizza delivered every Friday night, they decided they wanted to spend that money differently. The information that they took the trouble to gather allowed them to choose to buy frozen pizza two weeks per month, get chicken from the deli once per month, still have pizza delivered once per month, and have an excess of roughly $40 per month, which allowed them to eat out at a nice restaurant once every couple of months. Keeping track of expenses revealed an opportunity to get more of what they wanted with the same income.

Another couple was considering buying a new minivan. They'd been driving a ten-year-old Volvo station wagon, and it was completely paid off, but it was starting to break down every now and then, and that was a hassle. They looked at what the Volvo had cost them in the past year in terms of repairs. Then they looked at what they'd have to give up in order to come up with payments for the new van. Because they were unwilling to cut back on investing in their future, they would have to take the van payment out of their budget for other items. The new van would have taken a big chunk out of their entertainment fund, their vacation fund, their clothing fund, and their home furnishings fund. When they were able to see what the new van would truly cost them in terms of their actual lifestyle, they suddenly became quite fond of their old Volvo. Taking the time to track their expenses didn't prevent them from getting something they really wanted. It allowed them to *see* what they really wanted and, in this case, to keep it.

For some couples, income is much smaller and expenses are much higher. In general, the closer you are to living paycheck to paycheck, the more carefully and accurately you need to track your expenses. If you're living on the edge, you have to be more careful, or you could be in for a nasty fall. For other people, finding $40 per month may be small potatoes. Some couples spend $50,000 per year on fresh flowers for their foyer. If you're in that financial category, you can likely eat all the pizza you want, but you still may want to keep track of your expenses; in fact, that may well be how you came to have that kind of money to spend in the first place.

Cash Flow

Cash flow refers to the timing of your money's coming in and going out of your pocket. If you have to pay your mortgage on the fifth of the month but you don't get your paycheck until the tenth, you may have a cash-flow problem. When managing your money, you need not only to make sure you have *enough* money to cover your bills but also to have enough money *when* your bills are due. One way to keep track of cash flow is to mark a calendar with green for income and red for outgo. That can help you see the patterns in the times money comes in and goes out. There are many other creative ways of looking at cash flow. One easy way is simply to put your income and expense charts together. Then, each month you can subtract your expenses from your income to see whether you have positive cash flow or negative cash flow each month. One of the helpful parts of budgeting (which we will get to in Chapter Seventeen) is that you can plan ahead of time for the months that you will have negative cash flow. If you know you're going to come up $500 short in July, then you can save extra (create your own escrow account) in the months prior so that bill-paying time will be much, much less stressful.

In a Nutshell

Congratulations! Now that you understand how to create a balance sheet, you can find your net worth and track your progress in accumulating wealth over the years. Keeping track of your income and expenses and managing your cash flow will help you take control of your money. It will likely take a bit of time to organize your own chart, and if you're not used to tracking your expenses, it might take you more time than you want it to. If you have a computer, then putting your chart on a spreadsheet will save you tons of time in adding and subtracting. If you haven't tried Quicken or QuickBooks, we suggest that you give one of them a try.

If you're willing to take a look at how much money actually comes into your family and how much goes out, you will most likely reap great rewards. You'll get quicker as you get used to your system, and you'll begin to see areas where you don't feel you're getting your money's worth. You'll likely begin to see that you want to get more for your money. When you hit that point, then you can start making sure you do get more.

Most couples are reluctant to track their expenses carefully because they are afraid they'll end up having to stop buying something that is really important to them. But what really happens is that they end up cheating themselves out of the future they truly want because they do not see how much more their money could be doing for them. If you're not happy with your financial situation right now, then you need to do something different. Try tracking your expenses for a while to see what opportunities you may discover.

Things do not change; we change.

HENRY DAVID THOREAU

Time to Talk

1. What do you think about doing a balance sheet? Does it feel scary, exciting, depressing?
2. How do you feel about keeping track of your expenses? How do you want to track your expenses? Should each of you keep track of your own, or will you do it jointly? How accurate do you want to be? For example, you could each get $100 in cash each month that you agree not to keep track of—but you also agree not to get any more cash than that.
3. Are you willing to commit to tracking your expenses for six months? A year?

Different people experience different feelings at different times. When you see the charts in this chapter, you may be feeling motivated to find ways to save money to invest. Your partner may feel depressed and want to go shopping to cheer himself or herself up. Please take a minute to answer and discuss the following questions:

1. When I think about how much money we have in our savings account, I feel . . .
2. When I think about how much money we need to retire, I feel . . .
3. I don't have any idea how much money we will need to retire. I feel . . .
4. When I think about saving, I am afraid that I will . . .
5. I am not willing to give up . . .
6. I'm afraid that . . .
7. I hope that in the future we can . . .
8. I am optimistic that we can . . .
9. I want to learn more about . . .
10. Retirement seems so far away. I'd like to set shorter goals, such as . . .

CHAPTER FOURTEEN

SMART BORROWING, DUMB DEBT

The budget should be balanced, the treasury should be refilled and the public debt should be reduced. And the assistance to foreign lands should be curtailed, lest we become bankrupt.

CICERO, 63 B.C.

Human beings have been trying to keep on top of their debt for a long, long time—even before Cicero. Today, credit is part of the fabric of our society. Our economy is dependent on consumers buying goods and services. More than 70 percent of our gross domestic product is based on what consumers purchase. Our jobs depend on people using credit to buy, buy, and buy more. Unfortunately, today's couples find it easier than ever before to spend more money than is good for them, ending up adding loads of stress to their lives.

Although credit can be useful, debt can bring great stress to your relationship. More than 70 percent of people in the process of divorce report that money and the abuse of credit by one spouse is a contributing factor to the decision to get divorced. In the United States, credit is truly both a blessing and a curse. As we noted earlier, research on couples in the first five years of marriage, conducted by Gail Risch and Michael Lawler at Creighton University, revealed that debts brought into marriage were one of the greatest problem areas for these otherwise young and happy couples. Let's look more closely at the pros and cons of debt.

Ten Good Reasons to Use Credit— and a Few Words of Caution

Although taking on too much debt can get couples in trouble, there are good reasons for using credit. What follows are ten good reasons to borrow money. We'd like you each to look over this list separately at first. Get out a pad of paper, and as you go through this list, write down any of these reasons that reflect why the two of you use credit—credit cards and other types of loans. We'll ask you to compare notes later.

1. *Simply for convenience.* Using credit and credit cards is sometimes much more convenient than using checks. Doing so can also help you establish a record of your expenditures. Many couples simply use credit cards like checks and pay off the balance on their cards every month. Those folks are using credit for convenience and organization, but are not allowing it to entice them into building up hard-to-manage debts.

Sometimes convenience is used as an excuse to use credit when it's not really the reason you use credit. Some couples use credit simply as a way to live beyond their means—as a way to avoid (for a while) the harsh reality that they cannot afford their lifestyle. If you leave a balance on your credit card every month, you may actually be paying up to 22 percent every year for the privilege. That's a big hit on your long-term financial viability, and when the growing debt is tied to the ongoing necessities of life, you will hit a wall sometime down the road.

Furthermore, it is a well-researched fact that when using a card, people are far more likely to spend more than they would have if they had used cash. Credit just doesn't feel like money, so we're less likely to be as careful.

2. *Cushion for emergencies.* Credit is valuable to use in true emergencies related to auto and home repairs or needed medical services.

3. *For identification.* Many firms will not cash checks or provide other services unless you can show them a credit card for purposes of identification. Many businesses consider having a credit card as an elementary sign of some financial means.

4. *To make reservations for business or pleasure.* Generally, it is impossible to reserve rooms, cars, or airline tickets without using a credit card. Many hotels and resorts require the use of a credit card to establish and hold a reservation for any length of time.

5. *To purchase expensive necessities.* There are many relatively expensive items that you may have come to see as essential for everyday life. Obviously, what's essential for you might be seen very differently by others. Yet many people see a washer, dryer, or microwave oven as relatively necessary. Sure, one can survive without them, but many people see such items as things worth taking on some debt in order to purchase.

6. *To take advantage of "free" credit.* Many stores will entice people to purchase items on credit for which there will be no interest charges for some period of time. This free credit lasts anywhere from ninety days to a year. During that time, most people plan to pay off the credit before the interest begins. You should, however,

be cautious about these deals. In the majority of such "free" credit contracts, there is a clause that you will pay back credit for the entire purchase, and if there is even $1 left on the account for one day after the expiration of the "free" credit period, you will be socked with large interest fees.

7. *To consolidate bills.* Many people will borrow on the equity in their home to pay off credit cards and other loans. If done wisely, this can result in a lower-interest loan, smaller bill payments, a specific length of time for repayment, and, perhaps best of all, tax-deductible interest. However, we add a major word of warning on this one. It won't help you in the long run to consolidate higher-interest debt if, as you are making those payments, you are also building debts back up in ways that incur higher interest. We've seen so many couples who consolidate their debts and reduce their monthly interest payments, only to refill credit cards up to their limits, making matters that much worse. In recent years, many people have taken out more home equity loan funds, often with the rationalization that they will pay off other, higher-interest debts, but then often using the money instead for things like vacations. The end result when you do this can be mortgage payments that exceed what you could qualify for outright, with no reduction in the other, higher-interest debts. You're headed for bankruptcy on that path.

8. *For protection from fraud, scams, and product failure.* Under federal law (the Fair Credit Billing Act), any mail, telephone, or Internet order can be contested if the purchase is done with a credit card. This means that, within some limits, purchasing by credit card can give you extra leverage when you have a dispute with a store or business. Further, although not related to any federal laws, some cards offer you an extra one-year warranty on anything you purchase using your credit card.

9. *To enjoy the good life.* Many people use credit cards or take out other types of loans to enhance their lifestyle, either to own things they never could afford, to travel, or simply to keep up with the Joneses. They do this expecting increased pay raises or income from other sources, such as winning the lottery. Individuals and families using credit for these reasons can easily get themselves in financial trouble because the increased spending is not always offset by the expected increase in income. So this strategy makes more sense when the money you are expecting to come in is sure, such as when the government owes you a tax refund and you're expecting it within weeks. In contrast, if you're depending on something like the lottery to bail you out, you're a financial train wreck waiting to happen.

10. *To get additional training or higher education.* This use of credit is a way of increasing your "human capital." Yes, you are taking on more debt, but you are also increasing your assets, from which you can generate more and higher income in the future. Research indicates that this does pay off in the long run, not only with increases in income in many cases but also with lessened likelihood of being laid off or fired from a job. Some have estimated that each additional year of education can result in an average increase in income of 5 to 15 percent. This is cer-

tainly true when it comes to acquiring professional degrees (for example law or medicine) and certain computer technology certifications. We're not suggesting that income generation is the be-all-end-all of life. Rather, when you take on a reasonable amount of debt for some activity that directly increases your odds of paying it off and more, it can be a wise use of debt.

Losing for Winning

Although there are good reasons for using credit, it needs to be managed carefully, or you can end up wasting a lot of your precious money. You may feel as though you've won when you get that new car you've wanted or that stereo surround-sound system to go with your big-screen television, but if you are not careful, you can lose big in the long run. For example, let's say that you want to buy a new thirty-six-inch television, but you don't have enough money in savings to just go buy one, so you charge it. You get a very nice model, perhaps a Sony Trinitron, with picture-in-picture and all the other bells and whistles, for $1,000. A typical credit card that charges 18 percent interest per year will have a minimum payment of 2 percent, which is $20 per month. You think that $20 per month doesn't seem like much. But look closer.

If you make only the minimum payment (which is common for many people because they have too much debt to do more than that), it will take you nearly eight years to pay off that television, and by that time you will have paid a total of about $1,800 for that $1,000 television to boot. Perhaps you have made these kinds of decisions. Is it worth it to you to buy in this way? Do you think this means you could truly afford that purchase, or not? We're not assuming the answer is no. Sometimes you decide that for the sake of your overall quality of life, you are willing to pay that extra in interest for something you could not otherwise purchase now. Our goal here is simply to get you thinking about it.

If the two of you want to spend $1,800 for something with a $1,000 price tag, you should go for it. However, if you want to make your money work for you, you're going to have to hold on to more of it. Paying almost twice what you have to pay for an item because you are using credit may stand in the way of reaching your goals.

When to Say When

It is a good idea for the two of you to understand your current level of indebtedness to your creditors. If you did not already do so in Chapter Thirteen, take some time now to write down every kind of loan payment you make every month, excluding your mortgage. This would include car loans, credit cards, student loans, and so forth. Now, using your income chart, look at the total income you have in a typical month. Using your expenses chart, subtract from your monthly income all of your nondiscretionary expenses. Nondiscretionary expenses are those expenses for which you owe. You have already promised to pay someone these amounts, so you can't use that money for something new. That will leave you with the amount of your monthly discretionary income. This is the amount of money you have in your pocket that you haven't already promised to give to someone, but it is money that you need to buy essentials like food and clothing as well as nonessentials like another sports bag when you have six already.

Now divide the total amount of your monthly debt payments by your total amount of monthly discretionary income.

$$\frac{\text{Total monthly debt payments}}{\text{Total monthly discretionary income}} = \text{Percentage of debt}$$

What percentage do you get? Compare it to Figure 29, which contains the current best thinking on this subject. Companies that determine your credit wor-

FIGURE 29. DEBT PAYMENTS AS A PERCENTAGE OF DISCRETIONARY INCOME.

Share of Discretionary Income (%)	Payments for Current Debt	Ability to Take On Additional Debt
<10	Considered safe; normally the borrower feels little pressure from his or her debts.	Individual should use caution when taking on additional debt.
11–15	Possibly safe; borrower begins to feel some pressure from creditors.	New debt should not be undertaken.
16–20	Fully extended; hope is that no financial emergencies occur.	It would be foolish to take on additional debt.
21–25	Overextended; borrower worries constantly about debt.	Borrower should see a nonprofit financial counselor.
26+	Ruinous; borrower feels desperate. Typically, this level threatens the most committed of relationships.	It is impossible to take on additional credit; next step is bankruptcy.

Note: Current debt excludes home mortgage loans and the use of convenience credit that is paid in full upon arrival of the bill.

thiness use guidelines just like these when evaluating whether or not you can or should take on more indebtedness.

Time to Talk

We suggest that the two of you take some time to talk out how you each feel about the amount of debt you have right now. Discuss these three things:

1. How do you see your debt affecting your financial future? We're not asking you to try to find a formula and make some precise prediction. Rather, talk about what you each think—or fear—the effects of your level of debt will have in the long term.
2. Talk through the possible good reasons to use debt that we covered earlier in the chapter. Compare the notes that you took while reading through the ten reasons. Which reasons are you comfortable with? Any? All? Some? Do the two of you agree? How do those reasons compare to your actual use of debt?
3. Finally, talk about the ways your level of debt as well as your reasons for using debt affect the quality of your relationship.

   Does your debt level or your reasons for using credit cause stress between the two of you?

   Is there a negative impact on your relationship?

   Do you think debt might cause problems for the two of you in the future?

   Is one of you more prone to incur debt than the other?

Talk these things out. We recommend that you use the Speaker-Listener Technique for this kind of talk. Are there key expectations that are not being met in these matters? Are any deeper, hidden issues triggered?

What to Do If You Have Overused Credit

Overuse of credit is simply too expensive to ignore. It can keep you from getting the tangible goods you want in life. There are a number of signs that you have overextended your use of credit. One way to tell if you're overextended is simply if you're denying or conveniently forgetting you are in debt. In some cases, couples have semiconsciously lost track of the amount they owe. More likely, they are afraid to add up and record their debt level on a piece of paper. When you looked at your percentage of debt, if you discovered that you're maxed out, then it is time to get debt under control.

If you have overused credit, you can refocus your financial efforts on paying off your debts. Simply adding 5 percent more a month to your minimum credit card payments can help you get out of debt sooner. If your creditors are calling you about nonpayment, call them first. Explain to them your circumstances and see if you can work something out. For example, some may reduce the interest on the account.

If you have a severe debt problem, your best choice is to approach one of the many nonprofit credit counseling services in your area. Look in the Yellow Pages for them under "Credit Counseling." We recommend those agencies that are accredited by the National Foundation for Consumer Credit (NFCC); they are more likely to give you the best feedback on your getting out of debt and creating the best circumstances with your creditors. They charge a minimum monthly fee, usually under $20, for their services. Funding for their services comes from United Way, foundations, and credit card companies that pay them a "fair share" in return for their assisting them with payments.

Most reputable credit counseling services will expect you to destroy your present credit cards, pledge not to apply for additional credit, and bring in your monthly check to pay the bills that you are paying through their services. If you are too embarrassed to go through this process in person, there are several nationwide telephone and Internet debt counseling agencies.

Credit Repair Clinics and Payday Advance Companies: Some Words of Warning

If you are overextended and deep in credit card debt, do not go to a so-called credit repair clinic. As the Better Business Bureau states, the advertisements you see on TV, in newspapers, and on the Internet that offer something like the following are most likely a scam:

> "CREDIT PROBLEMS? NO PROBLEM! WE CAN
> ERASE YOUR BAD CREDIT, 100% GUARANTEED.
> CREATE A NEW CREDIT IDENTITY—LEGALLY."

These companies promise that for a substantial fee, they can clean up your credit report. They are essentially lying to you: they cannot deliver what they have promised, no matter how much money you give them. Most take your money, delay, delay, and usually vanish overnight with your money in their pockets. They cannot change your credit history because no one can remove accurate and timely negative information from your credit report.

Many individuals who become involved with the payday advance process become so entangled in it that they are never able to escape from the vicious cycle of debt. No matter how desperate and deep in debt you are, these types of solutions make things worse, not better. You'll be much better off turning to credit counseling agencies for help and support.

The Big Purchase: A House

There is one type of purchase that almost no one can pull off without taking on debt. Buying a home is, for most of us, the biggest purchase of our lives. (If you have a house or no current interest in purchasing a house, you may wish to skip this section and go on to the next chapter.) The majority of Americans want to live in a home of their own at some time in their lives. It is a symbol of independence and freedom for many families. It is also often considered the single largest asset that most of us will ever own. Buying a house is usually one of the wisest uses of debt.

Renting Versus Buying

There's a lot to think about if you're considering buying a house. How much can you afford? Where do you want to buy? When's the best time? Paying more than you can comfortably afford can cause a lot of stress and heartache. Buying a house that you end up not wanting to live in for a long while will likely lead to the hassle and expense of selling and buying again. Before you start looking for the right house, it is a good idea to look at some numbers to compare renting versus owning. Generally speaking, renters will almost always win on a cash-flow basis. That is, they will take fewer dollars out of their pocket every month. However, in the long run, the purchaser of a house generally wins financially due to the deduction of interest on the mortgage and the increase in the value of the house.

What follows is an example of how you might compare the cost of renting an apartment at $750 per month rent to buying a $125,000 house at 7 percent interest. All of the numbers are approximate.

Apartment
$750/month rent
20.85/month insurance
$770.85/month

House ($125,000)
$765 principal and interest
167 property tax
42 insurance
$974/month

As you can see, at first glance it appears that living in the house will cost about $200 per month more than living in the apartment. In addition, to purchase the house, the couple will have to come up with around $12,000 to cover the down payment and closing costs, whereas in order to get into the apartment, the couple has to come up with only a $1,500 deposit; when you take these numbers into account, it is clear that living in the apartment is easier from a cash-flow perspective. The total outlay of cash for the first year looks like this:

Apartment
$750/month rent
20.85/month insurance
$770.85/month
× 12 months in a year

$9,250.20 per year
+ 1,500 deposit
$10,750.20 for year 1

House ($125,000)
$765 principal and interest
167 property tax
42 insurance
$974/month
× 12 months in a year

$11,690 per year
+ 12,000 for down payment and closing costs
$23,690 for year 1

There are advantages and disadvantages to both options in terms of lifestyle and convenience. If you are renting, you can call the landlord when something breaks. If you own, you get out the duct tape or call a plumber. Renters don't get to take any tax deductions for their rent, but those with a home mortgage get to deduct the interest. So, for year 1, the differences actually look more like this:

Apartment
$750/month rent
20.85/month insurance
$770.85/month
× 12 months in a year

$9,250.20 per year
+ 1,500 deposit
$10,750.20 for year 1

House ($125,000)
$765 principal and interest
167 property tax
42 insurance
$974/month
× 12 months in a year

$11,690 per year
+ 12,000 for down payment and closing costs
$23,690 for year 1

+ 0 toilet replacement	+ 320 toilet replacement
+ 0 lawn care	+ 400 lawnmower and other tools
+ 0 paint	+ 283 paint
+ 0 new carpet	+ 2,500 new carpet
$10,750.20 for year 1	$27,193 for year 1
	− 2,055 tax refund*
	$25,138 for year 1

*Assuming the couple would pay about $8,000 in interest and get 28 percent of that back.

You can see that in terms of cash flow, the renters did much better. It cost only $10,750.20 for rent for the year, whereas the homeowners saw $25,138 leave their pocket. But let's keep going a few more years. For simplicity's sake, let's assume that if the couple rented, their rent would stay the same for three more years, and that if the couple bought a house, they wouldn't have to make any repairs or improvements for three years.

Apartment	House
$10,750.20 for year 1	$25,138 for year 1
+ 9,250.20 for year 2	+ 11,690 for year 2
− 0 tax refund year 2	− 2,000 tax refund year 2
+ 9,250.20 for year 3	+ 11,690 for year 3
− 0 tax refund year 3	− 2,000 tax refund year 3
+ 9,250.20 for year 4	+ 11,690 for year 4
− 0 tax refund year 4	− 2,000 tax refund year 4
$38,500.80 cost for four years	$54,208 cost for four years

Now let's say the couple wants to move to a different city. If the couple had rented, they would get their $1,500 deposit back, so their total cost for housing for the four years would have been $38,500.80 − $1,500 = $37,000.80. If the couple had purchased the house, they would sell it. Let's say the house appreciated 3 percent per year, so they can now sell their house for $140,700.

$140,700 sale price of house
− 8,442 Realtor's fees of 6 percent
− 109,800 principal left on their mortgage

$22,458 left over

Thus the actual cost of housing for the couple had they purchased the house was

$54,208 cost for four years
– 22,458 left over after the sale of the home
—————————————————————
$31,750 for four years

So, in this case, buying the house turned out to be less expensive overall. Living in the apartment would cost $37,000.80 for four years, but living in the house would cost only $31,750. Please remember, of course, that this is just an example; and as you can see from even this simple one, there are a number of factors that could affect what the best decision is for you, including the following:

- Income tax bracket
- Purchase price of the house
- Property taxes
- Cost of homeowner's insurance
- Interest rate
- Amount of down payment
- Length of term of loan
- Amount the house appreciates or depreciates
- Length of time you stay in the house
- Comparable rent prices
- Cost of maintaining the house
- Expenses incurred when eventually selling the house

You will need to run the numbers to see what would be best in your situation. There are a number of "rent versus buy" calculators on the Internet. An excellent one is located at www.nolopress.com. Once the two of you have looked over the math, then it is a good idea to sit down and talk a lot about the decision.

Time to Talk About Renting Versus Buying

If you are facing a major housing decision of the sort we've been discussing here, talk through your thoughts at this time.

1. How do you feel about renting as opposed to owning?
2. What are the advantages and disadvantages of each for the two of you?
3. How secure is your income?
4. Do you plan to change jobs in the near future?

5. Will one of you quit working if you have children, or is one of you thinking of going back to school? If a change is in the foreseeable future, it may not be a good time to buy.

6. What are the economic indicators saying about the housing market in your area? Are prices at an all-time high?

7. Can you buy something you'd like to live in for a long while for a reasonable amount?

8. What other information do you need to be able to make the best decision? Who will get what information? When will you follow up and talk more?

If a house purchase might be in your near future, the following information could be useful.

How Much Will the Bank Let You Borrow?

Mortgage lenders use various guidelines to determine how much you can borrow to spend on a house. The first is the *front-end ratio*. This compares the total annual cost of housing to your total annual income. The house payment (principal, interest, taxes, and insurance—PITI) should fall somewhere between 25 percent and 29 percent of your annual gross income. For example, if you and your partner make $55,000 annually, using the front-end ratio of 28 percent would indicate that you could manage a total payment of about $1,285 a month ($55,000 ÷ 12 × 0.28).

The second rule of thumb is the *back-end ratio*. This ratio looks at all of a couple's current monthly payments—which include total house payment (PITI) and all credit card payments, car loans, and education loan payments—and compares it to monthly income. The back-end ratio usually falls between 33 percent and 41 percent of monthly income. Using the back-end ratio for the same couple and applying a ratio of 36 percent, the couple could qualify for a loan that does not result in total debt repayment of more than $1,650. So if this couple already had a car payment of $350 and $100 in minimum credit card payments, the maximum house loan payment they would qualify for would be $1,250.

The third and perhaps most important factor in determining whether you get a loan, and for how much, is your credit rating. Your credit rating is an arbitrary number that tells a lender how great a risk there is in lending to you. Do you have a history of paying back money you owe? The amount of credit you have, your payment history, and how long you have been carrying credit balances all affect your credit rating. High ratings go to people with a high probability of paying off their debt. Some lenders are willing to grant loans to couples with lower scores; others are less inclined to do so.

How Much *Should* You Borrow?

Of course, these are guidelines that banks use to determine how much *they* feel comfortable loaning to you. That doesn't mean that *you* will feel comfortable with your lifestyle if you borrow that much. You need to look at your budget to determine what you can *comfortably* afford. (Hint: if you're going to have to sell lemonade in your front yard in order to make the payments, you need to think about buying a less expensive house!)

Seriously, as you consider how much house to buy, you need to consider both the short-term effects on your cash flow and the long-term potential for economic gain. To get a realistic idea of how much house you can comfortably afford, it is a

**"MAYBE THIS ISN'T GOING TO BE THE BEST WAY
TO MAKE OUR HOUSE PAYMENTS."**

good idea to actually live with the budget that you would live with if you bought a house. For example, let's say that you are paying $950 per month for an apartment, and you are thinking about purchasing a house with a $1,200 monthly payment. You're already living with an outgo of $950 per month for housing, so if you can live comfortably for a year while putting an additional $250 per month into the bank, then you will feel more confident that you can afford the $1,200 payment.

Limit Your Housing Expenditures

Real estate agents provide an invaluable service to couples and families. However, you should avoid the temptation to "overbuy" a house. This is one of the biggest financial mistakes that many couples make. Remember: the real estate agent has two compelling interests. The first is the agent's commission. It is based on the size of the sale, so the more expensive the house she sells, the more money she makes. The second is the agent's contractual and legal obligation to the seller—not to you the buyer. The Latin maxim *caveat emptor* springs to mind: let the buyer beware.

It is your responsibility to develop a realistic housing budget and to determine the size mortgage payment you can afford. Remember that the payment will include payments on principal, interest, property taxes, and insurance. In addition, don't forget to add to your housing budget maintenance cost, furniture, window coverings, appliances, landscaping, and so on. Some of us homeowners have asked ourselves more than once, "Do I own the house, or does it own me?"

Here is one rule of thumb (from Stanley and Danko's *The Millionaire Next Door*) for figuring how much you might wisely spend on a house: "if you're not wealthy, but want to be someday, then never purchase a home that requires a mortgage that is more than twice your household's total annual income." If you buy so much house that it takes every penny just to make ends meet, then you can't afford to invest any money to help you reach your other goals. You need to decide how much of your hard-earned dollars you want to give to your mortgage company to help it reach *its* dreams and how much you're going to keep to help you reach *yours*.

Time to Talk About What's Important in a House

For most couples, a house is not just shelter. It is not just some walls and a roof. It will become your home—and all of what *home* means to you—which suggests that you'll have issues, hidden issues, and expectations to contend with. Many couples find that they seem to lose their heads when they start looking for a new house. All of a sudden they find a house that is far more expensive than they can comfortably afford, but they feel as though they *have* to have it, and aren't even sure why. "It's just right somehow." They allow all the invisible forces to push them off course.

If you get pushed off course on one of the most important decisions you'll make together, you'll really end up in a bind. It will feel far better to know what you want and need in a house before you start looking. Think about what's important to you in a house:

- Do you want to live in the city or the suburbs?
- Do you need a garage?
- Do you want modern or traditional?
- Do you want a ranch or a two-story?
- How close to work do you want to live?
- How big of a yard do you want?
- Do you want something that you'll need to fix up?
- How busy a street will you feel comfortable living near?

Get together and compare notes. It is rare that two partners will want or need exactly the same things in a house.

If you start out determined that protecting your team is more important than choosing any particular house, then you're far more likely to end up with something that really works—or you'll keep trying until you find it. You don't want to buy a house only to lose a home.

Avoiding Budget Creep

If you have your needs and wants nailed down, you'll be far better prepared to avoid budget creep when you start looking for the right home. Budget creep is what often happens when a couple discovers how little house a whole lot of money can buy. Couples decide on an absolute maximum that they are willing to spend. Then they start saying to themselves, "Well, maybe we could afford $100 more per month." So they go back to their budget, carve out $100 more, and then adjust psychologically to the new limit. Then they do it all over again: "Well, maybe we could afford just $100 more." Next thing they know, they're looking at houses that are $500 per month more than they can afford. Some couples don't have trouble with budget creep and some do. If you do, you might consider refusing to look at a house that you can't afford. You can also write out your budget options this way:

If Our House Payment Is . . .	**What Will Happen**
$800	We can afford to go on vacation, buy furniture, eat out.
$900	We'll have to give up our vacation.
$1,000	We'll have our ugly green striped couch in the living room for at least three more years.
$1,100	We'll have no vacation, no new furniture, no eating out—no fun!!

This sort of calculation can help make the consequences of your decision feel more real in the short term. In the long term, it helps to realize that because you'll be paying interest, paying $10,000 more for a house means you're really spending a whole lot more.

The decisions about whether to buy or rent or how much to spend will have a major impact on your lives over the years. The more the two of you work through both the math and the emotional pieces, the more likely it is that you'll make a decision you can both live with happily for a long time.

What Type of Mortgage Loan Should You Get?

When you decide that you're ready to buy a house, you'll likely need to borrow some money to do it. You'll need a mortgage loan. Once upon a time, there was only one type of mortgage loan; now there are several different kinds. We're going to discuss two of the most popular.

The conventional mortgage loan is a loan for a fixed number of years at an unchangeable interest rate. If you select a conventional loan today, you will know almost exactly how much your house payment will be twenty or thirty years from now. The only significant changes in the payment amount will occur because of changes in property tax or in home insurance rates. The real value of the conventional loan is its financial predictability.

Another common loan is the adjustable rate mortgage (ARM). The payment on the loan changes periodically due to the fluctuation of the interest rate, which can go up or down. For example, if you select an ARM with a "teaser rate," the interest rate for the first-year payments will be 2 to 4 percent below the market rate for conventional loans. At the end of the first year of the loan, the interest rate can increase, usually by a maximum of 2 percent. Your payments increase accordingly. It is not unusual to get an ARM that has a maximum total increase in interest rate of 5 or 6 percent. Although ARMs seem very tempting to many young couples because they can get into a home for very low monthly payments,

ARMs can be a trap. The monthly payments can dramatically increase from year to year, and it is often impossible to keep up. If that has happened to you, it's possible that you can refinance your house to lower the rate. But you may not be able to. Before deciding to go with an ARM or one of its variations, make sure you have a plan for the worst-case scenario.

◆ ◆ ◆

Please take your time in making the decision to buy a house. Go to the library and read up on the subject. Buying and owning a house can be one of life's most rewarding experiences for a couple. But you want to do it right, so that your love nest doesn't end up becoming a hornet's nest of financial woe.

CHAPTER FIFTEEN

INSURANCE: HOW TO PROTECT
WHAT YOU'VE GOT

I detest life-insurance agents; they always argue that I shall some day die, which is not so.

STEPHEN LEACOCK

In the Introduction, I (Natalie) wrote that I found it quite distressing to see all our gear (and my husband, Shawn) floating down the river after our canoe had capsized. I learned the life lesson *bring rope.*

You never know when your little boat is going to hit rough water or capsize. This is the chapter in the book where we tell you about different kinds of rope (alias insurance) and help you figure out what needs to be tied down.

Although for most people the topic of insurance is about as dry as the Sahara Desert in the summer, it's one of the most important aspects of your total financial picture to think clearly about. In the event of a fire, it can make the difference between living in your car and living in your completely rebuilt house. It can make the difference between getting the best medical care for your loved ones and making do with less. Everybody makes mistakes from time to time. But the potential for financial and emotional devastation if you make an insurance mistake is too great to ignore. Every year, 1 out of every 105 people will die, 1 out of every 88 houses will burn, 1 out of every 70 cars will be in an accident, and 1 out of 8 people will suffer a serious disability. This is one area where you just need to suffer through the less-than-exciting information, make wise decisions, and get it done.

Perhaps you need to get coverage you don't now have. Perhaps you need to reevaluate what you have and decide whether to stay the course or make a change.

Important Note

This chapter covers a topic that is vast, varied, and volatile. By this we mean that there are many kinds of insurance, many variations of needs and issues in the lives of people, and a vast range of products and options that are always changing. For many reasons, we think there is no other topic in this book about which you could find more widely divergent opinion among financial professionals—including insurance agents—as to what is best in various situations. In each of the chapters on money management, our chief goal is to make you more aware of the key issues that might affect your decision making so that you can figure out what more you need to learn and who else you might want to talk to make the best decisions possible.

> *You simply must study, learn more, and get input if you expect to make the wisest decisions for the long term.*

When it comes to insurance, we don't hope to give you any depth of advice on which you should make decisions without further input. We don't know enough, and likely you don't either. Sure, in some areas, the decision may be so simple and so straightforward that more basic advice will do. But you simply must study, learn more, and get input if you expect to make the wisest decisions for the long term. Our goal is rather circumspect: we want to help you think through the major types of insurance that exist and what some of your needs might be regarding them. As we go, we raise some very specific issues that will illustrate why the stakes can be so high for the decisions you eventually make.

Do I Need an Insurance Agent?

The answer to this question is that it depends on what type of insurance you are looking for and how complex the decisions are about that type of insurance. On the one hand, in many instances it might make a lot of sense to buy some kinds of insurance by using a search engine on a Web site, thus skipping an agent altogether. On the other hand, a competent insurance professional can be invaluable when you're making decisions on such complex matters as disability, permanent life, or long-term care insurance. Long-term care insurance is one of the fastest-growing, most complex areas of insurance you could imagine. It's improbable that you could make a well-reasoned decision about such insurance without an agent who has special expertise.

A good agent does have special expertise to offer you. As you know, however, insurance agents make their living by selling you things. More specifically, they make a living by selling you the things that they sell. They don't make any commission if they refer you to a product offered by someone else. So you do have to be careful and to know enough to watch out for your own best interests. You need to be able to say, "No, I don't want that policy" or "I need you to show me what the numbers would look like if I did this, at this age, for this long."

You'll likely want to consider different agents for different kinds of insurance. For example, many people shop around a bit and choose one of the large, name-brand companies for their basic home and auto insurance. If the agent you choose represents only that company, he or she may be wonderfully helpful with that insurance need. However, you might do far better to seek the opinion of another agent—or agents—when it comes to life or disability insurance. It probably makes the most sense for you to talk to at least one or two independent insurance agents. They represent many companies, and a good agent can both advise you and help you comparison-shop among the companies he or she represents. If such an agent puts three nearly identical life insurance policies in front of you, from three highly rated, stable companies, yet the price of the policies varies by hundreds of dollars, which do you think you'd choose?

So shop around. Learn at least the basic issues about a type of insurance when you go shopping for it. Give real thought to the input of insurance professionals, especially for the more complex types of insurance. Most of all, be assertive and ask a lot of questions. We'll put some of the key issues on the table for you, but there is much for you to follow up on unless your insurance situation is already well put together.

The Big Six (Types of Insurance)

In this section, we'll briefly discuss the six major kinds of insurance that the two of you need to understand and evaluate.

1. Homeowner's insurance
2. Auto insurance
3. Health insurance
4. Long-term care insurance
5. Life insurance
6. Disability insurance

Homeowner's Insurance

The normal homeowner's policy has two parts. The first part deals with losses to your home and buildings on your property, loss of personal property, and what it costs you to live while your home is being replaced or repaired. The second part is liability insurance. This covers you if you are sued for damage that occurs while an individual is on your property.

If you have a mortgage on your house, the lender will require that you insure your house for at least as much as you owe on the mortgage. One of the biggest mistakes we see couples make with regard to homeowner's insurance is assuming that if the bank is happy, then this is enough insurance. Not so. The bank is most interested in protecting its investment, not yours. It is your job to protect your *home*. It is unlikely that you would want to insure your house for less than 80 percent of its replacement cost. It is far more likely that you will want to insure the property for closer to 100 percent of actual replacement cost and to have the clause in your policy that automatically raises the replacement value of the home to account for inflation. You likely don't need to include the value of the land when figuring out how much insurance you need. Even if your house burns down, the lot will still be there.

Time to Talk: Who's Got Your Back?

Here's a little exercise you can do together to get your minds going on thinking about insurance. Take out a piece of paper and each of you separately take ten minutes to write out what kinds of insurance you currently have, who the agent is, what is covered, and in what amount. Here's a list of the six major kinds of insurance.

1. Homeowner's insurance
2. Auto insurance
3. Health insurance
4. Long-term care insurance
5. Life insurance
6. Disability insurance

Now discuss what you've come up with, then get your policies out and look up the correct answers. If nothing else, you'll leave this exercise knowing more about your current insurance situation should the need arise for some type of insurance.

Be careful to *read* in your policy that your assets will be replaced at actual cost of replacement. A *guaranteed cost replacement* policy means your home will be rebuilt no matter what it costs. A *cash value* policy means you can get up to the current market value of the house, which may be a lot less than what it would cost to rebuild your home. Check calculations on how much the policy estimates it would cost to replace the *quality* of your home. There's a big difference between a home that costs $60 per square foot to build and one that costs $150 per square foot to build. Also check to be sure that you're covered if the repairs will have to be made to the standards of new building codes. Some policies will cover bringing your house up to code if your entire home has to be rebuilt, but if the home is only partially damaged, you could get stuck paying to bring your house up to code. If you don't see something very specifically pertaining to your coverage in black and white, you need to check further to find out what is actually covered by your policy.

You also need to know what kind of calamities are covered. Fire yes but smoke no? Water damage if from a pipe inside your home, but not from one outside your home? Damage when heavy snow causes a tree to fall on your house? Backed-up sewer? Floods? Some kinds of protection cost extra.

Another common mistake is to undervalue all the stuff that you have inside your house. Many of us moved out of our parents' home able to fit everything we owned into the back of a VW Bug. It took a U-Haul trailer to move out of our first apartment, and by the time we've been in a house awhile, we have accumulated moving vans full of valuable *stuff*. Unless you keep an inventory in a fireproof location, you are leaving yourself open for financial disaster. One of the easiest ways to keep an inventory is to take a video camera and walk around the house, pointing out the different items and saying what they are and when you purchased them. Then put the videotape into your safety deposit box (if you don't have one— get one!). It isn't a perfect solution, but it's far better than nothing. Again, make sure your policy states that it will replace your stuff at the current cost to replace it, not at the depreciated value (read *garage sale* price).

Finally, you will want to price the cost of personal liability, medical expense, and no-fault property damage coverage. Liability insurance protects you against the consequences of your actions. The minimums are often quite low, and it will cost you very little to protect yourselves financially in these areas. It is often a good idea to get extra personal liability coverage through what are called umbrella policies. Ask your agent for more details about those.

Please do a lot of additional reading, asking, and thinking about your homeowner's insurance in addition to what we've provided here. Even if you already have good coverage, make a few calls to check prices. Prices are changing almost as often as a teenage girl changes clothes or a teenage boy takes a shower.

Automobile Insurance

Most states require that you carry a certain amount of liability coverage, and if you have a loan on the car, the lender will require comprehensive coverage to protect its investment.

Automobile insurance combines the following four types of insurance into one package: (1) liability insurance, (2) medical payment insurance, (3) protection for you against uninsured and underinsured drivers, and (4) damage to your car. Each one of these types has specific policy limitations, conditions of payment, and exclusions. For example, liability coverage is typically stated as "100/400/100." The 100 refers to a $100,000 per-person injury limit that is paid for liability losses from an accident. The 400 refers to a maximum payment of $400,000 for bodily injury per accident. The 100 refers to the maximum amount of $100,000 per accident paid for property damage.

The pricing of auto insurance is a complex process. Essentially, it depends on accident and theft figures associated with the age, gender, and driving record of the driver; the type of car; the distance driven annually; and the region of the country in which the car is insured. The key to purchasing auto insurance is to shop around and compare apples to apples. Research has indicated that the cost of insurance for the same car and driver can vary as much as 400 percent in the same city or region of the nation.

Health Care Insurance

If you have millions in the bank, then you may decide that you would rather pay for any medical care out of pocket when the need arises rather than pay for health insurance. However, when we say millions, that is exactly what we mean. You can easily run up a bill into the thousands of dollars for a week at a hospital. You will need to look at how much a loss could cost in economic terms and see if you could cover that cost.

Staying on top of the changes in health insurance can be a real pain in the neck, but it's something you must do. These are very important financial decisions. You need to keep up with changes in your health care policy, including premiums, deductibles, copayments, maximum payout limits, and preventive health care coverage. If you work for a large company or for the government, you likely receive a packet each year that allows you to fully evaluate your options. Often you'll have choices between HMOs, PPOs, and traditional medical insurance. If you work for a smaller company or for yourself, your options may be far more limited. Still, where you have choices, you want to know what they are. What the best policy is for you and the level of medical care your family uses will be entirely different for someone down the street with different medical needs.

How do you decide what's best for you and your family? You need to see what your options are. Compare the costs and the coverage of the various options very carefully. Read the fine print. Decide how important it is to you to be able to choose your own doctors. Most insurance experts recommend against policies that are very narrow in scope. For example, catastrophic medical policies or policies that are focused on a specific disease are often poor choices. The same holds for hospitalization policies that pay directly to you on a daily basis. Accident policies are also not recommended. All of these types of potential injuries and illnesses should be covered under your major medical or comprehensive health care policy.

Before you decide what kind of policy to buy, you can check out such resources as consumer guides, like one put out by the Georgetown University Institute for Health Care Research and Policy, titled *A Consumer Guide for Getting and Keeping Health Insurance*. Their resource covers all fifty states as well as the District of Columbia. Here are some other sources of good information:

The National Committee for Quality Assurance, (800) 839-6487

The National Health Council, (202) 785-3910

Health Care Financing Administration, (800) 638-6833

Health Insurance Association of America, (202) 824-1600

Disability Insurance

Sixteen times as many families lose their home to foreclosure because of a disability than because of a death in the family. Yet only two out of five adults have disability insurance. This type of insurance is designed to replace a portion of your income if you become disabled as a result of an accident or illness.

Home Safe

When I (Scott) was a little boy, my parents owned and ran their own business, selling electronic testing equipment to industry. As a manufacturer's rep, my father could bring in very little income unless he could be out meeting with customers. When I was in grade school, my father became very ill and was unable to work consistently for four long years. I still remember going to the hospital with my mother. Children weren't allowed on the wards back then, so I'd play in the lobby while Mom visited Dad. As we were leaving the hospital one day, my mother stopped in the parking lot and had me look up to one of the top floors. There was my father, looking down, waving to me. I smiled and waved back to him. It was years later that I learned that my father thought this would probably be the last time he'd ever see me. He was scheduled for major surgery the next day, and the doctors expected that they'd find that he was full of cancer.

My father eventually recovered far beyond what the doctors thought possible, and he and my mother went on to develop the business into a very successful venture. Now they are retired and enjoying truly wonderful golden years together.

I remember the years during my dad's illness as being pretty tough for my family, but it would have been so much worse if my dad hadn't bought disability insurance years before his illness.

I found out later that this insurance was the key reason we did not lose our house. So how hard do you think it was to convince me to buy solid disability insurance? It costs a great deal, and since I have been self-employed most of my adult life, I pay for it directly out of my income. But what is peace of mind worth? A lot.

The first question is how much disability insurance you need. If you're financially independent, meaning that you do not rely on your ability to work for an income, then the answer may be none. For most of us, however, the answer is a minimum of 60 to 70 percent of your current annual income. If your employer has paid for the insurance, then your benefit is taxed, and this amount may not be enough. However, if you pay for it yourself, this payout would be nontaxable. The reason for this has to do with the nature of the funds used to purchase the insurance. If the disability insurance is paid for with pretax dollars—or dollars on which you did not pay income taxes—you will need to pay tax on any benefits paid out to you later. If after-tax dollars are used to buy the insurance, you will not pay tax on benefits that you draw. Bottom line? Factor in the tax repercussions of the benefits when deciding how much disability insurance you want to have. If you have an employer who provides disability insurance but the amount is less than you'd be comfortable with, you can look into supplemental policies to bring the benefit up to a higher level. There are many complexities to figuring out what is best for you and your situation; we encourage you to give thought to these issues and to talk them through together.

Disability insurance is very expensive. That's just more evidence of how likely people are to need it. The price of disability insurance takes into account your gender, your age, and the amount per $1,000 of income that you want to replace. Other factors include the waiting period before benefits can be paid and the length of time of maximum benefit. Normally, there is a five- to six-month waiting period before disability insurance will pay benefits. In addition, the length of payout period can range from one year to the age sixty-five. The smaller the amount of coverage, the longer the waiting period, and the shorter the payout period, the cheaper the policy will be to you or your employer.

Many disability companies require that their payments be coordinated with Social Security disability payments. When evaluating a policy, ask questions about how such payments would affect the payout of the policy, should you need to use it. You also need to consider whether to have (or if you have) an *owner-occupation policy* or *any-occupation* policy. An owner-occupation policy will pay out if you are unable to perform the duties of the *owner's* job. For example, if you are a chemical engineer, can you perform the duties of a chemical engineer? The any-occupation policy pays you until you can work at *any* job. In other words, if you were a brain surgeon with an any-occupation policy, you wouldn't get disability payments as long as you were able to say, "Do you want fries with that?"

An Example of How the Right Agent Can Help

Say you are healthy and looking to buy disability insurance. Some companies still offer what is called a *return of premium rider,* although they are less available now than they used to be. One such option on the market allows the owner to get back his or her premium after ten years if he or she stays healthy and does not use any disability support from the policy. Every ten years, the insurance company will write a check back to the insured for the premium that's been paid. Yes, the rider costs extra. Of course the insurance company is the one earning the interest on the money the insured has paid for ten years—that's how the company makes its money on such a policy—but the rider allows the insured to have protection and get that money back if it turns out to be unneeded.

Such an option may or may not make sense for you. Many agents won't even have such an option to show you. Others can not only show you the option but also can run the charts for you to see how well you'd have to do investing the premium money to come out ahead of how you'd do purchasing the rider. As we said earlier, so many of these decisions get very complex. Complex decisions require complex information in order to make the best choice.

Long-Term Care Insurance

Long-term care insurance is relatively new, and it might be the most complex of all the types of insurance we discuss. It is designed to pay for care for older adults in their own home or in a nursing home. Apparently, 85 percent of the time, it ends up paying for long-term care in the home—which is what many people prefer when coping with long-term health problems. The policies are both complex and relatively expensive.

Who should consider purchasing this type of insurance, and when? This is an interesting question, and the answer depends on whether or not you have done a good job of planning for retirement. Some experts say that unless you have either a great deal of wealth or none at all (to protect), the policies are worth giving serious consideration to in your overall economic planning. The cost of private-pay nursing home beds is skyrocketing, which means that many couples have seen the health problems of one partner wipe out the life savings of the two.

It is generally agreed that individuals who want to be certain that long-term illness or disability doesn't destroy their spouse financially, or who want to leave something for their heirs, should consider long-term care insurance. This type of insurance will protect the majority of their assets from being spent down to the poverty level as required by Medicaid (which will help you only after you have expended your savings and assets).

Long-Term Care Insurance

Amy I. Locke, CLU, CLTC, CSA

Without proper planning, the need for long-term care can be the greatest threat to your financial security. Long-term care is extended chronic care to help with daily activities such as bathing or dressing, getting in and out of bed or a chair, toileting, eating, or it may be needed for a cognitive impairment such as Alzheimer's disease. Only 15 percent of people receiving long-term care are in nursing home facilities. Most are being cared for at home, in the community, or in assisted-living facilities. Long-term care (LTC) insurance policies are designed to pay for care in any of these settings.

People of all ages can need this type of protection as a result of a car accident, sports injuries, multiple sclerosis, strokes (one-third of the people in the United States who have a stroke each year are under age sixty-five). Forty percent of people needing LTC are between the ages of eighteen and sixty-four. Some examples of people you might have heard of include Christopher Reeves, who at age forty-three broke his neck horseback riding, and Michael J. Fox, who at age thirty-six was diagnosed with Parkinson's disease.

LTC is expensive. The average cost for a private pay nursing home bed is $145 per day, or $54,000 per year. Adult day care averages $50 per day, assisted living centers run $90 per day, and home health care can cost $120 per eight-hour shift. Without planning, the costs of LTC can exhaust your assets in a short period of time.

Most LTC in America is paid for out-of-pocket or by Medicaid (which is welfare). To be eligible you must first become destitute—which means spending down lifelong savings and liquidation of assets. Medicare (which provides benefits of various kinds to Americans sixty-five and older) pays only for skilled care while you are recovering, and once you've made what progress is possible, the payments stop. So, a person suffering from Alzheimer's or paralysis from a stroke may not be eligible for long-term assistance.

Reasons to Consider Long-Term Care Insurance

- To maintain independence and not become a financial burden to family
- To protect assets for retirement and to leave to family
- To be able to stay at home as long as possible
- Peace of mind

LTC insurance policies have evolved over the past twenty years to the point that today's policies cover care in all types of settings, with various benefits possible. Life is uncertain. The time to plan for LTC benefits is while you are relatively young and healthy. Your money pays the premium, but your health buys the policy. The longer you wait to obtain coverage, the more expensive it will be. An insurance broker who specializes in LTC will be able to help you design a plan that fits your personal situation.

Source: www.LockeandAssociates.com

It's not just older folks who think about these policies. They are very popular with people between the ages of forty and sixty these days. And it's not just old age that some people want to protect themselves from. What about a stroke that leaves someone partially paralyzed but otherwise healthy enough to live a long time? Or what about some sort of dementia that develops prior to what most would consider old age?

Even if you do not fit the description of a wise candidate for this type of insurance, your parents might. Don't hesitate to point out the reality of their financial future if they are among the folks who have a nest but not a huge nest egg. Their financial future, as well as some aspects of yours, may be tied to their decisions about nursing home care, retirement, and estate transfer financial planning. In this situation, it may be true that the financial sins of the father (or mother) may be visited upon the sons and daughters.

Life Insurance

Life insurance does not, of course, protect us from death. It protects our loved ones from financial hardship caused by our death. Psychologically, you may not feel comfortable at all in discussing life insurance. If you don't, you should get over it. We've known of too many families in which one parent died and the surviving parent and children had to drastically alter their overall lifestyle because there was either no insurance or too little. This is one of those things that many people find easy to put off, perhaps to some degree out of sheer busyness, but all too often out of denial of the possibility of death.

Unless you have special circumstances, acceptable life and disability policies should ensure that your dependents could live in the same home, attend the same schools, keep the car, and so forth. Even if the two of you are newly married, both working, with no children and few assets, you may want to get a small policy to allow for your partner to pay for funeral expenses and to be able to afford to remain in your apartment for a couple of years. Or you may want to get a large term life insurance policy because it's so cheap. It's up to you, and it's up to you to weigh out what's best in your situation.

There are two primary kinds of life insurance: term and permanent. Not to sound like a broken record, but the issues here are complex, and the best choice for one person may not be the best for another. Here we only hope to cover a few keys for you to consider as you find out more and assess what you need.

Term Life. Term life insurance is pure protection. It is not a way to accumulate cash. As long as you pay your premium, the policy will pay out a certain amount of money if you die within a certain period of time. When the term is over, if you're still walking, you walk away with nothing. It's simple and cheap. The premium tends to be less expensive when you're young and gets more expensive as you get older.

Many companies used to sell annual renewable policies that the insured would renew at a new rate each year; the rate would typically go up as the individual grew older. We're told that few companies even offer that anymore because it makes so little sense for most people. What is most common now are what are called level-term policies. You select the number of years of coverage (for example, 5, 10, 15, 20, or 25 years) and the death benefit amount, and your premium stays the same over that period. The great advantage of level-term life insurance is that you know exactly what you are getting, for how long, for how much. It's therefore easy to compare policies among major companies, too. In fact, it's so easy that there is no excuse for not comparing rates among well-rated companies. You could lose a lot of money by failing to do so.

Permanent Life. The name might be misleading, as you can't buy a permanent life. But you can buy a life insurance policy that is a relatively permanent fixture of your financial life in comparison to term insurance. It is more complicated and expensive, sometimes five to ten times more expensive than term insurance. There are three main types, but it's well beyond the complexity of this book to describe them in enough detail for you to make a decision based on this information—if you otherwise have concluded that permanent life insurance makes sense for you. These three types are as follows:

1. *Whole life.* This is essentially annual renewable term insurance plus a savings account function. For each payment you make, some portion goes to pay your death benefit, some portion pays your insurance agent's commission, and some portion goes into the cash value, or saving vehicle. Usually, the insurance company invests the money very conservatively.
2. *Universal life.* This is similar to whole life except that the insurance company will invest your money more aggressively. That can be good if they are savvy investors, and less good if they are not.
3. *Variable life.* This seems to be the hot product right now. These policies tend to include a wide range of investment options and significant tax benefits compared to the identical investments if made outside the boundaries of such a vehicle. That means that you have another option to consider besides IRAs and other retirement accounts if your goal is long-term investment with tax benefits.

There is much more you can learn about each of these types of life insurance. So how do you choose? For many people, level-term life insurance is easy to obtain and perfect for the current need for protection. In fact, some people will tell you—often forcefully—that there is almost no situation under which the permanent policies make sense. But that advice is too one-size-fits-all. In fact, you may have very good reasons for considering a permanent policy. Because those products are complex, you have to do your homework.

Various financial experts have run analyses that suggest that the average person is likely to do best buying term life insurance and investing the difference in cost between that and permanent life insurance. However, those analyses often use average policies rather than the best policies to make the comparisons. Further, and more important, term may not be the best choice if you don't actually invest the difference. Most people do not. If you need a savings vehicle that helps you be more disciplined, then a variable life policy might be a good choice for you.

If you think a permanent type of life insurance policy might be useful, here are at least a few of the really crucial questions to ask yourself—and an agent—before buying:

1. What is your purpose? If you have no savings motivation and want pure death protection, what are your options, and what would be the long-term financial outcomes of each one?

2. What is the guaranteed interest rate that the permanent policy pays on the cash value or savings portion of the policy? You want to know what has been typical, but you also need to know what the lowest rate is. Because it's unlikely that you'd be looking at a permanent policy if you were not interested in the savings aspect of it, you surely want to know how a particular policy compares on this crucial aspect with others you may be looking at.

3. Insurance experts tell us that this question is crucial: What's the interest rate you will pay on any money you borrow on the value of your policy in the future? Once you've built up value in a permanent-type life insurance policy, your key way of getting it out is to borrow it. Of course, you can cash out the policy, but that's not usually what makes the most sense, for a host of reasons including potential tax implications. Policies vary tremendously, though, in what the rate of interest will be on any funds that you borrow. That can make the difference between such a choice being a reasonable investment or a pretty poor one in your situation.

Want to get killed when buying a permanent life insurance policy? Here's what you do. Buy it from an agent you hardly know and who hardly knows you; get a policy with a low interest rate on the investment portion but a high interest rate on borrowing against that money. That'll do it. If you want to do well, ask a lot of questions and get a lot of answers so that you can decide what's best for you and your family.

How Much Insurance Do You Need? There are many ways to calculate your death benefit need, ranging from a very easy approach to the very complex. The easy method assumes that your family will need about 70 percent of your salary for seven years after your death. To calculate the amount of insurance you need to buy, multiply your current income by seven and then multiple that answer by .70. This calculation assumes you are a "typical" family, which may or may not be who you are. That figure seems pretty low to us, though. (We will have more to say about this shortly.)

A slightly more complex approach is found in the calculators provided by Metropolitan Life and the Teachers Insurance and Annuity Association, as illustrated in Figure 30.

You need to consider whether to insure the life of a stay-at-home spouse. It has been estimated that the value of the stay-at-home spouse to a family with children is about $10,000 annually, which includes the value of his or her labor in child care, housecleaning, and so on. That nevertheless underestimates the value of what this person brings to the family. The $10,000 estimate is very narrowly focused on the cost of replacing specific services in the family routine. Most families would fair far better with a more generous insurance policy. This is especially true if anyone in the home is in poor health or has special needs.

We ascribe to this rule of thumb: the total assets your loved ones would be left with, if you died, should be enough that they can maintain their lifestyle by living on the interest and dividends that would come from reasonable investment of the principal, while never having to tap into the principal. So, many would recommend that between savings, retirement funds, inheritances, and the insurance benefit, the

FIGURE 30. A WORKSHEET TO CALCULATE YOUR LIFE INSURANCE NEEDS.

1	Five times your personal yearly income.	$
2	Total appropriate expenses above and beyond your daily living costs for you and your dependents (e.g., tuition, care for disabled child or parent).	$
3	Your emergency fund (3 to 6 months of living expenses).	$
4	Estimated amount of funeral expenses (U.S. average is $5,000 to $10,000+).	$
5	Add lines 1 through 4. This is the total estimate of your family's financial needs.	$
6	Your total liquid assets (e.g., savings accounts; CDs; money market funds; existing life insurance, both individual and group; pension plan death benefits; and Social Security benefits).	$
7	Subtract line 6 from line 7 and enter the difference here.	$
	The net result (line 7) is an estimate of the shortfall your family would face upon your death. Remember, these are rules of thumb. For a complete analysis of your needs, consult a professional.	

total amount your family is left with should be enough that an 8 percent yearly return would cover the lifestyle your family would desire to maintain.

There are many great sites on the Internet to check for quotes on insurance and to figure out how much insurance you need. Don't stop there. Check with an agent or two. If you find one who understands your situation and in whom you develop trust, listen carefully to the options he or she can put in front of you. As you can tell from what we've covered briefly here, there are many variables and lots of trade-offs, and a good insurance professional can help you weigh out the pros and cons of your options. A good agent will try to sell you term if that's best for you, but will also help you see how the other options would work out in your life. Read up on your options so that you are a well-prepared client and are able to ask the right questions; that way you can be satisfied that you're getting the right answers for you. Unless you know you're already set up just right for your situation, take the time to learn and plan based on what's best for your spouse and family.

Insurance of a Different Sort

While we're on the subject of dying, you could think of a last will and testament as a kind of very important insurance. Although not really insurance of the sort we've focused on in this chapter, a proper will does help ensure that your assets will be handled in the way that you direct and that your children will be cared for according to your wishes after you die. Dying without a valid will is known in legal parlance as having died *intestate*. If you do so, the state in which you reside takes upon itself and its legal system the distribution of your property according to its laws. Usually this forces your heirs to share your money and property in ways that you did not want. In addition, if no relatives are found, all your money and property will go into your state's coffers. The court will also determine who will care for your children and their property if the other parent is unavailable or unfit.

If you have children and you don't yet have a will, stop what you are doing and get a basic will done in some way that designates who you would want to have raise them should you die. With a will, you express your wishes not only as to who will raise them but also as to who will manage the assets that pass to them from your estate. Usually that's the same person, such as a trusted relative. The courts have the final say regarding guardianship of children. The key here is that if you haven't put your desires in a will, the judge will decide without knowing them. In the belief that it's better to do *something* than to do nothing at all on this matter, you might even go get one of the more respected software programs that allow you to prepare a will. That is at least a temporary step you can take rapidly.

With a basic will, you can leave your property to the people and organizations you choose. You also name the person you want to have care for your children if your spouse is unable to do so. A will also names a person to manage your minor children's property. Individuals who are under age fifty, are in good health, and do not expect to pay any estate taxes upon their death can usually get by with a basic will.

Who needs more than a basic will? If you meet any of these criteria, you need a more complex will:

- You expect to pay estate taxes.
- You want more control over property after your death.
- You have a child who has a special situation, such as a disability, that you need to address more specifically in your will.
- You have divorced and remarried, and have children from a previous relationship. These are good reasons to seek a lawyer's assistance in writing a will.

Do you need an attorney? You might get by all right with a will generated by a computer program or through a Web site, but you might not want to take that chance. As is true of everything else in this chapter, there are many complexities, and the well-being of your family could very well depend on the quality of information you get regarding these matters. Usually you can have an attorney draw up a will that will meet the unique needs of your family for a couple hundred dollars. Peace of mind is worth much more. And while you're in the attorney's office, you may discover that setting up a trust is a much better way to protect your assets for your loved ones.

Trusts are contractual agreements that enable an individual or organization to hold your assets for either your benefit or that of your heirs. They are very flexible arrangements that can vary in function from protecting your assets from taxes and creditors to managing your assets for young children or disabled elders. One of the great advantages of a trust is that your estate will not have to go through the court system in order to be settled. You can avoid probate fees and ensure that what you want to have happen with your assets actually does happen, and there is no long period of limbo. A will, in contrast, is a legal document, which means that the courts will very likely be involved. Furthermore, though you've stated in your will what you want to have happen, the will can be contested, and a judge will make the final decisions, not you. There can be a period of limbo as long as a couple of years while the will goes through the courts. For solid yet reader-friendly information about the pros and cons of wills and trusts, you can start by reading *The 9 Steps to Financial Freedom*, by Suze Orman.

The Factors That Affect the Cost of Your Insurance

As you begin to put all your many options together, keep in mind the various factors that will affect the cost of your insurance.

- *Coverage.* The more money the insurance company will have to pay if you file a claim, the more your premiums will be.
- *Deductibles.* The deductible is the amount you must pay out of pocket before the insurance company starts to pay. For example, suppose your roof is damaged in a hail storm and will cost $4,500 to replace; if you have a $500 deductible, you will pay $500, and the insurance company will pay $4,000 of the cost to fix your roof. The higher the deductible, the less the insurance will cost.
- *Coinsurance.* Coinsurance is the process by which the buyer and the insurance company share in the coverage of a loss. For example, there will be tremendous differences in premiums for health care policies with 70 percent, 80 percent, or 90 percent coinsurance clauses. The more you are willing to pay to cover the risk, the less the insurance costs you.
- *Hazard reduction.* If you lower the chances of the insurance company having to pay a claim, then your premiums will be lower. For example, premiums for life insurance for nonsmokers are lower than for smokers.
- *Loss reduction.* If you lower the amount of damage likely should an accident occur, then your premiums will be lower. For example, if you install smoke detectors and fire extinguishers in your home, your home insurance premiums will be lower. Because you have lessened the amount of damage a fire might do to your home, the insurance company gives you a decreased premium.
- *The company you choose.* These days, insurance companies are competing with each other, and that means rates are dropping. If you've done your homework well in the first place, regularly comparing makes less sense with a permanent life insurance product. But it makes a lot of sense with term life, home, and auto insurance. When it comes to home and auto insurance, you could actually save more than $1,500 annually on rates if you do some regular comparison shopping. However, beware that the cheapest insurance may not be the best deal. If your company isn't there for you when you need it, the money you saved on the premium is meaningless. Insurance companies are not all created equal. There are various ways to rate insurance companies, and there are groups who do it. To find ratings, check out A. M. Best, Moody's, Standard & Poor's, or Duff & Phelps Credit Rating Company. The DALBAR ratings (800-296-7056; www.dalbarinc.com) of insurers measure consumer satisfaction with sales, service, and communications. You can get a lot of great information from the Insurance News Networks site at

www.insure.com; however, beware that insurance companies advertise on this site, so not all information is bias-free.

Four Key Questions to Discuss Together

Before you spend your Friday nights visiting with various agents, you'll need to ask yourself whether you really need each of the six types of insurance. You need to answer four key questions.

1. How much loss can you afford financially? You may not need certain types of insurance if you can afford to bear the risk yourselves. If you can cover, say, only a $2,000 loss, then you'd better get insurance to cover any loss over than amount. If a potential loss could destroy any wealth you've already accumulated, destroy your ability to build financial success, or lead to bankruptcy, you cannot afford that loss: you need insurance.

2. How much risk can you afford emotionally? Just because you can cover the cost financially doesn't mean that you can afford the risk emotionally. There's a psychological value to insurance coverage. Some people handle loss better than others. One person who totaled his car might say, "Oh, well, easy come, easy go!" while another might feel devastated if he didn't have insurance to cover the loss. Many couples who rent believe that renter's insurance falls into this category. They may not own many household goods that could be destroyed by fire or vanish with theft, but to lose these items represents a loss that may be too emotionally painful to face without financial compensation. When discussing insurance with your partner, it's a good idea to discuss potentially different comfort levels with risk.

> *When discussing insurance with your partner, it's a good idea to discuss potentially different comfort levels with risk.*

3. What is the minimum amount of insurance you must have in order to meet your responsibilities to your loved ones? What you and your partner can afford financially and how much you can risk in emotional terms are both important. However, there is one factor that is even more important than what you want: your responsibility. If you are married or if you have children who are dependent on you (or both), then you have the responsibility to provide for your dependents to the degree that you can.

4. Beyond the minimum, how much money do you want to put into insurance? Once you have determined the minimum amount of protection that you *must* have, you need to decide how much more money you *want* to invest into the various kinds of protection available.

Rational Versus Emotional Reasoning

Some financial advisers base insurance needs on a strict economic model, assuming that what matters most of all is how things end up on the final balance sheet of life. That's fine, but it's perfectly acceptable for people to have different psychological needs and to take those needs into consideration when making financial decisions, as long as the individuals have the economic means to do so.

As the two of you discuss your needs as a couple, it's very important to look for solutions that balance the needs you each have. When making such financial decisions, one of you may be solely focused on the bottom line; for the other, psychological needs weigh more heavily. In such cases, having the ability to have deep, safe talks about what you each feel, need, and desire can put you way ahead as a couple in terms of making the kinds of decisions that you can both feel good about. In other words, when talking through issues like those introduced in this chapter, you might do well to try out some of the suggestions we presented in Part Two.

Moving Forward

To ensure that you have the best insurance set up for your family, you need to work through the following steps.

1. Decide what type of insurance policies to buy.
2. Decide what levels of coverage you need and want.
3. Determine where to acquire the coverage at a reasonable rate.
4. Purchase the insurance.
5. Evaluate and adjust your insurance periodically.

CHAPTER SIXTEEN

TAXES: KEEPING MORE OF WHAT YOU MAKE

The only difference between death and taxes is that death doesn't get worse every time Congress meets.

WILL ROGERS

We don't know anyone who's neutral about income taxes. Governments sure aren't. Although we all have our opinions about taxes and how the money is used, most of us are honest, law-abiding citizens who try the best we can to cope with taxes with a minimum of stress.

If you desire to manage your money in the best ways possible, you need to focus on two key goals when it comes to taxes:

Goal 1: Pay what you owe when you owe it.

Goal 2: Never pay one cent more.

Goal 1: Pay what you owe when you owe it. Goal 2: Never pay one cent more.

The first goal can be called *tax compliance,* the second *tax avoidance.* As you plan your financial lives, it's important to take into account the tax consequences of various options you have and the decisions the two of you make. For example, as we examined the issue of renting or buying a home, it was clear that your ability to deduct interest payments on a home mortgage can play a major role in understanding which option is the best one for your situation. Or, in considering different types of insurance you might obtain, complicated tax issues can have a great impact on what may be the best course of action for you. For example, you may be very disciplined as an investor and have thus concluded that you'd do best buying term life insurance and investing the difference between that and the cost of whole life. However, your specific circumstances may make it wise to consider a universal variable life policy because of the specific tax advantages that those have. Other areas of your finances that tax strategies might influence include investing, retirement planning, and estate transfer.

Learn More and Get Advice

Generally speaking, if your income exceeds $60,000 a year, you will likely come out ahead getting more sophisticated tax advice (and other professional advice, such as that of financial planners). As with the other chapters in this financial management part of the book, we can cover only some of the basics for the two of you to think about as you make your decisions. Really, we'll feel we have succeeded in this money management section if we can motivate you to learn more. Go to the library, go to the bookstore, go online, and learn, learn, learn. Seek advice from qualified professionals in specific areas when appropriate. When it comes to taxes, you may save a bundle by spending some extra money now, and regularly, getting a tax checkup from a certified public accountant.

Go to the library, go to the bookstore, go online, and learn, learn, learn.

One of the reasons why it can be very wise to get professional tax advice is that our tax laws here in the United States are very complex. Worse, they are ever changing. What might be a great tax strategy this year may be the worst tax strategy in two years. The rules of the game today will not be the same tomorrow.

The federal government has made four major changes in the tax code since 1985, and it is bound to make more as the twenty-first century progresses. Sometimes these changes have occurred under the banner of simplification, but the rules really only get more complex. In part, these changes are made because of changing economic conditions that affect revenues to the government, and—no surprise—politicians generally don't want their stream of money to dry up.

Let's look at the recent major tax changes that occurred at the federal level to give you an idea of how things change and can then change back again. The last major tax legislation as of the time we're writing this book was the Economic Growth and Tax Relief Reconciliation Act of 2001. You might otherwise know this as the version of President Bush's tax relief that was passed by Congress. Many of the provisions of this act are phased in over ten years. Yet if the law remains unchanged over this ten-year period, many provisions of the 2001 law will disappear in 2011. Figures 31 and 32 show how rates and tax brackets will fluctuate under the provisions of the 2001 law.

FIGURE 31. TAX RATES UNDER THE PROVISIONS OF 2001 TAX RELIEF LAW.

Year	Individual Regular Income Tax Rates (%)					
Pre-Act	——	15	28	31	36	39.6
Jan.–June 2001	10	15	28	31	36	39.6
July 2001–Dec. 2003	10	15	27	30	35	38.6
2004–2005	10	15	26	29	34	37.6
2006–2010	10	15	25	28	33	35
2011 and after	——	15	28	31	36	39.6

FIGURE 32. REGULAR INCOME TAX BRACKETS FOR MARRIED INDIVIDUALS FILING JOINTLY.

2001 Taxable Income ($)	Rate (%)	2006 (Projected) Taxable Income ($)	Rate (%)
0–45,200	15	0–12,000	10
45,201–109,250	28	12,001–57,850	15
109,251–166,500	31	57,851–124,900	25
166,501–297,350	36	124,901–190,300	28
Over 297,350	39.6	190,301–339,850	33
		Over 339,850	35

The more things change, the more they stay the same. Who knows what will actually happen. The only logical thing you can do to make a real difference in your bottom line is to keep your eyes open, keep reading, and think about that expert advice. When the rules change, your strategies will likely need to change with them.

Tax Decisions That Can Tax Your Relationship

Before we move into some specific thoughts for you to consider when it comes to tax management, we'd like to mention two of the ways that tax decisions often intersect with couple dynamics. Almost every adult who pays enough in taxes to be faced with options has to decide how aggressive he or she will be in tax avoidance.

For example, how comfortable are you in claiming deductions that you are enti-tled to claim? How aggressive are you in claming deductions that push the limit? People vary in their tax-avoidance comfort level the same way people vary in their risk tolerance when it comes to investing.

There are two scenarios related to tax-avoidance strategies that can cause con-flicts for couples. One occurs when you simply differ in how comfortable you are pushing the limit in claiming deductions but your differences are within the range of what a tax expert would consider ethical and legal compliance. If you differ in this way, the best thing you can do is talk about it openly, getting at the feelings and any hidden issues that may be involved.

The second scenario, which can cause couples real trouble, has to do with ag-gressive tax avoidance that crosses the line into illegal tax evasion. Many people do not easily know when their partner is doing something illegal with their taxes; they often find out only after the beans are spilled with the IRS. That's because in many households, one partner knows about and handles much more of the taxes than the other. However, we've known other couples in which both are aware of what one wants to do that is illegal, and the other is quite disturbed by it, lead-ing to a lot of conflict between the two. Sometimes the conflict over this matter is so severe that major trust issues are triggered, often in irreparable ways. If you are faced with such a situation, remember how great the stakes might be, because, as we said in Chapter One, depending on how you file your taxes, the IRS does not tend to think of you as two separate people.

Specific Points to Consider

What follows are suggestions that the two of you might discuss or assign to your-selves as topics to study further.

Know Your Marginal Tax Rate

When you are making financial decisions, it's very important for you to know your *marginal tax rate,* which is the percentage of income tax you pay on the last dollar you earn. In other words, if you made one more dollar of taxable income, at what rate would that dollar be taxed? To determine your marginal tax rate, look back at Figure 32 and estimate your annual taxable income. For example, if you are married and filing a joint return and have taxable income between $45,201 and $109,250 in 2001, your marginal tax rate is 28 percent. In other words, for every additional dollar you earned between $45K and $109K, you paid $.28 on those dollars.

Knowing your marginal tax rate can help you make better investment decisions. For example, if you are in the 31 percent tax bracket, you may want to invest in double-exempt tax-free bonds rather than taxable bonds. Most double-exempt tax-free bonds yield lower interest than other bonds (depending on the amount of risk), but every dollar you receive is a dollar that goes into your pocket, and none of it goes to federal or state income tax. In contrast, if you are in a lower tax bracket and pay a lower marginal tax, a tax-free bond may not be nearly as good an idea as a taxable one, because the taxable one may pay you more, even after you factor in the tax difference.

It can also be helpful to know your *average tax rate*, although it's not nearly as important a number to know for financial planning. It can be useful for keeping your resentment down, though, as it's going to be a good deal lower than your marginal tax rate. Your average tax rate is determined by dividing your gross annual income by the actual amount of taxes you pay. The average tax rate is always lower than your marginal tax rate because of the progressive nature of income tax law. Most American taxpayers pay an average federal tax rate of about 15 percent.

Should You Do Your Own Taxes or Pay for Someone to Do Them for You?

There are no concrete rules to guide you in making this decision, but you will want to consider three things. First, how complex is your family's financial situation? Typically, a working family with income only from employment and two children as dependents can handle their own taxes. Even if you have some deductions and other matters to consider that you may be unsure of, some of the tax software that is now available for use on home computers is inexpensive and very easy to use. Two very popular programs are TaxCut and TurboTax.

As the number of sources of income and deductions increases, you become more likely to benefit from using a professional tax service. At the very least, a service makes it easier for you and your family simply to get your taxes done and in, so that you can get on with what's far more important and less taxing (!) in your life. How much stress and strain occurs in your family during tax filing season? For some families, this is one of the most stressful and hostility-filled times of the year. If you happen to live in one of these households, we recommend that you use a professional tax preparation service.

Another consideration is your track record with the IRS. Have you had several income tax reports sent back because of math errors or denied deductions? Have you been audited because of math errors or illegal tax deductions? If the answer is yes to these types of questions, we would recommend that you use a tax preparation service. The IRS seems to take note when people begin using a service and has a somewhat higher regard for taxpayers who get help.

When you use a tax preparation service, you are gaining a professional associate who can intervene for you if there are any questions about your taxes. (Of course, the person who does your taxes can do a good job only if you reveal everything about your financial situation and have the information organized.) Normally, a tax professional will assist you in correcting any problem with a tax return and assist you if there is an audit. In addition, many people get to deduct the expenses of tax preparation from next year's income tax (certain rules apply).

We suspect that reading the new IRS info is a great cure for insomnia, so if you find it boring, scary, intimidating, or anything else pretty negative, give yourself a break and hire someone to do it who likes numbers and regulations.

To Overwithhold or Underwithhold?

If you work for an employer who takes taxes out of your check for you and files those taxes with the IRS for you, the amount you are having withheld is going to be too much, too little, or just right—sort of like the three bears and their bowls of porridge. If you overwithhold, you will get a tax refund in the following year. If you underwithhold, you will owe additional tax when you file your return—and maybe penalties as well. If you withhold just the right amount, you might owe the IRS a few bucks or they you, but you're not looking at any serious money changing hands at that time of year.

Many people (therefore couples) deliberately overwithhold because they want to receive a tax refund upon filing their taxes. It's at times amusing, though sad, to hear people say things like, "Gee, I didn't get a refund and you got a big one. I'd rather work where you work." In 1999, the average refund was about $1,500. So if you have a friend who's getting a check for $1,500 back and you owe $63, you might be kind of disappointed or jealous. But many people don't understand that if they are getting a large check back, they had essentially given the IRS a substantial interest-free loan over the past year. The IRS had more of that person's money than it was entitled to and eventually had to give it back. If this is your situation, realize that you could have invested that money and had it gaining interest instead, provided that you are disciplined enough to save money in safe places.

We realize that some people decide to overwithhold as a way to force the saving of money, as some do with certain kinds of insurance. If you really can't save any other way, overwitholding may be a good enough strategy. Just recognize what you are doing, and why. Many families have the opposite problem because they underwithhold. Sometimes folks underwithhold and delay filing; they end up owing the IRS the tax, interest, and a penalty. How does it work for the two of you?

When You Are Self-Employed

If you are self-employed, you probably didn't make that decision by looking at tax considerations. More likely, it had something to do with your willingness to take a risk, your confidence in your business idea, and some degree of comfort with running things more on your own. When it comes to taxes, there are benefits as well as increased difficulties for the self-employed. On the positive side, there is a lot more flexibility as to how you can handle expenses and deductions, as long as those things pertain to the business. On the negative side, there is a lot more flexibility as to how you can handle expenses and deductions. Oops, we just said that. Well, the advantages are strongly linked to the disadvantages. You have more options and flexibility, but you also have more paperwork and more responsibility to get it all done correctly and on time. In addition, the IRS knows self-employed people have these added decisions—and, at times, temptations—when making deductions, so they tend to audit more returns of the self-employed.

One of the difficulties of self-employment is having to file estimated tax payments each quarter. We've seen more people get in tax trouble because of this than for any other reason. Here's how it works. If you have to file estimated payments (and if you make much at all, you have to, or you incur penalties), you have to make a pretty good guess as to just how much to send in. In the earlier phases of a new business, this can be hard to predict. You can be safe and estimate high, or you can wait and see how you do trying to hit it dead on. Many self-employed people have gotten to April and found that they've underpaid their taxes to the tune of $5,000. As you might imagine, many folks don't have that $5,000, and now it's due.

Now imagine that it's $10,000 or $15,000 that's due, and the money isn't there. Of course, this means that in the previous year, the person or couple essentially spent a serious amount more than they had available to spend. We've heard through the grapevine that the IRS is a pretty aggressive creditor to have chasing you down for money. These situations have ruined or stressed many marriages. How about yours? Imagine that you've been trusting your mate to pay his or her share of the taxes, and you find out that for the next two years you have to make an extra monthly payment of $500 to the IRS because your mate mismanaged his or her self-employment taxes.

Now here's a trick. Actually, no trick—nothing up the sleeve. If you are self-employed, we recommend that you do three things. First, get a really good estimate of how much you should be sending in each quarter for federal (and state) estimated taxes. Get the help of a tax adviser if you are unsure of how to get a really good estimate. Second, open up an account at your bank that you think of as your own personal escrow account. Usually, an escrow account is one in which one party temporarily keeps money that is going to change hands between two other parties. The point is that the money is already gone, safe, no longer there, on hold—are you getting the idea here? Once in escrow, the payee no longer really thinks of it as his or her money. It's gone. You can do this with your tax payments. You put aside—no matter what—enough money in this account each month that will allow you to make your estimated payments. Once you put it in that account, consider it the government's already. You just haven't written the check. If you are firm with yourself, you won't spend this money on something else that you cannot afford, because you understand that the money isn't yours. When the deadline rolls around for the next payment, you write a check on this account.

The idea of creating a personal escrow account can be used to cover other large, regular payments for which you'd rather put aside the same amount each month. This strategy can work well for things like large insurance bills that you will likely have to pay twice per year.

Complexities

Although we understand a good deal about taxes, we are not tax experts, so we're not even going to try to cover some of the very complex nuances of our tax code that may have very important consequences in your life. We'll mention a few here more to call your attention to them than to give you specific advice for your situation.

Capital Gains Taxes. Capital gains taxes are taxes that you pay on the profit you've made from the increase in value of assets you own. Selling or transferring an asset triggers the requirement to pay the tax. Since one has to pay such taxes only when the asset is sold, people often hold on to some investments that they might rather cash out of because they don't want to trip the tax trigger. There are different implications for short- and long-term gains, and various interesting things happen when you die while you still own the asset. If you have many investments outside of retirement accounts (in which you need not worry about tax consequences until you retire), you'll want to be studying carefully the implications of these taxes or relying more routinely on the advice of a tax expert.

Estate Taxes. If you inherited $2 million today, you'd pay at least $829,000 in federal estate taxes. It used to be that most people didn't consider it very likely that they'd ever inherit much at all, and surely, for most people, that's probably still the case. But something that has changed in our society is that there are larger numbers of older Americans who have more wealth than ever before. Even a simple home someone grew up in can now kick a typical estate up to several hundred thousand dollars just like that. What this means is that more people than ever before will be paying significant inheritance taxes in the years to come. Will that be you? As of 2001, everything over $675,000 of an estate is subject to hefty estate taxes. If you have parents who might leave you substantial wealth, we hope they have been wise in making thorough preparations to avoid as much of this tax as possible. If they are not prepared, you have a difficult conversation to bring up, but it's still worth doing so. Although people don't like to talk and think about death (at least their own), there are many strategies for lowering estate taxes as well as probate taxes that are worth looking into. Even the way a will is set up can make a huge difference. If you are likely to inherit substantial wealth or to leave substantial wealth to others, you'd be wise to ask a tax expert, a legal expert, and an insurance expert what options you have for keeping more of the hard-earned wealth on your side of the table.

State and Local Taxes. Don't you just love it? Each state, county, and city has its own tax rules in addition to those of the federal government. There are real estate property taxes, business property taxes (yes, businesses have to pay yearly taxes to have and use the equipment that they have purchased to run the business), occupational taxes, sales taxes, automobile license fees, and on and on it goes. Many times, you have to bear with these kinds of taxes, but they might not actually affect your decision making very much. Other times, they can. Here are just two examples.

In metro Denver, where three of the coauthors live, there is a huge difference between the school (property) taxes due to the city and county of Denver compared to surrounding counties. Although some people deliberately choose to live in a different county because the schools are more highly rated, they will pay much higher property taxes to live outside Denver. If you were in such an area and you decided that there was a private school you wanted your children to go to, perhaps for religious reasons, you'd do far better financially to live in Denver than to live in one of the outlying cities. Of course you'll pay taxes either way, but if you were otherwise able to find comparable homes, you might rather pay less tax than more for schools you've decided not to use anyway. If you are making a decision about where to buy a home and you've not investigated such things, you are risking throwing away thousands of dollars each year for many years to come. Think about it. Then get information to think about it more thoroughly.

Another common kind of tax reality that can affect your decisions if you are paying close attention is sales tax. Many people live and shop in areas where the sales taxes are very different from county to county or city to city. On a large purchase, such as for a refrigerator, it might save you $35 to buy it in one place rather than another—as long as you are picking it up yourself. If you have the appliance delivered to your home, however, you'll likely pay the sales tax for your area, so taxwise it won't matter where the actual store is located.

Tax Sheltering

You know, Mick Jagger and the Stones sang "Gimme Shelter" at a point in life where they were dying to save some money on taxes. You can cry out for, and find, shelter too. For example, arrange your financial situation so that you can collect as many deductions in one year as possible and also postpone any income for that year into the next. This bunching of deductions and postponing of income will help you lower your overall tax bill in the short term. You'll eventually pay it, but delaying tax payments can keep more in your account, longer. You can arrange to pay for a group of medical expenses or business expenses in the same year. At the same time, you can ask that a commission check for a major sale be issued after the first of the next year in order to avoid the tax consequences in a particular year.

Another important strategy is to seek investments that are tax sheltered. For example, make as large a contribution to your 401(k) retirement fund as possible and, at the same time, contribute the maximum to your IRAs. The contributions use pretaxed dollars and defer the payment of taxes on them until after you are retired. It is assumed that most of us will have lower levels of income after retirement and will therefore be in lower marginal tax brackets. That's the beauty of IRAs, SEP-IRAs, Roth IRAs, 401(k)s, and so forth. See Chapter Eighteen for more ideas.

Understand the Mechanics

We're not talking about those mechanics at your Ford dealer. Rather, we're talking about tax mechanics—how they work. Pull out your 1040 or 1040EZ from the past couple of years. Go through them, line by line, together, taking careful note of each entry and where it came from and how it affects your bottom line. Many people aren't really very aware of what actually affects their income taxes, but this is a simple way you can understand yours better. Are there any categories that you'd like to change in one direction or another in the coming year? Do the two of you agree?

Planning for the Future

In wrapping up this topic, we'd like to plant a little seed. As you consider what your children might major in while in college, you might consider suggesting that they get a degree that allows them to work in a field related to the federal income tax. If your kids become tax accountants or attorneys who specialize in tax law, they are bound to have a safe and secure job for the remainder of this century, as we will continue to tweak the income tax every congressional session until the next Ice Age. We're talking major job security!

Time to Talk

You may have found this chapter pretty boring. If so, rest assured: there are vast numbers of additional details that you can use to bore yourself to tears. However, sometimes boredom is worth suffering through if it saves you thousands of dollars. Talk through these questions:

1. Do you know how much tax you actually paid last year to your state and federal governments? What do you think of that amount? Would you like to lower it?

2. Do the two of you share a similar philosophy about how aggressive you want to be in claiming deductions?

3. Does the one of you who doesn't do as much with the taxes want to understand more from the other who has been managing them?

4. Talk through all of the major ideas presented here. Discuss each one and its implications for your lives. Do you have any major decisions coming up for which knowing more about the tax consequences might save you some serious dough? What do you want to do differently? What do you need to learn more about?

5. Do you need professional tax advice? Who are you going to call? Do you have any friends who might be good sources of a recommendation for getting great advice? (Hint: that would probably be a friend who's doing very well financially.)

CHAPTER SEVENTEEN

A PENNY SAVED IS . . . NOT MUCH! HOW TO CONTROL SPENDING

Annual income twenty pounds, annual expenditure nineteen and six, result happiness. Annual income twenty pounds, annual expenditure twenty pounds ought and six, result misery.

CHARLES DICKENS, *DAVID COPPERFIELD*

In this chapter, we're going to talk about controlling spending. Remember, we warned you: success is not for wimps. If your income and expense picture looks like Figure 33, your chances of living out your dreams are about as good as your odds of winning the lottery. However, if your income and spending looks more like Figure 34, you have something to work with. The larger the gap between income and expenses—as long as income is the higher number—the better your shot at living the future you want.

FIGURE 33. WHEN EXPENSES EQUAL INCOME.

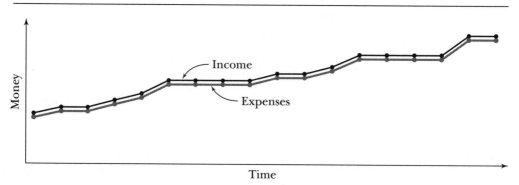

FIGURE 34. WHEN INCOME IS GREATER THAN EXPENSES.

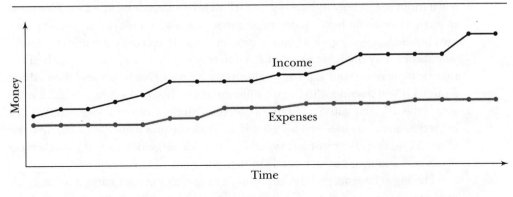

Increasing Income Versus Decreasing Spending

There are really only two ways to increase the gap between income and expenses. One is to increase your income, and the other is to decrease your spending. Let's talk briefly about increasing your income. By income, here, we are talking about earned income—pay you receive from work. We'll be talking in Chapter Eighteen about increasing your investment income.

> *There are really only two ways to increase the gap between income and expenses. One is to increase your income, and the other is to decrease your spending.*

You have many factors to think about when you consider income opportunities. Although it only makes sense for you to earn the best income you can (assuming that we're talking about doing it ethically), the amount of income isn't the only criterion for evaluating a job opportunity. For example, it is important to consider living costs along with income. It doesn't make much sense to take a job that pays $20,000 more per year if you'll have to move to a city where your living expenses would end up costing $25,000 more. There are also the quality-of-life factors to consider. For example, if you have to commute two hours to and from work each day to make a better income, you are sacrificing a great deal in terms of overall quality of life. Some jobs may not be worth the stress they bring to your life, whether because of coworkers, bosses, the tasks, or other such factors. In contrast, your finding fulfillment in your work, perhaps in what you are contributing to the world, may make one job better than another, even if the income is lower. Opportunity, time requirements, cost of living, and impact on quality of life are just some of the factors to think about along with income potential when you are considering career opportunities.

One factor with perhaps the greatest impact on earning potential may be your education. Whether you do it through formal or informal education, continuing to learn and increase your skills will be key to reaching your dreams. Continue to learn more about how to have a great relationship with those you love. Continue to learn more about how to earn more money through employment, owning your own business, investing, or a combination of these. If you are currently employed, you may or may not want to look for a different job that pays more. Your best bet may be to increase your skills and value to your current employer and then ask for a raise. Or you may need to learn a different trade. If you don't have a college degree, odds are that you'd do better to get one. Studies have shown the difference in lifetime earnings between a high school graduate and a college graduate to be about $1 million. For most individuals, getting a college degree is the single most important financial decision made in their lifetime.

Having acknowledged the importance of increasing your earned income, we now want to focus on controlling your expenses. The reality is that no matter how much you bring in, if you spend it all, you'll never get ahead. Remember that Bill and Mary Toohey, whose story we discussed in Introduction to Money Management, were able to become financially free on an income that never topped $60,000. Most millionaires don't become millionaires because they make huge incomes. They become millionaires because they control their spending.

Does the idea that people become millionaires by controlling spending seem hard to believe? If so, then your expectations are at work. Here's reality: Only 8 percent of millionaire households have incomes in the $500,000 to $999,999 range. The median millionaire household's annual taxable income is $131,000. Although $131,000 isn't exactly small potatoes, it's a long way from a million. So if these folks aren't making "big bucks," how did they become millionaires? They didn't inherit it. More than half never inherited as much as a dollar. The answer is that most millionaires simply create a big gap between their income and their expenses, just like the Tooheys. They live well below their means. They live in houses much smaller than they can afford, buy suits off the rack at department stores, and drive older cars.

Think about this a moment. In the coming month, which can you alter more dramatically: your income or your spending? Most people have more immediate control over their spending. You can pull more of those levers faster to have a greater effect on your bottom line. To help you control spending, we're going to encourage you to use that infamous tool called a budget. We're going to focus on budgeting because that's where you can get the most bang for your buck, so to speak.

Imagine

We have two exercises to help you put into perspective how important controlling your spending is to your future.

Exercise One

The two of you can do this together or separately. Close your eyes. (OK, that makes it hard to read. Read the directions and *then* close your eyes!) Imagine yourself at age sixty-five. Imagine your partner. Imagine yourselves deeply in love and doing something wonderful together that you've always wanted to do. Maybe you're living in your cabin in the mountains or your house on the beach. Maybe you're sitting in a little café in Paris. Make this image as real as you can. Feel the warm, contented feelings you would feel. Enjoy this daydream for a minute. OK, now put this book down and actually do this exercise—even if you have to go hide in the bathroom to get a little privacy. It will take only a few minutes.

Now write down the answers to the following questions:

- Where were you?
- What were you doing?
- Name three feelings that you felt.
- What would it mean to you if this dream came true?
- What would it mean to you if you were to get to the end of your life and this dream hadn't come true?

If your partner has done this exercise too, then take some time to discuss your answers together. Simply talk as friends about your dreams. (If you have vastly different ideas about what you want to do when you retire, *don't worry.* We haven't gotten to that part yet. For now, just enjoy hearing what your friend and partner dreams up.)

Exercise Two

OK, here's another exercise. Again you are sixty-five years old. You've retired. You are standing in front of your home watching all your material possessions being loaded into a truck. All but a few sticks of furniture are going into storage. Your partner looks very pale. You and your partner are moving into a crummy little one-bedroom apartment in a crummy little neighborhood. You've lost your house to foreclosure. You don't have a house on the beach. You won't be traveling. You're hoping that your job at McDonalds will pay enough for you to keep your apartment. This is how you'll finish out your life because you never planned for your retirement.

Sound far-fetched? We wish it were. The truth is that 85 percent of men in the United States at age sixty-five don't have $250 set aside for retirement. According to the Social Security Administration, only 2 percent of those who reach the retirement age of sixty-five are totally self-sustaining. You know those commercials you sometimes see on TV where an elderly couple is smiling on the golf course—clearly having the time of their lives? Well, they represent only 2 percent of sixty-five-year-olds. Another 23 percent are lucky enough to still be working (if you consider *having* to work at age sixty-five lucky). The other 75 percent must live on charity or depend on their relatives. These are scary statistics.

◆ ◆ ◆

The reason we wanted you to imagine the two of you experiencing a wonderful retirement and then to compare it to a miserable one is that human beings are motivated by the hope of gaining pleasure and the fear of experiencing pain. We're usually willing to exert some effort in order to get some pleasure. We're usually willing to exert even more energy to avoid experiencing pain. For the two of you to succeed in controlling your spending, you're both going to have to understand what's at stake. You're going to have to understand, deep within your soul, that *this is your life*. This isn't a dress rehearsal. If you want to live your dreams, your desire to reach those dreams is going to have to be stronger than your aversion to budgeting. You'll need to start thinking, "Ten, twenty, or thirty years from now, what will be wishing we had done today?" Have you got that? You get only one life. Don't waste it.

A budget is the tool you use to help make sure you're living to the fullest today and reaching your goals for tomorrow. For some couples, it's no problem to establish a budget and stick to it. For others, it is hard. No matter which group you're in, working hard all your life and ending up living off of charity would be hardest of all.

Savers and Spenders

When couples sit down to carve out a budget, they typically discover that they don't see eye to eye on what a "good" budget would be. People say that opposites attract. It isn't always true, of course, but it does seem that savers tend to marry spenders. Even if both of you are frugal compared to most people, when you're just comparing the two of you, one of you will likely feel better about spending, the other about saving. One tends to think more about today, the other more about tomorrow. That's normal. Sometimes couples are afraid that if they don't both agree exactly on how much to spend on what, it means they aren't compatible. That's an unrealistic expectation.

You and your partner are unlikely always to agree on all money matters. Fortunately you need not do so to succeed financially. Each of you needs to understand yourself as well as your partner, respect each other, and accept responsibility. Maybe you enjoy spending money. That's fine; however, you must accept that your behavior affects your partner, so you need to be willing to come to the table and respect your partner's need to save some. Maybe you feel more secure saving. That, too, is fine. But you need to be willing to allow your partner to be himself or herself and enjoy spending some money. If you always look down on your partner because he or she is not just like you, you'll poison your relationship.

The Spender Versus Saver Quiz

Here's a little quiz we've put together to help you determine where you are on the saver-spender continuum. Following are several groups of sentences. On a separate piece of paper, write down the letter of the description that most accurately represents you if handling money were entirely up to you. For example, the first group talks about saving a portion of your paycheck. If you would save a portion of each paycheck but your partner spends so much there isn't any left, go ahead and write *a*. Answer these questions as if you were the only one involved. Go ahead and complete this quiz now. Please be as honest about yourself as possible; don't just try to pick what you think are the "right" answers.

1. a. I nearly always save a portion of each paycheck.
   b. It usually takes all I've got just to pay the bills.
   c. I do well saving for a while, then I find something that I really want, and I take the savings back out.
2. a. It is very rare (or never) that I do not pay my credit card balance in full.
   b. My credit card balances nearly always carry over from one month to the next.
   c. Usually I pay off my credit cards, but I do have periods when I carry balances.
3. a. I have a general sense of where all my money goes.
   b. I keep a record of where every penny goes.
   c. I have no idea where my money goes.
4. a. I always think carefully before buying something.
   b. I think carefully before buying expensive items.
   c. If I see it and want it, I buy it.

5. a. When something breaks down, I usually have to use my credit card to replace the item.

   b. When something breaks down, I have money in savings to replace it.

   c. When something breaks down, although I have money in savings to replace it, I'd rather find a way to do without it or use money I'd earmarked for something else.

6. a. My checkbook is balanced once per month.

   b. My checkbook is balanced every few months.

   c. My checkbook hasn't been balanced in over a year.

7. a. If I get some "extra" money, I want to spend it.

   b. If I get some "extra" money, I want to save it.

   c. If I get some "extra" money, I want to spend half and save half.

8. a. I live on a budget.

   b. I don't make enough money (or too much) to bother with a budget.

   c. I know I should live on a budget, but I keep putting it off.

9. a. If I want something, I'll buy it whether or not it is on sale.

   b. I try to wait to buy what I want until I can find it on sale.

   c. I'll buy something on sale, even if I don't really need it.

10. a. It feels good to buy something new.

    b. It feels good to put money in savings.

    c. It feels good to buy and save according to a budget.

11. a. I put money into savings before I pay for other things.

    b. If there's anything left after spending, I'll save that.

    c. I have a plan for saving and spending.

12. a. I save because I want to become financially independent.

    b. I plan to start saving when I get better off financially.

    c. I will never be able to save.

13. a. Money isn't really very important in the grand scheme of things.

    b. Money is very important to me.

    c. I haven't really thought much about money until recently.

14. a. Saving money is most important.

    b. Living comfortably is most important.

    c. Living very well is most important.

15. a. I sometimes write checks when I'm not sure there will be enough money to cover them.

    b. I never write checks unless I have enough money in my account.

    c. I'm really not sure how much money I have in my checking account.

16. a. It is a realistic goal to be debt-free except for a house payment.

    b. It is a realistic goal to be completely debt-free—without even a house payment.

    c. It is not realistic to think that I could be debt-free.

Scoring

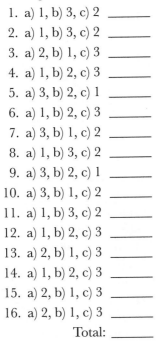

 1. a) 1, b) 3, c) 2 _____
 2. a) 1, b) 3, c) 2 _____
 3. a) 2, b) 1, c) 3 _____
 4. a) 1, b) 2, c) 3 _____
 5. a) 3, b) 2, c) 1 _____
 6. a) 1, b) 2, c) 3 _____
 7. a) 3, b) 1, c) 2 _____
 8. a) 1, b) 3, c) 2 _____
 9. a) 3, b) 2, c) 1 _____
10. a) 3, b) 1, c) 2 _____
11. a) 1, b) 3, c) 2 _____
12. a) 1, b) 2, c) 3 _____
13. a) 2, b) 1, c) 3 _____
14. a) 1, b) 2, c) 3 _____
15. a) 2, b) 1, c) 3 _____
16. a) 2, b) 1, c) 3 _____
             Total: _____

After you add up your score, you can look at the following ranges to get a feel for how your spending or saving habits compare to each other. There is much room within each range, and in fact they overlap somewhat to allow for individual differences. These ranges aren't designed to be taken as "the last word" but rather to give the two of you a feel for how your approaches to money might be different, and to facilitate conversation.

If You Scored Between 16 and 28

Unless you are living at the poverty level, you are probably too tight with money. You are more likely to neglect the needs of those you love and deprive them unnecessarily. You may be something of a wet blanket—always saying no to the idea of "letting loose a little." You are more likely to fear running out of money or worry about not having enough. You may be obsessed with finding the absolute best bargain before buying something. You are more likely to set unrealistic financial goals that require your family to endure hardships for long periods of time. You may be seen as controlling. You may take great pride in your "self-discipline," though in reality you are meeting your own emotional needs through saving while possibly neglecting others' needs to spend.

If You Scored Between 24 and 40

You are probably neither too stingy nor too much of a spender. You may be somewhat inconsistent in your spending and saving habits. You probably have periods when you are doing well saving, and then you'll go on a spending spree, but you tend not to hit either extreme. You may have some financial plans but need to refine and improve them. You can enjoy the security of having money in the bank, but you can also enjoy the euphoria of spending a chunk of money.

If You Scored Between 36 and 48

Assuming that you're not so wealthy that you have money to burn, you likely spend money too easily and resent any kind of accountability. You may think of yourself as generous, yet you probably find it difficult to truly share control of the money with your partner. You likely fear structure, such as a budget. You tend to be spontaneous or impulsive in your purchases. You are unlikely to have any financial plans and probably avoid or withdraw from discussions regarding the future. Your finances tend to be haphazard and marked by a series of financial emergencies. You are likely to spend a lot of time juggling different bank accounts and credit card balances. You have the habit of overestimating how far money will go. When you want something, you consider how much the monthly payment will be, rather than counting the whole cost.

Time to Talk

If you have both taken this little quiz, we suggest you take some time now to talk about your scores. The ranges we've described might be helpful to you, but what's more important is how similar or different your scores are. Is there a lot of difference between your answers? How is that difference played out in your relationship?

Regardless of how similar or different your scores are, where do you score as a couple? What your spending looks like as a couple might be reflected in the higher score of the two or might be best represented by an average.

Exploring Your Hidden Issues Around Budgeting

One of the key premises of this book has been that couples too often get pushed off course financially by the invisible forces: issues, hidden issues, and expectations. You've already learned a lot about how to harness the energy of these forces to make them work for you instead of against you when it comes to financial issues in general. Now we want you to look at these forces specifically in terms of how they can affect your efforts to create a budget for the two of you. Here's what we want you to do: get some paper and write out your answers to each of the following questions. Take some time to do this thoughtfully. After you're finished, make the time to discuss your answers together.

1. The idea of budgeting might set off the hidden issue of *caring* for me because . . .
2. The idea of budgeting might set off the hidden issue of *control or power* for me because . . .
3. The idea of budgeting might set off the hidden issue of *recognition* for me because . . .
4. The idea of budgeting might set off the hidden issue of *commitment* for me because . . .
5. The idea of budgeting might set off the hidden issue of *integrity* for me because . . .
6. The idea of budgeting might set off the hidden issue of *acceptance* for me because . . .
7. When I think about the structure, the "rules," or the accountability involved in budgeting, I feel . . .
8. If we create a budget, I am afraid that . . .
9. When I think about saving more money, I feel . . .
10. When I think about limiting our spending, I feel . . .
11. If we create a budget, one good thing that could result is . . .
12. An obstacle we'd have to overcome in order for our budget to be helpful is. . . . Here are three things we could try that would help overcome this obstacle:
13. In five years, what will we wish we had done today?
14. Can we agree to create a budget and stick to it for two months?
15. We're going to reward ourselves for creating a budget and sticking to it for two months by . . .
16. During these two months, we expect that we will learn more about what works for us and what doesn't. This is the date we're going to sit down and adjust our budget:

Benefits of Budgeting

Now that you've thought about some of the emotional baggage associated with budgeting, let's talk about what a budget really is. A budget is simply a spending plan. In Chapter Ten we talked about the golden ground rules. These are agreed-on ways to handle events and issues safely in your relationship, and they help protect all that is good in your relationship. A budget is the same kind of thing. It is an agreed-on plan for handling your money as a team. Both savers and spenders benefit. Savers know that a certain amount is going to go toward what is important to them: investment for tomorrow. They are allowed a certain amount of "guilt-free" saving. Spenders know that a certain amount of money is going to go toward what is important to them: meeting the wants of today. They are allowed a certain amount of "guilt-free" spending. For both of you, it helps to ensure that you are putting your precious dollars toward the things that matter to you most.

> *A budget isn't about preventing you from getting what you want. It is a plan to help you get what you want most.*

Some couples have gotten the idea that a budget is planned and enforced deprivation. If it is, then you're doing it wrong. Although it's true that to get ahead you must keep some of what you earn, that doesn't mean you have to make yourselves miserable. It means you need to be wise. It means you can't waste money on things that are less important than your dreams. A budget isn't about preventing you from getting what you want. It is a plan to help you get what you want *most*.

Is a Budget Really Worth the Work?

In their book *The Millionaire Next Door*, Stanley and Danke found that 54.5 percent of millionaires use a budget like the one we're talking about here. Of those who do not, more than half set aside a minimum of 15 percent of their pretax dollars to invest and then feel free to spend the remainder. This is called reverse budgeting, or the "pay yourself first" method. Twenty percent of the millionaires make so much money that it doesn't really matter how much they spend. Of the ones who don't have money to burn, approximately 68 percent budget, about 29 percent use the reverse budget method, and only around 3 percent don't budget at all.

From these simple data we can learn one very important truth: the vast majority of people who don't make enough money to burn yet want to become and remain millionaires use some form of budget. Maybe it's worth a try.

Creating a Budget

You might be happy to know that you've already done all the hard work in creating a budget. The hardest part is overcoming your hang-ups about the idea in the first place. If you've been talking about your issues, hidden issues, and expectations, then you've tackled that part. That's the Problem *Discussion* we talked about in Chapter Nine.

Then there's organizing all your information. We handled that in Chapter Thirteen. When you started tracking your income and expenses, you created the basic framework for your budget. As we discussed in Chapter Thirteen, when you are tracking your expenses, you are simply recording what you spend your money on. With a budget, you will now define a target. You decide together how much or how little you *plan* to spend in each area. Now you're ready for the Problem *Solution* stage. We suggest that you follow the four steps of the problem-solving model presented in Chapter Nine.

Agenda Setting

You begin with the agenda. You could phrase the agenda this way: "What are we going to do differently about managing our money in the next two months?" We don't expect that you're going to reach all your financial goals in two months. What we're hoping to do here is help you try budgeting for a short while, to see if you find it useful for reaching your goals.

Brainstorming

Here's where you take blank copies of your income and expense charts and start writing in "budget estimates" in each category. If you've been tracking your expenses, then you can base your estimates on actual numbers. We'd suggest that each of you create three or four different options by yourself. Take time to see how you would handle the money if it were entirely up to you. This will help you make sure you understand what your own priorities are. Remember that your expenses can't be more than your income—well, they can be, but that's not the path to financial freedom!

Compromise and Agreement

Now you each bring to the table your several different "optional" budgets and start discussing the advantages and disadvantages of each. This may be challenging, because you are choosing to make some things happen and other things "not happen." To make a choice always means that something will be left unchosen. That can be painful. It may involve grief. You can help each other through the tough part. If, however, you find yourselves becoming frustrated with each other, then you'll want to pick up the floor and use the Speaker-Listener Technique to discuss the issues some more.

As part of your plan, remember to incorporate answers to these questions:

1. How much "mad" money will each of you get? You each need a certain amount that you don't have to be accountable for. Many couples come up with

great financial plans for budgeting, but fail to make sure each has some money to spend that's in the budget but doesn't have to be accounted for in any way at all (except if someone is engaging in such potentially destructive activities as gambling). Many budgets fail because people don't allow for some room to wiggle. Most people, no matter how committed and strong their partnership, need some room to make some financial decisions completely on their own.

2. How accurate are you going to be in tracking your expenses? To the dollar? To the penny?

3. Who is going to be responsible for entering the information onto your budget sheet?

4. When and where are you going to keep the expense information? For example, at the end of every day are you going to put all receipts in an envelope kept in the kitchen? We suggest that you come up with a system that doesn't require or allow you to grill each other with "How much did you spend, and on what?" at the end of each day.

5. When are you going to record credit card purchases: when you use the credit card or when the bill comes due? In many cases, knowing you'll be accountable for the purchase that very day will help you control your spending. Somehow, buying on credit doesn't feel like *really* spending money. This is why the stores want you to use that plastic card. They know you'll spend more! So if you can get into the habit of thinking of the money as really gone when you charge, you'll likely find it easier to control your outgo. (From a cash-flow perspective, you can set aside the money into your own "credit escrow account"—similar to an escrow account for taxes mentioned in Chapter Sixteen—so that when the bill comes, you're not hit so hard.)

Follow-Up

Some couples go over their budgets very carefully every month, others just go over them.

SALLY POPLIN

Once you've agreed on a budget to try for two months, you need to set a date and time to discuss how it worked and didn't work for you. For the two-month experiment, you will need to keep track of your expenses. You may find that you estimated too low in some categories and too high in others. Be prepared to use the Speaker-Listener Technique to discuss your feelings about "not making the budget." Perhaps one of you spent more than you were supposed to. Use the floor to discuss this issue. Perhaps you had expenses you weren't planning on, and that was discouraging. Pick up the floor and discuss that. You may find that you want to create entire new categories. You may find that the categories are fine, but you want to change how you keep track of the data.

Get out your calendar now and mark a date in two months to talk about how your budget experiment went. Also write out what you're going to do to celebrate your attempt. Even if it doesn't go perfectly, you should celebrate your first try.

At the follow-up, make the changes you want to make, and agree to another two-month trial.

The Envelope Method for Kids (and Mom and Dad Too!)

One method of budget control that is especially good for children is the envelope system. You place into envelopes the exact amount of cash that you have planned to spend in that category. As you take money from the envelope, you record on the outside of the envelope the amount spent, the date, and where the money was spent. Many county cooperative extension agencies will sell you a set of twenty preprinted envelopes that can be used for this method. They're very inexpensive, too! Remember to store the envelopes in a safe place.

Many couples who decide to get out of debt cut up their credit cards and use only cash. Many couples see using the envelope system as too inconvenient, but we have had couples tell us that it was one of the best things they ever did. They use electronic banking for paying all their bills and use cash for everything else. They *never* have to worry about a credit card bill coming due. They *never* spend more than they have.

For the Skeptical at Heart: Common Questions or Objections

Before leaving this topic, we'd like to deal with some often-expressed, honest concerns about the difficulties of budgeting.

I Really Hate Rules

Déjà vu all over again? There's a lot of suggested structure in this book, and some people really dislike structure. Some feel truly confined when trying to follow a budget. First, the primary point is that any and every couple needs to have a way to keep a handle on how much money is coming in and going out of their family. You simply can't forever spend more than you have. At some point, someone will come and take your house away if you do not make the payments—same with your car, your furniture, everything. If what you're doing is working, then you may not want to do something different. We know of a couple who uses one checkbook for six months of the year and another checkbook for the other six months. They just put all their money into the first account and write all the checks they want out of it. Then they tuck that checkbook away for six months to be sure all the checks have cleared from that account. They start putting money into the second account and writing checks out of the second account. They put so much more money into the accounts than they need that they know they'll not bounce any checks. They never balance any statements. Apparently it works. Although we'd hate to be around their house at tax time, we say if it ain't broke, don't fix it.

If, however, you don't have money to waste and you want your money to do more for you, then you have to know what it's doing now. Using a budget can help a lot, and you don't have to rule it out just because you don't like rules. If you don't like rules, then don't *think* of a budget as a bunch of rules. The budget is your tool to help you get what you want. No one is forcing you to do anything. You're in charge. You're the ones deciding what you want your target to be.

It Goes So Slowly When We Work Out a Budget

Yes, it does. That's a big part of why it works. Stop to think about all the money that has gone through your hands in the last few years without your having any idea where it went. That's very sad and very unproductive. Yes, taking the time to think through what matters most to the both of you, and to talk it out, can take a lot of time, but taking that time may well be the fastest route to getting more of what you want. Remember too that there's a big difference between the amount of time and effort it takes to plan and create a budget and the time it will take you to maintain your system. Once you create a budget that works for you, it will likely save you a lot of time. Sometimes the fastest route is the slow lane.

What If My Partner Isn't Interested?

Over the years, we've noted that if one partner is not so wild about trying this and working at it, it may be that the partner has a hard time saying what he or she really wants. When budget time arrives and he or she really wants to spend more in a certain category, this partner feels foolish or selfish for wanting what he or she wants and so prefers not to bring it up. Be careful to consider psychological needs when creating your budget. It is hard to argue practically for emotional needs, so they risk getting shut out. It may not be at all rational for someone to want to buy a brand-new car when the used one is working just fine. However, emotional needs are valid too, so it might be wise to work the costs of a new car into the budget. This doesn't mean that the kids should go without food or shoes so that you can drive a new car. We're simply saying that practical needs matter and emotional needs matter too. And the two of you should respect both.

We feel strongly that any change in either partner will have a positive effect on the relationship. Your effort to bring planning and structure to your spending will be helpful, and perhaps it will even encourage your partner to participate, as he or she comes to feel validated and accepted by you. You may find that simply budgeting for whatever portion of the finances are under your control is a good start.

We Do Well for a While, but Then We Blow It

This is important enough that we'll say it again: one of the reasons budgets fail is because couples do not allow themselves enough wiggle room. You must each have some money that you can play with. Another reason budgets can fail is that the couple forgets about those "extra" expenses. For example, the dishwasher breaks. Do you have money in your budget for appliance repair or replacement? Are you going to take that money from another category, or do without?

Plan to Fail; Just Don't Fail to Plan

When my (Scott's) son Luke was five, he participated in gymnastics class. One day, the teacher had all the kids stand in a line, and each took a turn climbing up a ladder, hanging onto the monkey bars, swinging from one bar to the next down the row, then climbing down the ladder at the other end.

When Luke's turn came, he made it to about the fourth bar and then fell off. He ran back to get in line again. On his next turn, he made it to about the fourth bar, then fell off. He went back and got in line.

As Luke's turn came again, instead of climbing up the ladder, he darted off to a corner of the room, grabbed a chair, lugged it over to just under the fourth bar, then ran over to the ladder and climbed up. When he reached the fourth bar, instead of falling, he stood on the chair for a moment, then reached for the fifth bar and proceeded to the end of the bars and climbed successfully down. The only one smiling more proudly than Luke was his daddy.

We can all stick with a budget for a while. But usually something happens, and we fall off the bandwagon. Successful couples know their weaknesses and prepare for them. If you know that you're going to *need* a new CD from time to time, then put that in the budget. Put a miscellaneous or emergency category into your budget so that when you know you're about to fall off the budget, you've got a support ready.

Another reason that couples fail to stick with their budget is that they don't feel rewarded for playing by the rules. This is a real key. You'll kill your partner's motivation for sticking with the budget if you take away his or her incentive. For example, let's say that your partner really wanted the two of you to take a trip to Mexico. So you put a certain amount of money into the budget for your trip. During negotiations, your partner was willing to forgo money in other categories to make sure this was included. Then the car breaks down, and you haven't planned for that expense anywhere in the budget. For most couples, taking the Mexico money to pay for car repairs would mean death to the budget, not to mention death to any plans for romance! You may want to discuss taking some money from almost any other category, but don't go for your partner's "motivational" categories. You both need to have the sense that the budget is helping you get what you want most, and each of you will need to protect the other's reasons for making the budget work.

◆ ◆ ◆

Learning to control spending is really the heart of financial success. Many couples balk at the idea of using a budget, but as we have learned, financially successful couples do, in fact, use a budget to help them reach their financial goals. We hope you'll give it a try for a couple of months at the minimum. The more money you can hold on to, the more you'll have to invest, which is the focus of the next chapter.

Additional Resources

Your local county cooperative extension office (there are more than thirty-five hundred offices in the United States) will send you a publication that lists typical family budget categories. These publications are usually free or very inexpensive.

If you have Internet access, there are numerous family budgeting forms located on the Web that you can download for free. In addition, there are many free or inexpensive shareware budgeting programs available for downloading off of the Internet at either www.download.com or www.tucows.com.

CHAPTER EIGHTEEN

INVESTING: HOW TO GET MORE

Sometimes when I consider what tremendous consequences come from little things . . .
I am tempted to think . . . there are no little things.

BRUCE BARTON

Y ou've just gotten seated for dinner, and the phone rings. You start to answer it, but hesitate; you don't want your dinner to get cold. You decide to answer it because it might be your mother. It's not; it's your friend the apprentice genie we mentioned in Chapter Two. He has learned some new magic and is eager to know if you are interested in trying it. Dinner was only Hamburger Helper anyway, so you decide to hear your old buddy out.

After catching up with each other about careers and family and such, he gets down to business. Here's his offer: he can give you a magic penny that will double every day for forty days, or, if you would rather, he'll give you a million dollars instead, right this moment. Which one would you choose? Most of us would choose the million dollars. A million dollars is not loose change, after all, unless you're Bill Gates! But guess what: as you will see on the next page, most of us would not be making the best choice. Let's watch what would happen to a doubling penny in forty days:

Day	Amount of Money
1	$0.01
2	$0.02
3	$0.04
4	$0.08
5	$0.16
6	$0.32
7	$0.64
8	$1.28
9	$2.56
10	$5.12
11	$10.24
12	$20.48
13	$40.96
14	$81.92
15	$163.84
16	$327.68
17	$655.36
18	$1,310.72
19	$2,621.44
20	$5,242.88
21	$10,485.76
22	$20,971.52
23	$41,943.04
24	$83,886.08
25	$167,772.16
26	$335,544.32
27	$671,088.64
28	$1,342,177.28
29	$2,684,354.56
30	$5,368,709.12
31	$10,737,418.24
32	$21,474,836.48
33	$42,949,672.96
34	$85,899,345.92
35	$171,798,691.84
36	$343,597,383.68
37	$687,194,767.36
38	$1,374,389,534.72
39	$2,748,779,069.44
40	$5,497,558,138.88

Wow! What a difference a little time and knowledge can make—in this case, a $5,496,558,138.88 difference.

Time and knowledge—these are the keys to great investing. In this chapter, we're going to present some of the fundamentals of successful investing. There are many easy ways for you to gain specific investment advice through the Web or in terrific magazines like *Money, Worth, Kiplinger's,* and *Smart Money.* Our goal here is not to teach you everything you need to know about investing, but simply to get you started. The information will likely be more interesting or useful to some readers than to others. Understanding basic principles of investment is certainly important to the development of wealth, and although wealth is not everything, a solid financial situation gives you more options to pursue the most important things in life, such as time together, good education and opportunities for your children, and the ability to give to causes that are important to you. You may already have heard about some of what we'll say here, but we don't think it hurts to review the basics. We'll start by focusing on how time is critical to investment success.

Time Is Your Friend

If the genie had offered the magic penny for only twenty-seven days, it would have been better to take the million. But he gave you more time. In most aspects of life, time is not your friend. You age, you get wrinkled, things stop working, and your kids grow up way too fast. But one area where time is your friend is investing. Now, to be clear, time is only friendly if you let it work for you. Many couples do not, and most do not let it work as powerfully as it could. Time isn't going to ask you whether you want a comfortable amount with which to retire or a small amount. It will wait to see what you choose. You have already chosen what to do with past opportunities. You've taken them, or you have not. The choices you make from this day forward are what matter most now.

Time is important. Let's look at another example of how time makes a difference. The following is a chart that many financial planners use to encourage couples to get going with investing for their future. It shows what happens when two couples get an 8 percent annual return on their investment. Even though the Millers invest half as much as the Taylors, the Millers end up with about $47,000 more. Why? Time.

Age	The Millers	The Taylors
22	$2,000	
23	$2,000	
24	$2,000	
25	$2,000	
26	$2,000	
27	$2,000	
28	$2,000	
29	$2,000	
30	$2,000	
31	$2,000	
32		$2,000
33		$2,000
34		$2,000
35		$2,000
36		$2,000
37		$2,000
38		$2,000
39		$2,000
40		$2,000
41		$2,000
42		$2,000
43		$2,000
44		$2,000
45		$2,000
46		$2,000
47		$2,000
48		$2,000
49		$2,000
50		$2,000
51		$2,000
Total invested	**$20,000**	**$40,000**
Total value at 8 percent	**$145,841**	**$98,846**

If you haven't seen this kind of chart before, you may be amazed to learn that if you invest $2,000 per year for ten years, you'd have more than if you invested $40,000 but had ten fewer years for the interest to compound. The conclusion that most financial planners (and other rational people too) would draw is that it's better to invest like the Millers than the Taylors. It's much better to start early. So why don't we?

The Challenge

What is most likely to be happening in your life from age twenty-two to age thirty-one? Let's say that you graduate from college at twenty-two. When you graduate, you get one piece of paper that says you're a graduate and another that says you get to start paying off your student loans. You can't live in the dorm anymore—you need a place to live. You buy a house with a yard. You need a lawnmower and a hose and a wheelbarrow. You need more than a couple of futons to sit on, and you don't want to use bedsheets tacked over the windows as drapes forever. Your cars now have 140,000 miles on one and 117,000 on the other. It's time to brave the car dealerships, or you'll be walking. Then you start a family. In other words, your income is lower than it will likely be later because you're just starting out, and your expenses are higher in some ways because you're just starting out. Truth be told, from ages twenty-two to thirty-one, most of us aren't going to find an extra $2,000 sitting in the bank at the end of the year.

The thing is, from age thirty-one to infinity, most of us aren't going to find an extra $2,000 sitting in the bank at the end of the year either. Investing isn't one of those things that will simply happen on its own. We have to make it happen. Although many couples don't start investing early, many others do. Couples who are older than you, couples who are younger than you, couples with more money than you have, and couples with less money than you have—many of them are investing in their future. You can too. Our goal isn't to guilt-trip you if you haven't started investing yet. What we want to do is encourage you to sit down together and map out a plan that works for both of you, taking into account your real needs for today and the real opportunities you have today.

Your plan needs to take into account the fact that you can't relive the early years. If you decide to forgo the video camera until you're forty, that's fine. You may end up with several thousand more in the bank. But you can't go back and capture your baby's first steps. Those days are gone. If you've got only ten more years until you plan to retire, you can't go back and start investing. You've lost that opportunity forever. It's a very difficult task to balance the needs of today with those of tomorrow. Today's needs will always feel bigger because today is here—in your face, so to speak. Most of us need to give a little more weight to tomorrow's needs just to balance the scale.

Sooner Is Less Expensive

Many couples say, "We just can't afford to save right now." Actually, if you want to take less money out of your lifestyle in order to reach your goals, then that's all the *more* reason to start now. Figure 35 shows how much you need to save if you want to retire a millionaire.

If you are twenty-five years old and you want to retire a millionaire at age sixty-five, you have to invest only $158 each month at 10 percent interest. In other words, you would make 480 payments of $158, which is $75,840. You would take $75,840 out of your lifestyle over the span of forty years so that time and compound interest could do the work of turning that $75,840 into $1 million.

However, if you wait just five years, until you're thirty, then you would have to invest $263 per month at 10 percent interest. That would be 420 payments of $263, which is $110,460. You would have to take $110,460 out of your lifestyle so that time and compound interest could turn that money into your $1 million goal.

So to reach your goal, if you start at age twenty-five, you would spend $75,840. If you start at age thirty, you would have to spend $110,460. The same goal costs you $34,620 more if you wait just five years.

If you wait until you're thirty-five, that same goal will cost you $159,120 (360 payments at $442), which is $83,280 more. Procrastination is a very expensive habit. The longer you wait, the more money you have to take out of your lifestyle and the less work that time and compounding interest can do for you. Of course, as Figure 35 also shows, the better the return on your investment, the better you'll do. That's the *knowledge* part, which we'll get to in a bit.

FIGURE 35. MONTHLY SAVINGS AMOUNT NEEDED AT VARIOUS RATES OF RETURN TO RETIRE A MILLIONAIRE.

Time to Retirement	4%	8%	10%	12%	15%
10 years	$6,793	$5,469	$4,833	$4,347	$3,634
15 years	4,065	2,892	2,412	2,002	1,496
20 years	2,728	1,699	1,317	1,011	668
25 years	1,946	1,053	754	532	308
30 years	1,441	672	442	286	144
35 years	1,095	437	263	156	68
40 years	847	287	158	85	32

Will You Have Enough When You Retire?

The 2001 Retirement Confidence Survey (2001 RCS) from the Employee Benefit Research Institute (www.ebri.org) of one thousand individuals found that only 22 percent were very confident that they would have enough money to retire comfortably. In fact, the number who were "not at all confident" almost doubled from the 2000 survey to the 2001 survey.

There are two important facts you should remember as you and your spouse plan for retirement. The first is that you and your spouse may now spend many more years in retirement than people would have expected decades ago. Life expectancy for a man sixty-five years of age is about eighty, or fifteen years beyond standard retirement age. For women, life expectancy is closer to eighty-five, or about twenty years beyond retirement. That's a lot of years during which you probably won't be working full-time.

The second fact is associated with money. The general rule of thumb used by most financial planners is that you will need about 70 to 85 percent of your present income during retirement. The Web site of the American Savings Education Counsel (www.asec.org) has an online worksheet that can help you arrive at what the counsel calls a ballpark estimate of what you'll need. We urge you to complete this worksheet or something like it, because what you learn may have a big impact on your life. Doing this kind of calculation may be the one thing that changes your financial behavior. According to the 2001 RCS, after calculating what they would need for retirement, 53 percent of those surveyed reported they had started saving more, and 24 percent reported they had changed the investment allocation of their money in savings and retirement accounts.

Get Started Now Even If It's Just a Little

Investing is a lot like exercising. Those who do best find some ways to get the job done—ways they can sustain, day in and day out. But the same attitude that some people have toward exercising can also plague investing: many people don't get started because they feel they have too little to put into it right now. If you regularly exercise, do you ever decide you won't bother today because you have only twenty minutes to spare instead of your usual sixty? That's a mistake in strategy. If you have only twenty minutes today, do twenty minutes today, then work to do more another day. It's the same with investing. Get started and keep at it, even if you don't have as much as you'd like to invest now. Even small amounts can have big effects when you have time on your side.

Knowledge Is Your Other Friend

Knowing which of your options will likely give you the greatest gain is crucial to successful investing. If the genie had asked you, "Do you want $5,497,558,138.88 or $1,000,000?" your answer would have been obvious, but he didn't. He asked you whether you wanted A or B, and you had to figure out which deal was better. And although you may not have a genie calling you, you are making these A and B kinds of decisions all the time, whether you know it or not. You can't make these decisions perfectly, but you can make them wisely. That starts with planning based on knowledge.

We found this interesting bit of trivia in *USA Today* (Aug. 8, 2001): sixty years ago, IBM chairman Thomas Watson said, "I think there is a world market for maybe five computers." So much for predictions. Sure, some things are predictable. The sun will rise in the east. Spring will follow winter. You can probably pretty well predict how your mate will respond to some kinds of suggestions. Generally, though, when it comes to the economy and markets, it's hard to predict what will happen. That's because economies are fundamentally about human behavior, and it's very hard to predict many aspects of how humans behave.

One of the most important aspects of successful investing is having a plan and sticking to it.

Planning is something else, though. You don't have to know the future to have a wise investment plan. One of the most important aspects of successful investing is having a plan and sticking to it! A good plan is based on sound knowledge of investment options and strategies. Now we will cover a variety of important tips that can help you develop and enact your investment strategy.

Where Do I Put My Money?

Roger Ibbotson, of Ibbotson and Associates, is considered one of the foremost experts in the area of statistical securities research. He released a study showing what would have happened if, in 1925, an investor had placed $1 in four different scenarios. In the first scenario, the investor simply kept pace with inflation (the consumer price index, or CPI); the second dollar was invested in thirty-year U.S. Treasury bonds, the third in corporate bonds, and the last in the Standard & Poor's 500 Composite Stock Price Index (the S&P 500). Figure 36 shows what the values of those dollars would have been in 1992.

FIGURE 36. FOUR $1 INVESTMENT SCENARIOS, 1925–1992.

Investment	1925 Value	1992 Value
Inflation (CPI)	$1	$7.46
30-year Treasury bonds	$1	$17.99
Corporate bonds	$1	$27.18
S&P 500	$1	$517.50

As you can see, some places where we might put our money are better than others. The return on the dollar invested in the S&P 500 is almost seventy times better than the return on the inflation-adjusted dollar. Does that mean that the stock market is always automatically the best investment? Nope. Smart investors give careful consideration to their options, don't react to whims and short-term trends, and ignore information that would divert them from well-considered plans.

Unlike our hypothetical encounter with the genie, in the investment world you have more choices than simply A or B, although to keep things simple, we could say that you can choose between A, B, and C. Broadly speaking, there are three main types of investments: bonds, cash, and stocks.

Bonds. Bonds are essentially loans; you loan your money to the government, a utility, or a corporation, which promises to pay you a specific interest rate and refund your principal by a certain date. Bonds come in all shapes and sizes and levels of risk. The bond market and interest rates usually move in opposite directions, so if the bond market goes up, interest rates are dropping. You can find loads of information at www.publicdebt.treas.gov/sec/secdirec.htm, which is the Web site for the bond program at the U.S. Department of the Treasury. Another excellent site is www.investinginbonds.com. There are several bond-rating companies (who will tell you whether the bond you're interested in is high risk or low risk or something in between). You can start with Standard & Poor's at www.standardpoor.com and Moody's at www.moodys.com.

Cash. Cash, savings accounts, money market accounts, and certificates of deposit (CDs) are often viewed as the most safe of all the investment vehicles. Cash, of course, is that green stuff that seems to mysteriously disappear from our wallets. Savings accounts, money market accounts, and CDs are all ways of keeping your money in the bank. With savings accounts and money market accounts, you let the bank use your money, but you don't promise to leave it with them for any length of time, and they don't pay you much. CDs are also typically offered by banks, but you agree to leave a certain amount of money with them for a period of time

(say six to twenty-four months), and they agree to offer you a slightly higher rate of return than if you just let the money sit in your savings account. The advantage of cash investments is that you can get at your money with ease and little, if any, penalty. Money in savings accounts, money market accounts, and CDs is insured up to $100,000 as long as your bank is insured by the Federal Deposit Insurance Corporation (FDIC).

Stocks. You are not *loaning* your money to anyone when you invest in stocks. When you purchase stock, you *buy* a part of a company or a group of companies. You buy part of their current assets and their potential to earn or lose money in the future. No one promises to give you your money back at a later date. Later, you can sell your share of the company, and if it is worth more, then you will have made money. If it is worth less, you will have lost money. While you hold on to your piece of the company, you may or may not receive a share of the company's profits, known as a dividend. We'll talk more about stocks in a bit.

Asset Allocation

You've probably heard the proverb, "Don't put all your eggs in one basket." It's good advice. It is generally not a good idea to put *all* your money into cash or *all* into bonds or *all* into stocks. In investment terms, deciding how many eggs to put into different baskets is called asset allocation. Most experts agree that it is wise to have a combination of different types of investments and that how you divide up your investments will ultimately have more to do with your success (or failure) than any other factor.

As you saw in Figure 36, stocks have historically outperformed bonds and cash types of investments. According to the Vanguard Group, the average annual rates of return of U.S. stocks, bonds, and cash from 1926 to 1998 were as follows: stocks (S&P 500), 11.2 percent; bonds (U.S. corporate bonds), 5.7 percent; and cash (U.S. Treasury bills), 3.9 percent.

Considering that stocks have historically done so much better, why not simply invest all your money where you're most likely to get the best return? Two reasons. One, there is a difference between *history* and *future*. No one knows for certain that the stock market will continue to outperform other investment opportunities. Two, dividing up your investments helps you ride out the rough times. For example, from early 1973 to mid-1974, the S&P fell from 119.6 to 63.38. What that means is that if you had your entire life savings, let's say $100,000, invested in those stocks, you would have seen your savings' value drop to around $53,000. Could you ride out that kind of loss? In contrast, if you had been a medium-risk investor and had 40 percent of your investments in bonds and cash, then your savings would still have been worth around $72,000. Sure, that's still a hit, but one that's perhaps more tolerable. Of course, if you could have hung on until the market rebounded, you wouldn't have lost anything at all, and if you'd stuck with it even longer, you'd have made a bundle.

To have all of their investments in the stock market would be considered too bumpy a ride for most. Take a look at what the S&P has done in the past twenty-plus years. In mid-1974, it had dropped to a low of 63.38. By September 1978, it was at 108.05. If you had invested in a mutual fund that mirrored the S&P, and you checked the price of your stock on random days over the years, here's what you would have discovered:

Date	S&P at Close	Date	S&P at Close
Sept. 1978	108.05	Sept. 1990	311.32
Oct. 1979	112.16	Dec. 1991	418.32
Nov. 1980	141.96	Dec. 1992	442.64
Sept. 1981	118.19	Oct. 1993	471.1
Dec. 1982	147.08	Apr. 1994	450.8
July 1983	171.64	Dec. 1995	622.88
June 1984	153.24	Dec. 1996	759.2
Dec. 1985	211.27	Dec. 1997	986.25
Dec. 1986	254.86	Dec. 1998	1,244.93
Aug. 1987	337.88	Dec. 1999	1,447.47
Jan. 1988	253.33	Mar. 2000	1,553.09
Oct. 1989	360.43	Sept. 2001	1,155.4

If you're investing for the long term, it is easier to ignore the ups and downs of the stock market, although a wise investor won't entirely ignore a big downturn. But what if you need some money and it's a bad time to sell? That's where keeping some of your investments in cash and bonds can help. If you need to dip into your funds, you won't be forced to sell "low." Instead, you've created a cushion for yourself.

Some couples are quite fearful of losing anything and so decide that it would be best to keep all of their investments in cash and bonds. That's generally not such a wise decision either. These kinds of investments often have relatively low rates of return, and when you take inflation into account, you may actually be doing worse each year. Furthermore, there are ways of spreading out your risk even within the stock market.

So how do you decide how many eggs to put into each basket? It depends primarily on two factors: your time horizon and your risk tolerance.

By *time horizon* we mean how much time you have to reach your goals, which should influence the amount of risk you take on. If you are close to the goal for which the wealth was desired, such as retirement, your investments should be lower risk and less volatile. If you are sixty-seven, you probably cannot afford to have a ten-year market downturn if you have most of your investments still in the stock market. That wouldn't be prudent. In contrast, if you are thirty-four, you can handle some pretty significant downturns for a long while because you don't really need the money for many years. You can let the long-term view—generally so beneficial to investing—work for you because you have a lot of time ahead of you (we hope).

Regardless of their time horizon, people also vary in risk tolerance. Two investing couples in otherwise identical situations (same age, income, assets, and so on) can have very different comfort levels with risk. One couple, let's call them the Joneses, might have high risk tolerance. They truly are able to invest a lot in something volatile like aggressive growth stock funds and ignore the stomach-turning ups and downs. They might be more comfortable with risk in other ways, too. Suppose the Joneses are in their early forties. Another couple in their early forties, let's call them the Smiths, might be much more cautious. Although theoretically they have just as much time as the Joneses to rebound from losses, the Smiths might not be able to stomach the ups and downs. Both couples will likely do well over time if they plan reasonably well and stick to their plans. It's entirely likely that the Joneses will retire with more money, but perhaps they take other financial risks that make things even out.

Life gets most interesting in this area when you are married to someone who has a very different level of risk tolerance than you have. One of you may be all in favor of really going for it, and the other may be tense even about government bonds. Well, it's time to talk. You will have to incorporate this difference in "stomach-ability" in your investing plans. If you don't, you might build recurrent stress on your relationship into your investing behavior. Don't go there. Perhaps if you are such a couple, you will develop a plan whereby you have a minimum amount in very secure, low-risk investments. Once the minimum cushion is established, then monies above that amount can be invested more aggressively, perhaps again until a certain amount of money has accumulated. Once you've hit a goal at that level, then you can begin to invest even more aggressively still.

Figure 37, which shows recommendations based on a consensus among investment experts, takes time horizon and risk tolerance into consideration. This figure can serve as a rule of thumb, not law carved in stone. The two of you would do well to discuss your financial goals and your comfort level with risk, and come to

FIGURE 37. ASSET ALLOCATION FOR THE TYPICAL INVESTOR.

	Stocks (%)	Bonds (%)	Cash (%)
High-risk investors, young investors	70–80	15–25	0–5
Medium-risk investors, investors approaching retirement	60	30–40	0–10
Low-risk investors, retiring investors, retirees	40–50	40–50	10–20
Investors over age seventy	20–30	60	10–20

Source: W. Reichenstein, "Basic Truths About Asset Allocation: A Consensus View Among the Experts," *American Association of Individual Investors Journal,* Oct. 1996.

an agreement together. Some couples keep 95 percent of their investment in stock and only 5 percent in bonds. It's up to you. Then, once a year, as the value goes up or down in each category, you can readjust to match your desired percentages.

Dollar Cost Averaging

Dollar cost averaging (DCA) is one of the most popular and popularized methods for investing known. It's generally considered to have two advantages: it works, and it's simple. When you use DCA, you decide how much you want to invest and at what interval. For example, you might decide to put $150 a month in a specific mutual fund that's within a retirement vehicle of some sort, such as an IRA. Here's the key. The method requires you to stick with the plan no matter the conditions. If you are investing in stocks, you send in that $150 whether the market is going up or going down, crashing or soaring. You ignore the trend and commit the funds. With stocks or with mutual funds comprising stocks, the beauty of DCA is that you actually get more shares when the market is down, so you have potential for growth when the market goes back up again.

Consider Tax Avoidance

As we said in Chapter Sixteen, there's no reason for you to pay any more taxes than you are lawfully required to pay. From there, the best advice for you to follow will get very complex and require you to carefully evaluate alternatives. Many people will do quite well over time by taking full advantage of various ways of investing for retirement that allow them to accumulate wealth tax-free until they need it at retirement, when their tax rate will likely be lower.

You probably have some money in one or more of the following types of retirement plans or vehicles: Roth IRA, IRA, SEP-IRA, Keogh, 401(k), or a formal pension plan that may allow you to choose among options. Keoghs and SEP-IRAs are mostly for people who are self-employed or who have substantial self-employment income. A 401(k) plan may be offered through your place of employment. At any rate, the nuances here are more complex than what we will even attempt to cover in this book, but you will want to know about them and how they affect you.

What's a 401(k) or 403(b)? What's a SEP-IRA?

A 401(k) is a salary reduction plan that allows employees of private companies to contribute money toward their retirement. The 403(b) is a similar program for those who work for nonprofit organizations. Where do they come up with these names? Both are named for the sections of the IRS tax code that created them.

Your employers can also make contributions to these plans in the form of either cash or stock. These plans are valuable retirement planning tools because the money invested in them is paid with pretax dollars and so can lower your income tax bill every year. In addition, as the value of the 401(k) grows, the gains are tax-free until you withdraw the funds at retirement. If you change employers, these plans can be moved between companies. There are complex rules regarding this issue, as well as how and at what age you can withdraw money from your 401(k). The maximum allowable employee contribution to a 401(k) in 2001 is $10,500, but that will change in 2002.

In some 401(k) plans, the employer matches the employee's contribution up to a certain percentage. That's free money, but research indicates that up to 40 percent of us who have the opportunity to participate in a 401(k) at work are *not doing so!*

A SEP-IRA is one of the easiest ways for partially or fully self-employed individuals to prepare for retirement. The contributions are tax deductible, and the earnings grow on a tax-deferred basis. There is little paperwork associated with SEP-IRAs, and they are very flexible. You control the money in the SEP-IRA, and you can invest the money in mutual funds, stocks, bonds, real estate, and annuities. However, law prohibits investments in life insurance, precious metals, collectibles, and securities that are purchased on margins. The Quicken Web site (www.quicken.com/retirement/IRA) has an excellent overview of all these IRAs and especially the SEP-IRA. Because there are complexities involved with IRAs, you may want to seek professional advice before deciding what type of IRA or combination of IRAs is right for you and your family.

The Feeling Is Mutual

One of the developments in the past couple of decades that has greatly fueled many people's participation in investing are mutual funds. With mutual funds, you can invest money in one vehicle that spreads your investment across many specific investments chosen according to some characteristic. You can find mutual funds focused on high-tech stocks, small company stocks, major industrial businesses, bonds, real estate, financial sector stocks, international stocks or bonds, and so forth. There are mutual funds that focus on just about any element of the economy. Some are very focused, some inherently more diversified. Some are more aggressive, and some are low risk and slow growth in focus.

There are many mutual fund companies, often called families, such as Fidelity, Janus, Scudder, and Vanguard. There are many families and many options within families. There are load and no-load funds: load funds charge you a percentage to put your money in, to take it out, or both; other funds charge only a small management fee. There is almost universal expert opinion that there is no advantage to the funds that charge loads. You may decide differently for some reason at some time, but that's the consensus. The load funds, on average, simply show no advantages over the no-load funds in terms of historical performance.

You can invest in mutual funds outside the context of retirement investing or inside it. In other words, if you have an IRA, you probably chose a mutual fund family, opened an account, and started putting money into it. Those mutual fund gains over time will accumulate tax-free until you pull them out later, when you are retired. On the funds you might invest in outside a retirement context, you will pay taxes on those funds in the shorter term based on how long you keep the money in the funds, when you sell shares, when and how you get paid dividends, and whether or not the funds are inherently oriented toward taxed or nontaxable investments.

The bottom line: you have many options, and mutual funds have made it far easier for the average person to invest in sensible, planned ways.

So Many Choices, So Little Time

It can be downright overwhelming to try to figure out which stocks or which mutual funds to invest in. Furthermore, you can get hit with broker fees or management fees that eat up your profits. How in the world can you begin to compare all the options? One way you can start is with a well-known, well-regarded, no-load mutual fund. One of the most highly regarded is the Vanguard 500 Index Fund. It is a no-load mutual fund that buys only the five hundred stocks on the S&P 500 list. An index is a kind of ruler for measuring how well segments of the market are doing. Until 1976, indexes were used strictly to measure progress. Then investors decided to invest in the same companies used to measure the progress. This seemed like a pretty good idea, considering that the S&P index had outperformed 75 percent of mutual funds since the 1970s. Although there is never any guarantee for the future, the Vanguard index fund offers a stellar track record, and Vanguard is known for excellent service and low fees (though they will get you if you move your money in and out a lot, but *don't do that!*). You can go to www.vanguard.com for more information and to set up an account online. You will have to make an initial minimum investment, which is currently $1,000 to $3,000 depending on the type of account. Then, on a monthly basis, Vanguard can transfer whatever amount of money you designate out of your savings or checking account and invest it for you in its 500 Index Fund, and you've started investing in your future!

Keep Your Paws off

If you are investing to meet long-term goals, you want your behavior to reflect long-term thinking. Those who do poorest at investing, even when investing in stocks—and maybe especially when investing in stocks—focus on the short term. Like marriages, stocks are inherently long-term investments. If you focus on the short term, you will tend to move your investment in and out and in and out, and will tend to get killed. There is a great deal of research showing that, generally speaking, people cannot time the market. You might know people who think they can, but they cannot.

Various people have analyzed how the stock market has performed over the past six decades. David and Tom Gardner, founders of the Web site known as the Motley Fool, have done such an analysis. (By the way, the Gardners have various books and tapes available, as well as what may be the single most popular Web site for investors that exists: www.fool.com. We highly recommend this site for advice, thoughts, and strategies on long-term investing.) As we were saying, the Gardners have analyzed, among other things, how people do moving their money in and out of the market as opposed to staying fully (or nearly so) invested in stocks over many years' time. The data suggest that there have been a number (not a large number, either) of crucial days or periods when the market, as a whole, took huge leaps of growth.

These moments in history were not predicted nor likely predictable. But the point that savvy investors like the Gardner brothers make is that if you happened to have pulled much of your investments out of the market during those magic moments, you missed most of the advantages the stock market has held over other investments throughout those decades. The train does not leave the station on a regular schedule, and although it can be boring to let your investments stay put, if you don't happen to be on the train when it leaves, you miss the really great opportunities that the stock market provides. Market timers are very likely to miss some of these key moments.

People with a long-term view of investing also tend not to overreact to short-term changes in the economy. *Short-term* in this context may mean even a few years of a downturn. Now this does not mean that you should pick certain investments, funds, or bonds and just stick with them no matter what happens. Many people had wisely moved some of their profits made from tech stocks in the past few years to other types of investments before the big downturn in that part of the market at the turn of the millennium. Smart investors do adjust how they allocate their investments according to market conditions as well as their own stage in life, but they generally are creative at keeping all their money working for them over time.

The moral here is to get started, keep at it, and keep your eye on your time horizon when you allocate your assets.

Some Good Tips (but Not Stock Tips)

"If it sounds too good to be true, it probably is." We don't really have to say more on this, do we? When you find you're being seduced, pay attention. Unless it's by your partner, it's not likely to be good for you.

Will Social Security Still Exist When You Retire?

Ric Edelman, author of *Ordinary People, Extraordinary Wealth*, says that when he conducts financial planning seminars, individuals who are over forty-five answer yes to this question, and those under forty-five say no. Edelman goes on to state, "I believe Social Security will continue in some form, if only due to political pressure, but I make no predictions about what the benefit levels will be or how old you'll have to be to receive them." All of our collective guesses are as good as his, which is to say "maybe," especially to the younger individuals and families in the United States.

Assuming Social Security remains in existence, what do you need to know about it? First, you need to know that Social Security payments are designed as a minimum financial safety net. You certainly get that impression when you find that the average monthly payment for Social Security beneficiaries in 1997 was $750, or $9,000 annually. Second, you need to know that women are especially at risk of receiving low benefits because they are in and out of the workforce to have and raise children and because normally they are paid lower wages throughout their working lives. So even though you may be able to plan on receiving something, it's not likely to be enough to support the lifestyle you'd prefer to have in your golden years.

Learn from Your Mistakes

Have you ever heard of Berkshire Hathaway? The largest shareholder in this successful company is Warren Buffet, often considered one of the greatest CEOs of our times.

There's an interesting story behind Warren Buffet's decision to name the company Berkshire Hathaway. Some years ago, Buffet bought a textile mill in New England, intending to make the business a great success, which was almost routine for this business genius. In this case, however, the textile mill failed miserably. To remind himself and all of those around him of the importance of studying one's failures carefully and learning all that you can, Buffet named his new company after the disastrous failure, Berkshire Hathaway.

We recommend this strategy to you as well. When have your own plans failed? Why? Was there a problem with the plan or your ability to stick with it? If you are going to invest, you are very likely going to make mistakes, at least in terms of making some choices that you wish you had not made. Study those. Are there lessons to be learned that can make it less likely that you'll make the same mistake again?

There's More to Know

There are many aspects of investing at which most people will excel as long as they are willing to do a little homework. However, you'll find that some decisions will require you either to do a lot of studying or to seek professional advice. You might want to get expert advice on such decisions as whether to have a Keogh or a SEP-IRA, for example. At the end of this book is a guide to selecting a financial planner. Another option is to join or start an investment club.

Investment clubs have been around since 1898, and through the years their popularity has waxed and waned. They might be a great way for you and your partner to learn together about investing in the stock market and to have fun at the same time.

Here's the idea. You get together regularly with some people you like, to hang around and talk about investing—sharing ideas on strategies, specific opportunities, research that you've found, and encouragement on planning and discipline.

Finding and joining an existing club may not be easy. Most are "closed" clubs, meaning that you can't just drop in, and most have established rules for membership. However, if a club sounds like something you're interested in, you could always start one of your own. You can start learning more about investment clubs from the National Association of Investors Corporation, which was founded in 1951 for the purpose of starting and supporting investment clubs, at www.better-investing.org.

The Key Difference

Really, the key difference between couples who succeed financially and those who don't is the age at which they start planning and then stick with their plan. Time will escape through your fingers if you let it. "Someday" is the road to nowhere. Maybe you can start investing today, maybe not. But you *can* start planning today. Creating a plan means putting some thought into what you are doing. Because the two of you are a couple, or you are reading this book in that context, you need to create a plan that the two of you can cooperate in carrying out. This is crucial. If one of you is working a plan and the other is undermining it, you're not going to get ahead. You need to pick up the floor to discuss any issues or hidden issues surrounding the competition of the needs of today with those of tomorrow. You'll need to use your agreed-on budget or other tools to control your spending, consider your investment options, decide on a regular pattern of investing a certain amount each month—and then stick to the plan.

The Three Key Points to Take from This Chapter

1. Start yesterday.
2. If you didn't do that, start today.
3. Create a plan.

Thinking through the various issues we raise in this chapter will help you develop a plan for your financial future. Doing this will take time and energy. There is much more for you to learn and act on, and we hope we've given you food for thought as you move ahead.

Time to Talk

Take some time to talk through these questions:

1. How much money would you like to have when you retire? You can find various systems for estimating this on the Web or by talking with a certified financial planner. Your goal is to accumulate enough assets that income from your investments (for example, interest on something safe like Treasury bills) can cover the expenses of the lifestyle you desire.

2. If you change nothing and remain on your current path, how much do you think you will have when you retire?

3. If you have children, do you need to be investing to finance their college education? How much do you want to accomplish in that area in relation to your retirement goals? Most experts will tell you to give more weight to the retirement goals. Still, it's important to think about both.

4. Can the two of you define your existing plan, or, if you have none, the plan you wish to start following? Any plan that includes the word *lottery* in it could probably use some reworking.

5. Who is responsible for doing what? What information do you need to obtain? What phone calls need to be made?

6. How will you go about learning more? See if you can figure out some ways of making it fun to work together on this.

PART FOUR

FINDING YOUR TARGET

CHAPTER NINETEEN

THE HEART OF COMMITMENT

Commitment is making the choice to give up choices.

SCOTT STANLEY

The epigraph says just about all of what's at the core of commitment. It all comes down to what choices you make and what else in life you are willing to give up to protect the path you have chosen. All other aspects of what commitment means and does can be derived from that one simple statement. Any commitment you make in life requires that you make a choice among alternatives.

In the past two decades, there has been an explosion of scholarly theory and research on commitment. Here we focus on four specific aspects of commitment identified by scholars such as Scott, each having great bearing on the future quality of your relationship as well as the stability of your financial situation. First, let's take a look at the big picture of what commitment in relationships—and especially marriage—is all about.

> *Any commitment you make in life requires that you make a choice among alternatives.*

How Does Commitment Develop? How Does It Die?

Commitment can be thought of as having two major dimensions: dedication and constraint. We're not planning to say much about constraint here, although it's a very important aspect of commitment. Constraints have to do with the costs of leaving a path one has chosen. They can be an important force that helps keep relationships stable through tough times. Here we will focus more on dedication: the force of commitment in action and commitment as expressed in the daily choices we each make. Dedication is defined by a deeper, intrinsic desire to identify in life with one's partner, to give to him or her, and the desire to grow old together.

The Binds That Tie

What can go into the overall constraint commitment people have depends on who they are, what they value, and what their circumstances are. Here is a list of elements that commonly serve as constraints for people staying in their marriage.

- Social pressure from friends and family
- Financial considerations
- Concerns for children's welfare or fear of loss of contact
- The difficulty of the steps to leave
- Moral factors, such as belief that divorce is generally wrong, or that one should always finish what one has started
- Poor quality of alternatives

You could think of these elements this way: all other things being equal, more of any of these makes it more likely that people will choose to stay in their marriage, even through tough times. We believe that without constraint commitment, most couples would not make it in marriage beyond a few years because of the normal ups and downs in satisfaction in life together. But as you'll see in this chapter, there is much more to a thriving, protective commitment than just constraints.

Early on, commitment develops as partners look for ways to reassure each other of a future together. Think about the earlier days of your relationship. In most relationships, there's an awkward period during which the desire to be together—and your attachment—is great but the commitment is unclear. That produces anxiety on some levels about whether or not you'll stay together. "I really love her, but what if she doesn't want to be with me?" Such anxieties are likely greatest for those who have reasons to wonder about how secure relationships can be, such as those whose parents divorced or those who've been through a divorce themselves. Having a clear and secure commitment will be all that much more important for such people.

As you expressed your mutual dedication more clearly, your relationship became safer to invest in. In relationships, almost any form of commitment can be understood as a symbol of security. When I (Scott) was in high school, girls and boys would sometimes "go steady." The common emblem of this "commitment" was a class ring. I understand that teenagers no longer go steady. In fact, we've been told frequently that they sort of just go out, dating casually and even in groups. We're not arguing in any way for young people to make premature commitments beyond the wisdom of their years. Yet it does seem that even such a simple change in dating patterns is a sign of our times, that people are perhaps less willing than in the past to see how commitments can contribute to deeper, fuller relationships.

It is only with a deep sense of security that two people can fully experience the wonder, magic, and mystery of a great relationship. Both of you must feel secure that the other has indeed chosen you and will invest his or her life in yours, into the future. Even though more and more couples are attempting to have great relationships with lower levels of commitment (such as nonmarital cohabitation), the best of what two people can be together usually does not grow without commitment. The good stuff develops most deeply from a foundation of security. Partners who do best in life go slowly and carefully up front, in choosing one another (sure, there are exceptions), and, once they are sure, they make a strong commitment to be there through thick and thin.

If most couples have high levels of dedication early on, such as when engaged or early in marriage, what happens over time to kill dedication for some couples? For one thing, if a couple doesn't handle conflict well, satisfaction with the marriage will steadily decline. Because satisfaction fuels dedication, dedication begins to erode along with satisfaction. With dedication in jeopardy, giving to one another erodes further, and satisfaction takes a bigger dive. It's a downward spiral from there. You try less, you see less reason to try, and soon your relationship is dying.

When dedication has eroded, the type of commitment that remains is constraint, not dedication (see box). For some of those who let so much slip away, their constraints end up being primarily related to the presence of their children, and when their children leave home, so does most of the glue holding them together. Even if such a couple does not break up, the erosion of commitment can lead to insecurity about the future that makes it far harder to work to make the marriage all it can be. Dedication erodes further when people feel their efforts no longer make a difference.

The secret to satisfying commitment is to maintain not just constraint but also a high level of dedication. Constraint commitment can add a positive, stabilizing dimension to your marriage; it can also keep you from doing immensely impulsive, stupid things when you are unhappy in the short run. But it's dedication that correlates most strongly with the quality of a relationship. Our research shows that dedicated couples report not only more satisfaction with their relationships but also greater levels of self-disclosure—they trust more to share more deeply. The rest of this look at commitment focuses on dedication. It's dedication that is all about the choices we make; choices in how we think and how we act toward those we love.

Making the Choice: The Dances of Dedication

You've surely heard the story about the monkey who gets his paw trapped in the jar because he grasps so much food in it that he cannot pull his fist out through the opening. Only by letting go of so much, and choosing less, would the monkey get what he wants. That's a message born out by research as well as common sense. You want to hang on to it all? You'll end up with little. If you choose to give up some of your choices so as to invest in a deeper, narrower path, you'll prosper. This message is not an easy one to digest in our American culture. We glorify choices and options and having it all. There is great danger in these messages, because if you listen too closely, you may fail to do the things that the most deeply satisfied couples know how to do. Let's look further at what the most satisfied and committed couples do. And as we do, note that each of the four core forces of dedication runs against the grain of a culture that says to give up nothing and hang on to every option. Each requires you to give up something to gain something else.

Choices and Priorities

When people are more dedicated to their partners, they are more likely to make decisions that protect the relationship when it comes to decisions about time and resources. For example, early in their relationship, most people will move mountains in their schedule to spend time with their partner. As the cares and hassles of life take over, however, too many of us allow our relationship to take a backseat. A great relationship is a front-seat deal (unless you are in the backseat together, but that's another story).

To some degree, problems with priorities can reflect as much a problem with overinvolvement elsewhere as one of a lack of dedication at home. Unfortunately, as people get busier and busier, too many people end up doing what I (Scott), in my book *The Heart of Commitment*, call *no*-ing each other rather than *know*ing each other: "No, I don't have time to talk tonight." "No, I'm too tired to even think about making love tonight." "No, I promised Jeff I'd come over Saturday and help him put up that new fence."

Yolandra and Freddie were like so many couples living in the fast lane. Both had worked hard to get through college with degrees in business and finance. Both relied on financial aid, including student loans. After college, they both began careers with financial firms, and both did well. They were making good incomes, enjoying their work, and paying down their student loans. Life was good, and they were enjoying it. Over a few years' time, though, they both began to drift a bit in their connection. Both traveled a lot, both worked very long hours, and both spent more time with colleagues at work than with each other at home. Essentially, they were both saying yes to everything their careers offered and increasingly, almost without noticing, saying no to one another.

For many busy couples, it's easy to miss this dynamic at work. In part, the problem here is what I call *presuming on the commitment of the other.* Sometimes the worst thing we do to our loved one is to take him or her for granted. It's as if we are thinking, "I have to get this project done to please that client. She (spouse) is going to have to wait. I know she'll understand because she's committed to me for the long haul." It's this kind of thinking that gets us into trouble. Because our mate has promised to be there, we believe he or she will wait while we put more energy into something that's not nearly as important. So we let our most important relationship die on the vine starving for love, because we take our partner's commitment for granted.

Don't get us wrong. In some ways, the dynamic we're identifying is the very reason why committed couples tend to do so well over time. They *can* count on each other to be there, which allows them short-term decisions and actions that will bring other benefits (like a more secure or larger income). The problem comes when you regularly fail to protect the needs of your partner against the demands of the world. To protect your relationship, you've got to be good at saying no to things that might seem important but aren't, and saying yes to your partner in ways that matter to him or her. Remember, matching each other on key expectations is not nearly as important as trying to meet your partner's most cherished expectations.

> *The problem comes when you regularly fail to protect the needs of your partner against the demands of the world.*

Yolandra and Freddie caught themselves in time. They realized they were drifting, and Freddie spoke up first, after dinner one night while they were talking about how their days had gone. It became a turning point for them when he said, "I've been thinking a lot about where we've been heading. There are so many ways in which we're doing well. I'm proud of you and your success, and I know I'm enjoying mine. But I don't feel like we're nearly as close as we used to be. I miss 'us,' and I want what we had back before too much slips away."

Notice all the *we*'s in what he said. It's not very often that such words by one partner to another will be met with anger or defensiveness. The love and commitment to "us" is too apparent. The desire to protect the relationship is clear. If Yolandra and Freddie's story reminds you of where your relationship has been heading, think about how you might convey this type of message to your partner. Then, work together on plans to reinvigorate and protect your love through the goals you set and the choices you make to reach them.

Couple Identity: The Story of Us

Couples vary in the degree to which the partners view the relationship as a team rather than as two separate individuals who each mostly focus on self. In the happiest and strongest marriages, "we" transcends "me" in how the partners think. If a couple doesn't have this sense of being a team, conflict is more likely, because the partners see problems as "me against you" instead of "us against the problem." Our research clearly shows that couples who are thriving in their marriages have a strong sense of "us."

How does having a couple identity relate to choices? In at least one major way. To have a strong identity in life together, you each have to make the choice to align your worlds in significant ways. Sure, that means giving up some degree of individualism. Teams don't work as well when the focus is mostly on the individuals in them. This is one way in which cohabiting couples, on average, are simply different from married couples. Married couples have made a much larger decision, both symbolic and tangible, to entwine their lives. As we said at the outset, it's for those very reasons that married couples tend to do best, financially, over time. There are benefits from identifying together as a team moving through life.

The dynamics of "me" versus "we" also explain why many couples—but surely not all—find it difficult to deal with decisions about how separate or together to keep their finances. For some couples, it's only pragmatics that drive their decisions on these matters. Other couples struggle with this subject against a whole backdrop of larger issues about the nature of the relationship. "Are we a 'we' or a 'me versus you'?"

We aren't suggesting that you merge your identities. Rather, we're suggesting that most couples do best with a clear sense of the two individuals coming together to form a team—what a difference this makes in how you view life together! There's an old joke about a wedding ceremony in which the minister gets to the point of saying, "and the two shall become one," and someone in the back row leans over to her friend and says, "I wonder which one?" That's not the idea here.

Who's on My Side?

Natalie Monarch, a colleague of ours, has been studying couple identity by looking at the degree to which it is reflected in three major areas:

1. Your view of how you have dealt with the past together, especially regarding the sense that you have overcome things together, as a team
2. The degree to which you view your relationship together as special
3. Your view of your future together, especially in the sense of having dreams and a vision

Notice a word that's repeated in those three major themes: *together*. What people seem to want most in marriage is a lifelong best friend and confidante, which is directly related to having a sense of being together in the flow of life. Reflect on your relationship for a moment; how do you view it in light of these three aspects?

Many times, important transitions in life will remind you of how much of a team you are, or how much that special sense of being a team has slipped away. One couple, Melissa and Will, had a pretty stable and harmonious life up until the time their youngest child left home to take a job in another state. As happens with many couples, some of the glue that had bound them together left with their children. They drifted for some time, with increasing distance and conflict—developing lives that were largely independent from one another. One day, they started to turn it all around.

Consider the humility and power of a talk like this. They were at the breakfast table together, reading the paper and having coffee.

    Will: *(looking up from his paper)* Can we talk a second?
Melissa: *(putting her paper aside)* Sure, what's up?
    Will: Well, something . . . um, something important.
Melissa: *(nodding and listening)*
    Will: I've been thinking that we're at a big point in life here. What we do in the next year might lay down the pattern for us for the next thirty years. I'm not sure I like the path we're on, and I've been thinking that maybe we should really plan for the kind of relationship we want in the future. You know, to be very intentional about where we head now.

Melissa: *(barely suppressing a smile)* I love that idea. I've been wondering—actually worrying—a bit, too, about where we're headed. I'd like us to be really close and not just share a house in the years ahead.

Will: Me too, but I'm thinking that if we're not careful, we'll be only roommates for the next thirty years. I want to be best friends and lovers.

Melissa: What do you think we should do next?

Will: How about we go away for a weekend? Maybe to that cabin. No TV, no distractions. Just us. We can talk and play and plan for our future. What do you think?

Melissa: Sounds perfect. Let's look at the calendar.

As is true of everything we have suggested to you in this book, the strategies we suggest are most powerful if you make the key decisions together.

Time to Talk. For many couples, their couple identity has been nurtured and protected from the start. If you have it, work at keeping it. But things always are changing, and you can take this time of life as an opportunity to openly discuss and plan for how you want to express your "we" in the years ahead. If you've lost the couple feeling, work at getting it back.

Here are a few ideas for preserving and deepening couple identity:

1. Do just about any of the exercises throughout this book—together. That will increase your sense of having the common goal protecting your relationship.
2. Pursue some activities together that have a lot of meaning or enjoyment for both of you. Together is as together does.
3. Tell each other some ideas of things you could each do that would increase the sense that your relationship is special in some way.
4. Talk regularly about both short-term and longer-term goals. Having clear mutual goals increases your sense of being on the same team.

Choices and Sacrifice

Our culture encourages devotion to self. Notions of sacrifice, teamwork, and the priority of one's partner have not enjoyed much positive press lately. In fact, our society seems to glorify self and to vilify whatever gets in the way. Selfishness may sell in our culture, but it doesn't buy lifelong happy marriages.

We want to be clear, though: working on yourself, making improvements, and considering what you can do to make your relationship great is not being selfish. That's taking personal responsibility—one of the most powerful things you can do to be the best partner you can be.

Positive attitudes about sacrifice—and sacrificial behavior—build up a relationship over time. In fact, in our research, people who are happiest in marriage gain some sense of satisfaction in doing things that are largely or solely for their partner's benefit. We don't mean being a martyr, but rather finding real joy in a genuine choice to give of yourself for your partner. In the way the term is commonly used, a martyr does things for you not out of concern for what is best for you but because he or she wants to put you in debt. That's *debt*-ication, not dedication.

What You Can't See Can Hurt You

Perhaps the saddest thing we've seen in our work with couples is unexpressed dedication. In so many couples, one partner has withered on the vine because he or she can't see much evidence that the other is really committed. Sometimes there really has been an erosion of dedication. But many other times it's not so much that there is a lack of dedication to one another as much as that the dedication has become harder to see.

One way this happens is that people stop doing many of the things they used to do to show how dedicated they really are. Little things—cards, a flower, a poem, an e-mail, a call in the middle of the day, a sticky note on the steering wheel that says "I love you"—can say "I'm thinking of you, I'm here for you, and I'm committed to you." Bigger things matter too, of course. A lot.

This brings us to the other way couples can get in trouble here. All too often, people lose track of the things that their partner already does—and regularly does—that demonstrate a high level of dedication. Sadly, we all tend to get accustomed to a certain standard of living and behavior in relationships, and things that may be terrific evidence of dedication appear instead to be routine and "to be expected." If you're feeling that your mate is not so dedicated these days, ask yourself first if you are making a negative interpretation. Yes, that means pushing yourself hard to see all the things he or she is probably doing that show dedication.

Here again we see the importance of the choices you make. Can you take satisfaction, at times, in laying aside your favored choice because of what you think is best for your partner or for your relationship? Maybe you are thinking you cannot, perhaps even with good reason. Some people are takers and rarely givers. Those people make it very hard for their partners to continue over time to give to them without resentment. There are even times, if married to someone who takes and does not give, that the greatest sacrifice might be in confronting the partner's self-centeredness. But for most of us, much of the time, it's too easy to err in the other direction—to focus on what we want and what would feel is best for us right now as opposed to what may be best for our partner and our relationship into the future.

Relationships are generally stronger when both partners are willing to make sacrifices. In the absence of this willingness to sacrifice, what do you have? You have a relationship in which at least one of you is in it mostly for what you can get, with little focus on what you can give. That's not a recipe for happiness or growth.

In a culture that reinforces self, it's hard to ask, "What can I do to make this relationship better?" It's a lot easier to ask, "What can my partner do to make me happier?" You can (and do) choose how you think about your relationship. Think about not only what you do for your partner but also why you do it: Do you think with the attitude, "You'd better appreciate what I'm doing"? Do you often feel your partner owes you? There's nothing wrong with doing positive things and wanting to be appreciated. There is something wrong with believing you are owed. In couples who are doing wonderfully well, you'll find two partners who give freely to one another and appreciate that fact.

Note how similar some themes are here with those we discussed when talking about financial management. Doing well over time financially usually requires significant sacrifices in the present for the sake of the future. Far too many couples are currently on a path that will leave them thinking they handled this dynamic poorly when they get to older age.

Sacrifice is one area of relationships where men and women seem to differ a lot in perspective. We are just beginning to look at such things in some depth, but the early research is intriguing. A colleague of ours at the University of Denver, Sarah Whitton, has been studying sacrifice in relationships along with Scott and Howard. Among other things, she has found that both a long-term view and couple identity were strongly related to males' willingness to sacrifice for their female partners. This makes great sense. After all, in the absence of a shared sense of a future together, sacrificing for your partner will seem like depositing money in a bank with a "going out of business" sign out front. When thinking about the future, investing makes sense. Sacrificing is a kind of investing. If you're thinking only about the present, why bother to invest?

In this research, for females, only the long-term view was related to sacrifice, and far more weakly than for males. This study, along with a number of other studies in our lab, highlight the particular importance of male dedication levels in the life and health of relationships. Without an otherwise strong commitment, males may be particularly likely to resent giving to females—or they just don't do it. To be candid, we think that on average, women have historically given more in marriages than men. There are many exceptions, but we have come to believe that it is particularly important for males to demonstrate their dedication to their mates by giving freely of themselves in ways that are clear and consistent.

Choices and the Long-Term View

When people are dedicated to their partners, they want and expect the relationship to last. They want to grow old together. It's a core part of dedication. This long-term expectation for the relationship to continue plays a critical role in the day-to-day quality of marriage for one simple reason: no relationship is consistently satisfying. What gets couples through tougher times is the long-term view that commitment brings. How? When you decide you will be together, no matter what, you can safely deal with the curve balls life throws at you. In addition, psychologically speaking, the long-term view stretches out the time perspective for you, so it's easier not to overreact to the small annoying events in life.

> *The long-term view makes it easier not to overreact to the small annoying events in life.*

We're not saying everybody should devote Herculean effort to save his or her marriage, no matter how abusive or destructive. However, for the great number of couples who genuinely love each other and want to make their marriages work, a long-term perspective is essential for encouraging each partner to take risks, disclose about self, and trust that the other will be there when it really counts. In the absence of a long-term view, people tend to focus on the immediate payoff. This is only natural. If the long term is uncertain, we concentrate on what we are getting in the present.

The Stock Market of Love.   You may have already noticed how similar these points are to those you'll hear from people who talk about investing in the stock market. Although the stock market has been the best single investment over the long haul (at least historically), how people approach investing in it determines how likely they are to gain or lose in the market. As we discussed in Chapter Eighteen, those who are most likely to get killed investing in the stock market are short-termers—people who attempt to time their investments, pulling them in and out and in again, only to lose by selling at the wrong times and buying at worse times. Your relationship, and especially marriage, is a long-term investment.

People who do best in marriage recognize that happiness in life and love is not a constant but something that goes up and down depending on current conditions. For example, most couples experience some strain on their friendship and loving bond in the period around the birth of a child. Most couples will find it a strain on their relationship to have one partner experience a career setback such as unemployment. Sadly, many couples at some point experience a major trauma to one of their children or to one of the two partners. You just don't know what life will throw at you in the future. There is uncertainty about that, but there is no uncertainty about which couples excel and which do not. Among other things, those who excel maintain a perspective on the future—the future of the partners together—that makes ongoing, deep investment in the relationship worthwhile.

Do you invest money in any accounts or institutions where you have no confidence in their future? Of course not. Neither do people invest in a depth of love and sacrifice to one another without confidence in the future. If the two of you have no shared sense of the future, the goal setting we recommend in Chapter Twenty makes no sense at all—at least not long-term goal setting of the sort that has the most positive and profound impacts on the quality of your lives.

People invest where they have trust that their investment will be rewarded. Trust is based on long-term trustworthiness. What we call the hidden issue of commitment (Chapter Four) is easily triggered when the future of the relationship is uncertain. When commitment is unclear, we don't feel accepted—a core issue for everyone—and instead we feel pressured to perform. The message is, "You'd better produce, or I'll look for someone who can." Most of us resent feeling we could be abandoned by someone from whom we expect to find security and acceptance. People generally do not invest in a relationship with an uncertain future and reward.

Another colleague of ours, Fran Dickson at the University of Denver, has studied lifelong married couples. Among many things, she found that the happier couples reported having talked regularly about their future over their years together. In a sense, what they described is one of the ways they have nurtured a vision for their future together. That does not mean locking in all the details, but rather dreaming and reminding one another that the relationship has a future as well as a history. In the exercises at the end of this chapter, this is one of the powerful things we recommend the two of you try to do together. You'll have to be creative about the ways, but we're convinced it's a very good strategy for preserving a lasting love, together.

Our "rededicating" couple, Will and Melissa, do not have the perfect marriage (who does?), but they have a strong expectation of a future rooted in balanced commitment. They talk about plans for life together. In fact, they are being intentional about what their future might look like. For couples like them, the long-term view allows each partner to "give the other some slack," leading to greater acceptance of weaknesses and failings over time.

When partners make their commitment clear, a powerful message is displayed in the flow of life: "I'll be here for you." Your daily choices demonstrate whether you really believe in the long-term strength of your union. That's the essence of commitment. It's not only believing that you will be there for one another in the future but that you can count on one another through the ups and downs of life.

Threatening the Long-Term View. Sometimes commitment becomes a weapon in a fight. When used, it's like an atomic bomb that leaves devastation in its wake. Rod and Mary are a couple who are not doing well and haven't been for some time. They are angry, distant, and distrusting. They aren't yet planning to get a divorce, but the topic comes up more and more often in bad arguments. Consider the following conversation and its effects on trust, power, and commitment:

Rod: Why does this house always look like a pigsty?

Mary: Because we have two big dogs and I'm at work every day.

Rod: I end up having to clean up all the time, and I'm tired of it.

Mary: Oh, and like I don't clean up all the time after the kids? When you're here, you usually disappear into your shop. I'm the one cleaning up constantly— not you. And I bring in just as much money as you do, but do twice the work around here.

Rod: Yeah, yeah, I disappear all the time. You don't even know what really happens in this marriage. I don't even know why we stay together.

Mary: Me neither. Maybe you should move out.

Rod: Not a bad idea. I'll think about it.

By the end of the fight, each was trying to convince the other they weren't committed. You can't get much less dedicated than emphasizing the short-term view. If you're trying to keep your marriage on track, don't bring up the topic of divorce, period. Likewise, don't threaten to have affairs. Such statements threaten the long-term view. They erode trust and reinforce the perception that it's risky to invest. Pushing yourself not to say such things when very frustrated is an act of dedication. Practice self-control!

◆ ◆ ◆

If you've been in a situation like this for some time, ask yourself a few questions:

- Do you want to make the most of your relationship?
- Do you want it to work into the future?
- Do you have a choice about whether you make these comments that threaten the future?

If you answer yes to all three questions, you know part of what you need to do. Don't make any comments that undermine any reason that you or your partner has to make the effort to make things better.

What can you do instead? Nurture a vision of your future together. Be confident that it will come to pass. Do things that reaffirm your long-term commitment. You can take walks while dreaming of your future together. You can set goals for the future, as we encouraged you to do in the next chapter. In fact, one of the most powerful benefits of goal setting is that it reinforces a couple's sense of a shared future. You can act on financial planning that in its very essence portrays your faith in your future. How you handle your money can be turned into a reaffirmation of your long-term commitment to one another.

The two of you will probably come up with your own unique ways to strengthen your long-term view, but all partners need ways to keep reaffirming the fact and intention that it's "you and me, into the future." That's what it's all about.

Take the Opportunity You Have Now

The ceremony on the wedding day is not as important for the long term as the daily evidences of dedication. You could think of these as small celebrations of your commitment in life together. Consciously consider and choose ways to demonstrate your dedication to one another through the priorities you live, the evidence you show of your identity as a couple, and your awareness of a future together. There's no better time than now to do all you can to affirm your commitment to one another.

Perhaps at some point in your life you've seen some of the great cathedrals in Europe, either in pictures or in person. Many of these took one to two hundred years to build. Historians tell us that when builders began work on these magnificent structures, they'd plant a forest nearby. They did this so that the wood that would be needed for the doors, ornamental work, and pews would be available many decades in the future when the builders were ready for it. What a fascinating example of how taking the long view leads to actions in the present that build the resources for the future. What can you do today and this week or this month to plant some trees for the future of your love?

Exercises

There are several exercises to help you get the most out of this chapter. You'll have the opportunity to examine your dedication commitment, consider your priorities, and think about a rededication of your devotion to one another.

Assessing Dedication Commitment

On a separate piece of paper, jot down your responses to these statements, assigning a point value between 1 and 7 to indicate how true the statement seems to you. Use the following rating scale for your answers: 1 = strongly disagree, 4 = neither agree nor disagree, 7 = strongly agree.

1. My relationship with my partner is more important to me than almost anything else in my life.
2. I want this relationship to stay strong no matter what rough times we may encounter.
3. It makes me feel good to sacrifice for my partner.
4. I like to think of myself and my partner more in terms of "us" and "we" than "me" and "him [or her]."
5. I am not seriously attracted to anyone other than my partner.
6. My relationship with my partner is clearly part of my future life plans.
7. When push comes to shove, my relationship with my partner comes first.
8. I tend to think about how things affect us as a couple more than how things affect me as an individual.
9. I don't often find myself thinking about what it would be like to be in a relationship with someone else.
10. I want to grow old with my partner.

To calculate your score, simply add up your ratings for each item. We can give you an idea of what your score means on these dedication items. In our research—with a sample of people who were mostly happy and dedicated in their relationships (including some married for over thirty years)—the average person scored about 58 on the items in this scale. If you scored at or above 58, we'd bet you're pretty highly dedicated. Your dedication may be quite low if you scored below 45, however. Whatever your score, think about what it may mean for the future of your marriage.

Considering Priorities

An important way to look at dedication is to consider your priorities. How do you actually live your life? What does this say about your commitment?

Take a piece of paper you can divide into three columns. In the first column, list what you consider your top five priorities in life, with number one being the most important. Possible priority areas might include work and career, your partner, adult children, religion, house and home, sports, future goals, education, possessions, hobbies, pets, friends, relatives, coworkers, television, car. Feel free to list whatever is important to you. Be as specific as you can.

Now, in the second column, list what you think your partner would say are *your* top five priorities. For example, if you think your partner would say work is your top priority, list that as number one. In the third column, list what you believe are your partner's top five priorities.

When both of you have completed your lists, compare them. Don't be defensive. Reflect on what the answers each of you gave mean to your relationship. Use the Speaker-Listener Technique if necessary. If you see a need to make your relationship a higher priority, talk together about specific steps you can take to make this happen. You might find it helpful to use the problem-solving process you learned in Chapter Nine.

Nurturing the Long-Term View

As we noted earlier, one of the most powerful things you can do to keep your relationship on a great path is to talk in various ways and from time to time about your future together. Doing this stretches your perspective out beyond just the here and now. We don't mean that you should be trying to lock in your path in all kinds of ways, but we mean that it's important to have a clear sense of a future. Where would you like to be in thirty years? What would you like to do when you retire? Where would you like to travel someday? How do you feel about becoming a grandparent one day, or about having reached that stage already? You'll have to decide how the two of you can best increase your sense of your future. You could take dream walks together, talking about your plans for your future. You could try to sprinkle your regular time together as friends with thoughts about a future. Be creative.

CHAPTER TWENTY

TURNING REALITY INTO DREAMS

A dream is a prophecy in miniature.

TALMUD

What do you really want in life? What's most important to you? These were the questions at the beginning of this book, and they are the questions with which we will end. It seems to us that too many couples spend their lives running around at an exhausting pace but have no idea what is *really* important to them. In our view, life is too precious to waste chasing things, things that in the big picture just don't mean that much. It has been our hope that as you've read through these pages, you've been challenged to think more about what your life is about and, in particular, what your most intimate relationship is about.

We've discussed the various invisible forces that can push couples off their course, the kinds of things that get in the way of finding the gates to happiness. You've learned how to understand these forces and how to disarm them or harness their energy. A couple who is no longer being pushed around by issues, hidden issues, and expectations is free to focus on the practical task of managing money rationally and successfully. We hope you've seen that you can manage your money wisely, which will better enable you to make those things happen that you deeply desire to have happen—in essence, to turn your reality into your dreams.

Attaining your dreams is important not only because it is good to be happy but also because, we believe, your reality is part of a bigger Reality. In the grand scheme of things, what you do and how you live your life matters. Although not everyone agrees, most people believe that life has a purpose. Richard Bolles, author of the perennial best-seller *What Color Is Your Parachute?*, said this: "It is wonderful to feel that beyond eating, sleeping, working, having pleasure and *it may be* marrying, having children, and growing older, you were set here on Earth for some special purpose, *and* that you can gain some idea of what that purpose is."

To discover what that purpose is, you must search your heart as well as your mind. It is a search that is not *only* about dollars and cents, not *only* about what you want, not *only* about your responsibilities or even your opportunities. Although your search must surely include these things, it will be incomplete without considering your own philosophy of life. As you think through for yourself answers to such questions as "What is the meaning of life?" or "Why are we humans here?" you will be better able to put your own life in context. Finding your purpose in life is in part discovering your part in the bigger picture of all life. Perhaps the single most motivating factor in your search for your purpose, and your definition of your dreams, is that you have only one lifetime in which to fulfill them.

This Is It

This is your life. This isn't a dress rehearsal. This is it. You have only one chance to be who you are meant to be and do what you are meant to do in this world. What are you going to do with the days that you have left? Are you going to take a trip around the world? Are you going to find a cure for cancer? Are you going to run a marathon? Are you going to learn to speak French? Are you going to put your kids or grandkids through college? How are you going to make sure that the world is just a little bit richer for your having been here? All these are questions interwoven with your overall purpose.

Some couples fully believe in the importance of defining their purpose, or mission in life, and they intend to do it *someday*. Many couples simply consider themselves too busy and are unwilling to carve out the time. We understand that. Each one of us authors knows what it is like to work round the clock for days, weeks, even months, and each one of us has made the mistake of becoming focused too narrowly on one particular facet of life. But we also recognize this as a *mistake*, and we've come to fully understand that at some point, you have to say, "Enough." You have to step back and say, "What am I really about here, anyway?" You really don't have time to waste wandering around in the desert of unclarity.

The clock is ticking. Take a look at the following list to get an idea of how much time (based on average life expectancies) you have left on this planet to fulfill your purpose.

Current Age	Average Number of Years Left	Average Number of Days Left
20	56.3	20,550
25	51.6	18,834
30	46.9	17,119
35	42.2	15,403
40	37.6	13,724
45	33.0	12,045
50	28.6	10,439
55	24.4	8,906
60	20.5	7,483
65	16.9	6,169
70	13.6	4,964
75	10.7	3,906

The numbers may look like a lot, or they may look like too few. The point is that you have only so many days on this earth to turn your reality into your dreams. Maybe you already know exactly what your purpose is, and you have a plan to fulfill it. If you don't, how many more days are you going to wander around without even knowing why you are here, before you die? We hope you'll decide that yesterday was the last day. If you accept that your days are limited, you're more likely to understand the importance of aligning them with your purpose. That makes goal setting both easier and more important. Furthermore, couples who entwine their dreams together and create their plans together have the opportunity to look out across the expanse of time and see themselves unified in love and in life. In this sense, the dream becomes a prophecy.

Defining Dreams, Defining Goals

You got to be very careful if you don't know where you're going, because you might not get there.

YOGI BERRA

If your dreams are to come true, you have to know what the dreams are. This is another of those powerful statements that can be overlooked because of its simplicity. Sure, there's a lot we need to do to be able to reach our goals—we need to be motivated to do so, we need to understand ourselves and our partner, we need to have the technical ability to get from point A to point B. All of this we have covered, or we have at least showed you how to begin. Yet let's not forget to take in the obvious: you have to make sure you know where point B is. Where are the gates of happiness for you? What are your goals?

When it comes to setting goals, there are two different kinds of people in this world. There are those who, when faced with the opportunity, say, "Oh cool, I love setting goals and planning how to reach them." And then there are those who say, "Oh man, I hate this. When I set goals, things never seem to work out the way I'd planned, and I end up feeling worse instead of better. I'd just as soon not go there." In case you fall into the second group, let us take a moment to tell you why this process might be a bit different from what you've experienced in the past.

Different Process, Different Terms

Our process for defining goals is contrary to most conventional wisdom regarding goal setting. Once you have discovered what it is that you really want and come up with a plan to achieve it, we are in essence going to tell you to lay aside what is usually called "the goal" and to keep the plan. It may sound crazy, but that's what we're going to encourage you to do. Here's why. Remember when we talked about how unmet expectations lead to feelings of sadness, disappointment, frustration, and anger? Well, the way many of us have been taught to define goals actually turns the goal into an unrealistic expectation, which sets us up to be disappointed when that expectation isn't met. To better understand what we're getting at, we need to define some terms.

In our opinion, goals should be defined so that you can take complete responsibility for achieving them. They do not require something to happen that is outside your control, such as an upswing in the economy, another person's cooperation, or improvements in your physiology or health. A proper goal is defined such that the only reason the goal can be thwarted is if you don't do what you said you'd do.

Goals need to be differentiated from results. Results are defined as the consequence that you *hope* will follow from reaching your goal. Results may require something to happen that is outside your control, so you should not take responsibility for them; your only responsibility is to create and reach your goals so that the results are most likely to occur. Our definitions acknowledge the simple truth that in real life we do not have control over results; we have control over only our actions. If we define our goals such that we have no control over whether or not we reach them, we are in essence creating unrealistic expectations for ourselves—a recipe for disappointment.

Examples of Goals and Results

Here are some examples to help flesh out this idea a bit more.

Let's say that you and your partner want to save enough money to meet the requirements for buying a house. You figure that you need to save $10,000 for the down payment and closing costs. You put together a realistic budget and commit to putting a minimum of $278 per month into savings. At this rate, it will take you three years to save $10,000. If you make it your *goal* to qualify to buy a house, then there are many outside circumstances that could thwart your goal. For example, in three years, the housing market may have exploded and you'd need $15,000 as a down payment for the type of house you want. Or the rules may have changed and you'd need to have a higher income, or interest rates may have gotten so high that it would be ridiculous to try to buy a house at that time. These are all things that are out of your control. However, if you made qualifying to buy a house the *result* you're hoping for and made it your *goal* to put $278 per month into the bank, then every month that you put $278 into the bank, you get to enjoy the satisfaction of reaching your goal. Of course you can still feel disappointed that the hoped-for result didn't come to fruition, but successful people don't beat themselves up for the things that are out of their control. They set goals they can reach and often adjust their goals so that their desired results are more likely to occur.

Let's look at another example. Many people want to lose weight, so they set a goal that looks something like this: "My goal is to lose twenty pounds by Halloween (so I can enjoy all that candy without worrying about it!)." Suppose someone plans to reach this goal by eating no more than 2,500 calories per day and exercising for twenty minutes three times per week. So what happens if this person follows his plan to the letter but is only eight pounds lighter or, worse, two pounds heavier when Halloween rolls around? Big-time discouragement sets in. For some people, following this plan would allow them to attain the results they desired. For others, it won't. Suppose, however, that this person were to state his goal this way: "My goal is to eat no more than 2,500 calories per day and exercise for twenty minutes three times per week for a period of four weeks." If he does what he sets out to do, he will have successfully reached his goal. He can then reevaluate how well reaching his goal helps him achieve the desired results. None of this is to say that results aren't important or that you shouldn't seek them. Results *are* extremely important, and we will discuss them more fully in a bit. The point now is to differentiate between goals and results.

If you make it your goal to have a more intimate relationship with your spouse, then you have defined a goal that is beyond your capacity to achieve. You can control what *you* do to increase the chances of having a more intimate relationship, but you cannot control what your spouse will do, nor how he or she will react. A better goal would be to make one specific deposit into your mate's main love account each week for a period of two months and then to reevaluate.

The Value of Results

There is a healthy balance to maintain when setting goals. In this world, there is much that is under our control, and we grow stronger as we exercise our control over these domains. Yet there is much that is beyond our control, and it is emotionally healthy to maintain a profound respect for all that is in that realm. In the United States, and indeed around the world, people were reminded of just how much we *cannot* control, when on September 11, 2001, the World Trade Center was attacked by terrorists. On that day, many of us were reminded that we cannot always choose our circumstances. We cannot choose what happens to us, but we can choose how we will react. We can always choose to rebuild.

In life, the results you desire provide the motivation to keep putting one foot in front of the other. Your desired results are, in essence, your vision for your future. A vision inspires you and calls you forward. As you see the desires of your heart in your own imagination, you create new perceptual realities. You see possibilities with greater clarity. As you visualize your desired results, you begin to see *more*. You begin to see things you missed before—opportunities, resources, possibilities—that can help you attain your goal.

We need both a vision and a goal. The vision motivates us to keep putting one foot in front of the other; goals provide the right path on which to walk. Big dreams just lead to big disappointments if you don't know how to plan your path and if you don't walk down that path.

Successful people don't just dream. Successful couples don't just act. They dream and then act with purpose—according to a plan. Even a plan with key flaws is better than no plan, because as you act on it, you learn more. As you move forward, you have the opportunity to discover those flaws and adjust.

Characteristics of Good Goals

We've found that many couples feel defeated before they begin because they assume that the end goal is to reach an impossible ideal—to become perfect. Relax. We don't expect perfection. In fact, we think that becoming "perfect" is not only an impossible goal but a boring one. Think about it. Think of someone you know who you think is practically perfect in every way. Now ask yourself, "Do I really *like* this person? Or do I find this person not so fun to be around? Do I really want to *be* like this person?" How fun would it be to live in a world where everyone lived in a perfectly decorated mansion with no "But that's my favorite recliner" in the family room or "I Love You Mommy" crayon art on the fridge, drove a luxury sedan with no French fries under the seats, had absolutely no excess body fat (which would mean you couldn't buy Oreos anymore because Nabisco doesn't keep producing what doesn't sell), and went to bed early instead of staying out too late with their friends because they'd want to be in tip-top shape for work the next day? We don't think perfection sounds like a realistic or fun goal. Instead, we'd like to help you discover the path to becoming *your* best, which will still allow you to retain your unique personality. That means that while you build on your unique strengths, you must also hold on to some of your quirks—those sometimes endearing and sometimes maddening qualities that make you a unique human. Throughout this book, we have encouraged both you and your partner to learn and grow. However, our desire has never been to get you to change from the person you are to someone you are not. Our hope is that you will continue to become more fully and richly all that you are, and that each of you will fully and deeply accept the other as you move forward in life together.

Your goal doesn't have to include perfection, and your plan to reach your goals doesn't have to be perfect either. We don't have to know everything that we'll need to know to bring about the desired result. We can't. No one can accurately anticipate *all* that needs to happen to bring about the realization of his or her dreams. Our goals will have to change as our circumstances change. What we experience as we move toward our goals will often lead us to set new and different goals. *That* is the primary function of goals—to continue to move us forward. As we move forward, we learn more about what's needed, about what's possible, about what's desired. Thus we can make more informed decisions, refine our goals, and move forward once again. Don't aim for perfection; don't wait to have the perfect plan before you work on defining your goals. Just begin.

A Good Goal Is One *You* Want

In this chapter, we provide some exercises to help you discover what really matters to *you*. Far too many goal-setting tools are based on what the author or instructor believes you *should* want instead of what you do want. You don't have to want to retire with a million dollars. You don't have to want to "make it to the top" at your workplace. You don't have to want to be able to run ten miles without breathing hard. You don't have to want anything you don't want. If what you want more than anything is to quit your high-paying engineering job and become a "fix-it person" for the senior citizens in your community who can't afford to hire someone, then we want to help you realistically figure out how you and your partner can make that happen.

If you or your partner wants to go back to school to get a doctoral degree, then we want to help the two of you figure out how to do that. If you want to be able to buy a VW Beetle, then we want to help you do that (and Natalie wants to know if she can drive it: "Can I please, oh please? Can I, huh? I promise I'll be reeeeeeeeeally careful!"). We're OK with whatever you care about (assuming it's ethical!). We just care about helping you get what *you* care about.

A Good Goal Is Big Enough to Be Challenging but Is Still Realistic

Let's get real. Some things are impossible in life. We are reminded of a story about a mother and her daughter. The little girl ran up to her mama and said, "Mommy, I've decided to become a nurse when I grow up." Her mother said, "Honey, you don't have to be a nurse. You can be a doctor. You can be anything you want." The little girls eyes lit up in amazement. "Really?" she asked. "Yes, really," her mom replied. The little girl scrunched up her brow and put her finger to her temple in deep concentration. She said, "I think I'll be a horse when I grow up."

When you start dreaming, consider every possibility. However, when it comes time to sit down and actually set your goals, you'll have far more success if you take into consideration what is realistic for you.

For example, suppose you aren't a morning person, and regular exercise hasn't been part of your routine for fifteen years, but you set the goal to make it to the 5:30 A.M. spinning class every single day of the year; unless you are one of those rare souls who can make such a drastic change in their lifestyle, you are likely setting yourself up for failure. It is better to start small and keep adding to your goals. For instance, it might be better to state your goal this way: "I am going to make it to at least one spinning class every week for three out of the next four weeks." Then, buoyed by your success, you can up it to two classes per week for the following three out of four weeks. A good goal is not only within your control and challenging enough to be motivating but also realistic enough to be achievable.

A Good Goal Fits Your Personality

Goals should fit your personality. Some people are more "bite the bullet and get it over with as quickly as possible" types, and others are more "I don't care how long it takes, I just want it to be as painless as possible" types. You can probably tell which type you are by how you approach a cold swimming pool. Do you just dive in and shiver through the shock? Or do you sit on the side and dunk your toes in, and twenty minutes later you're up to your knees?

Suppose you were setting a goal to save money. If you're the bite-the-bullet type, then you might do better with goals like this: "I am not going to spend a single dime beyond my fixed expenses for the next two months." In contrast, if you're the

I-don't-want-to-feel-the-pinch type, then you might do better with a goal like this: "I'm going to buy generic ice cream instead of Häagen-Dazs for the next six months."

A Good Goal Includes Several Options

Goals need to be specific, but not too specific. For example, the goal to buy generic ice cream would be improved further if you were to say, "I will buy one generic item instead of the more expensive item every time I go to the grocery store." That way, you give yourself room to save money even if you get an irresistible craving for Häagen-Dazs.

A Good Goal Is Time Limited

A good goal has a deadline. You need to know not only where you want to go but also when you're going to get there. Setting a time limit gives you the opportunity to stop and reevaluate. Short-term is usually better than long-term. In order to maintain the sense that you're moving forward, you need to see the milestones along the way. You may have lifelong goals, but set mini-goals along the way. Goals should be structured so that you'll know at the end of each week or month whether or not you've met them.

A Good Goal Is Measurable

By measurable we mean that you can answer the question, How will you know when you've achieved it? Suppose you say, "I want to have more money in the bank." How much is *more?* Will you really feel like you've moved forward if you have one penny more? What if you have more money in the bank simply because you used your credit card to buy everything that month? Use terms that are specific and measurable and that capture what you are really trying to do.

A Good Goal Gives You Some Wiggle Room

A good goal allows you to be imperfect and still reach the goal. For instance, instead of saying that you will attend every single investment club meeting in the next six months, make it your goal to make it to five out of the six.

Ten Steps to Turning Reality into Dreams

Now that we've talked about the difference between results and goals, and you understand the characteristics of a good goal, let's put it all together. You can use the following ten-step process to set goals associated with a desired result.

1. Write down the desired result. Remember, results are the consequence that you *hope* will follow from reaching your goal. For example, you might list as your desired result that you would like to feel closer to your partner, that you'd like to be described by your friends as "playful," or that you'd like to become financially free.

2. Write down a goal that you think might help you get the desired result. Remember, the only reason a goal can be thwarted is if you don't do what you said you'd do. A good goal

- Is one *you* want
- Is big enough to be challenging but is still realistic
- Fits your personality
- Includes several options
- Is time limited
- Is measurable
- Gives you some wiggle room

3. State what reaching the goal would get you. Why do you want this?

4. Brainstorm ways you could achieve this goal. What do you have to change in order to reach success? What specific actions will you take? When?

5. List what achieving this goal would cost you if you were to pursue it. You may find that some goals would cost you too much time, money, emotional energy, and so on. Are you willing to be uncomfortable? What is the payoff for keeping things the same?

6. List the obstacles that may come between you and your goal. List ways you could overcome these obstacles. What are you afraid of? What is the worst thing that could happen? If your best friend had this fear, what advice would you offer?

7. Evaluate your goal. At this stage you need to look at your desired result and see how likely you think it is that reaching your goal will get you the result you want. Is there a better way? Is what you would get more than what it would cost? Are you willing to pay the price?

8. If the answers to these questions are yes, fine-tune your goal and write it down. If you answered no, then

- Reevaluate your desired result. Is there another result that would work for you?
- Reevaluate your goal. Is there another goal that could end up giving you your desired result? Are there other ways of achieving your goal?
- Place the potential goal on the back burner. You may decide to resurrect it at a later time when it wouldn't cost as much to achieve or when the value of reaching the goal increases.

9. Plan how you're going to handle the times when you'll want to quit. What excuses will you offer yourself when you start to fail? What will you do to get beyond the excuses and achieve success? Ask yourself, "What 'push' can I give myself to get me through?"

10. Write on your calendar the dates you're going to meet to check up on and celebrate your progress.

Once you have your plan, of course, you have to actually *act* on it. Part of the power of goal setting is that the process helps you eliminate those things you don't really want in life and helps you focus on what you do want. You don't have to rely on willpower alone because the goal is truly yours—you can feel it deep in your gut. By the time you've completed this process, you know what you want, why you want it, and how you're going to get it. You're primed for success.

Goal Setting in Action

An example will help you see the process from beginning to end, so here we're going to show you one couple's ten steps.

1. *Write down the desired result.* We would like to take our kids to Disney World for a week.

2. *Write down a goal.* We figure that it will take $5,000 to stay at one of the resorts at Disney World and pay for airfare, food, etc. for one week, so our goal is to save $5,000 in twenty months.

3. *State what reaching the goal would get you.* We want to enjoy one very special, magical vacation together. We both have special memories of the time our parents took us to Disneyland, and we want to do something similar. We want to be able to look back at the kids' childhood and have that memory. We want to feel close. We want to have fun. We want to go someplace where we can relax—everything is taken care of once we get there. Disney World is a place where both the kids and the adults would have fun. There's plenty to do—we won't easily get bored. There's a variety of activities for slower, more relaxing days and fast-paced, more exciting days. We won't have to drive anywhere or worry about getting lost.

4. *Brainstorm ways you could achieve this goal.* To save $5,000, we will need to save $250 per month for twenty months. To do that we could

- Stop investing $250 per month in our IRA for twenty months.
- Put the $2,000 we have saved for a new car toward the trip.

- Tighten up the grocery budget, the clothing budget, the home improvement budget, and the entertainment budget.
- Win the lottery.
- Take the money out of our retirement fund and pay huge penalties.

5. *List what achieving this goal would cost you if you were to pursue it.* If we chose option A, the trip would cost us our sense that we're adequately preparing for our future. Option B might be OK, but we decided that we really don't want to go into debt to buy our next car, so that would feel like going backwards. As far as option C is concerned, we might be able to squeeze a little bit more out of the grocery budget and entertainment budget, but we don't think we can cut that much from clothing or home improvement. It gets too stressful when we can't make the improvements we'd planned on the house. We just don't want to live with a budget that's that much tighter. It's kind of hard to win the lottery when we never buy tickets, and we don't want to leave reaching our goals up to chance like that anyway—so much for option D. And we ain't touching our retirement account. One special week just isn't worth our future.

6. *Evaluate obstacles.* We don't see how we can save that much. We could look for ways to make more money. We could save for a longer period of time. We could find ways to make the trip less expensive, like by going somewhere less expensive altogether, staying for a shorter time, or staying in a less expensive hotel.

7. *Evaluate.* We still want to take the kids to Disney World sometime. Disneyland doesn't offer the same attractions as Disney World. For this vacation, no substitute will work. That's what we want. When we do it, we don't want to worry about having to watch the pennies. We want to stay in a resort on-site and not try to skimp. Since we're not willing to cut back on retirement, we're going to have to look for other ways to pay the price.

8. *Write down the goal and keep it where you can see it.* We're going to take $500 out of the "new car" fund. That's as much as we feel good about. We've decided to go camping next summer instead of taking a "bigger" vacation, which will save us about $1,600. We're going to take the trip during off-peak season, which will save us about $500, but we figure that prices will likely go up by at least that amount, so we're going to keep our target at $5,000. We're going to give up cable for a year, which will give us an additional $40 per month. (This came out of the entertainment fund.) We'll forgo half of our Christmas presents to each other, which adds another $200 to the pot. Finally, for the next twenty-four months, we'll try to squeeze an additional $75 per month out of the grocery budget, the clothing budget, and the home improvement budget.

9. *Plan how you're going to handle the times when you'll want to quit.* We know we're going to have a hard time if we look through furniture catalogues, bicycling cat-

alogues, and electronic equipment catalogues, or watch the home improvement shows on TV. (Hey! No more cable. Well, that won't be a problem!) We're going to cancel catalogues that will be tempting for us. Christmas will be hard. We're going to make this Christmas entirely different by volunteering to help at a food kitchen. We won't feel deprived if we're helping others. We're going to get a big poster of Disney World and cut it up into 24 puzzle-piece shapes. Each month that we make our goal, we're going to tape one of the pieces of the puzzle to the wall in the kitchen. Each month we'll be able to see more of the picture. That way our progress will be very visible.

10. *Put follow-up dates on your calendar.* We're planning on taking the trip in late February. In anticipation of the day we're going to leave for our trip, we're going to check to see how we're doing and paste up our puzzle piece on the twenty-second of each month. In March, June, September, and December, we're going to do more research into the trip to see if our estimates of expenses are still on track, see if this is still where we want to go, and so forth.

It Isn't Always So Easy

You may have noticed in the previous example that both partners agreed on the desired result and the goal. When two people plan and work toward one goal, their teamwork creates tremendous power. It's wonderful to experience such teamwork in action. Unfortunately, there will be times when the two of you won't agree on your goals. Sometimes that's frustrating, and sometimes it's frightening. It can be very unsettling to discover that your partner wants to retire at age forty and have both of you join the Peace Corps, when your heart is set on having a high net worth and living in an expensive loft in the heart of San Francisco. It isn't uncommon for one partner to be ready to retire, thinking he or she will finally be building that cabin in the woods, and the other partner says, "And who are you going to live with? Certainly not me!"

The fact is that in addition to knowing how to establish goals for yourselves as individuals, you and your partner also need to know how to interlace your goals together. Some goals, of course, are fine simply to achieve on your own. If you want to learn to play tennis, that is unlikely to interfere with your partner's reaching his or her goal. If it does, you can pick up the floor and work to understand what the issues are for both of you and use the problem-solving model we presented in Chapter Nine.

One strategy for handling the times when bigger life goals clash is to set the agenda by asking, "If we were absolutely determined that both of us would each achieve the essential elements of our goals, what would we do? If there were no restrictions on our time or money, how would we pull this off?" Take some time to brainstorm, and allow your brainstorming to include ridiculous ideas. Then leave it for a week or two. Come back to it to find out whether you can see some new options that you didn't see before.

Another strategy is to prioritize your goals and then look to see if you can come up with certain combinations of goals that will work for both of you. For example, Stacy wanted to buy a larger house, but Peter didn't want to put any more money into a house. He wanted to put more money away for retirement. They decided to look at additional goals for both partners. Stacy had also wanted to go back to school sometime, so they decided that she would go ahead and go back to school to get her master's degree. When she graduated, she went to work and brought in enough income to buy a larger house. Though the house was not as expensive as she had originally wanted, it met her most important needs in a house and allowed her and Peter to meet their investment goals as well.

Sometimes couples will have conflicting goals, and there simply isn't a great solution. At that point the goal is to protect your relationship from the stress of the conflict. One strategy is to set an agenda this way: "How are we going to protect the rest of our relationship from this conflict about these particular goals?" Or you might ask, "What's best for me, for you, *and* for our relationship as a whole?" With this approach, you are pitting the two of you against an outside problem instead of letting a problem come between you. As you learned in Chapter Two, a happy marriage has much to do with overall satisfaction in life, so even when the two of you don't agree, keeping in mind the preciousness of a lasting love can help you keep things in perspective.

Start Dreaming

In the beginning of Part Three, which covered money management, we said that we were going to go through all the nitty-gritty of *how* to get what you want, and that once you saw that you *could* do it, we'd help you figure out what it is that you want to go after. We've shown you how to get your financial documents together and how to "ask the right questions" regarding insurance to ensure that you and your loved ones are protected from financial loss. We've shown you ways to control your spending and minimize your taxes so that you'd have something left over to invest, and we introduced you to the world of investing. Although there is still much you can and should learn about all these topics, we think you're now ready to think deeply about your life and what you want.

Here's what we want you to do. We want you to take out some paper and write out your answers to the following questions. We've included lots and lots of questions, and it may look a little overwhelming. It's OK to work on this a little at a time. You may want to answer just one question per day for a while, or even to go away for a weekend and spend the time contemplating these questions. The old saying "The more you put into it, the more you'll get out of it" applies here. Some people prefer to talk about things, and some prefer to write. If you and your partner want to talk together through each of these questions, that's fine by us. You may find that the conversations draw you toward one another to an even greater degree. However much the two of you talk, we'd still like for you to write down as much as possible. You'll want to refer back to your notes in the years to come as you continue to revise your dreams and goals.

Think Back

1. Think back to three or four of the happiest times of your life. How did you feel then? What was going on? Were you alone or with others? Were you the center of attention, or were you supporting someone else?
2. At what times in your life have you felt most alive? Have you ever had the sensation that a particular moment was predestined? That you were in the flow of exactly what you were supposed to be doing at that moment? When? What was happening?
3. When you were little, what did you want to become?
4. Was there a time when you really stretched yourself? What was something good that came from that?
5. What successes are you most proud of? Why? Why did you succeed?
6. What rewards are the most motivating for you? What flips your switch?
7. What qualities do you most appreciate about yourself? Here are some ideas: honest, loving, grateful, flexible, disciplined, healthy, romantic, happy, playful, focused, passionate, strong, smart, cheerful.

What Do You Want?

Continue asking yourself questions. Allow yourself to write down the answers quickly. List anything that comes to mind. Don't evaluate. Don't ask yourself, Why? Just write.

1. If I could do anything in the world I wanted, what would that be?
2. Who do I want to be?
3. What do I want from my life?
4. What do I want to accomplish?
5. Where do I want to go?

6. What do I want to give?
7. What do I want to create?
8. What's the purpose of my life?
9. What's my mission?
10. What do I want my life to stand for?
11. What do I want to be remembered for?
12. What people and places would I like to visit?
13. I would consider my life to have been a success if . . .
14. What is one thing that I deeply want to achieve in the next year?
15. What do I want to be doing in two years? In five? In ten?
16. What are the ways I'd like to improve myself?
17. What personal growth seminars do I want to take?
18. What educational classes would I like to take?
19. What books have I been wanting to read?
20. Is there a church or synagogue I've been meaning to attend?

Here are some financial goals common among couples. Is there anything here you want to pursue?

1. Do you want to increase your net worth?
2. Do you want to save for a future dream?
3. Do you want to buy, start, or invest more in your own business?
4. Do you want to maintain your current lifestyle after you retire?
5. What kinds of activities do you plan to take part in after retirement? Will these require additional funds?
6. Do you want to provide income for your dependents in the event of your death? For how long? How much?
7. Do you want to provide income for yourself and your dependents in the event that you become disabled? For how long? How much?
8. Do you want to make contributions to certain charities or other worthy organizations?

What Do You Want Your Relationship to Look Like?

Go back to the Going Deep exercises at the end of Part One. Look again at what you wrote regarding how you'd like things to be. For example, on the money-relationship style dimensions, are you happy with the teamwork level? If you'd like to see that change, what would be the desired result, and what would be the goal?

Time to Prioritize

If you've put a lot of work into these exercises, you could very well have pages and pages of notes. Good job! Now you'll need to distill this information into a more useful format. Go back through your answers and categorize the results that you'd like to see happen in your life. You can categorize these in any way you choose. Some examples of categories might be as follows:

- Individual results
- Relationship results
- Financial results
- Long-term results
- Short-term results

Once you have your desired results organized by category, prioritize them in order of importance to you. If you have a tough time putting your desires in order of importance, you may find the worksheet shown in Figure 38 helpful. Choose your top ten desired results; the worksheet will help you prioritize from there.

After you have prioritized your desired results, use the ten steps we discussed earlier in the chapter to begin creating goals to help you make your desired results most likely to happen. As part of this process, pull out your budget. Take a look at where you're spending your money. Are you using your money to help you get what you most want in life? Take some time to think through how you can bring your budget into line with your life goals.

Time to Talk

If you haven't already been talking about the questions in the Start Dreaming section, now we'd like for you to schedule a time to talk with your partner. See if you can carve out at least an hour of uninterrupted time together. You could even make it a date and go out to eat, planning to talk over candlelight.

Share with your partner what you've discovered about yourself. If your partner completed the exercise as well, then let your partner share what he or she learned. Usually when both partners do this kind of exercise, one will have written pages and pages, and the other will have put everything on a single five-by-seven note card. That's OK. Don't hassle your partner about how much or little he or she did—that's not the way to start a romantic evening! If you would like to use the structure of the Speaker-Listener Technique, that's fine. (You can use the menu as the floor!)

FIGURE 38. FOUR STEPS TO DETERMINING YOUR PRIORITIES.

Step 1: List ten competing goals in any order.

1.
2.
3.
4.
5.
6.
7.
8.
9.
10.

Step 2: Compare each goal with another; circle the one that is the more important of the two.

1 or 2	1 or 3	1 or 4	1 or 5	1 or 6	1 or 7	1 or 8	1 or 9	1 or 10
	2 or 3	2 or 4	2 or 5	2 or 6	2 or 7	2 or 8	2 or 9	2 or 10
		3 or 4	3 or 5	3 or 6	3 or 7	3 or 8	3 or 9	3 or 10
			4 or 5	4 or 6	4 or 7	4 or 8	4 or 9	4 or 10
				5 or 6	5 or 7	5 or 8	5 or 9	5 or 10
					6 or 7	6 or 8	6 or 9	6 or 10
						7 or 8	7 or 9	7 or 10
							8 or 9	8 or 10
								9 or 10

Step 3: Record the number of times you circled each goal.

Number of times you circled 1:
Number of times you circled 2:
Number of times you circled 3:
Number of times you circled 4:
Number of times you circled 5:
Number of times you circled 6:
Number of times you circled 7:
Number of times you circled 8:
Number of times you circled 9:
Number of times you circled 10:

Step 4: Record the goals in order. The one you circled most often is priority number 1; the one you circled least often is priority number 10.

1.
2.
3.
4.
5.
6.
7.
8.
9.
10.

Before you start, it's a good idea to agree on the ground rules. For example, as you listen to your partner, you may learn something new. You may not. Some of your partner's dreams may make you uncomfortable, either because you don't share them or because you're afraid that your dreams and your partner's don't mesh. Decide together before you start sharing whether you want to bring up dreams that may not converge with your partner's. If you feel safe enough together to discuss these kinds of potentially painful dreams, then go ahead. If not, save that discussion for later.

If you have time, you can begin to ask each other the following questions. If you don't have time during your first discussion, schedule another time to get together to complete the next stage. When you ask each other these questions, don't act like prosecuting attorneys. You're not supposed to grill your partner. You're enjoying discovering your beloved.

Choose something your partner mentioned wanting to do, and ask:

Why do you want to do this?

Why do you want to be this kind of person?

What will it give you?

How will your life be different when you succeed? What will you feel? What bad things will be absent or good things be present?

Before you end this discussion time, each of you should choose one or two of your partner's dreams or desires and tell your partner how you'd like to help him or her reach that dream. You don't have to get very specific about what steps you will take, though you can if you'd like. Mostly, we'd like for you to end this discussion by affirming to each other that you want to accompany your partner on the journey to reaching his or her dreams. We can't think of a more beautiful beginning to your future than your making a commitment to help each other turn your reality into dreams.

In the Years Ahead

To help you continue to pursue your dreams and stay the course, we suggest that you schedule an annual Long-Term Planning Day. Most couples find that life gets too busy for them to try to continually update their goals, their budget, and so forth. However, it is possible to set aside one day just to make sure you're both in alignment with where you want to be going in life. Choose one day. Put it on the calendar. Pick a day that will not likely get ruined. Maybe choose a holiday like Valentine's Day or Memorial Day or Father's Day—some day when you're unlikely to have work interfere.

Plan for a day of financial dreaming, planning, troubleshooting, and goal setting. One day a year. Make it a special day. Make it a tradition. You wake up and
you shower together. You make plans for the kids—plans that can still hold even
if they get sick. (In other words, get a friend who will keep the little darlings even if
they have a cold.) Maybe go away to a bed-and-breakfast. Go to a special brunch.
Go on a picnic. Do something relaxing together. Not a movie. Not a sporting event.
Not something that you'd do on any other day. This is a once-a-year tradition. Maybe
take along your scrapbook (or the box of undated pictures) and look through them.
Get nostalgic. Bring pictures of travel books, of places you want to travel to together
sometime. Bring pictures of the Ford 150XLT that you want to drive someday. Bring
the Ethan Allen catalogue and look through it together. Then get down to business.

Bring out your budget and work it through. Make your long-term plans. Revise your goals. See how you've done over the last year. What have you accomplished together? What do you still want to do? Make your plans for the following
year, so you'll both stay on course, always heading for the gates of happiness.

One Final Story

I (Natalie) would like to leave you with one last story.

As tears trickled down my cheeks and toward my lips, I tasted the salt. I don't
know why I remember the taste, but I do. I also remember feeling my great-
grandma, whom I called Grammy, tremble as I held her hand. We were listening to the pastor saying something about dust to dust. I was trying to believe that
my great-granddaddy had really gone, but somehow I couldn't quite fathom such
a loss. My mind wandered.

My little sister and I had looked forward to visiting Granddaddy and
Grammy's house every summer for as long as I could remember (all nine or so
years of my life at that point). They lived on a farm, and we could run around the
vast pasture without any adults around. Grammy and Granddaddy were always
lots of fun. Grammy let us eat cookies and drink Pepsi for breakfast! Granddaddy
let us play in the barn and jump from high places into the soft hay. I remembered
their house as a happy place, not only because they loved us so much but also
because they loved each other.

As a kid, I would giggle when they kissed, which they did often. They'd giggle too, in mock embarrassment. (It always amazed me that such old people still
giggled.) Grammy would tell him, "You're such a wonderful love."

They didn't always get along perfectly. I remember one time he called her
"Woman" when he was annoyed with her. Grammy was little, but she was feisty.
She shook her rolling pin at him and said, "Don't you talk to me in that tone."

I smiled at the memory and then tasted the salt again. As we left the burial site, I still clung to Grammy's hand. She turned and looked back one last time, and I heard her whisper, "You were such a wonderful love."

Some people in our world have come to believe that it's impossible for a rich and beautiful love to last a lifetime. You'll never convince me of that. I've seen it. Grammy and Granddaddy were married for over sixty years, and it wasn't long after Granddaddy died that Grammy went to be with him. She'd decided that love was more precious even than life.

◆ ◆ ◆

As you contemplate what you really want out of life and what your purpose is on this earth, we hope you will not dream too small. We hope that your dream will include a love that is rich and that lasts a lifetime.

RESOURCES

CHOOSING A FINANCIAL PLANNER

In a period of increasing financial complexity, especially in regard to taxes, insurance, and investments, many couples with combined annual incomes above $60,000 could use the skills and knowledge of a professional financial planner. If your family income is above $100,000, a financial planner is almost an imperative. A well-qualified and experienced financial planner can assist couples in planning their future.

There are least two caveats to consider prior to beginning the process of selecting and interviewing financial planners:

1. In many states, anyone—and we mean anyone—can hang out a shingle and call themselves a "financial planner." The financial planning industry is one of the most underregulated areas of professional services. Many state legislatures have ignored this industry, leaving it to police itself. In numerous cases, individuals who have been either scammed or simply given very bad advice are forced to use the civil court system to punish the abuses in this industry.

2. Financial planners generally earn their income in one of two ways. Most (more than 95 percent) receive commissions from the investments, insurance polices, and other financial products they sell to their clients. In some cases, these financial planners will also charge you an hourly rate for gathering financial information, writing, and presenting the plan to you. However, their real interest is

"YOU KNOW, IF YOU'RE THINKING WHAT I'M THINKING, WE MIGHT WANT TO PLAN OUR 'NEST EGG' WITH SOMEONE ELSE."

in selling you certain products or product lines that give them the highest level of personal income possible.

A small group of financial planners have fee-based practices. That is, after they evaluate your financial situation and your financial goals, they charge a fee for their services based either on the amount of time the plan took to develop and report or on a sliding fee scale linked to the gross annual family income. Typically, these planners will recommend certain types of investments, insurance plans, and estate planning programs, but they do not sell them, nor do they receive referral fees from agents or stockbrokers who finally sell the financial products to you.

Education and Accreditation of Financial Planners

People involved in the financial planning industry vary quite a bit in terms of their training and expertise. Usually, the alphabet soup following their name on their business card can give you an idea of planners' qualifications.

Most reputable financial planners choose to take additional training after graduating with a bachelor's degree. University postgraduate training produces individuals with a variety of degrees. Many financial planners will have an M.B.A. (master of business administration), a graduate degree indicating that the recipient has had training in all areas of business activities. A few will have an M.F.P. (master of financial planning). To earn this degree, the student devotes the whole two years of graduate school to the study of financial planning. Some financial planners will indicate they have a M.S. (master of science), which could be in any major, including financial planning.

Aside from university postgraduate work, most financial planners receive additional training targeted on financial planning issues. In the best-known training program, the financial planner becomes a certified financial planner (CFP). More than thirty thousand individuals have acquired this credential. The CFP training and designation are controlled by the International Board of Standards and Practices for Certified Financial Planners. After training in a number of educational modules either by correspondence or through a qualified university, the person must go through a two-day testing period, gain three years of work experience in financial planning, and agree to a code of ethical standards. In addition, he or she must acquire continuing education credits in financial planning in order to maintain the CFP accreditation. To locate a person with a CFP in your area, go to the Web site of the trade group, the International Association of Financial Planners (www.fpanet.org).

The financial planners who are fee-only are generally members of the National Association of Personal Financial Advisors. Their members can be found by going to www.feeonly.org and using the site's search function. There are slightly more than 750 members of this group, and they are in only forty-five states.

There are a few certified public accountants (CPAs) who also practice financial planning. Those who specialize in financial planning can be found through the American Institute of Certified Public Accountants at www.aicpa.org.

There are other professional designations associated with financial planning. One is the chartered financial consultant (ChFC), who has specialized training in life insurance and financial planning. There are more than fifteen thousand ChFCs in the United States, and information about their training can be acquired at the American College Web site (www.amercoll.edu). The American College also certifies chartered life underwriters (CLUs), who also have training in life insurance.

One professional organization that does not accredit financial planners but rather trains people who can help individuals and families get out of debt is the Association for Financial Counseling and Planning Education (AFCPE). More about this organization can be found at www.afcpe.org. It offers the accredited financial counselor (AFC) program through its Institute for Personal Finance. Many of these individuals work in nonprofit financial counseling service organizations as well as for the family services area of the military.

If you want help finding a financial planner in your area, you can contact these organizations:

Financial Planning Association: (800) 282-PLAN, www.fpanet.org

National Association of Personal Financial Advisors: 888-FEE-ONLY, www.feeonly.org

American Institute of Certified Public Accountants, personal financial planning division: (800) 862-4272, www.cpapfs.org

American College: (800) 392-6900, www.amercoll.edu

Society of Financial Service Professionals: (610) 526-2500, www.financialpro.org

If you want to determine the disciplinary history of a financial planner or adviser, you can contact the following associations and government enforcement groups:

Certified Financial Planner Board of Standards: (888) CFP-MARK

North American Securities Administrators Association: (888) 84-NASAA

National Association of Insurance Commissioners: (816) 842-3600

National Association of Securities Dealers: (800) 289-9999

National Fraud Exchange: (800) 822-0416 (there is a cost for this service)

Securities and Exchange Commission: (800) 732-0330

The Ten Questions to Ask Your Potential Financial Planner

If you need or want to use the services of a financial planner, you and your spouse should interview several potential financial planners for at least half an hour before selecting the one that is right for you. It is best that you go in to the interview with a well-defined list of questions, such as the ones listed here. (These questions have been slightly adapted from a free brochure available from the Certified Financial Planner Board of Standards.)

1. *What experience have you had as a financial planner?* Determine how long they have been in practice and with what kind of organizations they have worked. Ask them to briefly describe to you their previous work experiences in financial planning and how these relate to their current financial practices.

2. *What are your financial planning qualifications?* Now that you know the meaning of all those letters behind their names, you can knowledgeably ask planners to explain to you what degrees and accreditations they hold in the field of financial planning. It is strongly recommended that you seek out a CFP. These individuals must have had at least three years' experience dealing with such complex financial planning topics as tax planning, insurance, investment, estate planning, and retirement planning. In addition, all CFPs must follow a set of ethical guidelines that is enforced by the Certified Financial Planner Board of Standards; if they violate those standards, their CFP accreditation can be removed. Ask them if they have any ethical complaints outstanding against them or if they have ever appeared before the accreditation association for an ethical disciplinary hearing. In concluding this part of the interview, you should ask them about their continuing education program and how they stay current in this rapidly changing field.

3. *What services do you and your organization provide to individuals and families?* The types of services that financial planners can give are dependent on a number of factors, including planners' credentials, licenses, and special areas of expertise. Until recently, financial planners could not sell insurance or other securities products, such as stocks or mutual funds, without special federal and state licenses. In some cases, they were not allowed even to give investment advice without being registered with both state and federal regulatory groups associated with the Securities and Exchange Commission (SEC). Many financial planners today are working in banks where they can refer you to one or more associates who can sell insurance, mutual funds, and stocks and bonds, as well as set up trusts and other complex financial transactions. Some financial planners develop specializations, such as saving for college, estate planning, or retirement issues. The fee-only financial planners do not sell products at all. They can only encourage

you to complete the agreed-on financial plan; other individuals sell you the products outside the planners' organization.

4. *What is your process in developing financial plans and helping clients implement them?* In order to determine if this planner is the one you want to select for this important task, you should ask her what type of clients and financial situations she typically works with. You need to know if you fit her expected profile of a financial planning client. One area of importance is to determine if your planner's concept of risk and meshes with yours. She may suggest that you invest only in fast-growth high-tech companies that have very risky investments, whereas you prefer old-line blue-chip stocks that return reasonable dividends with little or no risk. Some planners may require that you have a certain net worth before they will work with you. Some will help you implement the plan you develop, whereas others will refer you to others to complete that task.

5. *Will you be the only person that works with me in this organization?* Fewer and fewer financial planners work alone. Most require the assistance of secretaries, accountants, and computer staff to assist them in creating financial plans. Under those conditions, your private financial information will have to be shared with others in order for you to accomplish your financial planning goals. You may request to meet with everyone who will be seeing your materials. It is your money and your life these individuals are working with, and you must be comfortable with that. If the planner works with other professionals outside his firm, ask for their names so that you can check on their backgrounds also.

6. *How will you be paid for your services to me?* Here are some of the different ways in which financial planners earn their living.

> *Salaried employees:* Some financial planners are salaried and are made available to you either by your bank or credit union or some other financial institution. The planner's employer pays her through fees or commissions associated with her services.
>
> *Fee-only planners:* Fewer than one thousand financial planners are fee-only. They are normally members of the National Association of Personal Financial Advisors. The fee can be based on an hourly rate, a percentage of income or net worth, or a combination of fees. The costs of fee-based financial planning can vary widely. Fees may be based on a fixed price, an hourly rate (such as $75 per hour), or some combination of fixed price and hourly fee based on the complexity of your financial plan.
>
> *Commissioned only:* The majority of financial planners are paid commissions by the companies that produce the products they sell. This means they must sell you the product and get you to sign on the bottom line. Normally, these

commissions are based on a percentage of the cost of the product they sell. Therefore, the more they sell to you, the more they make.

Combination of fee and commissions: A number of financial institutions and agencies charge a fee for developing a financial plan. The financial planner also is paid a commission from the products he sells. Some financial planners may negotiate with the client and lower their fee if the client buys a certain amount of financial products from them.

7. *What are the usual charges for working with a client with my income or assets?* Financial planners should be able to answer that question based on an intelligent estimate of costs incurred while working with a similar client. Some may not be able to answer that question very directly, because it will depend on how much they are able to sell to you of the financial products their agency represents.

8. *What potential conflicts of interest may affect your judgment while working with me as a client?* It is not unusual for planners to have developed some types of business relationships with partners or other corporations that would affect their professional recommendations in their work with you. That is, these business relationships may inhibit their ability to make the best possible recommendations that would be in your interest only. Ask planners to supply you with a written description of these conflicts of interest. If they refuse to place them in writing, it is suggested that you seek a financial planner who will.

In many cases, financial planners who sell mutual funds, securities, stocks, and insurance policies have a business relationship with the companies that provide these financial products. The more companies the planners represent, the more likely they are to give you a choice of products rather to say "This is *the one*" for you.

Occasionally, financial planners will have a business agreement to share fees or commissions with an accountant, attorney, or insurance agent to whom they refer you for additional services. These relationships should be revealed to you in writing when you request them.

9. *Have you ever been accused or disciplined for any unlawful or unethical actions by any governmental or other financial planning regulatory agency or organization?* Many state and federal agencies regulate the financial planning business and its professional members. The financial planning industry as a whole is underregulated from the perspective of most policy analysts. However, there are certain segments of it, especially those associated with products that are sold to the public—stocks, bonds, insurance, and so on—that are well regulated, especially at the federal level. However, there is a checkerboard of state regulations, and some states do a better job than others in regulating this industry. As a result, the financial planning industry

continues to have a high potential for scams, fraud, and fiscal abuse. For example, the National Association of Securities Dealers (NASD), the CFP board, state insurance boards, and Better Business Bureaus keep detailed records of all disciplinary actions against financial planners.

If a financial planner seems vague or evasive about answering this question, walk out! The financial planning industry has become highly competitive over the years. You will be able to find competent and honest financial planners who can help you achieve your financial goals without losing sleep over their ability to serve you.

Financial planners who are registered as investment advisers with the SEC or state securities agencies or who are associated with a company that is registered as an investment firm must provide you with a disclosure Form ADV or state equivalent. If they do not voluntarily give you the Form ADV, they violate SEC rules and regulations and should be reported immediately.

10. *Can I have in writing all the details of the services that you will provide to me?* After you have completed the interview, a professional planner should agree to provide a written response to your questions and a description of the services she can provide to you if you become her client. You should keep this document in your files for future reference.

OUR TEN FAVORITE BOOKS ON MONEY MANAGEMENT AND INVESTMENT

The man who does not read good books has no advantage over the man who can't read them.

MARK TWAIN

We hope that you've gained much from *You Paid* How *Much for That?!* But we also hope that you won't stop here. Please continue learning more about how to make your money work for you. We've read hundreds of books and articles about personal finance over the years, and we've kept track of our favorites. To help guide you in your continuing education, we've provided a list of our favorite top ten (all of which are from the popular and more recent genre rather than the academic or more classic types of writing).

1. *The 9 Steps to Financial Freedom,* by Suze Orman. New York: Crown, 1997.

2. *The Average Family's Guide to Financial Freedom,* by Bill Toohey and Mary Toohey. New York: Wiley, 2000.

3. *The Millionaire Next Door,* by Thomas J. Stanley and William D. Danko. New York: Simon & Schuster, 2000.

4. *The Motley Fool Investment Guide,* by David Gardner and Tom Gardner. New York: Simon & Schuster, 1997.

5. *The Motley Fool: You Have More Than You Think,* by David Gardner and Tom Gardner. New York: Simon & Schuster, 2001.

6. *Ordinary People, Extraordinary Wealth,* by Ric Edelman. New York: HarperCollins, 2000.

7. *Personal Finance for Dummies,* by Eric Tyson. New York: Hungry Minds, 2000.

8. *Rich Dad, Poor Dad,* by Robert T. Kiyosaki and Sharon L. Lechter. New York: Warner Books, 2000.

9. *Taxes for Dummies,* by Eric Tyson and David J. Silverman. New York: Hungry Minds, 2001.

10. *Your Money or Your Life,* by Vicki Robin. New York: Penguin, 1999.

RESOURCES AND TRAINING

We have a variety of relationship-enhancing resources available. Further, we conduct workshops both for couples and for those who work with couples. We have included this section for those who may wish to go further, either as a partner in a couple or as someone who works to help couples make great marriages.

The PREP® Approach

Books

In addition to the book you are holding, we have the following titles that deal more exclusively with the theme of building strong and happy marriages. Each is adapted and developed for a special purpose. The core ideas expressed in Part Two of this book, as well as in the chapters dealing with issues and events, are the primary focus of these works. All are from Jossey-Bass, the publisher of this book, and can be ordered from PREP at the address below or by calling (800) 366-0166, from Jossey-Bass by calling (415) 433-1740, or from any bookstore.

Fighting for *Your Marriage*, by Markman, Stanley, and Blumberg (new rev. ed., 2001)

A Lasting Promise: A Christian Guide to Fighting for *Your Marriage*, by Stanley, Trathen, McCain, and Bryan (1998)

Becoming Parents: How to Strengthen Your Marriage as Your Family Grows,
by Jordan, Stanley, and Markman (1999)

Beyond the Chuppah, by Crohn, Markman, Blumberg, and Levine (2002)

Empty Nesting, by Arp, Arp, Stanley, Blumberg, and Markman (2002)

Fighting for *Your African American Marriage,* by Whitfield, Markman, Stanley,
and Blumberg (2001)

Audiocassettes and Videos

Fighting for *Your Marriage* audiocassettes and videos are available from PREP
Educational Products, Inc. To order, please call (800) 366-0166 or write to us at
the address below. You can also order from Jossey-Bass.

Workshops

We conduct workshops for mental health counselors, clergy, lay leaders, and other
marriage educators who desire to be more fully exposed to the PREP approach.
For information about these "instructor" workshops, please call (303) 759-9931 or
write to us at the address below. We will be glad to give you information about
seminars or products to help you in your own relationship or in your work to help
other couples.

We also have a list of people who have been trained in this approach and who
conduct workshops or do counseling using aspects of this model. To obtain that
list, write to us at the address below or visit our Web site.

You can contact us at:

PREP
P.O. Box 102530
Denver, CO 80250-2530
E-mail: PREPinc@aol.com
Web site: www.PREPinc.com

RESEARCH AND REFERENCES

Amato, P. R., & Rogers, S. J. (1999). Do attitudes toward divorce affect marital quality? *Journal of Family Issues, 20*(1), 69–86.

American Savings Education Council. (Dec. 12, 2001). Programs and events. Employee Benefit Research Institute [http://www.asec.org/eventhm.htm].

Amoruso, D. (Nov. 12, 1999; Dec. 3, 2001). *Realty Times* [http://realtytimes.com/rtnew/rtcpages/19991112_trends.htm].

Angus, C. (1981). *The sense of well-being in America.* New York: McGraw-Hill.

Arp, D., & Arp, C. (1997). *10 great dates to energize your marriage.* Grand Rapids, MI: Zondervan.

Astin, A. W., Green, K. C., & Korn, W. S. (1987). *The American freshman: Twenty year trends.* Los Angeles: Higher Education Research Institute, University of California.

Bailey, W. C. (1987). Gender differences in investment behavior: The tale of "Black Hole Bonds." Unpublished manuscript.

Baucom, D., & Epstein, N. (1990). *Cognitive behavioral marital therapy.* New York: Brunner/Mazel.

Beach, S. R., & O'Leary, K. D. (1993). Marital discord and dysphoria: For whom does the marital relationship predict depressive symptomatology? *Journal of Social and Personal Relationships, 10,* 405–420.

Bedard, P. (Jan. 1996). In the land of Dixie, BMW builds a James Bond two-seater. *Car & Driver.*

Beemer, C. B., & Shook, R. L. (1997). *Predatory marketing.* New York: Morrow.

Behrens, B., & Halford, K. (Aug. 1994). *Advances in the prevention and treatment of marital distress.* Paper presented at the Helping Families Change conference, University of Queensland, Brisbane, Australia.

Bischoping, K. (1993). Gender differences in conversation topics. *Sex Roles, 28,* 1–19.

Blanchflower, D. G., & Oswald, A. J. (2000). *Well-being over time in Britain and the USA.* Cambridge, MA: National Bureau of Economic Research.

Bradbury, T. N., Beach, S.R.H., Fincham, F. D., & Nelson, G. M. (1996). Attributions and behavior in functional and dysfunctional marriages. *Journal of Consulting and Clinical Psychology, 64,* 569–576.

Brock, H. S. (1997). *Complete guide to your money happiness: How to achieve financial success, security, and peace of mind.* Carson City, NV: Legacy.

Business Women's Network Interactive. (Mar. 1999; Dec. 2001). [http://www.BWNi.com].

Buss, D. M., Shackelford, T. K., Kirkpatrick, L. A., & Larsen, R. J. (2001). A half century of mate preferences: The cultural evolution of values. *Journal of Marriage and the Family, 63,* 491–503.

Casale, A. M. Tracking tomorrow's trends: What we think about our lives and our future. *USA Today.*

Center for Marriage and Family. (1995). *Marriage preparation in the Catholic Church: Getting it right.* Omaha, NE: Creighton University.

Center for Marriage and Family. (2000). *Time, sex, and money: The first five years of marriage.* Omaha, NE: Creighton University.

Chapman, G. (1992). *The five love languages: How to express heartfelt commitment to your mate.* Chicago: Northfield.

Cherlin, A. J., & Furstenberg, F. F., Jr. (1994). Step families in the United States: A reconsideration. *Annual Review of Sociology, 20,* 359–381.

Christensen, A., & Heavey, C. L. (1990). Gender and social structure in the demand/withdraw pattern of marital conflict. *Journal of Personality and Social Psychology, 59,* 73–82.

Cialdini, R. B., & Richardson, K. D. (1980). Two indirect tactics of image management: Basking and blasting. *Journal of Personality and Social Psychology, 39.*

Clements, M., & Markman, H. J. (1996). The transition to parenthood: Is having children hazardous to marriage? In N. Vanzetti & S. Duck (Eds.), *A lifetime of relationships* (pp. 290–310). Pacific Grove, CA: Brooks/Cole.

Clements, M., Stanley, S. M., & Markman, H. J. *Predicting divorce.* Manuscript submitted for publication.

Cordova, A. D. (2000). *Teamwork and the transition to parenthood.* Unpublished doctoral dissertation, University of Denver, CO.

Cordova, J. V., Gee, C. B., Warren, L. Z., & McDonald, R. P. (2000). Intimate safety: Measuring the private experience of intimacy in men and women. Unpublished manuscript.

Cordova, J. V., & Scott, R. S. (2000). Intimacy: A behavioral interpretation. Unpublished manuscript.

Cordova, J. V., Jacobson, N. S., & Christensen, A. (1998). Acceptance versus change interventions in behavioral couple therapy: Impact on couples' in-session communication. *Journal of Marriage and Family Therapy, 24,* 437–455.

Crocker, J., & Gallo, L. (Aug. 1985). *The self-enhancing effect of downward comparison.* Paper presented at the American Psychological Association Convention, Los Angeles.

Cummings, E. M., & Davies, P. (1994). *Children and marital conflict.* New York: Guilford Press.

Diaz, A., & Noel, C. (Jan. 8, 2000; Dec. 3, 2001). *ABC News.com* [http://abcnews.go.com/onair/2020/diaz000628.html].

Diener, E., & Suh, E. M. (Eds.). (2000). *Culture and subjective well-being.* Cambridge, MA: MIT Press.

Economic History Resources. (Dec. 8, 2001). How much is that? [http://eh.net/ ehresources/howmuch/dollar_question.php].

Edelman, R. (2000). *Ordinary people, extraordinary wealth.* New York: HarperCollins.

Eidelson, R., & Epstein, N. (1982). Cognitions and relationship maladjustment: Development of a measure of dysfunctional relationship beliefs. *Journal of Consulting and Clinical Psychology, 50,* 715–720.

Farrell, C. (Mar. 2, 2001; Dec. 9, 2001). *Business Week online* [http://www.businessweek.com/ bwdaily/dnflash/feb2007/nf2001032_060.htm].

Fincham, F. D., Garnier, P. C., Gano-Phillips, S., & Osborne, L. N. (1995). Pre-interaction expectations, marital satisfaction and accessibility: A new look at sentiment override. *Journal of Family Psychology, 9,* 3–14.

Fincham, F., Grych, J., & Osborne, L. (Mar. 1993). *Interparental conflict and child adjustment: A longitudinal analysis.* Paper presented at the biennial meeting of the Society for Research in Child Development, New Orleans, LA.

Floyd, F., Markman, H. J., Kelly, S., Blumberg, S., & Stanley, S. M. (1995). Prevention: Conceptual, research, and clinical issues. In N. Jacobson & A. Gurman (Eds.), *Handbook of marital therapy* (2nd ed.). New York: Guilford Press.

Forgue, R. E., & Garman, T. E. (2000). *Personal finance.* Boston: Houghton Mifflin.

Forthofer, M. S., Markman, H. J., Cox, M., Stanley, S. M., & Kessler, R. C. (1996). Associations between marital distress and work loss in a national sample. *Journal of Marriage and the Family, 58,* 597–605.

Fraenkel, P., Markman, H. J., & Stanley, S. M. (1997). The prevention approach to relationship problems. *Sexual and Marital Therapy, 12,* 249–258.

Furnham, A. F. (1985). Why do people save? Attitudes to, and habits of, saving money in Britain. *Journal of Applied Social Psychology, 15,* 354–373.

Gardner, D., & Gardner, T. (1997). *The Motley Fool investment guide.* New York: Simon & Schuster.

Gardner, D., & Gardner, T. (2001). *The Motley Fool: You have more than you think.* New York: Simon & Schuster.

Gilligan, C. (1993). *In a different voice: Psychological theory and women's development.* Cambridge, MA: Harvard University Press.

Gillis, J., & Krugman, S. (Feb. 2, 2001; Dec. 8, 2001). *Consumer Federation of America* [http://www.consumerfed.org/backpage/savings.html].

Glenn, N. D. (1998). The course of marital success and failure in five American 10-year marriage cohorts. *Journal of Marriage and the Family, 60,* 569–576.

Glenn, N. D. (1991). The recent trend in marital success in the United States. *Journal of Marriage and the Family, 53.*

Glenn, N. D. (1990). The social and cultural meaning of contemporary marriage. In B. Christensen (Ed.), *The retreat from marriage.* Rockford, IL: Rockford Institute.

Glink, I. R. (Nov. 27, 2001; Dec. 4, 2001). *Think Glink, Inc.* [http://www.thinkglink.com/ hbc392.htm].

Gottman, J. M. (1993). A theory of marital dissolution and stability. *Journal of Family Psychology, 7,* 57–75.

Gottman, J. M., & Krokoff, L. J. (1989). Marital interaction and satisfaction: A longitudinal view. *Journal of Consulting and Clinical Psychology, 57,* 47–52.

Hahlweg, K., & Markman, H. J. (1988). The effectiveness of behavioral marital therapy: Empirical status of behavioral techniques in preventing and alleviating marital distress. *Journal of Consulting and Clinical Psychology, 56,* 440–447.

Hahlweg, K., Markman, H. J., Thurmaier, F., Engl, J., & Eckert, V. (1998). Prevention of marital distress: Results of a German prospective longitudinal study. *Journal of Family Psychology, 12,* 543–556.

Halford, K., & Bouma, R. (1997). Individual psychopathology and marital distress. In K. Halford & H. J. Markman (Eds.), *Clinical handbook of marriage and couples intervention* (pp. 291–321). New York: Wiley.

Halford, K., & Markman, H. J. (Eds.). (1997). *Clinical handbook of marriage and marital interaction.* London: Wiley.

Hao, L. (1996). Family structure, private transfers, and the economic well-being of families with children. *Social Forces, 75.*

Inglehart, R., Basanez, M., Moreno, A., & Moreno, M. (1998). *Human values and beliefs: A cross-cultural sourcebook: Political, religious, sexual, and economic norms in 43 societies: Findings from 1990–1999.* Ann Arbor: University of Michigan Press.

Inglehart, R. (1989). *Culture shift in advanced industrial society.* Princeton, NJ: Princeton University Press.

Jacobson, N. S., & Christensen, A. (1998). *Acceptance and change in couple therapy: A therapist's guide to transforming relationships.* New York: Norton.

Johnson, M. P. (1995). Patriarchal terrorism and common couple violence: Two forms of violence against women. *Journal of Marriage and the Family, 57,* 283–294.

Johnson, M. P., Caughlin, J. P., & Huston, T. L. (1999). The tripartite nature of marital commitment: Personal, moral, and structural reasons to stay married. *Journal of Marriage and the Family, 61,* 160–177.

Jones, W., & Adams, J. (1999). *Handbook of interpersonal commitment and relationship stability.* New York: Plenum.

Kanapur, R., and Bailey, W. C. (1995). Mothers' perception of financial socialization. Unpublished manuscript.

Kapoor, J., Dlabay, L., and Hughes, R. J. (2000). *Personal finance* (6th ed.). New York: McGraw-Hill.

Karney, B. R., & Bradbury, T. N. (1995). The longitudinal course of marital quality and stability: A review of theory, method, and research. *Psychological Bulletin, 118,* 3–34.

Kendall, S., and Stapf, S. (Apr. 6, 2000; Dec. 8, 2001). *Consumer Federation of America* [http://www.consumerfed.org/backpage/savings.html].

Kiecolt-Glaser, J. K., Malarkey, W. B., Chee, M., Newton, T., Cacioppo, J. T., Mao, H. Y., & Glaser, R. (1993). Negative behavior during marital conflict is associated with immunological down-regulation. *Psychosomatic Medicine, 55,* 395–409.

Kim, P., & Patterson, J. (1991). *The day America told the truth: What people really believe about everything that matters.* Upper Saddle River, NJ: Prentice Hall.

Kirkcaldy, B. D., & Furnham, A.M.T. (1998). National differences in personality, socio-economic, and work-related attitudinal variables. *European Psychologist, 3,* 255–262.

Kiyosaki, R. T., & Lechter, S. L. (2000). *Rich dad, poor dad.* New York: Warner Books.

Kurdek, L. A. (1993). Predicting marital dissolution: A 5-year prospective longitudinal study of newlywed couples. *Journal of Personality and Social Psychology, 64,* 221–242.

Lane, R. E. (Ed.). (2000). *The loss of happiness in market democracies.* New Haven, CT: Yale University Press.

Lewis, A., Webley, P., & Furnham, A. (1995). *The new economic mind.* Upper Saddle River, NJ: Prentice Hall.

Mahoney, A., Pargament, K. I., Jewell, T., Swank, A. B., Scott, E., Emery, E., & Rye, M. (1999). Marriage and the spiritual realm: The role of proximal and distal religious constructs in marital functioning. *Journal of Family Psychology, 13,* 321–338.

Markman, H. J. (1981). The prediction of marital distress: a five year follow-up. *Journal of Consulting and Clinical Psychology, 49,* 760–762.

Markman, H. J., & Hahlweg, K. (1993). The prediction and prevention of marital distress: An international perspective. *Clinical Psychology Review, 13,* 29–43.

Markman, H. J., & Kraft, S. A. (1989). Men and women in marriage: Dealing with gender differences in marital therapy. *Behavior Therapist, 12,* 51–56.

Markman, H. J., Floyd, F., Stanley, S. M., & Jamieson, K. (1984). A cognitive-behavioral program for the prevention of marital and family distress: Issues in program development and delivery. In K. Hahlweg & N. Jacobson (Eds.), *Marital interaction.* New York: Guilford Press.

Markman, H. J., Floyd, F., Stanley, S. M., & Storaasli, R. D. (1988). The prevention of marital distress: A longitudinal investigation. *Journal of Consulting and Clinical Psychology, 56,* 210–217.

Markman, H. J., Renick, M. J., Floyd, F., Stanley, S. M., & Clements, M. (1993). Preventing marital distress through communication and conflict management training: A four and five year follow-up. *Journal of Consulting and Clinical Psychology, 62,* 1–8.

Matthews, L. S., Wickrama, K.A.S., & Conger, R. D. (1996). Predicting marital instability from spouse and observer reports of marital interaction. *Journal of Marriage and the Family, 58,* 641–655.

McCullough, M. E., Worthington, E. L., Jr., & Rachal, K. C. (1997). Interpersonal forgiving in close relationships. *Journal of Personality and Social Psychology, 73,* 321–336.

Met Life. (Dec. 9, 2001). Financial planning for college [http://www.metlife.com/Lifeadvice/Money/Docs/plancollege1.html].

Mueller, J., Niemi, R. G., & Smith, T. W. (1989). *Trends in public opinion: A compendium of survey data.* Westport, CT: Greenwood Press.

Myers, D. G. (1992). *The pursuit of happiness: Discovering the pathway to fulfillment, well-being, and enduring personal joy.* New York: Avon Books.

National Association of Home Builders. (Dec. 3, 2001). Economic and housing data, June 2001 [http://www.nahb.com/main_features/facts.htm].

National Cooperative Bank. (Oct. 1999; Dec. 9, 2001). Market notes [http://www.ncb.com/homepage/marnotes.nsf/docadd/october1999.htm].

Nelson, C. (1994). *Women's market handbook.* Detroit: Gale Research.

New Strategist. (1999). *The American marketplace: Demographics and spending patterns* (4th ed.). New York: New Strategist.

Noller, P. (1996). What is this thing called love? Defining the love that supports marriage and family. *Personal Relationships, 3,* 97–115.

Notarius, C., & Markman, H. J. (1993). *We can work it out: Making sense of marital conflict.* New York: Putnam.

Orman, S. (1997). *The 9 steps to financial freedom.* New York: Crown.

Owen, B. R. (Oct. 9, 2001; Dec. 4, 2001). Two more strip malls close to completion. *SE Missourian.com* [http://semissourian.com/story.html$rec=48604].

Pasch, L. A., & Bradbury, T. N. (1998). Social support, conflict, and the development of marital dysfunction. *Journal of Consulting and Clinical Psychology, 66,* 219–230.

Pasley, K., Sandras, E., & Edmonson, M. E. (1994). The effects of financial management strategies on quality of family life in remarriage. *Journal of Family and Economic Issues, 15,* 53–70.

Pistole, C. (1989). Attachment in adult romantic relationships: Style of conflict resolution and relationship satisfaction. *Journal of Social and Personal Relationships, 6,* 505–510.

Popcorn, F., & Marigold, L. (2000). *EVEolution: The eight truths of marketing to women.* New York: Hyperion.

Reichenstein, W. (Oct. 1996). Basic truths about asset allocation: A consensus view among the experts. *American Association of Individual Investors Journal.*

Roberts, S. (1998). *Harness the future: The 9 keys to emerging consumer behavior.* Etobicoke, Canada: Wiley.

Robin, V. (1999). *Your money or your life.* New York: Penguin.

Rogers, S., & DeBoer, D. (2001). Changes in wives' income: Effects on marital happiness, psychological well-being, and the risk of divorce. *Journal of Marriage and the Family, 63,* 458–472.

Rubinowitz, S. (Dec. 17, 2001). The most popular dog breeds in the year 2000. *PetPlace.com* [http://www.petplace.com/articles/artShow.asp?artID=2117].

Rusbult, C. E. (1983). A longitudinal test of the investment model: The development (and deterioration) of satisfaction and commitment in heterosexual involvements. *Journal of Personality and Social Psychology, 45,* 101–117.

Rusbult, C. E., Zembrodt, I. M., & Gunn, L. K. (1982). Exit, voice, loyalty, and neglect: Responses to dissatisfaction in romantic involvement. *Journal of Personality and Social Psychology, 43,* 1230–1242.

Sager, C. J. (1976.) *Marital contracts and couple therapy.* New York: Brunner/Mazel.

Sanders, M. R., Halford, W. K., & Behrens, B. C. (1999). Parental divorce and premarital couple communication. *Journal of Family Psychology, 13,* 60–74.

Schaninger, C. M., & Buss, W. C. (1986). A longitudinal comparison of consumption and finance handling between happily married and divorced couples. *Journal of Marriage and the Family, 48,* 129–136.

Schor, J. B. (1991). *The overworked American.* New York: Basic Books.

Silliman, B., Stanley, S. M., Coffin, W., Markman, H. J., & Jordan, P. L. (2001). Preventive interventions for couples. In H. Liddle, D. Santisteban, R. Levant, & J. Bray (Eds.), *Family psychology intervention science.* Washington, DC: APA Publications.

Smith, J. W., & Clurman, A. S. (1998). *Rocking the ages: The Yankelovich Report on generational marketing.* New York: Harper Business.

Srivastava, A., Locke, E. A., & Bartol, K. M. (2001). Money and subjective well-being: It's not the money, it's the motives. *Journal of Personality and Social Psychology, 80,* 959–971.

Stanley, S. M. (1998). *The heart of commitment: Compelling research that reveals the secrets of a lifelong, intimate marriage.* Nashville, TN: Nelson.

Stanley, S. M. (2001). Making the case for premarital training. *Family Relations, 50,* 272–280.

Stanley, S. M., & Markman, H. J. (1992). Assessing commitment in personal relationships. *Journal of Marriage and the Family, 54,* 595–608.

Stanley, S. M., & Markman, H. J. (1997). *Marriage in the 90s: A nationwide random phone survey.* Denver, CO: PREP.

Stanley, S. M., & Markman, H. J. (1998). Acting on what we know: The hope of prevention. In *Strategies to strengthen marriage: What we know, what we need to know* (pp. 37–54). Washington, DC: Family Impact Seminar.

Stanley, S. M., Blumberg, S. L., & Markman, H. J. (1999). Helping couples fight *for* their marriages: The PREP approach. In R. Berger & M. Hannah (Eds.), *Handbook of preventive approaches in couple therapy*. New York: Brunner/Mazel.

Stanley, S. M., Bradbury, T. N., & Markman, H. J. (2000). Structural flaws in the bridge from basic research on marriage to interventions for couples: Illustrations from Gottman, Coan, Carrere, and Swanson (1998). *Journal of Marriage and the Family, 62*, 256–264.

Stanley, S. M., Lobitz, W. C., & Dickson, F. (1999). Using what we know: Commitment and cognitions in marital therapy. In W. Jones & J. Adams (Eds.), *Handbook of interpersonal commitment and relationship stability* (pp. 411–424). New York: Plenum.

Stanley, S. M., Markman, H. J., & Whitton, S. *Communication, conflict, and commitment: Insights on the key Cs of marriage from a national survey.* Manuscript submitted for publication.

Stanley, S. M., Markman, H. J., & Whitton, S. *Maybe I do: Interpersonal commitment and premarital or non-marital cohabitation.* Manuscript submitted for publication.

Stanley, S. M., Markman, H. J., Prado, L. M., Olmos-Gallo, P. A., Tonelli, L., St. Peters, M., Leber, B. D., Bobulinski, M., Cordova, A., & Whitton, S. (2001). Community based premarital prevention: Clergy and lay leaders on the front lines. *Family Relations, 50*, 67–76.

Stanley, S. M., Markman, H. J., St. Peters, M., & Leber, B. D. (1995). Strengthening marriages and preventing divorce: New directions in prevention research. *Family Relations, 44*, 392–401.

Stanley, T. J., & Danko, W. D. (2000). *The millionaire next door.* New York: Simon & Schuster.

Stanton, G. T. (1997). *Why marriage matters: Reasons to believe in marriage in postmodern society.* Colorado Springs: Piñon Press.

Stefan, K. (Dec. 12, 2001). Mars, Venus, and the art of investing. *MyPrimeTime.com* [http://www.myprimetime.com/money/investing/comtent/mars/index.shtml].

Sternberg, R. J. (2000). *Cupid's arrow: The course of love through time.* New York: Cambridge University Press.

Stevens, D., Kige, G., & Riley, P. (2001). Working hard and hardly working: Domestic labor and marital satisfaction among dual-earner couples. *Journal of Marriage and the Family, 63*, 514–526.

Storaasli, R. D., & Markman, H. J. (1990). Relationship problems in the early stages of marriage: A longitudinal investigation. *Journal of Family Psychology, 4*, 80–98.

Tennov, D. (1999). *Love and limerence: The experience of being in love* (2nd ed.). New York: Scarborough House.

Thurmaier, F., Engl, J., & Hahlweg, K. (1999). Eheglück auf Dauer? Methodik, Inhalte und Effektivität eines präventiven Paarkommunikationstrainings—Ergebnisse nach fünf Jahren. Zeitschrift für *Klinische Psychologie, 28*, 54–62.

Toohey, B., & Toohey, M. (2000). *The average family's guide to financial freedom.* New York: Wiley.

Tripp, M. A. (Dec. 8, 2001). *Gender differences in communication.* [http://www.umm.maine.edu/BEX/students/MarkTripp/mt320.html].

Tyson, E., & Silverman, D. J. (2001). *Taxes for dummies.* Boston: IDG Books.

Tyson, E. (2000). *Personal finance for dummies.* Boston: IDG Books.

U.S. Bureau of the Census. (1992). *Marriage, divorce, and remarriage in the 1990s* (Current Population Reports, P23-180). Washington, DC: U.S. Government Printing Office.

U.S. Bureau of the Census. (Dec. 8, 2001). Historical income tables: Families, 2000 [http://www.census.gov/hhes/income/histinc/f01.html].

U.S. Department of Education. (Dec. 8, 2001). Median family income, by race/ethnicity of head of household, 1950 to 1991 [http://www.ed.gov/pubs/YouthIndicators/indtab14.html].

Underhill, P. (1999). *Why we buy: The science of shopping.* New York: Simon & Schuster.

University of Georgia BOS/SBDC, Applied Research Division. (Oct. 2001; Dec. 13, 2001). Industry fact sheets: Single family construction (NAICS 233210), [http://research.sbdc.uga.edu].

Van Lange, P.A.M., Rusbult, C. E., Drigotas, S. M., Arriaga, X. B., Witcher, B. S., & Cox, C. L. (1997). Willingness to sacrifice in close relationships. *Journal of Personality and Social Psychology, 72,* 1373–1395.

Waite, L., & Gallagher, M. (2001). *The case for marriage: Why married people are happier, healthier and better off financially.* New York: Broadway Books.

Waite, L. J. Tabulations from the National Survey of Families and Households, 1987–1988 and 1992–1994.

Weiss, R. L. (1980). Strategic behavioral marital therapy: Toward a model for assessment and intervention. In J. P. Vincent (Ed.), *Advances in family intervention, assessment and theory* (Vol. 1, pp. 229–271). Greenwich, CT: JAI Press.

Weiss, R. L., & Dehle, C. (1994). Cognitive behavioral perspectives on marital conflict. In D. D. Cahn (Ed.), *Conflict in intimate relationships* (pp. 95–115). Mahwah, NJ: Erlbaum.

Wellner, A. S. (1996). *Who's buying for the home.* New York: New Strategist.

West, C. G., Reed, D. M., & Gildengorin, G. L. (1998). Can money buy happiness? Depressive symptoms in an affluent older population. *Journal of the American Geriatrics Society, 46,* 49–57.

Whitehead, B. D. (1997). *The divorce culture.* New York: Knopf.

Whitton, S. W., Stanley, S. M., & Markman, H. J. (in press). Sacrifice in romantic relationships: An exploration of relevant research and theory. In H. T. Reiss, M. A. Fitzpatrick, & A. L. Vangelisti (Eds.), *Stability and change in relationship behavior across the lifespan.* Cambridge University Press.

Worthington, E. L. (1990). *Counseling before marriage.* (Vol. 23, Resources for Christian Counseling series, G. R. Collins, Series Ed.). Nashville: Word.

ABOUT THE AUTHORS

Natalie H. Jenkins is vice president and marketing director of the Prevention and Relationship Enhancement Program (PREP, Inc.). Jenkins began her business career with a degree from Colorado State University, but states emphatically that her true education comes from "the real world." Her passion for practical application has served her well, as for the last decade she has spearheaded PREP's efforts to bring its research-based materials out of the research lab and into the hands of couples. She is codeveloper of the *PREP One-Day Leader's Manual, Christian PREP One-Day Leader's Manual,* and *PREP Coaching Video.* She is also coauthor of the *Fighting* for *Your Marriage Workbooks.* Jenkins's understanding of money dynamics, her quick wit, and her ability to translate academic research findings into usable strategies make this book one of a kind.

Scott M. Stanley, Ph.D., is codirector of the Center for Marital and Family Studies, adjunct professor of psychology at the University of Denver, and president of PREP Educational Products, Inc. He has published extensively in academic journals, as well as writings for couples. He is internationally known for his work on the PREP approach for reducing the risks of marital distress and divorce, as well as his research and theory on marital commitment. Stanley has coauthored the bestselling book, videos, and audios titled *Fighting* for *Your Marriage.* He is also coauthor of *A Lasting Promise* and *Becoming Parents,* and author of *The Heart of Commitment.* He contributes extensively to both print and broadcast media as an expert on marriage.

William C. Bailey has a masters of theology from Southern Methodist University and a Ph.D. in family economics from Texas Tech University. Dr. Bailey is associate professor in the School of Human Environmental Sciences at the University of Arkansas, where he teaches personal finance and family science. He is also past national program leader for family economics for the Cooperative States Research, Education, and Economics Service in USDA and continues to conduct research on attitudes about money and marriage.

Howard J. Markman, Ph.D., is codirector of the Center for Marital and Family Studies, professor of psychology at the University of Denver, and president of PREP, Inc. He is coauthor of the *Fighting* for *Your Marriage* series, *Why Do Fools Fall in Love?*, and *The Clinical Handbook of Marriage and Couples Intervention*. He is codeveloper of PREP and coauthor of over one hundred scientific articles and chapters.

INDEX